Jacques Maritain
and the
Many Ways of Knowing

American Maritain Association Publication

General Editor: Anthony O. Simon

★ *Jacques Maritain: The Man and His Metaphysics*
Edited by John F. X. Knasas, 1988, ISBN 0-268-01205-9 (out of print)

★ *Freedom in the Modern World: Jacques Maritain, Yves R. Simon, Mortimer Adler*
Edited by Michael D. Torre, 1989, Second Printing, 1990, ISBN 0-268-00978-3

★ *From Twilight to Dawn: The Cultural Vision of Jacques Maritain*
Edited by Peter A. Redpath, 1990, ISBN 0-268-00979-1

★ *The Future of Thomism*
Edited by Deal W. Hudson and Dennis Wm. Moran, 1992, ISBN 0-268-00986-4

★ *Jacques Maritain and the Jews*
Edited by Robert Royal, 1994, ISBN 0-268-01193-1

★ *Freedom, Virtue, and the Common Good*
Edited by Curtis L. Hancock and Anthony O. Simon, 1995, ISBN 0-268-00991-0

◆ *Postmodernism and Christian Philosophy*
Edited by Roman T. Ciapolo, 1997, ISBN 0-8132-0881-5

◆ *The Common Things: Essays on Thomism and Education*
Edited by Daniel McInerny, 1999, ISBN 0-9669226-0-3

◆ *The Failure of Modernism: The Cartesian Legacy and Contemporary Pluralism*
Edited by Brendan Sweetman, 1999, ISBN 0-9669226-1-1

◆ *Beauty, Art, and the Polis*
Edited by Alice Ramos, 2000, ISBN 0-9669226-2-X

◆ *Reassessing the Liberal State: Reading Maritain's Man and the State*
Edited by Timothy Fuller and John P. Hittinger, 2001, ISBN 0-9669226-3-8

◆ *Faith, Scholarship and Culture in the 21st Century*
Edited by Alice Ramos and Marie I. George, 2002, ISBN 0-9669226-5-4

◆ *Jacques Maritain and the Many Ways of Knowing*
Edited by Douglas A. Ollivant, 2002, ISBN 0-9669226-4-6

★ Distributed by the University of Notre Dame Press
◆ Distributed by The Catholic University of America Press

Jacques Maritain and the Many Ways of Knowing

Douglas A. Ollivant
Editor

With an Introduction by
George Anastaplo

AMERICAN MARITAIN ASSOCIATION

Distributed by The Catholic University of America Press
Washington, D.C. 20064

American Maritain Association
Distributed by The Catholic University of America Press
Washington, D.C. 20064

Library of Congress Cataloging-in-Publication Data

Jacques Maritain and the many ways of knowing / Douglas A. Ollivant,
  editor ;   with an introduction by George Anastaplo.
      p. cm.
Includes bibliographical references and index
    ISBN 0-9669226-4-6   (pbk. : alk. paper)
    1. Maritain, Jacques, 1882-1973. 2.   Knowledge, Theory of. I.
Ollivant, Douglas A.
    B2430.M34 J317 2002
    121'.092--dc21

                                                        2002006668

Manufactured in
the United States of America

Dedicated to

Henry Babcock Veatch

A Great-Souled Gentleman and Philosopher

Requiescat in Pace

Contents

PART II   Politics, Culture, Literature

PART III   SCIENCE, ART, THEOLOGY, MYSTICISM

Editor's Note

In how many ways—and with what degree of certainty—do we know? The essays assembled within address these questions from a variety of disciplinary viewpoints, but the thought of Jacques Maritain is never far in the background.

Grounded in the philosophy of St. Thomas Aquinas, Maritain presented an account not only of the (more or less traditional) Thomistic-Aristotelian theory of knowledge, but also expanded it to include what he would call connatural, or artistic knowledge. Maritain was not afraid to claim that we do in fact know what we know, even if the experience cannot be taught or shared. The essays herein are therefore more wide-ranging than might otherwise be expected, as artists, historians, theologians, architects, musicians, social scientists and literary critics join professional philosophers in exploring the avenues opened by Maritain's work.

The essays contained in the volume are divided into three parts. The first grouping deals with basic questions of knowledge at a theoretical level, or what would be called "epistemology" in most contemporary Departments of Philosophy. The essays in the second section attempt to address the social consequences of how we know, taking the political and ethical implications of knowledge—or the lack thereof—into account. Finally, those in the third section deal with ways of knowing not often taken seriously by modernity. These authors touch on the knowledge conveyed through alternative modes of experience—from modern physics, through music and poetry, to even mystical knowledge of God Himself. Taken as a whole, the three sections present a credible alternative to the pervasive contemporary academic skepticism, or what Maritain describes as the "deep vice [that] besets the philosophers of our day."[1]

My debts incurred in the preparation of this volume are legion. My most sincere thanks go to Anthony O. Simon, Secretary of the American Maritain Association, and General Editor of this series. Without his advice, encouragement, and (most critically) instruction, the production of this volume would have been (even more) greatly delayed. I also wish to thank the contributors to this volume for their assistance and patience.

My warmest gratitude goes out to my fellow editors in this series for their assistance and counsel. Peter A. Redpath, Alice Ramos, Curtis L. Hancock, John P. Hittinger and John F.X. Knasas were particularly helpful at critical moments. Special thanks are due to Dennis Wm. Moran, not only as fellow series editor, but also for his generous assistance in the composition of this volume. My thanks go out as well to his staff at *The Review of Politics*. Fr. James V. Schall, S. J. was an ever-stalwart source of encouragement and advice. Thanks are also due to David McGonagle and Beth Benavides of The Catholic University of America Press. And Paul Seaton generously donated his time to indexing this volume. Not least, I am eternally grateful to Professor George Anastaplo for graciously providing the magisterial introduction to this collection. He is a model for many of us—a prolific scholar, gifted author, mesmerizing teacher, and a family man of unquestioned integrity.

Finally, my thanks go to my wife and children for their patience as I took this volume through production. To my bride Jacalyn and children Evan, Caleb, Austin, Samuel, Hope and Grace—may you all know the depth of my love, and yet know that mine is but a pale reflection of that of God for each of you.

---

[1]Jacques Maritain, *The Degrees of Knowledge*, trans. Gerald B. Phelan (Notre Dame, Indiana: The University of Notre Dame Press, 1995), p. 1.

The Forms of Our Knowing

A Somewhat Socratic Introduction

George Anastaplo

The whole of science is nothing more than
a refinement of everyday thinking.
—Albert Einstein

Prologue

Is there a basic way of knowing that we typically if not naturally develop, a way which permits human beings to survive and to work in, if not
even to understand, the everyday world and in the light of which we somehow shape and assess other ways of knowing?

We do seem to grasp many things naturally—and we sense that we know
some things, even as we also sense that we do not know other things but that
perhaps we could get to know some of them. We sense as well that many others
know some if not all of the things that we do in much the way that we do—and
we very much rely upon their knowing such things, sometimes even "betting"
our lives on how they will respond to the "situations" we must share.

We can be reassured that much of what has been believed or known long
ago or far away is very much like what we accept. But we are cautioned,
even as we are thus reassured, by recalling the many things we have "known"
that we now recognize are simply not so. We also may be aware of our own
persistent incapacities. The personal incapacities of which we do happen to
be aware can warn us about others of which we may be woefully ignorant.

The naturalness of knowing seems to be intimately linked to that which we
grasp by *seeing*. "I see," we can say when we at last come to understand
something that has been explained to us. The things seen have forms which we
distinguish and sort out, forms which can be linked (as Socrates sometimes
seems to have linked them) to the Ideas, which in turn are fundamental to what
can truly be relied upon by the reasoning being. There is, then, a way of knowing that we naturally develop, just as the best eyesight is naturally developed in

1

the proper conditions. This way of knowing can be refined, corrected, and applied in our constant effort to understand all that is around us. But that original grasp of things, probably well entrenched in most of us before we even begin to wonder about what we know and how we know it, always remains available as the standard by which we are inclined to judge what it is *to know*.

Human beings have long—perhaps they have "always"—striven to test and to confirm what they believe themselves to know, and even to examine what it means "to know." Socrates, for example, is remembered for having insisted that he knew that he did not know. But it is evident that some awareness was drawn upon by him both of what it means "to know" and of the superiority of knowing to non-knowing. It is also evident, in the two dozen essays in this volume, that many forms of knowing, including knowing what it means and is required to know, are examined.

It should be of use, in considering this rich array of essays inspired to a considerable extent by the remarkable career of Jacques Maritain, to be reminded of three challenging approaches to problems of knowing, approaches which are apt to be particularly influential for contemporary inquiries into these matters. One approach is that of the modern physical sciences, which has affected all scholarly disciplines. Another approach is that of, speaking loosely, modern subjectivism, with its considerable emphasis upon self-consciousness. The third approach is that of art, which can itself be intimately related to divine revelation. Illustrations of each approach are offered in the three parts of this Introduction, with even more extended illustrations in the volume of essays that follows.

We can begin with modern science, recalling as we do so Jacques Maritain's inspired observation, "Few spectacles are as beautiful and moving for the mind as that of physics…advancing toward its destiny like a huge, throbbing ship."[1]

I

i.

Much of what I have to say about ways of knowing in this part of my Introduction (in which the typical approach of the modern physical sciences is considered) is anticipated by three items: by a story, by an observation I have made on another occasion, and by a biographical fragment.

---

[1] Quoted in James Arraj, "Nonlocality and Maritain's Dream of a Philosophy of Nature," in this volume at p. 270.

First, there is my observation (taken from a memoir of Leo Strauss I first published in 1974):

> ...What seems to be missing in the current scientific enterprise is a systematic inquiry into its presuppositions and purposes. That is, the limits of modern science do not seem to be properly recognized. Bertrand Russell has been quoted as saying, "Physics is mathematical not because we know so much about the physical world, but because we know so little: it is only its mathematical properties that we can discover." But the significance of this observation is not generally appreciated–as one learns upon trying to persuade competent physicists to join one in presenting a course devoted to a careful reading of Aristotle's *Physics*.
>
> Is there any reason to doubt that physicists will, if they continue as they have thus far in the Twentieth Century, achieve, again and again, "decisive breakthroughs" in dividing subatomic "particles"? But what future, or genuine understanding, is there in *that*? I believe it would be fruitful for physicists–that is, for a few of the more imaginative among them–to consider seriously the nature of what we can call the "ultron." What must this ultimate particle be like (if, indeed, it is a particle and not an idea or a principle)? For is not an "ultron" implied by the endeavors of our physicists, by their recourse to more and more ingenious (and expensive) equipment and experiments? Or are we to assume an infinite regress (sometimes called progress) and no standing place or starting point? Or, to put this question still another way, what is it that permits the universe to be and to be (if it is) intelligible?[2]

Then there is the story: Some years ago I found myself in Pisa with an old schoolmate, Laurence Berns. Of course, we had to attempt the experiment said to have been conducted by Galileo from the Leaning Tower. One of us climbed to the top, carrying a variety of rocks (gathered up at the site); the other stayed below to warn away pedestrians and to observe the results of the experiment (as well as to watch out for the police). Two pairs of rocks of different weights were dropped: one pair of rocks of uneven weights seemed to hit together (that is, only one noise could be heard upon impact); the other pair of rocks of uneven weights seemed to hit at quite different times (that is, two distinct noises upon impact could be heard). We thereupon reported to our common teacher, Leo Strauss, that the question of modernity was still open. (Another common teacher we had had at the University of Chicago

---

[2] George Anastaplo, *The Artist as Thinker: From Shakespeare to Joyce* (Athens, Ohio: Ohio University Press, 1983), pp. 252-53. See also Anastaplo, *But Not Philosophy: Seven Introductions to Non-Western Thought* (Lanham, Maryland: Lexington Books, 2002), p. 261, as well as notes 18 and 25 of this Introduction. See, for bibliographies of George Anastaplo's work, *Brandeis Law Journal* 39 (2000-2001), pp. 219-87; *Northern Illinois University Law Review* 20 (2000), pp. 581-710. (Both of these law reviews may be found on LexisNexis and on Westlaw.)

was Yves Simon, whose salutary influence is evident in various of the essays in this Collection.)

Now for the biographical fragment: I have been told that Enrico Fermi had a remarkable intuitive sense, an ability to sense what line of inquiry would be worth pursuing. Thus, people working on a problem, even with respect to matters that Mr. Fermi was not particularly versed in, liked to sit next to him at the faculty club at the University of Chicago, confident that he could be induced to say something useful about their current inquiries. It has been suggested to me that this remarkable intuition was linked to his considerable expertise as an experimenter. But it has also been suggested that it was important that he was an experimenter with a gift for theoretical speculation.

I was struck by the emphasis, in this description of Enrico Fermi, upon the term "intuition," since I had been impressed by the same quality in another Italian, Galileo Galilei. The critical role of such enlightening intuition first became apparent to me (appropriately enough) upon consideration, in a seminar, of Galileo's inquiry into the speed of light.

With these remarks as preface, let us turn to a more systematic (albeit necessarily preliminary) set of observations on Galileo's *Dialogues Concerning Two New Sciences*.[3]

ii.

Intuition can be said to appear in two forms, one which works from a "natural" common sense, the other which works from a cultivated "common sense."

"Natural" common sense is somehow our starting point. But one soon learns that one's senses can mislead one, or at least that they can induce one to believe something to be true which one cannot explain or account for.[4] And if one's senses can mislead, why not also that common sense which seems to depend upon those senses? Even so, the senses and one's primitive common sense must be repeatedly utilized if there is to be an ascent to a more sophisticated mode of sensing and explaining. Such an ascent, some of Galileo's partisans might have said, was provided by the observations and insights of the ancients, and especially Aristotle. But, they might have added, the intuition thereby put to use, however useful, indeed indispensable, it had been, was necessarily

---

[3] Galileo Galilei, *Dialogues Concerning Two New Sciences*, trans. Henry Crew and Alfonso de Salvio (New York: Dover Publications, 1954).

[4] See ibid., p. 1.

limited: that intuition was too much dependent upon the surface of things, and hence upon appearances or illusions, to be free from error. It may even be the final stage of the progress of "natural" common sense for it to come to a recognition, or at least to an awareness, of its limitations– and so a different approach to accounting for observable things is both called for and made possible.

This different approach takes its departure from a cultivated "common sense." The implications of experience are perhaps taken more seriously than they had been: measurement and skepticism become more important than they had been. Thus, we are told by Salviati, one of the characters in Galileo's *Dialogues*, "A large marble column was laid out so that its two ends rested each upon a piece of beam; a little later it occurred to a mechanic that, in order to be doubly sure of its not breaking in the middle by its own weight, it would be wise to lay a third support midway; this seemed to all an excellent idea; but the sequel showed that it was quite the opposite, for not many months passed before the column was found cracked and broken exactly above the new middle support."[5]

This was, it is observed, by another participant in the *Dialogues*, Simplicio, a "very remarkable and thoroughly unexpected accident, especially if caused by placing that new support in the middle."[6] But, it is said in reply by Salviati, "the moment the cause is known our surprise vanishes":

> [For] when the two pieces of the column were placed on level ground it was observed that one of the end beams had, after a long while, become decayed and sunken, but that the middle one remained hard and strong, thus causing one half of the column to project in the air without any support. Under these circumstances the body therefore behaved differently from what it would have done if supported [at its ends] only upon the first [two] beams; because no matter how much they might have sunken, the column would have gone with them.[7]

It can be said that enough such experiences–and the ancients no doubt had them also–, coupled with the suspicion that the old-fashioned way of accounting for the observable things could progress no further, eventually induced the bolder and more imaginative spirits in the community to reconsider what was being observed. This reconsideration promoted recourse to a greater reliance not only upon measurement but also upon experimentation– that is to say, upon the steady generation of ever more observations than would naturally be available.

[5] Ibid., p. 5.
[6] Ibid.
[7] Ibid. See also ibid., pp. 134-36.

Much is made in the *Two New Sciences* of the cleverness and ingenuity of the experiments resorted to. (To what extent are they Galileo's? To what extent does he collect and organize what others have done?) Again and again, the cleverness of the devices used is recognized.[8] Of course, chance plays its part, but only in a subordinate role. Thus Salviati says of one device that he happened to develop, "The device is one which I hit upon by accident; my part consists merely in the observation of it and in the appreciation of its value as a confirmation of something to which I had given profound consideration…"[9] The "profound consideration" devoted to these matters, in a mode which makes experimentation fruitful, evidently works from the premise that the secrets of nature can indeed be discovered, but only if the appearances of things are called into question (both the appearance of an explanation in some instances and the appearance of permanent concealment in other cases). Thus, Salviati reports on a conversation with the Academician (Galileo), after he had studied a matter "for a while in vain," "First he told me that he also had for a long time been groping in the dark; but later he said that, after having spent some thousands of hours in speculating and contemplating thereon, he had arrived at some notions which are far removed from our earlier ideas and which are remarkable for their novelty."[10]

Earlier it had been recognized that novelty can be dangerous. To be called "an innovator of doctrine" is to be invested with "an unpleasant title."[11] After all, does not human experience show that departures from long-established opinions are all too often the result either of ignorance or of perversity?

iii.

More needs to be said about the cultivated "common sense," or the second form of intuition, to which I have referred. Consider Salviati's use of an experiment to ascertain whether the speed of light "is instantaneous or momentary or [whether it] like other motions require[s] time."[12] It is clear, from everyday experience, "that sound, in reaching our ears, travels more slowly than light."

[8] See, e.g. ibid., pp. 80, 82.

[9] Ibid., p. 101. Louis Pasteur is quoted as having said, "In the fields of observation, chance favors only the mind that is prepared." *Familiar Quotations*, ed. John Bartlett (Boston: Little, Brown and Company, 1980), p. 591. See for the quotation of Albert Einstein used as the epigraph for this Introduction, ibid., p. 763.

[10] *Dialogues Concerning Two New Sciences*, p. 271.

[11] See ibid., p. 83. See also ibid., pp. 261-62. The career of Socrates provides *the* warning here. See, e.g. Anastaplo, *Human Being and Citizen: Essays on Virtue, Freedom, and the Common Good* (Chicago: Swallow Press, 1975), p. 8.

[12] *Dialogues Concerning Two New Sciences*, p. 42.

But such experience does not inform us "whether the coming of the light is instantaneous or whether, although extremely rapid, it still occupies time."[13]

Salviati then describes an experiment he devised (which I need not describe here[14])—an experiment which could be conducted at distances of two or three miles or, with telescopes, at distances of eight or ten miles. Sagredo concedes, "This experiment strikes me as a clever and reliable invention."[15] Salviati is asked to tell them what he concluded from the results. He replies, "In fact I have tried the experiment only at a short distance, less than a mile, from which I have not been able to ascertain with certainty whether the appearance of the opposite light was instantaneous or not; but if not instantaneous it is extraordinarily rapid–I should call it momentary…"[16] Something is then said about the significance of the movement of a lightning flash across the sky–but not much is made of this, perhaps because it is sensed that it may not be merely an instance of a light moving across the sky? (It is, instead, we now believe, a burning process, by which light is produced: Is it the sequence of burning which takes the elapsed time that we observe?)

But consider the experiment which *is* made. We now know that it would not have been possible, with the arrangement devised by Salviati on that occasion or with any other then available, to observe *any* lapse of time in the transmission of light across the distance of one mile. (That is, 1/186,000th of a second would have had to have been measured. One is reminded of the problem, for centuries, of observing a fixed star's parallax because of the movement of the earth. That is, it was *not* recognized, we are told, how distant the fixed stars were—and hence how minute any parallax would be.) Two curious responses by Salviati should be noticed here. The first is that he considered his experiment indecisive; the second is that he did not try it again at a greater distance, although he evidently had the means to do so.

Was it indecisive? If anything, the experiment should have inclined him to (if not confirmed him in) the opinion that the transmission of light was "instantaneous." Is not that what good-faith recourse to this experiment required? (If one can, in such circumstances, say that one's instruments are not precise enough, then one is in effect saying that it may be impossible ever to "prove" instantaneity, since one can always conclude that the failure to record elapsed time is due only to the relative crudity of one's instruments.) May not Salviati have reached the conclusion he does, of indecisiveness, for the same reason that he does not try

[13] Ibid.
[14] See ibid., p. 43.
[15] Ibid., p. 43.
[16] Ibid., pp. 43-44.

the experiment again at a greater distance (which might have been expected to permit a minute elapsed time to be noticed)? That is, although the transmission appeared instantaneous, he believed otherwise; or, to put this another way, he "knew better." Or, to put this still another way, he was guided in his responses and subsequent conduct by a general theory of nature and of cause-and-effect. Fundamental to that theory is the premise that motion takes time; light is not to be treated as an anomaly, as something virtually miraculous. Was this not an instance, like others of which we have heard, of "fudging" with one's data when one "knows" the right answer? Or, to put this in the terms we have been using, were not Salviati's responses here sensibly guided by an intuition which had been shaped and refined by a quite new way of looking at things?

It should be noticed, however, that we today should not consider the anomality of instantaneity with respect to light to be conclusive against it. For, we are usually told, there *is* a comparable anomaly in the still authoritative account of the speed of light, the notion that light cannot be accelerated. Galilean (and Newtonian?) intuition would suggest that the speed of any thing in motion can always be increased. To say that it cannot be increased is to accept a different kind of instantaneity–that is, a second-stage instantaneity, so to speak, with respect to the speed of light. But, we are also usually told, such constancy in the speed of light has thus far been required by theory and confirmed by experiment. Does this conclusion depend upon a further refinement, beyond Galileo and Newton, of intuition?

iv.

Perhaps this further refinement has depended upon a subjection of physics to a mathematical mode of inquiry to a far greater extent than even Galileo did in his pioneering efforts and Newton did in his grand synthesis. Such subjection may not only completely subordinate our "natural" common sense but may also disclose or at least induce if not even require "anomalies" which might not otherwise have occurred to us. Indeed, it sometimes seems that some things are the way they are "by definition"–with the definitions invoked here being, in a sense, arbitrary.[17]

In any event, Galileo and his successors seem to be relying upon an intuition which is itself dependent upon premises which the ancient scientists also recognized to some extent: there is an order to the things which happen by nature; that order is uniform, wherever one goes; and (perhaps it is only here that the moderns put a greater emphasis than did the ancients) all of the natural order is, in principle, knowable, with more and more of it knowable

---

[17] See, e.g. ibid., p. 162.

in practice, if the inquiry is properly organized, adequately financed, and persistently pursued. Thus, Salviati opines, "I assume matter to be unchangeable and always the same..."[18] And Sagredo observes that "nothing occurs contrary to nature except the impossible, and that never occurs."[19] But, as Salviati tells us, the impossible must be distinguished from the very difficult.[20] (The impossible, by the way, is not the same as "a freakish and interesting circumstance," which can occur in nature.[21] But the freakish, in appearance to human beings, may have natural causes?)

We *now* realize, Galileo and his successors would insist, that a properly organized inquiry into the natural order is one which relies very much on mathematics (as well as upon ever more ingenious experiments). In this respect, Plato is important.[22] Geometry is more useful than logic, it seems.[23] Logic, insofar as it is distinguished from mathematics, brings Aristotle to mind, that inquirer who was sometimes willing to settle, in these matters, for "mere probabilities" in the place of demonstrations.[24] (Aristotle can also be invoked for "the infallible maxim..., the non-existent can produce no effect."[25]) The rigor that mathematics brings to these pursuits may be reflected in the language Salviati uses in describing the doings of nature: he prefers "the aversion of nature for empty space" to "that much-talked-of repugnance which nature exhibits towards a vacuum"[26]; he prefers "a certain incompat-

---

[18] Ibid., p. 3. It has recently been reported, "An international team of astrophysicists has discovered that the basic laws of nature as understood today may be changing slightly as the universe ages." James Glanz and Dennis Overbye, "Anything Can Change, It Seems, Even an Immutable Law of Nature," *New York Times*, August 15, 2001, p. A1. The finding, yet to be generally confirmed, is with respect to the fine-structure constant. Even so, one must wonder, is there a constant pursuant to which the minute change reported takes place? See the text following note 18 of this Introduction. We notice in passing recent speculations among physicists about whether the speed of light can itself be modified.

[19] *Dialogues Concerning Two New Sciences*, p. 12.

[20] See ibid., p. 36.

[21] See ibid., p. 192.

[22] See ibid., pp. 90-91, 137.

[23] See ibid., pp. 137-38.

[24] See ibid., p. 6.

[25] Ibid., p. 12. See, on a very useful translation of Aristotle's *Physics* by Joe Sachs, Book Review, *Interpretation* 26 (1999), p. 275. A related question here is, Why is there something rather than nothing? How does the Platonic Doctrine of the Ideas bear upon this and like questions? See, on the Ideas, Anastaplo, *The Thinker as Artist: From Homer to Plato & Aristotle* (Athens, Ohio: Ohio University Press, 1997), p. 303. See on Aristotle, ibid., p. 318.

[26] *Dialogues Concerning Two New Sciences*, p. 11.

ibility" to "antipathy."[27] It is by proceeding in this manner that Galileo is said to have "done so much to open a pathway hitherto closed to minds of a speculative turn."[28]

In proceeding as they have, however, have not Galileo and his successors relied upon that Aristotelian intuition which, with its antipathy toward infinite regresses, posited constants upon which reliable speculation must be grounded? Indeed, was the constancy of the speed of light itself considered necessary if there was to be something by which all motion might be measured? Do we not see emerging here another facet of that "ultron" which I have posited–that ultron, a kind of constant, which must be properly grasped if our many ingenious, and no doubt productive, experiments are to be truly understood?

V.

The problem with the ancients, then, was not their supposition of constants (or absolutes) but rather their confusion of some constants with others. Thus, for example, Aristotle evidently saw a constancy in the ratio between the weight of a body and its rate of fall; Galileo saw, instead, a constancy in the rate of acceleration of a body, uniform all over the earth (with adjustments for altitudes?), independent of its weight.[29] Ordinary experience tends to support Aristotle, or at least helps account for his conclusion. That is, air resistance *can* be such as to have the rate of fall affected somewhat by the weight (or is it also the shape?) of the falling body.

However that may be, it is difficult to notice that bodies *do* fall at the same rate, irrespective of weight; it is difficult, that is, to set aside the effect of air resistance in ordinary circumstances (such as my friend and I encountered at Pisa). Besides, we can usually throw a lighter stone farther and faster than the heavier one; and if *we* can thus differentiate in everyday events between the heavier and the lighter stone, why should not "gravity" be able to do so also? Our greater difficulty in lifting the heavier stone, and the greater impact it makes when it falls, "suggest" that the pull of the earth upon it is greater–and why should not that pull be transformed into speed?

Constant motion is dramatized at the outset of the *Two New Sciences*.[30] Motion is important, especially naturally accelerated motion.[31] In this respect,

---

[27] See ibid., p. 71.
[28] Ibid., p. 178.
[29] See, e.g., ibid., p. 264.
[30] See ibid., p. 1.
[31] See ibid., pp. 153f, 160f.

there is here "a new science dealing with a very old subject."[32] It is observed that it is remarkable that Archimedes, Apollonius and Euclid did not notice the things developed by Galileo.[33] But do not the ingenious devices Galileo has to resort to in order to make his points testify to the difficulty of observing what he has somehow come to "see."[34] Indeed, as I have indicated, it must be rare, in nature, to observe two bodies of different weights falling at exactly the same rate. Galileo would not have had to improvise and to labor as he did, and thereby earn the recognition he has, if everyday impressions with respect to falling bodies were not quite different from what "unnatural" experiments and measurements eventually revealed.

vi.

We must wonder whether Galileo's discoveries did not depend in part upon a greater interest in discovering *how* (such as the rate at which) bodies fall than in considering *why* bodies fall? Had the latter inquiry—in some ways, the more important inquiry, since it addresses itself more directly to the question of *being*—made more likely any Aristotelian errors with respect to these particular matters? Does not Newton, for example, recognize that *his* remarkable account of moving bodies does not purport to suggest *why* they move as they do?

Of course, we naturally continue to prefer the *why* to the *how* questions in some inquiries. For example, why a woman kills her husband is usually regarded by us as a much more important question than how she kills him.[35] Have we settled for the less important questions in physics only because they are more manageable, more productive? Or is it also that we sense that the ancients had somehow learned all that there is to be learned about the whyness of things and that we must rely (and inevitably do rely) upon what they have learned, however mistaken they may have been in some "details"? In any event, Salviati (he may be somewhat sarcastic, yet nevertheless revealing) is not concerned with "the more profound questions of nature" that some philosophers are.[36]

---

[32] Ibid., p. 242.

[33] See ibid., pp. 242-45. Compare the text at note 37 of this Introduction.

[34] See, e.g., ibid., pp. 62-65, 68, 72f, 83, 89.

[35] One can be reminded here of Aeschylus' *Oresteia*. See, e.g., Anastaplo, "On Trial: Explorations," *Loyola University Chicago Law Journal* 22 (1991) pp. 765, 796; Anastaplo, *The Thinker as Artist*, p. 169. Of course, the *how* may sometimes illuminate the *why*.

[36] See *Dialogues Concerning Two New Sciences*, p. 94. Compare, on the respect for Aristotle, ibid., p. 95. See also the text at note 25 of this Introduction.

And yet, there is an intimate relation between Galileo and his companions (and successors), on the one hand, and the ancients whom they must correct and supplement, on the other. They are, after all, moved by similar passions. Thus, they can marvel at Archimedes's work.[37] They are open to the *beauty* of the truth, in whatever form it appears to them.[38] And they take pleasure in contemplating such beauty, in discovering at their leisure the truth about how things really are.[39]

vii.

It is quite clear that these men believe they have nothing better to do than to make and share the inquiries they engage in. They treasure "conversation between friends" in circumstances which find them "free from urgent business."[40] To speak thus is to speak somewhat in ancient accents.

Those who inquire–those who seriously inquire–are somehow friends, wherever they may be found. Thus, one relies upon the competence and the integrity of the experimenter.[41] Thus, also, one recognizes that it suffices to have someone else discover something, even if he does not present it as one would have.[42] The truth is more important than the name of the man who happens to discover it. After all, he who does discover it usually has had to rely upon the accomplishments and the often necessary mistakes of his predecessors.

The extended conversation in Galileo's *Dialogues Concerning Two New Sciences* concluded with the recognition that there is much yet to be explored,

---

[37] See ibid., p. 41 ("the marvels accomplished by the mirrors of Archimedes").

[38] See, e.g., *Dialogues Concerning Two New Sciences*, pp. 4 ("naked and simple beauty"), 6 ("a field of beautiful and useful ideas") (compare Aristotle here), 8 ("more interesting and beautiful"), 29 ("so clever and novel...so beautiful a structure"), 55 ("This demonstration is so beautiful"), 193 ("The idea is really beautiful and worthy of the clever mind of Sagredo").

[39] See, e.g., ibid., pp. 7, 41-42, 57, 91, 92, 106, 107, 171, 178.

[40] See ibid., pp. 26, 27. Socrates is reported to have said, "Just as others are pleased by a good horse or dog or bird, I myself am pleased to an even higher degree by good friends....And the treasures of the wise men of old which they left behind by writing them in books, I unfold and go through them together with my friends, and if we see something good, we pick it out and regard it as a great gain if we thus become useful to one another." Xenophon, *Memorabilia*, I, vi, 14.

[41] See *Dialogues Concerning Two New Sciences*, p. 179. ("I would like to have been present at these experiments; but feeling confidence in the care with which you performed them, and in the fidelity with which you related them, I am satisfied and accept them as true and valid.").

[42] See ibid., pp. 148, 294

that there are subjects which have eluded the participants in that conversation and which may lie "almost beyond the reach of human imagination."[43] Here, too, ancient accents may be detected and that enduring intuition about the magnitude and the majesty of nature which is likely to be shared by all of those who dedicate themselves to serious inquiry, whatever doubts they are bound to encounter and to examine from time to time.

II.

i.

The Socratic influence upon René Descartes, an influence that is bound to be noticed repeatedly in any Introduction to accounts of ways of knowing—the Socratic influence may be suspected in the Cartesian insistence upon an attempt at universal doubt as the proper starting place for a reliable understanding. That is, Descartes seems to radicalize Socrates's recognition that awareness of one's ignorance is far preferable to mistaken confidence in one's opinions.

Thus, both Socrates and Descartes can be understood to begin their serious intellectual lives by recognizing that they do not know. But, as has been noticed, is not Socrates somehow restrained by what he is nevertheless aware of by nature? That is, the mature Socrates always knew what it was to know. He also knew that knowing is better than ignorance. These are among the many things that Socrates never seemed to doubt.

ii.

Both the Socrates of Plato's *Meno* and the Descartes of his *Meditations* seem to suggest that if an inquirer can learn one thing, he can come to know all things.[44] Socrates does not indicate what that one thing should be, or even whether it is any one thing or whether *any* thing will do, so long as it *is* known, which would include an awareness of how and why it *is* known. (If it

<hr />

[43] Ibid., p. 293.

[44] See, on Descartes, Richard Kennington, "René Descartes (1596-1650)," in Leo Strauss and Joseph Cropsey, eds., *History of Political Philosophy*, 3d ed. (Chicago: University of Chicago Press, 1987), p. 421. See also Anastaplo, *The American Moralist: On Law, Ethics, and Government* (Athens, Ohio: Ohio University Press, 1992), p. 83. Laurence Berns and I have been preparing a translation of Plato's *Meno*, to be published by the Focus Publishing Company. See, on the *Meno*, Anastaplo, *Human Being and Citizen*, p. 74; Anastaplo, "Teaching, Nature, and the Moral Virtues," 1997 *The Great Ideas Today* 2 (1997).

should be one thing only, the context of the *Meno* suggests that it should be an understanding of virtue. But would it be something else if the context is that of, say, Plato's *Timaeus*?)

Descartes indicates that the one thing to be learned as *the* starting point has to do with one's awareness of one's own existence and the reliable knowledge one can have of *that*. Thus, it is through one's awareness of one's own that one can come to grasp what it is to know anything with clarity and distinctness.

May it not matter, and matter for centuries to come, that the course of inquiry Descartes inaugurates is rooted in radical introspection, in an emphasis upon one's *self* as the starting point?

iii.

It should be noticed that Descartes describes the order of establishing a reliable understanding, based on a perhaps natural desire for certainty. He does not describe here the order in which one comes to be, including how one comes to be as a reasoning being.

In the order of establishing a reliable understanding, the mind's awareness both of its limitations and of itself is primary. In the order in which one comes to be, one's senses may be critical, perhaps primary. That is, some physical development may be necessary before one can be capable of the kind of mental activity (in which one's mind is substantially liberated from dependence upon the physical and upon the senses) described by Descartes in his opening *Meditations*.

Is not nature more evident in that preliminary physical development, that development which Descartes takes for granted?

iv.

But, we have noticed, it is not the order of one's physical development that Descartes is concerned with, but rather the order in which one comes to be a properly-thinking being, which is not the same as a reasoning being simply.

To become a properly-thinking being, one must (he argues) start by demolishing a structure that one has long been accustomed to, the structure of presuppositions, opinions, traditions, etc. The most efficient, and sure, way of comprehensive demolition is to remove the intellectual foundations to which one is accustomed. Once they are removed, the entire structure will collapse.

The foundations are removed by calling into question everything one has ever taken for granted. Once one's confidence in how one knows anything has been undermined, then everything one has ever believed may be cleared away—and rebuilding can then begin on sounder foundations.

v.

But, we must wonder, how does Descartes know he has identified all of the foundations upon which his former opinions had rested and upon which had rested as well those opinions which have long been established among human beings?

That is, does he abolish the foundations of the foundations? Or, put another way, do not the products (or, at least, the remnants) of a natural development of the mind continue to assert themselves?

Indeed, one must wonder, must not Descartes continue to use things somehow left over (so to speak) from the structure that he had so thoroughly demolished?

vi.

The demolished structure *had* depended to some extent upon the senses, those senses whose unreliability he had made so much of in the first *Meditation*. And in the fourth *Meditation*, he observes (at the outset), "In these last few days, I have become so accustomed to ignoring my senses, and I have so carefully noticed that we know very little with certainty about corporeal things and that we know much more about the human mind..."

Yet, we in turn notice, here as elsewhere, that in the very account in which he reports ignoring the senses, he can mark the passage of time, the awareness of which very much depends of course upon the senses. Again and again, the passage of time seems critical to his account, as does the awareness of his fatigue and subsequent refreshment and as does his memory of what he has worked through thus far. Does not all this (disciplined though it may be by mathematical operations) draw somehow upon the supposedly repudiated senses?

The senses have to be recruited as well in the effort that he makes to record what he has been working out. But, even more important, must not all that he is doing, to repudiate the old (and unexamined) and to build anew, depend upon a non-mathematical language that comes from the old and that no doubt brings much of the "old" with it?

Thus, as subject to error and to illusion as the old way may be, is there not something even more deeply illusory about Descartes's opinion that he is truly starting from scratch? Perhaps that sense of one's own self upon which he builds so much—perhaps even the very sense of self—has had to be shaped by the supposedly repudiated old way.

vii.

Besides, are the foundations of the structure of one's opinions as critical as Descartes makes them out to be? For one thing, the conventional edifice he is concerned with may not have been built originally from the foundations *up*, but rather from a kind of inner necessity which somehow superseded the apparent foundations. That inner necessity, or the design if not the end of the thing under consideration, may have something to do with nature, which shapes the edifice, compelling its existence, with the location and elements of the foundations being secondary.

Buildings, we know, are not always built from the foundations up. Consider what we know as "pre-fabs": previously constructed parts are assembled according to a plan. Perhaps that resembles how thinking works: some things may be, or may arise, in the mind, by nature and always, ready to be joined in the rational being to other things in the appropriate circumstances or upon the appropriate stimuli.

Thus, the structure, built from the plans "down," may have a buoyancy of its own. Perhaps, even, it is "suspended" from something. Or, perhaps, foundations may have been needed at one stage, but may no longer be needed once the thing is well made, just as the forms may no longer be needed once a ship is built.

One way or another, then, one can conceive of the structure of one's opinions as having a beauty, an integrity, a vitality of its own, independent of what it had required in its formative stages. Its true foundations, then, may be evident not in its beginnings but in its ends, ends which generations of unreflecting human beings are naturally drawn to and which do not depend upon their self-consciousness.

viii.

Also natural may be the way we grasp things such as premises or the self-evident. These graspings would be reflected in common sense, in myths, in art, in traditions, and in "instincts." Does not Descartes question the *reasonable and customary trust* that the ancients evidently had, to a considerable degree, in what the senses routinely give us access to?

Does Descartes substitute something artificial for that which naturally makes itself evident to us? Does nature assert herself and shape our thoughts, leading us to truths (or exposing truths in us) which we are not fully aware of, truths which we somehow (if not instinctively) sense that we share with others? May there not even be propositions we initially accept as we would rely upon undemonstrated opinions before further experience with them and reflection upon them help us understand that they are quite sound?

ix.

One may even wonder whether Descartes may not be the shaper of a new myth, one grounded more in the psyche of the individual and less in the common sense of the community than the set of conventional opinions which he would replace.

That is, are we asked to follow him, but without really going ourselves through the experiences which justify for him what he now believes? Thus, we can begin to assimilate in a few hours of careful reading what took Descartes himself several days (supposedly, as the account goes) or more likely many years to work out. In fact, one might wonder as well whether his own account, with respect to the order for him of demolition and of reconstruction, is reliable. Of course, one might also wonder whether I have distorted Descartes's thought unduly in attempting to simplify it as I have for this occasion.

What assurance have we, in following Descartes as he apparently expects us to, that we are not misled by him (whatever his own intentions may be)? Is there not something contrived in all this—both in his account and in any reliance by us upon an account which makes so much of a radical doubt? If we follow fully in Descartes's steps, should we not even question whether he is truly communicating anything to us? Well, some would say, let what he says be considered your own thought. But how critical to such thought, and perhaps to any thought, is the possibility of eventually communicating with others?

x.

In any event, the Cartesian approach is characterized by negativity: the emphasis is upon not-erring, which is called (in the fourth *Meditation*), "the greatest and principal perfection of man."

Thus, man's thinking and perhaps his doing as well are to be guided primarily by what is to be avoided, not by what is to be aimed at. Is not this a distinctively modern approach, evident also in someone such as Thomas Hobbes, who can emphasize the *summum malum*, not any *summum bonum*?

Does this approach make more plausible the possibility of a demolition project which depends upon uprooting the foundations? Aspirations do not seem to count as much, as something by which structures can be truly seen and thereafter sustained?

xi.

The certainty that follows upon taking the greatest care to avoid error may make possible reliable progress, even that attractive development special to modern times, *planned progress*.

The degree of certainty to be insisted upon, Descartes would have us believe, may be seen in the rigor exhibited in his opening *Meditations*: that rigor provides a standard for all research and judgment that will contribute to a steady advancement.

A key question remains: what is sacrificed in order to secure such progress? Are among the things sacrificed those opinions that could once be grasped and made good use of, even though they could not be identified as more than probable truths?

Another way of asking this is to suggest that Descartes can build in his way only those edifices which can be built thus—that is, those edifices which can be built on foundations dependent upon self-consciousness. But the more serious thinking, as well as the more noble deeds, may not be secured this way. May not the highest things depend to some extent upon intuitions and an imagination which can be naturally grasped and used but which cannot be "demonstrated"?

xii.

The Cartesian emphasis on a certainty secured by ultimately grounding everything in self-consciousness seems to have helped make psychology much more important than it had ever been.

This kind of self-centeredness suggests that the community and its shaping of citizens will be played down, although a community influenced by Descartes will shape others in accordance with his opinions—and will do so in such a way, it would seem, as to permit a fruitful organization of research with a view to steady progress.

How is this self-centeredness to be compared to the Delphic Oracle's *Know thyself*? Socrates, it seems, urged this kind of knowing so that one might re-order one's passions and one's particularities (and especially one's opinions) in the light of what we might call universals. One must wonder, however, what the status of universals, or of the Ideas, is for Descartes.

Both subjectivism and individuality would seem to be encouraged, if not required, by the Cartesian approach—for are not these what self-centeredness tends to lead to when applied both to the means (and the possibility) of knowing and to the determination of legitimate interests?

Related to all this is the evident superiority for Descartes of the volition over the understanding. Is this not related, in turn, to the *willing* that has taken place from the outset of the *Meditations*? It would seem as well that the human being knows only what he makes, that truth is for the most

part (if not altogether) a construction of the human mind, rather than something which exists independent of any human mind and always available
for discovery.

xiii.

The Cartesian view of truth and of how it is to be secured requires that
everything be re-oriented to the new approach. May this not even be seen in
how "God" is understood by Descartes? Earlier, he had required for his argument, in developing his demolition project, the possibility of a powerful
evil demon: this may have testified, in effect, to the hold that a natural sense
of things may usually have upon us.

There need be no distracting quarrel about whether the divinity described
by Descartes exists. That divinity, which Descartes argues is the ground of
understanding, sounds very much like the workings of nature.

That is, are most if not all controversies, at least in the West, about the
existence of God really either about what God is or about which revelation
is authoritative? Certainly, one would not be likely to pray to, or to fight
for, the Cartesian divinity or to expect any intervention by such a divinity
in human affairs.

xiv.

Thus, one can see Descartes, even as he makes much of God, tacitly
setting aside the God of revelation, and this despite the likelihood that there
is something Christian in Descartes's insistence upon the primacy of the individual soul as the starting point of his project. There are, of course, modern
scholars who argue that Descartes accepted the conventional Christian revelation, something which seems to me unlikely. Even so, that such arguments
are made by competent observers testifies to Descartes's scare, influence,
and effect in these matters.

Not that Cartesian science (in the form, say, of sociology and anthropology) would completely ignore the teachings of revelation. Those teachings
would be dealt with, once the appropriate foundations are laid and a reliable
method is developed—but when one returns to these teachings thus, they are
not seen as they are seen by those who "believe." That is, such teachings are
"explained" as natural phenomena rather than "accepted" as inspired truths.
Thereafter they can be deliberately refashioned from time to time in order to
serve the needs of the day.

To say that the divine is seen primarily in terms of the natural is not to
say, however, that the ancients are resurrected in Descartes: for the nature to

which he returns is somehow different from theirs. The ancients do seem to have made more of common sense as the starting point even of philosophy: this may be seen in a community-shared experience. Common sense is rough; it can be wrong; it is certainly in need of periodic refinement—but yet, it is substantially reliable, perhaps because the Ideas exist, perhaps because minds share, and sense that they do share as minds, various things (including a somewhat reliable grasp of bodies).

Descartes's nature is different in another respect as well: it is, we have anticipated, somehow not open to the noble. Thus, Descartes, who is more sure of himself about critical beginnings than are Plato and his students—or at least he believes he should be more sure—Descartes is so concerned about the beginnings that he can ignore the ends that nature may point to. In short, he may lose sight of, and perhaps make more difficult the achievement of, the highest things both in words (philosophy) and in deeds (including the noble).

xv.

The reservations suggested here, it is prudent to assume, are reservations that Descartes himself was probably aware of. Why, then, did he proceed as he did?

For one thing, he might have answered, only in this way may a steady progress be made to "relieve man's estate" (to borrow from Francis Bacon). And, he might ask, is not that a prospect that is truly noble, or at least worthy of any humane philosopher? Then there is, of course, the challenge, and perhaps the glory (if not the nobility), of founding a new way that many will find remarkably productive and hence attractive.

Even so, we must still wonder precisely how Descartes made a difference? What *did* his method consist of and how did it work? Of course, something may be effective, especially if self-confidence is promoted thereby or if a part of the whole is somehow gotten ahold of—something may be effective without being simply or fully true.

But the question remains, Just how did Descartes (if he did) help bring about the modern scientific and technological revolution?

xvi.

One thing Descartes did do was to help legitimate a more "utilitarian" approach to human understanding, perhaps a more prosaic approach which could also be more "scientific" in the modern sense (with special reliance on mathematics).

A critical objective for him seems to have been what we know as "the conquest of nature," that "mastery and possession of nature" which would greatly benefit mankind. Did Descartes sense that a nature thus to be mastered and used would have to be depreciated? Thus, nature is not looked to as a source of final causes (or of the "whyness" of things), just as it is not looked to as the unaided source of the premises, or self-evident truths, from which common sense and a refined community opinion could readily work.

In the name of what, then, is the conquest of nature to be made? In the service primarily of the self, it would seem—that very self upon which reliable understanding is to be grounded. But is anything but chance to determine what it will be that that self will desire and in the light of which the conquest and exploitation of nature will be conducted?

xvii.

Perhaps it is because chance desires provide, under the Cartesian dispensation, the ends by which the conquest of nature may be guided in practice that more and more is made (wherever the modern project has "succeeded") of the physical. Thus, an aggressive materialism reigns, even though the ostensible starting place for the Cartesian revolution was an emphasis upon the soul and a total abstraction by the mind from the body.

Whether Descartes ever intended to abandon, or even to depreciate, the body is a question for others to address. Did he say what he did about the body, and about the soul, as part of his effort to replace nature as a source and guide— or rather, as part of his effort to replace those who had made so much either of nature (as formerly understood) or of the supernatural?

Be that as it may, the Cartesian approach eventually contributed, in effect, to an unparalleled harnessing of nature and an unparalleled gratification of the body—as well as perhaps to a lowering of the calibre of old-style philosophy (even though, with many more resources now available not only for assuring our physical well-being but also for permitting considerable "cultural" activity, there are many more people now "doing" philosophy than there ever were in pre-modern times).

It remains to be seen whether the approach of Descartes and his fellow-moderns is truly utilitarian. For one thing, it seems that the ancients were more dubious than their successors have been about the benefits of an ever-changing technology. For another thing, the ancients may have recognized that the body must be given its due with respect to the origins of human understanding, lest either a self-centered materialism grounded in skepticism or an irresponsible otherworldliness grounded in superstition follow from a failure to make proper use of common sense.

III.

i.

The disciplined subjectivity which Descartes developed may have been prepared for by Christianity with its perhaps unprecedented enthronement of the individual soul. The ramifications of such subjectivity are endless, including its tendency to sanctify a right to privacy and a tendency (at least in some quarters) to reduce political science, artistic criticism, and even theology to studies in personal psychology. There may be seen, in the essays that follow this Introduction, the vigorous Maritain reservations about the Cartesian approach to the ways of knowing.

When much is made of *the person*, there can be encouraged an overriding concern about the fate of the individual human being, a concern which tends to intensify the problem of death. Two (among the many) approaches to the problem of death, and to the ways of *knowing* about it, suggest the divergent responses that are generally available to human being. The first approach, very much grounded in the Christian tradition, may be seen in a poem by Gerald Manley Hopkins:

> I wake and feel the fell of dark, not day.
> What hours, O what black hours we have spent
> This night! what sights you, heart, saw; ways you went!
> And more must, in yet longer light's delay.
>
> With witness I speak this. But where I say
> Hours I mean years, mean life. And my lament
> Is cries countless, cries like dead letters sent
> To dearest him that lives alas! away.
>
> I am gall, I am heartburn. God's most deep decree
> Bitter would have me taste: my taste was me;
> Bones built in me, flesh filled, blood brimmed the curse.
>
> Selfyeast of spirit a dull dough sours. I see
> The lost are like this, and their scourge to be
> As I am mine, their sweating selves, but worse.

What does this Narrator *know* which justifies the despair expressed here? It is one thing to be moved in this way while one sleeps: all kinds of passions can be churning then (including such as may be caused, as Ebenezer Scrooge put it, by "an undigested bit of beef"). But once a mature human being is fully awake, even though it is still dark, should not he "know better"— and especially know that there is nothing dreadful always confronting the typical human being, however troubled he may naturally happen to be by the prospect that he might someday simply cease to be?

But, it will be answered, "God's most deep decree" means that unredeemed human life is doomed to gall, to heartburn, to being desperately lost—in short, to a nightmarish existence, whether one is awake or asleep, whether alive or dead. Socrates, of course, would wonder how it is that one knows the things that inspire the horrors and despair reported by this desperate Narrator: a fevered, if not self-indulgent and even self-flagellating, imagination may be suspected at work here. Socrates would also wonder what it is in the human soul, and in modern subjectivity (with its grounding for some in "fear and trembling"?), that makes us receptive to such dreadful flights of fancy.

ii.

On the other hand, Socrates could probably consider the approach to these or like matters exhibited in the following poem by Emily Dickinson to be healthier, as well as less dependent upon unconfirmed, perhaps unconfirmable, reports of an apocalyptic character:

Because I could not stop for Death–
He kindly stopped for me–
The Carriage held but just Ourselves–
and Immortality.

We slowly drove–He knew no haste
And I had put away
My labor and my leisure too,
For His Civility–

We passed the School, where Children strove
At Recess–in the Ring–
We passed the Fields of Gazing Grain–
We passed the Setting Sun–

Or rather–He passed Us–
The Dews grew quivering and chill–
For only Gossamer, my Gown–
My Tippet–only Tulle–

We paused before a House that seemed
A Swelling of the Ground–
The Roof was scarcely visible–
The Cornice–in the Ground–

Since then–'tis Centuries–and yet
Feels shorter than the Day
I first surmised the Horses's Heads
Were toward Eternity–

This poem is one of many by Dickinson touching upon the mysteries of Death. Here is how one scholar introduces his chapter on Death in his useful commentary on her poetry:

The most vivid embodiment of life to Emily Dickinson in her later years was the cherished nephew next door. When he was suddenly ravished from life and from her love by an early death, the most poignant cry she ever uttered broke from her lips:

'Open the Door, open the Door, they are waiting for me,' was Gilbert's sweet command in delirium. *Who* were waiting for him, all we possess we would give to know–Anguish at last opened it, and he ran to the little Grave at his Grandparents's feet–All this and more, though *is* there more? More than Love and Death? Then tell me its name!

These questions [Emily Dickinson] was never able to answer. Rather, she made many answers, in prose and verse, but for the most part they simply asked the same questions in other forms or resolved them in paradoxes. Love may be the crowning glory of life, but one becomes fully aware of such transcendent value only when confronted with its extinction in death.[45]

A poet may indeed describe dying and death in various ways. This may be seen in, for example, Shakespeare, where both the most serene and the most fearful dying can be depicted by him. Each way of depiction may, in the hands of a competent poet, be plausible. That *is* the way poetry works: each way that is depicted, among several quite diverse ways, may be more or less plausible when standing alone.

One "device" used by Dickinson for her meditations on Death is the funeral procession. This use is described for us by the scholar from whom I have already quoted:

What makes death fascinating to the poet is that, to borrow a term she used elsewhere, it is the 'Hyphen' between the mortal life and man's dream of immortality. However short the hyphen of death, however instantaneous the soul's passage from one world to another, the customs of society have habitually prolonged the interval with last rites, funeral procession, and burial service, perhaps to allow time for meditation on its meaning. In the village world of a century ago these

[45] Charles R. Anderson, *Emily Dickinson's Poetry: Stairway of Surprise* (New York: Holt, Rinehart and Winston, 1960), p. 225.

ceremonies were carried off with far more solemnity and pomp than today, and they were an inescapable part of people's lives. The pageantry of that dark parade to the graveyard particularly caught the eye of Emily Dickinson, with its plumed horses, flower-decked hearse, and formal mourning attire. From her tenth to her twenty-fifth years, when she lived on Pleasant Street, it regularly passed her home on its way to the cemetery nearby. As a schoolgirl she reported in a letter: 'Yesterday as I sat by the north window the funeral train entered the open gate of the church yard, following the remains of Judge Dickinson's wife to her long home.'[46]

iii.

Our scholar goes on to say that the Dickinson poem, "Because I Could Not Stop for Death" (also known as "The Carriage"), is "her finest poem on the funeral ceremony."[47] The first extended comments he makes thereafter are helpful, however in need of qualification they may be:

At first reading, the orthodox reassurance against the fear of death appears to be invoked, though with the novelty of a suitor replacing the traditional angel, by emphasizing his compassionate mission in taking her out of the woes of this world into the bliss of the next. 'Death,' usually rude, sudden, and impersonal, has been transformed into a kindly and leisurely gentleman. Although she was aware this is a last ride, since his 'Carriage' can only be a hearse, its terror is subdued by the 'Civility' of the driver who is merely serving the end of 'Immortality.' The loneliness of the journey, with Death on the driver's seat and her body laid out in the coach behind, is dispelled by the presence of her immortal part that rides with her as a co-passenger, this slight personification being justified by the separable concept of the soul. Too occupied with life herself to stop, like all busy mortals, Death 'kindly stopped' for her. But this figure of a gentleman taking a lady for a carriage ride is carefully underplayed and then dropped after two stanzas.[48]

iv.

A special feature of this poem, as has been noticed, is the conceit of presenting Death as a most courteous gentlemen taking a lady for a ride in the country, perhaps even seeming to court her.

The Narrator describing this outing seems to be the immortal soul of the woman whose body is being transported by the carriage. Death is in the driver's seat. How long Death remains there is, at least for me, a question. Does the Narrator sit beside him? (Does "ourselves" refer to the Narrator

---

[46] Ibid., pp. 238-39.
[47] Ibid., p. 24.
[48] Ibid., p. 242

and Death, or to the Soul and the Body of the Narrator, or to all of these?) However that may be, the unencumbered soul will ride on, in the carriage, after the lifeless body has been duly disposed of.

A leisurely trip is described, with no sense either of grief or of urgency. Before the poem ends particular things stop happening to the Narrator: there is nothing more to describe as she continues "toward Eternity."

v.

The central lines of this account describe the role of the Sun, immediately before and after the central words of the poem ("the Setting Sun"; words 63, 64, and 65 of 127 words):

> We passed the Setting Sun–
> Or rather–He passed Us–

This observation about the centrality of the Setting Sun, and what can be made of that, may suggest that all six stanzas of this poem are needed. I must question, that is, the decision by some editors of the poem to cut its fourth stanza. In short, this poem is constructed with great care.

I have observed that a poet's ways of describing dying and death may be diverse, with each of them (standing alone) being quite plausible. Which, of a variety of such poems, should be regarded as most plausible, if not as simply true, by the poet herself? Perhaps, it can be answered, the finest of the contending poems–for it is through *it* that the poet can be safely presumed to have said the best of what she knows.

The top rank of the "Carriage" poem, at least in its genre, has been recognized by the scholar from whom I have quoted. Several features of this poem, to which I now turn, encourage one to argue that it is even finer than its professional admirers believe it to be.

vi.

Before the Setting Sun is passed, the carriage is driven along familiar scenes, both in the town and in the adjoining countryside. Both human activities and the products of cultivated nature come to view.

The narrator, in looking back on this stage of the Ride from the perspective available to her at the end, considers children *playing* as particularly characteristic of human activity, not even children *studying* and *learning*, for that could point to maturity and the enduring.

In the light of Eternity, all human activity (all "labor" and "leisure") seems somehow childlike if not even ultimately inconsequential. From this perspective, that is, we are but "creatures of a day" (as Homer's gods put it in characterizing human beings).

vii.

After the Sun passed the Carriage (with the description of the Sun's movement relative to the Carriage reversed), a chilly, dimly-lit world is moved through. (There are here no "Fields of Gazing Grain.") *Day*, as such, will soon be gone, as Eternity looms up ahead. Lifelessness sets in.

It need be no more than suggested that the lifeless body is left in its grave. This is done by an austere, not easily recognized, description of a graveyard where the procession "paused" before the appropriate "House." The lifelessness in the second half of this poem is reflected in the considerable reduction, if not total absence, of motion after the passing by them of the Sun. Once the Sun is gone, both life and time fade away. The minimum of motion may be suggested by the use of "paused."

Nothing is indicated about a burial ceremony. It does not seem to matter to the Narrator, who has left her lifeless body to its fate in a tomb. Whether mourners, if any, feel otherwise seems of no concern to the Narrator.

The "first surmised" of the final stanza may refer back to the transaction in the graveyard, where the body is deposited. It may be only then, whatever may have been somehow suspected earlier, that the Narrator grasps firmly the facts of her Death. No shock or fear or even regret is expressed–a kind of bemused resignation sets in. Death may be left behind, with the body, at the graveyard. Death can then go on about its business among the living.

Not only does the body sink out of view, so do human habitations: houses, holding the bodies of families, are lost to view in the graveyard, or so it seems when a tomb is described. Personal clothing can also be described, if not even discarded, as insubstantial. Material necessities are no longer depended upon. The world and its equipment seem to be left behind by the Narrator.

viii.

The final stanza begins, "Since then–." Centuries have evidently passed since the burial. No details are given; but then, is there anything to report? Centuries can move by quickly, it seems, if there are no bodies to contend with or to tether one's experiences.

All now seems to be in slow motion, even as the centuries speed by, feeling shorter than the first day, the day of the burial. How many centuries? At least two–which means that seventy-thousand Eternity-oriented days (if not hundreds of thousands more) seem to have passed more quickly than one earth-bound day.

The familiar worldly things no longer matter. Death, too, has faded away. Indeed, had Death done anything at all? Is it merely an automatic signaling—an initiation of nothingness? It does seem to drift out of this picture, once the Narrator is alone as a soul, having no body to deal with. The Narrator seems to experience the state of *being* dead—not the experience of dying, but at most the immediate aftermath of death (the funeral procession and burial), which can be calmly surveyed and easily left behind. (Whether one can truly know one's own dying-and-death remains a mystery.)

What is suggested in this poem, however fleetingly, about the nature of life after death? It seems rather tranquil, relaxed, with little if any concern expressed about or contact with the life on the earth that one has left.

Centuries have already passed, by the end of the poem (which is when the Narrator begins to recollect the last day of her life), with little if anything to be recorded. Do centuries more have to be transcended before Eternity is reached–and will anything be different "then"? Does all that the soul will ever experience that is variegated depend upon its embodied state, or upon that *and* the events immediately following disembodiment? Afterwards, all there is depends upon memories–and those, like death, may fade. There is no hint in this poem that there is anyone to be met, any reward to be anticipated, any punishment to be dreaded after death.

Once Eternity is reached, does complete timelessness set in—and hence the cessation of all activity (including the workings of memory)? No change is possible "then"? Is such lifelessness implied by what has been said? Does the poet sense the implications of what is depicted here, by means of the "taste" of Eternity provided in the last stanza of the poem?

Each of the dead, it seems, is essentially on its own, without suffering an acute sense of loneliness. It also seems that the disembodied soul, no matter how long it survives, lacks the elements (related to the bodily) which permit both longing and deterioration.

It may be, as Aristotle observed when he touched upon these matters in the first book of the *Nicomachean Ethics*, that the prevailing opinions here are quite different from what this Dickinson poem suggests. Most people *are* inclined to believe that the dead are affected by what happens among their still-living descendants. It may be unfeeling–again to borrow from Aristotle– to leave our commentary without adding that something fine on earth can endure–at least so long as human beings continue–in the finest poems of our poets, even as they recognize what is not likely to endure.

Emily Dickinson herself, in another poem on death, can be seen (in her sensitivity to the unfeeling) to minister to those who need the kind of reassurance implied in the following poem:

The Bustle in a House
The Morning after Death
Is solemnest of industries
Enacted upon Earth–

The Sweeping up the Heart
And putting Love away
We shall not want to use again
Until Eternity.

The hopeful sentiments offered here can seem, or at least can be made to seem, not inconsistent with the more austere implications we have noticed in the "Carriage" poem.

ix.

Does Gerard Manley Hopkins endorse the sombre view of things expressed by the Narrator in that poem of his that we have glanced at? This is to ask, "What kind of a world is this, anyway?" Hopkins's personal opinion here cannot be determined without reckoning also with the recognition of the beautiful found in such poems as this by him ("Pied Beauty"):

Glory be to God for dappled things—
   For skies of couple-colour as a brinded cow;
      For rose-moles all in stipple upon trout that swim;
Fresh-firecoal chestnut-falls; finches's wings;
   Landscape plotted and pieced—fold, fallow, and plough;
      And all trades, their gear and tackle and trim.
All things counter, original, spare, strange;
   Whatever is fickle, freckled (who knows how?)
      With swift, slow; sweet, sour; adazzle, dim;
He fathers-forth whose beauty is past change;
                              Praise him.

Here, somehow, "God's most deep decree" does not seem to run. That is, we need not always (if ever) see and hence know the world through the darkened eyes of a Narrator who has been traumatized by "black hours" witnessing dreadful things.

Epilogue

We return, in closing this Introduction, to Socrates. A capacity is repeatedly relied upon by him to sift through what the poets say, including what they presume to say that they know both about death and about the divine. Thus, I have suggested, he would prefer Dickinson to Hopkins, even though he could also reasonably be expected to prefer (although not without reservations) Shakespeare to both. The reader of the essays that follow this Introduction is challenged to determine what Jacques Maritain's preferences would be here.

Socrates's response to Galileo would no doubt find him respectful, however much he might pursue further our inquiry into what it is that is presupposed by modern scientists as well as into what is not sufficiently examined by them. He would endorse, I believe, the observation quoted in the Prologue to this Introduction from Bertrand Russell about the limitations of a sometimes-tyrannical modern science.[49]

The willfulness, if not self-centeredness, of the Cartesian approach would intrigue Socrates, especially insofar as it seems to be a philosophical equivalent of the Thrasymachean approach to issues of justice. Certainly, Socrates would want to question the related suggestion, in effect, of modern subjectivism, the rather discouraging suggestion that we know only what we make. He would prefer to emphasize that we should always try to discover all that is there to be learned, particularly the enduring things— and in fully grasping those things, he might add, we not only identify ourselves with like-minded rational beings before and after us (everywhere in the Universe) but we also grasp as much (and as long) as we ever can the things that may naturally be known.

---

[49] See the text at note 2 of this Introduction. See also Ernest L. Fortin, *Dissent and Philosophy in the Middle Ages* (Lanham, Maryland: Lexington Books, forthcoming), chap. 2. Consider especially the intriguing suggestion by Father Fortin that both Al-Farabi and Maimonides claim for political philosophy the right to judge even divine things. See ibid., chap. 2. This is related to the insistence upon basing the worth of the work of such an artist as Dante upon the intellectual content no less than upon the formal beauty of his poetry. See ibid., chap. 4. Also important here, and with respect to Descartes and Gerard Manley Hopkins as well, is the following observation: "The quarrel between the ancients and the moderns concerns eventually, and perhaps even from the beginning, the status of 'individuality.'" Leo Strauss, *Natural Right and History* (Chicago: The University of Chicago Press, 1953), p. 323. See, on Leo Strauss, Kenneth L. Deutsch and John A. Murley, eds., *Leo Strauss, the Straussians, and the American Regime* (Lanham, Maryland: Rowman & Littlefield, 1999).

The Mysterious Value of the Human Person

Joseph M. de Torre

An openness to reality without limits (*logos, nous*) is what marks man out from the other animals, as Greek philosophy discovered. Man-made things, like houses, bridges, computers, business corporations, legal codes and civil governments, as well as nature-made things, like vegetables and animals, are stamped with limitation. The human person alone, among all beings in the cosmos, has the capacity to transcend or "go beyond" oneself into infinity, not of course through his or her physicality (confined to space and time and quantifiable), but through that other human component which is able to go beyond the confines of space and time to an indefinite degree, namely his or her metaphysicality. This wondrous power, traditionally called spirit (human knowledge and love), opens humanity towards infinite reality, and thus places the dignity of the human person, or the intrinsic value of every human being, above the entire physical cosmos.[1] This, Aquinas pointed out *passim*, and Maritain emphasized in his socio-political philosophy.[2] For the various "ways of knowing", we can recall Maritain's masterpiece, *The Degrees of Knowledge*, as well as *Science and Wisdom* and *The Range of Reason*.[3] For his part, Gilson provided the epistemological ground for this total openness to reality, especially in his works *Methodical Realism* and *Thomist Realism and Critique of Knowledge*.[4]

---

[1] Joseph M. de Torre, *Work , Culture, Liberation,* (Manila: Vera-Reyes, 1985), chap 5, and *Openness to Reality: Essays on Secularism and Transcendence* (Manila: SEASFI, 1995), chap. III.

[2] See especially his classic *Humanisme intégrál* (Paris: Aubier, 1936), and *Man and the State* (Chicago: The University of Chicago Press, 1951).

[3] Jacques Maritain, *The Degrees of Knowledge*, trans. Gerald B. Phelan (Notre Dame, Indiana: University of Notre Dame Press, 1995); *Science and Wisdom* (London: Geoffrey Bles, 1940); *The Range of Reason* (New York: Charles Scribner's Sons, 1952).

[4] Étienne Gilson, *Methodical Realism* (Front Royal, Virginia: Christendom Press, 1992); *Thomist Realism and Critique of Knowledge*, trans. Mark A. Wauck (San Francisco: Ignatius Press, 1986).

The human person is invited by his or her Creator, who is the fulness of personal existence, to plunge into that potentially infinite reality of the physical world (both macrocosmic, in an ever expanding universe; and microcosmic, in an ever explorable intra-atomic world of pure energy). As well as into the unfathomable and purely transensible and intangible world of moral values, anchored in the depth of human nature.[5]

Astride these two experiences (which fascinated Kant),[6] the physical and the ethical, is the metaphysical drive in search of ultimate beauty—the impulse toward total beauty and good, through the experience of partial beauty and good. Plato called this impulse, *Eros*, a term which subsequently lost its original meaning.[7] He also identified the possession of total knowledge as wisdom, and since this is unattainable by man, he has to be humbly satisfied with the "love of wisdom," namely philosophy. Man is both the poorest and the richest of all beings—the poorest, because he realizes the abyss of his ignorance (other beings don't), and the richest, because he can embark on an indefinite adventure to dispel that ignorance. The study of nature and history is the privileged path for this adventure.

The Global View of Reality

On the one hand, man has an infinite variety of choices in his quest for truth or revelation of reality to the human mind.[8] This gives rise to the special-ization of the sciences (mathematical, natural, social).[9] Likewise, the search for values and ultimate meaning, and the sensible expression of them through the fine arts, which are also called The Arts of the Beautiful (as distinct from the arts of the useful), also opens up an infinite number of vistas.[10]

On the other hand, however, man also perceives that beyond those su-preme values of beauty, good and truth lies the ultimate unity of all being. The

---

[5] Stanley L. Jaki, *The Relevance of Physics* (Chicago: University of Chicago Press, 1966); *The Road of Science and the Ways to God* (Chicago: The University of Chicago Press, 1978). Also William A. Wallace, *The Modeling of Nature* (Washington, D.C.: The Catholic University of America Press, 1996).

[6] Joseph M. de Torre, *The Humanism of Modern Philosophy* (Pasig City, Philippines: University of Asia and the Pacific, 1997), chap. XI, 7.

[7] *Symposium.*

[8] *Aletheia* or "revelation" is the Greek term for truth.

[9] Jacques Maritain, *Introduction to Philosophy* (New York: Sheed & Ward, 1947).

[10] Étienne Gilson, *The Arts of the Beautiful* (New York: Charles Scribner's Sons, 1965) and Jacques Maritain, *Art and Scholasticism* (New York: Charles Scribner's Sons, 1930). Also the "Letter of His Holiness Pope John Paul II to Artists," *L'Osservatore Romano*, English ed. (28 April 1999).

perception (or glimpse) of the latter is what gives man the global view of reality, which is therefore the indispensable vantage point from which to descry and explore any particular area of reality. This means that the philosophical or metaphysical approach to reality, with the candidness of an unprejudiced child who is not afraid of asking ultimate questions, must start and orient every endeavor to know, express and communicate the grasping of any truth.[11]

In other words, things have to be studied in their context and background.[12] The mind must strive always to see things with a global perspective of totality, without rushing into premature analyses, which miss the wood for the trees, or take the part for the whole. Most dreadful and terrifying mistakes can be made in the absence of this global and comprehensive (philosophical) orientation. The reduction of man to a mere economic unit (*homo oeconomicus*) is an instance of that distortion of reality that has produced huge quantities of human victims in battlefields, genocides, concentration camps and, above all, in mothers's wombs: the so called "collective guilt", so trenchantly opposed by Viktor Frankl's personalist philosophy.[13]

Spirit over Matter

The human person must be approached with this global view of his and her place in the cosmos. The human person must be looked at metaphysically and ethically, as a bearer of values and a God-seeker, as Max Scheler put it.[14] The human person is not just an animal that happens to have evolved from monkeys. This may be true with regard to the human body, but the spirit of man, oriented and open to infinity, and transcending all the limits of the space-time cosmos, can only originate from a Being infinitely beyond the quantified horizons of the material universe. The human spirit, both finite and capable of infinity, can be created from nothing only by an Omnipotent Creator.[15]

To be really human, therefore, the human person must allow his or her intelligence (drive for the truth) and will (drive for the good) to take command

---

[11] Dietrich von Hildebrand, *What is Philosophy?* (Chicago: Franciscan Herald Press, 1973). Also Jacques Maritain, *On the Use of Philosophy* (Princeton, New Jersey: Princeton University Press, 1961).

[12] Jacques Maritain, *On the Philosophy of History* (New York: Charles Scribner's Sons, 1957).

[13] Viktor Frankl, *Recollection: An Autobiography* (New York: Plenum Press, Insight Books, 1997).

[14] *The Humanism of Modern Philosophy,* chap. XXIII.

[15] Joseph M. de Torre, *Generation and Degeneration: A Survey of Ideologies* (Manila: SEASFI, 1995), chap. 14.

of his or her entire person (body and soul), impelled by that core of the self which is traditionally called the heart, and which is the inner drive for beauty.[16]

This humanism is not "secular" (closed to transcendence) or immanent, but is truly sacred (open to transcendence) and carrying the human person to an ecstatic self-surpassing and encompassing plunge into the entire expanse of reality. Only then can the human spirit begin to analyze and concentrate his or her attention on specific areas of reality, such as the physical sciences, the social sciences, the practical sciences or the fine arts. To perceive things properly, the human mind must always widen the scope of its vision, so as to take in as much context as possible: a panoramic and historical view is necessary with the ability to see the multiplicity of relationships and correlations; the global view of reality.

If the philosophical or metaphysical approach is missing in education, the products will not be real human persons, but voracious animals or dumb machines, with the catastrophic consequences that we are witnessing in our era of unbridled galloping technologism.[17]

A crippling of humanity occurred when positivists began to limit the field of human knowledge to what can be perceived by the senses and measured mathematically, lumping everything else into the sphere of subjective belief or "preference" or simply "mystical" incommunicable experience.[18] This distortion took different shapes.

From the Enlightenment to Romanticism

Kant in his *Critique of Judgment* tried to recompose the seemingly unbridgeable gap he himself had created between "pure reason" and "practical reason", namely between the world of necessity (physical phenomena) and the world of freedom (moral judgment).[19] But his attempt ended up in Hegel's absolute idealism and Marx's dialectical materialism, both obliterating human freedom and individual personality, as denounced by Kierkegaard and his personalist followers.[20]

It was Comte's positivism or scientism that consummated the split between physical necessity and spiritual or moral freedom, the former regarded as "objective" and the latter as "subjective."[21] This was the origin of the

---

[16] Joseph M. de Torre, *Christian Philosophy* (Manila: Sinagtala, 1980), chaps. 7, 19, 23.

[17] *Generation and Degeneration,* chap. 16.

[18] *The Humanism of Modern Philosophy*, chap. XIV, 5, and chap. XXII. See also Étienne Gilson, *The Unity of Philosophical Experience* (New York: Charles Scribner's Sons, 1937).

[19] *The Humanism of Modern Philosophy,* chap. XI.

[20] *The Humanism of Modern Philosophy.*

[21] *Generation and Degeneration*, chap. 16 and 21.

"two cultures" of the sciences *versus* the so-called humanities (popularized by C.P. Snow),[22] with the so-called social sciences awkwardly falling between the two stools, and becoming the target of both the physical sciences (for not being as quantifiable as the latter), and metaphysics and ethics (for failing to see the transcendent dimension of the human person).

Dilthey later tried to recover the validity of what neo-Kantians called the "sciences of the spirit" (humanities) as distinct from the "sciences of nature" (physical sciences),[23] and the attack on positivism was followed up with the rise of the phenomenological movement, merging with the existentialist revival of Kierkegaard's critique of Hegel,[24] while positivism got a new lease of life with the advent of logical positivism and the Vienna Circle. And the conflict goes on.

Thought versus Reality

But it is a conflict stemming from a wrong starting point. The philosophical or metaphysical approach to all branches of knowledge, outlined above, shows that the split between the sciences and the humanities is entirely unreal and artificial, since the sciences are not "inhuman", nor are the humanities "unscientific". The confinement of the field of human knowledge to what is empirical and quantifiable is an *a priori* dogma without basis in real human experience.

As Stanley L. Jaki has endeavored to show,[25] this dogma has not been accepted by the genuine scientists of our time who, in the field of macrophysics, microphysics and microbiology, have ventured into the transensible world of pure energy with the sole tool of the most abstract and meta-empirical science of mathematics, thus defying the positivistic reduction of knowledge to what is empirically verifiable.

If by "science" we mean true and certain knowledge through causes,[26] we have to rescue the concept of cause from its impoverishment at the hands of the empiricists and Kant, [27] and see it again in the context of a real metaphysics of actual being, not of abstract essences. And we ought to verify

[22] C. P. Snow, *The Two Cultures and A Second Look* (Cambridge: Cambridge University Press, 1959).

[23] *The Humanism of Modern Philosophy*, chap. XIX.

[24] Ibid., chap. XXIII and XVIII.

[25] *The Relevance of Physics; The Road of Science and the Ways to God.*

[26] This is the classic Aristotelian definition of science or *epistemé*: to know not just that something is like that, but why it is like that.

[27] *Christian Philosophy*, chap. 18.

once again that the human intelligence, keeping a global outlook on reality, can and does penetrate into the innermost core of the being of everything.[28]

Only this thrust can drive the human intelligence into the vast world of the physical and social sciences, and activate scientific discovery and technological invention. And only this thrust can stimulate human creativity in literature and the fine arts, or what has been called (somewhat inaccurately) the humanities.[29]

Reason and Faith

But there is still a higher knowledge to which philosophy can lead, as the gateway to it, just as it is the gateway to all other fields of human knowledge.

Aristotle spoke about "right reason" (*orthos logos*) as the openness of the human mind to reality, but not having received any tradition of allegedly revealed religion, he was not in a position to compare his rational knowledge with such a kind of revelation. His concept of person was not mature enough to ascribe it to a deity who could, therefore, speak to, or communicate with man, and so, could actually and historically make a revelation to man.[30]

Augustine and Aquinas, on the other hand, were in a different position. The former saw in the *Doctrina christiana* a Christian philosophy in perfect correlation or harmony with Judeo-Christian revelation. And eight centuries later, Aquinas enlarged and widened the scope of the *orthos logos* or *recta ratio* of Aristotle to include the sublime reality of God's own revelation to man. Faith in this revelation thus became the supernatural enlightenment of human reason; and philosophy, or rational thought and enquiry, became the indispensable tool of theology or rational understanding of revelation. This has been lucidly discussed in the encyclical *Fides et Ratio*.

Now was human reason open to the totality of reality by opening itself to the brighter enlightenment of Judeo-Christian revelation: thus, in the expression of Aquinas, supernatural grace came to bring nature to its perfection, without substituting itself for it.

But after the humanistic turbulence of the Renaissance, the Enlightenment emerged, calling that revelation blind and naive and irrational belief, having obfuscated and shackled reason (obscurantism!): the rationalists and the empiricists converging into Kant, and enclosing reason in the material universe. This is the real "closing" not only of the "American mind", in

---

[28] *Methodical Realism*; *Thomist Realism and Critique of Knowledge.*
[29] *Work, Culture, Liberation*, chap. 1.
[30] *Christian Philosophy*, chap. 2 and 3.

Allan Bloom's famous phrase,[31] but also of the entire modern mind. No one has fought more forcefully for this re-opening of the human mind and heart than Etienne Gilson with his classics, *Methodical Realism* (which he also calls "naïve realism") and *Thomist Realism and Critique of Knowledge.*

Back to Transcendence

Mankind now looks hopefully toward a future post-modern mind that can open itself again to transcendence.[32] This philosophical approach to all fields of knowledge, which is the openness to transcendence without artificial confinements, has in the past (and in the present) yielded the greatest accomplishments of culture.[33] It was present in the great poets and writers, artists and scientists, statesmen and economists, philosophers and theologians. It was present in Dante and Fra Angelico, Piero della Francesca and Raphael, Da Vinci and Michaelangelo, Cervantes and Calderon, Shakespeare and Milton, Copernicus and Newton, Corneille and Racine, Velazquez and Rubens, Goethe and Schiller, Beethoven and Wagner, Wordsworth and Blake, Burke and Lincoln, Jefferson and Disraeli, Dostoyevsky and Chekhov, Tchaikovsky and Stravinsky, Duhem and de Broglie, Planck and Einstein, Heisenberg and Weisszaecker, Dirac and Schroedinger, Undset and Stein, Churchill and Adenauer, Sun Yat Sen and Chiang Kai Shek, T. S. Eliot and C. S. Lewis, Chesterton and Belloc, Leo XIII and John Paul II, Ratzinger and de Lubac, Maritain and Gilson, Pieper and von Balthasar, Dawson and Jaki, etc.

It was because all these persons, among many others, were primarily philosophers, seekers of ultimate truth, that they attained greatness in their respective fields of knowledge and endeavor.

They combined the receptive power of the intellect (Aristotle's *nous pathetikos*) with its active power (Aristotle's *nous poietikos*). In other words, they were opened to the Dionysian or *yin* mystery of a reality always surpassing man (predominant in the feminine spirit), while driven by the Apollonian or *yang* impulse to definition and clarity (predominant in the masculine spirit): both insatiably thirsty for data-gathering, information and receptive experience, and anxiously eager "to do something about it". They were persons both speculative and practical, analytical and synthetic, con-

---

[31] Allan Bloom, *The Closing of the American Mind* (New York: Simon & Schuster, 1987).

[32] Of particular importance are the works of Viktor Frankl (especially *Recollection. An Autobiography*) and Paul Ricoeur, *The Philosophy of Paul Ricoeur*, ed. L. E. Hahn (Chicago: The Library of Living Philosophers, 1995).

[33] *Openness to Reality*, chap. III.

templative and active; in short, true philosophers or "lovers of wisdom", and thereby benefactors of humanity despite their human limitations.

Philosophy as Content and Form of Education

At the beginning of the thirteenth century, the founders of the first university, *the Universitas magistrum et scholarium Lutetiae Parisiorum degentium*, seemed to have had very much in mind this propedeutic or introductory role of philosophy for all other fields of knowledge, when they made it the core curriculum of the College of Arts and Sciences.[34] There the students (all of them) would get their bachelor's degree, which would qualify them for the masteral and doctoral programs of the faculties of law, medicine or theology. The Catholic Church even now requires the students for the priesthood to take a very thorough grounding in philosophy, before going on to theology. Thus, the Second Vatican Council in its *Decree on Priestly Training* (*Optatam Totius*, no. 15): "The philosophical disciplines are to be taught in such a way that the students are first of all led to acquire a solid and coherent knowledge of man, the world, and of God, relying on a philosophical patrimony which is perennially valid and taking into account the philosophical investigations of later ages."

This philosophical approach to all branches of knowledge also ensures that the mistake of confusion of method and object among them is avoided. Only the global or overall view of reality makes it possible to see the limits, correlations and overlappings of the different areas of it. While, from the objective point of view, theology can be considered the highest science, and philosophy its means of investigation and expression with regard to all sciences and arts, this does not in any way detract from the "autonomy of earthly affairs" mentioned by the Second Vatican Council (*Gaudium et Spes*, no. 36) and therefore from the autonomy of every science and field of knowledge.

Thus, it would be a methodological mistake and scientific blunder to try to solve the strictly physical, biological or economic problems with theological or philosophical principles. The task of philosophy (and for believers, theology) is to point out the links of any part of those sciences with philosophical anthropology and ethics. Thus any physical, biological, economic, social or political problems, to the extent that they affect the human person, cannot be solved by merely "scientific" principles, ignoring ethics. It is a

---

[34] F. J. C. Hearnshaw, ed., *Mediaeval Contributions to Modern Civilization*, (New York: Barnes & Noble, 1967).

matter of not confusing secularity or the rightful autonomy of earthly affairs with secularism,[35] or the ideology of enclosing man in a cosmos without any transcendence, which in fact closes the door to civilization.

A Liberal Arts Course

It is assumed therefore that the goal of a liberal arts course is to provide a basic higher education grounded in an anthropology open to reality, a philosophy of man flowing from the realization of man's openness to the infinity of being through his intelligence and free will, above the turbulent sea of sensitive feelings and *emotions*. This is the transcendence of man that makes him *homo sapiens* and *homo religiosus*: thus man surpasses himself indefinitely and dominates the universe.

Consequently, the core curriculum has to be articulated and organized taking into account man's search for wisdom (philosophy and science) and for moral perfection (ethics and religion), expressed in his creativity (technology and the arts), and open to both nature and supernatural religion as the source of this creativity.

Furthermore, as the achievements of mankind (economic, social, political, artistic, in short, culture and civilization) are accumulated in a living manner in the history of the various peoples interrelated by their geographies, it is indispensable, for the adequate perception of what is permanent and universal (*viz.*, values) in the changeable and plural (*viz.*, fashion and trends), to study all realities in their historical and geographical setting and context, and thus avoid the quicksand of cultural relativism and historicism.[36] Man is indeed existentially "in the making" (immersed in time), but essentially immutable *pace Heidegger*.[37] "You must remember this," said the song of *Casablanca*, "a kiss is still a kiss, a sigh is still a sigh: the fundamental things apply, as time goes by."

That permanence and unity in the changeable and plural is the field of both physics (science) and metaphysics (wisdom). It is by perceiving that permanence and unity (the supreme values of being: the true, the good and the beautiful)[38] that man is enabled both to master the world of change with his technology, and to express the universal and eternal in the particular and temporal with aesthetic experiences and creations through literature, poetry

---

[35] *Generation and Degeneration,* chap. 15.
[36] Ibid., chap. 6, 17, 29.
[37] Ibid., chap. 23.
[38] *Christian Philosophy*, chap. 19.

and music and other fine arts.[39] Thus, man creates culture and civilization, embodied in history and geography.

The March Towards Unity and the Centrality of Logic

However, due to the accelerated technological progress of the last two centuries, particularly in the fields of transport and communications, both culture and history are becoming increasingly global, highlighting more than ever the fundamental unity of the human race, and the moral call to promote the universal common good and purify mankind from narrow-minded and divisive nationalism and racism.[40] Every nation should therefore be anxious to know its own subjectivity (or personality) in all its richness, foster it and share it with the world at large.

Furthermore, since the conquest of culture through education is the achievement of human intelligence, it is indispensable to undertake the study of the laws ruling the proper use of this wondrous God-like human faculty of the intelligence.[41] Thus, the science of logic must be a part of the curriculum, as well as the art of speaking and that of writing. The classic *trivium* of (i) how to think (*dialectics* or logic); (ii) how to speak (*rhetoric*; not the modern or ancient empty bla-bla of sophistry, but the solid connection of reality to thought, and thought to speech); and (iii) how to write (grammar, not formalistic subjection to cliches, but dominating language for the purpose of clarity and precision in communication). And in this regard, that study of the Latin language is extremely useful as a perfect example of a logical language (intellectual training), as well as the key to understand Western culture and civilization at its roots.

Upon the *trivium* of logic, language, and writing, we can build the classic *quadrivium* of arithmetic, geometry, astronomy and music, transformed into the modern "arts and sciences", philosophy and history: all the "humanities" and all the "values", on a realist, objective foundation, conducive to peace and unity, freedom and progress in mankind.[42]

The Greek *paideia* or educational system put these seven "liberal arts" together as its core curriculum, with rhetoric at the head, aided by history, under the Sophists. Then the Socratic-Platonic-Aristotelian revolution re-

---

[39] *The Arts of the Beautiful; Art and Scholasticism.*

[40] Joseph M. de Torre, *The Roots of Society,* (Manila: Sinagtala, 1977), chap. XIII and XIV; *Person, Family and State: An Outline of Social Ethics* (Manila: SEASFI, 1991), chap. V.

[41] *Christian Philosophy*, chap. 26-28.

[42] *Work, Culture, Liberation*, chap. 7.

placed rhetoric with the "love of wisdom" (philo-sophia), later called meta-physics and ontology. This attempt was drowned by the returning tide of skepticism, relativism, and rhetoric of the Hellenic period. Right in the midst of this Greco-Roman era, Jesus of Nazareth was born under Emperor Augustus at the crossroads of all world empires.

The Advent of Christianity

Christianity came not to destroy the world but to bring it to its perfection. "Love of wisdom", or the pursuit of knowledge and good, became now both natural and supernatural; reason and faith in perfect continuity and harmony.[43] Thus, it crystallized in the *Doctrina christiana* of St. Augustine, wherein the seven liberal arts would be headed by theology. Henceforward, this Christian culture grew, through the "dark ages" of the barbarian invasions of Europe, until reaching its climax with St. Thomas Aquinas in the thirteenth century. In him, both reason and faith attained their highest peaks in the dialogue with both Christians (*Summa Theologiae*) and non-Christians (*Summa Contra Gentiles*). In these two works the major headings are roughly the same, namely God, the World, and Man. But while the first approaches each topic from the standpoint of revelation (faith), the second does so from the standpoint of natural reason. But both converge into the same truths. Theology, both natural and supernatural is thus the "love of wisdom" as the seventh or supreme liberal art.

The Humanism of the Enlightenment: West and East

Now, from the time of the European Renaissance onward Western philosophy took a twist in the direction of a humanism immanent to man, in growing alienation from man's transcendence and openness to infinite being, while Western experimental science remained firmly anchored to an objective realism (man, the disciple of reality, not the other way around). The result has been both a dazzling scientific and technological progress and an appalling moral decadence due to that immanentistic anthropology. As man recedes from God, he uproots himself from the ground of his own dignity and greatness. A renewed alliance of science and conscience is therefore required, as John Paul II has been emphasizing—an integrated approach to the totality of knowledge, with no more dichotomies between science and humanities:

[43] Joseph M. de Torre, *The Leaven of the Gospel in Secular Society* (Quezon City, Philippines: Vera-Reyes, 1983), chap. 8.

logic and philosophy, natural sciences and social sciences; technology and fine arts, theology and ethics, all within the framework of geography and history. The encyclical *Fides et Ratio* responds to this vision.

This renascence must, however, take account of the history of ideas in the West since the Renaissance, so as to recapture the realism that was almost lost by modern philosophy, and that had been kept in both the Greco-Roman and Christian centuries, and now is called to come back rejuvenated in a post-modern and truly progressive philosophy. And at the same time it is necessary to study the best achievements of both Indian and Chinese philosophy. Both of these, while always deeply influential, have remained largely unaffected by Western immanentism, and are therefore closer to the classic Western traditions of realism and common sense philosophy, although they can benefit from their exposure to Western monotheism and personalism so deeply rooted in the Bible.[44]

Modern European philosophy, beginning with Descartes replaced theology as the seventh liberal art with mathematics (Descartes), physics (Kant), history (Hegel), sociology (Comte), and economics (Marx), gradually dissolving humanity into inert matter or lifeless abstractions. We can recall here another classic of Gilson: *The Unity of Philosophical Experience.*

Cardinal Newman, in the middle of the 19th century, spearheaded the movement to restore theology as the seventh liberal art, a movement which thirty years later received a powerful impetus from Pope Leo XIII in his encyclical *Aeterni Patris* of 1879, which came in continuity with the constitution *Dei Filius* of Vatican Council I (1870); the restoration of "Christian philosophy" according to the mind of St. Thomas Aquinas.[45] Since Vatican II, the Popes have not ceased to promote this restoration, which, as Cardinal Newman explained in his *Idea of a University,* takes account of the creative force of both natural theology (philosophy) and biblical theology in shaping first Western and then global world culture and civilization, as expressed in science, technology, literature and the arts, as well as in economic and political institutions, through the emphasis on the dignity of the human person in his openness to infinity by freedom, knowledge and love. The encyclical *Fides et Ratio* has also been a response to this vision, as well as the two previous encyclicals, *Veritatis Splendor* (1993) and *Evangelium Vitae* (1995).

---

[44] The encyclical *Fides et Ratio* also takes up this point.
[45] *Openness to Reality*, chap. V.

It Takes One to Know One
Connaturality—Knowledge or Prejudice?

Catherine Green

The notion of connaturality in practical knowledge, as discussed by both Jacques Maritain and Yves R. Simon, is intuitively attractive. It seems to provide an account of the consistently good actions carried out and the bad actions avoided by the persons whom we tend to call both good and wise. Maritain follows the lead of Thomas Aquinas in his discussions of connatural knowledge. He argues that such knowledge is "experimental"[1] it is presupposed in real prudence[2] as well as in real art,[3] and it is the ground of knowledge achieved in mystical knowledge.[4] He also argues in *The Range of Reason* that the existence of connatural knowledge obliges us to realize the analogical character of knowledge itself.[5] Yves Simon takes up Maritain's interest in connatural knowledge and argues that it provides an objective certainty in practical knowledge that is analogous to the certainty found in scientific knowledge.[6] Connatural knowledge we are told is grounded in existence. The agent shares the ontological nature of the good that is sought and it is this ontological affinity that allows the agent to recognize the good in the other.

The problem that arises, however, is that the language used by both Maritain and Simon to describe such knowledge is poetic, a-rational and obscure. Maritain tells us that for the artist, "beauty becomes connatural to him, bedded in his being through affection, and his work proceeds from his

---

[1] Jacques Maritain, *The Degrees of Knowledge*, trans. Gerald B. Phelan (Notre Dame, Indiana: University of Notre Dame Press, 1995), p. 263 and *Freedom in the Modern World* in *The Collected Works of Jacques Maritain*, Vol. 11, ed. Otto Bird (Notre Dame, Indiana: University of Notre Dame Press, 1996), p. 15.

[2] *Freedom in the Modern World*, p. 15.

[3] Jacques Maritain, *Art and Scholasticism and The Frontiers of Poetry*, trans. Joseph W. Evans (Notre Dame, Indiana: University of Notre Dame Press, 1974), p. 47.

[4] *Degrees of Knowledge*, p. 281.

[5] Jacques Maritain, *The Range of Reason* (New York: Charles Scribner's Sons, 1953), p. 22.

[6] Yves R. Simon, *The Definition of Moral Virtue,* ed. Vukan Kuic (New York: Fordham University Press, 1986), p. 116.

heart and his bowels as from his lucid mind."[7] Simon says that the "[a]nswer to the ultimate [practical] question was obtained by listening to an inclination. The intellect, here, is the disciple of love."[8] Maritain suggests variously that such knowledge is "not rational knowledge,"[9] "non-conceptual,"[10] it is "obscure and perhaps unable to give an account of itself."[11] Simon suggests that "[i]nasmuch as the ultimate practical judgment admits of no logical connection with any rational premises, it is, strictly speaking, incommunicable."[12]

How, then, are we to understand this "affective knowledge?" How is this ontological "recognition" a way of knowing as opposed to a simple physical or physiological attraction rather like the attraction of silver to chlorine or boy to girl? That is, if it is not conceptual, what makes it a form of knowledge as opposed to a form of ignorance? I am reminded of a New Yorker cartoon in which a rotund bald judge dressed in a black suit and sporting a broomstick mustache surveys a plaintiff with these very same characteristics and dress. The judge's verdict; "Surely, not guilty." This would seem to result from an ontological affinity. But it looks much more like what we would commonly call prejudice. Of course, the notion of connatural knowledge stemming from preconscious inclinations suggests precisely a "pre-judging." What is the difference, then between prejudice, a form of ignorance and the pre-judgment that is essential to connatural knowledge? Second, if it is a kind of knowledge, how is it related to virtue? I am reminded of the "intuition" that the "good" scam artist has for his "mark" and the method of the "good" actor who attempts to take on the nature of the character he is playing in order to render a persuasive performance. These too seem to arise from a kind of knowledge by affinity. If connaturality is a kind of knowledge, does it admit of bad use? If it does admit of bad use, how could it provide any basis for moral certainty?

My goal in this paper, then, is to attempt to clarify the meaning and the analogous character of these connatural ways of knowing. Maritain argues that connatural knowledge obliges us to pay proper attention to the analogical character of knowledge. Yves Simon argues that the analogical ground of all knowledge is intentional existence and that knowledge by inclination can best be understood by examining the nature of intentional relations.[13] There-

---

[7] *Art and Scholasticism*, p. 47.

[8] Yves R. Simon, "Introduction to the Study of Practical Wisdom," *The New Scholasticism* 34 (1961), p. 21.

[9] *The Range of Reason*, p. 23.

[10] Ibid., p. 25.

[11] Ibid., p. 23.

[12] "Introduction to the Study of Practical Wisdom," p. 27.

[13] *The Definition of Moral Virtue*, p. 112.

fore, we will use Simon's discussion of the nature of intentional existence to help us explore this problem. Following the leads of Aquinas and Maritain, Simon argues that there are two distinct orders of existence.[14] The physical or entitative order is that in which things exist as they are and nothing else.[15] It is worth noting here that physical does not mean material but rather composite, that is, constituted by a matter and form unity. The intentional order of existence is that in which "what is and remains itself can also be the other."[16] The intentional order is necessary in order that existing things may be known by various minds and, may at the same time, maintain their own unique existence.[17]

Simon argues that the notion of intentional existence can only be understood analogically.[18] "Intentional existence" is primarily understood in the realm of formal causality, as the mode of existence assumed by the idea in the mind of the knower.[19] It also refers to the efficiency "of the principal agent present in his instrument," and in the realm of final causes, it refers to "the goodness that bestows dignity upon even the humblest of means."[20] We see in both Maritain and Simon that the good that ultimately allows a free agent to choose the good she desires is divine.[21] We will argue that these various realms of intentional existence correspond to the realms of connatural knowledge identified by Jacques Maritain. That is, metaphysical and intellectual knowledge is, of course, a kind of formal existence. Whereas, prudential and artistic connaturality are a kind of intentional existence determined by relation to the good and the beautiful, knowledge by way of final causality. Prudential connaturality can be understood by the character of the relation of the agent to the end as desired while artistic connaturality can be understood by the character of the relation of the artist to the beautiful both as object of knowledge and as object to be created. Finally, the connaturality of the mystic can be understood as a relation to divine efficiency in which the mystic is the instrument of divine charity.

We will begin by exploring Simon's understanding of the meaning and role of intentional existence. Next we will explore such existence in the realm

---

[14] Yves R. Simon, *An Introduction to the Metaphysics of Knowledge*, trans. Vukan Kuic and Richard J. Thompson (New York: Fordham University Press, 1990), pp. 9-10.

[15] Ibid. See also, Yves R. Simon, "To Be and To Know," *Chicago Review* 14 (Spring 1961), p. 87.

[16] *An Introduction to the Metaphysics of Knowledge*, p. 10.

[17] Ibid., p. 25.

[18] Ibid., p. 28.

[19] Ibid., p. 26.

[20] Ibid., pp. 26, 28.

[21] *Freedom in the Modern World*, p. 22 and Yves R. Simon, *Freedom of Choice*, trans. Peter Wolff (New York: Fordham University Press, 1969), p. 150.

of instrumental causality since it is here that Simon gives us the most developed discussions of the meaning of intentional existence. In light of what we have learned we will then briefly explore Maritain's discussion of the connatural knowledge of the mystic. We take this route because while practical knowledge is the area where connaturality is most familiar to everyday life, in both *The Degrees of Knowledge* and in *The Range of Reason*, Maritain gives his most thorough discussions of this knowledge in its relation to the mystic. From our understanding of what we will see is the instrumental character of mystical knowledge we will be able to develop a general outline of the role of connatural knowledge in moral action. We will conclude with a discussion of the possibility and nature of the steadfast and consistent recognition of the good found in prudence.

Simon tells us in *The Metaphysics of Knowledge* that "the intentional being of knowledge appears…as manifestation of a superabundance by which the divine generosity permits some creatures to be more than they are."[22] He is arguing here that intentional existence is found in things that can be known, where it is an excess of efficiency by which objects of knowledge can make themselves available to be known by a creature endowed with the ability to know. "It is this superabundance of creation that makes things spill over into or, better, radiate, ideas. The universe of nature so generously created is at the same time the universe of intentionality and that is how we are able to know it, and in knowing it to imitate divine infinity."[23] There are two realms of intentional existence here: the first, a kind of efficiency in the known thing "radiating ideas" to the knower and another in the knower where "[i]n the order of formal causality, the superabundance of being is shown in the ability of the knower to become the known in intentional existence."[24] He uses the term "intentional" to speak of that specifically immaterial kind of existence that the object of knowledge has in the soul of the knower.[25]

Our first problem, of course, is to clarify what he means by "intentional existence." In a note to this discussion he distinguishes "intentional" existence from other forms of superabundant existence. Intentional existence is an added existence that accrues to an active creature by virtue of an on-going relationship to a prior cause. It does not belong to the agent per se, but to the prior cause acting in or through the agent. Such existence is ephemeral and transient; gone when the prior cause is no longer present and acting on the agent. For example, the ability of a paintbrush to effect the precise idea of an

---

[22]*An Introduction to the Metaphysics of Knowledge*, p. 26.
[23] Ibid., p. 25. See also *The Degrees of Knowledge*, p. 118.
[24]*An Introduction to the Metaphysics of Knowledge*, p. 26.
[25] Ibid., pp. 12-13.

artist arises in the artist and culminates in the painting. When the artist takes a break, the paintbrush becomes simply a "a wooden stick with a tuft of hair at one end" with no ability to create such an effect on its own.[26] In the realm of final causes, he tells us that the means is given extra goodness from the end to which it is ordered. The good of hard work, for example, comes not simply from the action of working, but more from the good it strives to achieve, the house that is completed. As we all know, busy work has very limited good. Thus according to Simon, intentional existence can only be understood; 1. by its ultimate relation to divine power, 2. by its role as the means to knowledge in certain privileged creatures, and 3. by its continuing dependence on the prior cause from which it proceeds.

Now to better understand what Simon is arguing we will turn to his discussion of instrumental action. In *Metaphysics of Knowledge,* Simon examines the issue of instrumental causality in some depth in two contexts. In both he is interested to clarify its essential nature. This happens most completely in his discussion of the role of the image in the mind that produces the idea in the intellect.[27] Here he argues that there are two essential features of an instrument. An instrument must have an active nature of its own that serves as the proximate cause of both the ontological and specific nature of the effect.[28] Second, he argues that the essence of instrumental causality is that it is a matter of efficiency rather than specificity. He suggests here that an infinitely powerful agent could achieve any effect with any instrument.[29] But careful attention reveals that this is not strictly true. Simon is clear that an instrumental effect must proceed from some capacities that the instrument had prior to the action of the principal agent. Now an instrument as such has a potential to act in a specified way. For example lead cannot act as a buoy or channel marker because it cannot float and thus it could not be seen by sailors to warn them of danger. Simon's examples of various instruments and his references to St. Thomas all note that it is both the form and the efficiency of the instrument that is elevated by Divine power.[30] For example, baptismal waters cleanse the soul as well as the body, they lead to a rebirth of the soul as simple rain promotes the rebirth of plants after a drought.[31] To use a lead ball as a channel marker, then, would require not an elevation of existence

[26] Ibid., p. 27.
[27] Ibid., pp. 123-27.
[28] Ibid., pp. 123-24.
[29] Ibid., p. 124.
[30] Ibid., n. 42.
[31] Catherine Green, *The Intentionality of Knowing and Willing in the Writings of Yves R. Simon* (Ph.D. diss., The Catholic University of America, 1996), p. 116.

but a change of nature. This, of course, is possible by divine power. But it would not then be an instrumental action at all. The use of an instrument as an instrument requires the use of its own specific and active nature to affect the particular end. Instruments, then, are the means by which the principal agent transfers the form of an action to an effect.

Beyond this, however, there is another issue. The instrument must also serve as the bridge by which the ontological character of the action is transferred. As we know, existing things have both a potency to act and a potency to be acted on. In physical or composite things the action of a prior cause is limited by the ability of the receiver to accept that form. Thus Thomas's dictum, "the received is in the receiver according to the mode of the receiver."[32] Therefore in order for the instrument to transmit an immaterial action from the agent to the effect, the instrument must have the potential to receive and transmit immaterial action. Thus, according to Simon, all created natures have an intentional as well as a physical existence in order that they might be able to be party to the knowing of certain privileged creatures.[33] All created natures may serve as the instruments by means of which they can be known. In action of composite creatures the action received is limited and thus altered by the receiver. The action issuing from the instrument then expresses that limitation. For example a paintbrush with coarse wiry bristles would not be able to effect accurately the fine and precise brush strokes envisioned by the artist. Thus the immaterial idea in the mind of the artist is transmitted through the paintbrush with some alteration to the canvas. The paintbrush itself is the proximate source of both the specific and ontologic nature of the painting. The more powerful the agent, the more limited would be the alteration of the form by the instrument. That is, the more powerful artist would use the nature of the instrument rather perfectly to express her ideas.

The nature of an instrument, then, is understood as transmitting both the specific and the ontologic character of the effect from the prior agent to the effect. The intentional and immaterial character of the instrument accrues to it from its potential to effect immaterial and intentional action given with its created nature and then is increased or given active existence by the efficiency of some prior agent in using the instrument to achieve a particular effect. The more powerful the prior agent, the more perfect will be the use of the formal and ontologic character of the instrument and the more perfect the effect. In any case, the intentional and immaterial activity of the instrument

[32] Thomas Aquinas, *Summa Theologiae*, I q. 84, a. 1.
[33] *An Introduction to the Metaphysics of Knowledge*, p. 25.

is limited by the availability and activity of the prior cause. Finally, instrumental activity is essentially a kind of efficiency. The activity and the instrument are ordered to the ultimate effect.

To review, then, we have seen that intentional existence has three necessary characteristics. It is ultimately related to divine power, it is the means to knowledge in creatures who are able to know, and it constantly depends on the prior cause from which it proceeds. An instrument takes on intentional existence in the realm of efficiency and by means of its own formal and ontological character it transmits the formal and ontological character of the idea of the prior agent to the effect he desires. The limitation of the instrument and the amplitude of the prior agent affect the precision of this activity.

We are now ready to turn our attention of Maritain's discussion of mystical knowledge. The problem Maritain is addressing is how to identify the "proximate principles of mystical experience."[34] How is such experience realized? He answers by saying that it is both a "suprahuman mode of knowledge" and it is "knowledge by connaturality."[35] He explains mystical knowledge as an experience where the term "experience" means "knowledge of an object as present, in which the soul undergoes an action exercised upon it by that object and perceives in virtue of this very passion."[36] Here the soul does not initiate the action, but rather "is moved and set into immanent action through God's grace alone operating within it as the living instrument of the Holy Ghost. He elevates it to a higher rule by suspending its human way of acting: that is why mystics describe it as a passivity and a non-acting."[37] What Maritain is suggesting is that the soul of human creatures is given an extra "intentional" existence and power by which it is able to know God, albeit in a limited way in what Maritain calls "ananoetic" or analogical knowledge.[38] Beyond this, however, Maritain tells us, "Grace bestows upon us, in a supernatural manner, a radical power of grasping pure Act as our object, a new root of spiritual operation whose proper and specifying object is the Divine Essence itself."[39]

It is important to understand the nature of immanent action to understand what this means. Immanent action is a kind of action that allows a knower to enter into a unity with the known that does not alter in any way the known while it perfects the knower as knowing. The known is made present

---

[34] *The Degrees of Knowledge*, p. 275.
[35] Ibid., p. 276.
[36] Ibid., p. 280.
[37] Ibid.
[38] Ibid., p. 264.
[39] Ibid., p. 271.

to the knower as the goal of his action of knowing. In the presence of the object to be known, the knower forms his own faculty of knowledge in more or less exact correspondence to the form of the object.[40] In contact with the existence of the thing to be known, the knower moves to grasp the known and in intellectual knowledge to express that known in the mental word. In physical terms we might understand this as similar to the action of iron filings, conforming their active natures in correspondence with the active nature of a magnet brought close to them. Thus the knower unites with the object known without altering the known. The object provides the form for the action while the sensitive faculty provides the efficiency. There is thus formal identity while there remains existential distinction. Because the object is fully present to the faculty, the action is complete in itself. The faculty does not search for any end beyond this action, but rather simply attempts to grasp as fully as possible the object given.[41]

I would argue that we might understand Maritain's mystical knowledge in Simon's terms as intentional existence in the order of efficiency, that is, instrumental causality. We would not here have knowing or grasping of God as a formal concept, but rather as an active principal elevating our lives by His love. The divine Act adds the possibility of power to the human soul such that this soul in a state of grace is able to be the instrument of divine love in making itself present to the mystic. Maritain tells us that this state of grace is not simply given but is both given and received. That is, "there must be within the soul in a state of grace, sails all set to receive the wind of heaven, or, to use scholastic language, permanent dispositions or habitus which guarantee the possibility…of achieving this inspired knowledge."[42] Habitus, as we know, is not a first nature, but rather a second nature developed over time as a result of specific actions carried out for the sake of an end.[43] It is both a formal determination by a distinct object as well as an "existential readiness" to act in accordance with that object. In mystical knowledge this habitus would be the many acts of charity carried out by loving persons in the hopes of making themselves more like their God. "We are made connatural to God through charity."[44] "The connaturality of charity, under the motion of the Holy Ghost plays the formal part [of knowledge]."[45] What is essential here is

---

[40] *The Intentionality of Knowing and Willing in the Writings of Yves R. Simon*, p. 162.
[41] Ibid.
[42] *The Degrees of Knowledge*, p. 276.
[43] *Definition of Moral Virtue*, pp. 59-60.
[44] *The Degrees of Knowledge*, p. 277.
[45] Ibid., p. 281.

action formed by charity.

What the habitus of charitable activity does here is to prepare the person to receive the activity of the Holy Spirit in the immanent action of the mystical experience. Charity, of course, is the activity of giving of oneself to another. The immanent action of mystical experience is precisely a giving up of one's own active nature to the activity of the divine. The charitable soul under the power of divine efficiency conforms itself to divine will and serves as the "bridge" between heaven and earth. In the presence of a divine agent, the instrument of the mystic's soul most perfectly expresses divine love to the world. Since this is a union of efficiency the ultimate nature of the action is for the sake of the effect that will be given to the world, that is, for the specific acts of love expressed there. In so far as it is a specifically immanent action it is a union of the two radically distinct beings in which the mystic is perfected in her human nature while the divine nature remains unchanged.

Connaturality then can be understood as the forming of the soul of the mystic to be more charitable and thus Christ-like by virtue of many charitable actions. This results in the habitus of charity being present in the mystic. This habitus directed to the goal of knowing God prepares the being of the mystic to be ready to accept the divine activity in the moment of mystical knowing in which the connaturality of efficiency of the human by the divine is perfected ever more. The form here comes from the soul of the mystic formed by charity that is formally the same on earth as in heaven.[46] The efficiency is, of course, divine.

We are now ready to turn our attention to the nature of connaturality found in moral knowledge. Maritain tells us that "[w]hen a man makes a free decision, he takes into account, not only all that he possesses of moral science and factual information, and which is manifested to him in concepts and notions, but also all the secret elements of evaluation which depend on what he is, and which are known to him through inclination, through his own actual propensities and his own virtues, if he has any."[47] Simon puts it this way. The "[a]nswer to the ultimate question was obtained by listening to an inclination...The object of the practical judgment is one that cannot be grasped by looking at it. It is delivered by love to the docile intellect."[48] Quoting John of St. Thomas, he says, "'love takes over the role of the object.'"[49]

Simon argues that practical judgments are complex actions as are all acts of knowing. In an intricate interplay between desire and knowledge, we

---

[46] Ibid., p. 271.
[47] *Range of Reason*, p. 26.
[48] "Introduction to the Study of Practical Wisdom," p. 21.
[49] Ibid.

desire a good before we can seek the ways to achieve it. Having identified a good means, in fully chosen actions, it is necessary to evaluate this particular means in terms of its relation to the end desired: is it good enough? Finally, as a result of a "surplus of goodness" that accrues to the will by virtue of the natural desire all humans have for perfect and enduring happiness, the will produces the surplus of energy by which it elevates this particular means to the status necessary to make it good enough to determine an action here and now. "Because of [the will's] natural determination it possesses enough actuality to add to the least of particular goods all the surplus of goodness which it needs in order to be found constituted of absolutely desirable good."[50] Maritain says, the will "pours out upon that particular good, of itself wholly incapable of determining it, the superabundant determination it receives from its necessary object, good as such."[51] It is desire for complete and enduring happiness that sends the mind looking for ways to achieve this good. This desire and the power to effect it is given with our created human nature. Any particular object identified by the mind as good will always be radically inadequate to the task of achieving perfect happiness and thus could never by itself determine one to act. It is precisely by ignoring this limitation that one acts by simple habit or passion. However when we recognize this radical inadequacy, in making choices the natural will has the power necessary to make this inadequate means good enough for now and thus put the good idea into action.

It is clear that inclination is primary here in that desire is both the beginning and the end of this action. And it is clear that knowledge is present here since the mind first identifies the good and then evaluates it in terms of the good end. However, it is not so clear how connaturality functions. Simon tells us that connaturality here is a "harmony, a sympathy, a dynamic unity, a community of nature…between the virtuous heart and the requirements of virtue."[52] The knowledge of connaturality is not the cognitive identification of a good idea, or the comparison of the character of the particular good with the whole good. Rather it is the forming of the virtuous character of the person in consonance with the good desired. As we saw in our discussion of mystical knowledge, it was the habitus of charitable actions that made the mystical heart open to experience the act of divine charity. In the habitus of prudence the good character of the will which has been developed over time embraces the particular good as consistent with both its own character and

---

[50] *Freedom of Choice*, p. 150.

[51] Jacques Maritain, *A Preface to Metaphysics: Seven Lectures on Being* (New York: Sheed and Ward, 1948), p. 103.

[52] "Introduction to the Study of Practical Wisdom," p. 24.

with the character of the good it seeks. Thus in the realm of final causes the Divine Good as the final end of all human action gives intentional existence to the human will to allow it to form itself, by means of its particular actions, in consonance with the good it seeks. This ontological relation to the good is like the ontological relation between the charity of the mystic and divine charity.

The connaturality of practical judgments, then, is this shared goodness found in the will that desires the good, the mind that identifies the means to achieve that good and the good itself. The will desires a good thing, the mind identifies a means to achieve it and an action is chosen. Enacting a particular good changes and forms the mind and the will to be more like the good desired, connaturality begins. If the good desired and enacted is consistent with what is truly good for the person as a particular human person, that is, if it is consistent with some aspect of the perfect and enduring good, a connaturality with good itself begins. However, since the relation of the final good is not absolutely determinative, we must choose particular means in order to achieve happiness. Therefore it is quite possible that certain actions or means chosen will not only be inadequate to meet that final goal, but they may also be radically mistaken in their direction. Simon uses an analogy of people walking on a path in the woods on their way to a particular house.[53] They know that they want to reach the house and they walk to achieve that goal. However, the lights of the house come in and out of view. It is not clear that the path he is on will take him where he wants to go. As a matter of fact the path seems at times to take him in the wrong direction. Similarly, while we all try to achieve happiness, we may be at times quite mistaken about what kinds of goods will achieve that happiness.

The scam artist is acting then to achieve his happiness, which he understands to be found in easy wealth. He desires to "relieve" his patrons of their cash, he looks for ways to do this and then acts to carry them out. In so doing he forms a habitus or state of character directed to this end. Where the particular actions necessary to achieve the end initially must be mediated by knowledge ("will this work or will another means be more effective?") over time the need for reflection decreases. What initially happened by reflection now happens by second nature. The nature of the scam artist becomes identified with the "good" he seeks. This connaturality of nature allows for the steady recognition of his end, that is, a good mark, with little or no reflection.

Aristotle notes that this is a kind of "cleverness." It is "the power to perform those steps which are conducive to a goal we have set for ourselves

---

[53] *Freedom of Choice*, p. 103.

and to attain that goal...this capacity [alone] is not practical wisdom, although practical wisdom does not exist without it."[54] Simon suggests that making ourselves connatural with our particular goal relieves us of much of the intricate decision making that would normally be necessary to achieve such goals and thus provides the "habits" of character that are the ground of real virtue.[55]

The "method" actor then may be using such "cleverness" in a way more consistent with real virtue. In any case, it is clear that connaturality in the realm of final causes is a relation to an end as good in which the agent has acted in consonance with that good consistently and has thus formed himself in relation to that good. As a result he is able to "see" the good in its existential character without carrying out a logical deduction about its nature. Connaturality is mediated by habitus that is itself both explicitly determined by thoughtful attention to the form of the end and an existential readiness to act to achieve that form.

Since a habitus of acting to achieve particular ends is developed over time, the stability of the readiness to act in consonance with the desired end also increases over time. Thus, the stability of action of the scam artist merely developing his "art" will be limited. Prudence as such, however, depends on the stable character of the agent in relation to the various aspects of virtue: including temperance, fortitude, justice and the like. Therefore, the stability of prudence as a readiness to act in accord with these virtues will be assured by their presence as existential characteristics of the agent.

Connatural knowledge, then in all its forms would be a result of habitus. The more perfectly this habitus is developed, the more consistent would be its expression. It is thus a thoughtful direction of our actions to achieve a specified end, as truth, as good, as charitable or as beautiful. This habitus brings into existence a second nature through which we consistently recognize that end in a non-discursive action. It is a way of existing by relation to another that is itself immanent action. We may form our nature in relation to the good and express that nature in the connatural recognition of and action in consonance with the good, we may form our nature in relation to divine efficiency and express that nature in recognition of and consistent actions of charity. We may form our nature in relation to the beautiful and express that nature in the recognition of and consistent expression of the poetic word or the created art. Connatural knowledge can be understood as knowledge since it is a forming of ourselves in relation to another in an action that perfects our

---

[54] Aristotle, *Nicomachean Ethics*, 1144a25-29.
[55] *Definition of Moral Virtue*, p. 76.

own nature while leaving the other unaltered. It is a connaturality of existence since we take on some aspect of the efficient, the good or the beautiful existence of the other as our own.

While it is a pre-judging, that is a forming oneself and one's action in consonance with the existence of the other rather than with its intelligible form as such, what is expressed as a judgment is clearly not simply prejudice. That is, connatural knowledge occurs only after significant thoughtful judgments have prepared the way. In practical actions, since we are free to choose any means to the goal of happiness, a connaturality of good may be radically defective even as it is radically determinative of the actions of the agent. Since the intentional existence of instrumental action belongs properly to the cause, in mystical knowledge where the object of the charitable actions of the mystic is the love of God Himself, we find a connaturality of action and existence that is necessarily perfective.

Knowing Our Knowings

Gregory J. Kerr

In a previous paper, "The Elements of Discord: The *Sine Qua Non* of Education" I argued that the transcendentals were necessary principles for the communication of any theory from one person to another.[1] To be understood, we must be coherent (logical), affirm some absolute truth, goodness, and beauty. No one can successfully communicate a theory that is incoherent, values nothing, and holds nothing as true. If these transcendental properties are true of papers and theories, then they are also true of the knowers who form them. Theories and papers do not come out of thin air—they come from concrete acts of human knowing. In this paper, I will explore the different types of knowing associated with each of the transcendentals. I will further argue that the forms of knowledge associated with the true, the good, and the beautiful, are essentially different from each other, and how, according to Maritain, even truth is different for each one. I believe that if we can appreciate the differences between each of these kinds of human knowing, then we can prevent a multitude of serious but common errors and can come to appreciate the philosophies of others better. Maritain once remarked that, "everywhere I see truths made captive…. Our business is to find the positive in all things; to use what is true, less to strike than to cure." [2] It is in this Maritainian spirit of "recovery" that I shall explore the various forms of knowing and the philosophers who exemplified them.

One way to unlock the treasures of many of the great philosophers that may often seem to undermine and contradict each other is by doing what I would like to call a transcendental analysis of them. This means finding out what transcendental their philosophy is principally drawing from, principally "riding" on, principally following, and this will tell one a lot about their

---

[1] In *The Common Things: Essays on Thomism and Education*, ed. Daniel McInerny (Washington, D.C.: American Maritain Assocation / The Catholic University of America Press, 1999), pp. 92-101.

[2] Maritain, *Art and Faith: Letters Between Jacques Maritain and Jean Cocteau*, trans. John Coleman (New York: Philosophical Library, 1948).

philosophy including the blind spots it has and will have. Upon realizing this, one can appreciate the transcendental appropriation of that philosophy while not having to accept everything in it as a whole, or to criticize it for not "seeing" everything. For example, one could look at the philosophies of Plato, Aristotle and Nietzsche and see that each philosophy has its unique depth perception of the universe of being and yet, at the same time, has blind spots towards the value of other transcendental perceptions.

The notion of a "blind spot" first came to my attention in the work entitled *A View From Nowhere*.[3] In this work, the contemporary analytical philosopher Thomas Nagel argues that humans have two viewpoints: subjective and objective. He argues that each viewpoint cannot see the value of the other. According to Nagel:

> The problem of bringing together subjective and objective views of the world can be approached from either direction. If one starts from the subjective side, the problem is the traditional one of skepticism, idealism, or solipsism. How, given my personal experiential perspective, can I form a conception of the world as it is independent of my perception of it? …If on the other hand, one starts from the objective side, the problem is how to accommodate, in a world that simply exists and has no perspectival center, any of the following things: (a) oneself; (b) one's point of view; (c) the point of view of other selves…. [4]

As one can see then, from the scientific and objective point of view there is no "self," no interests, or values; and from a merely scientific vantage point, one can see exactly what Nagel is talking about. If one starts with the viewpoint of objective science and treats as a metaphysic, he may never escape it. This was the case with Bertrand Russell who knew what a world seen as a function of science meant. He wrote in a "A Free Man's Worship" that:

> Such, in outline, but even more purposeless, more void of meaning, is the world which science presents for our belief…. That man is the product of causes which had no prevision of the end that they were achieving; that his origin, his growth, his hopes and fears, his loves and his beliefs, are but the outcome of accidental collocations of atoms… only of the firm foundation of unyielding despair can the soul's habitation henceforth be safely built.[5]

Now scientific knowledge needs no apology, but man does need other forms of knowledge, even ones opposed to the methods of science to give him the whole truth about life. Maritain was acutely aware of the differences

[3] Thomas Nagel, *The View From Nowhere* (New York: Oxford University Press, 1986).
[4] Ibid., p. 27.
[5] Bertrand Russell, "A Free Man's Worship" in *Why I am Not a Christian* (New York: Touchstone, 1957), pp. 106-07.

of the various forms of knowledge. He was also acutely aware of how they did not see eye to eye. As we examine the kinds of knowledge that pertain to each of the transcendentals we see what a difference, the differences actually make. While there may be many different kinds of knowledge within the human being, we will focus upon three that Maritain himself focused on: the theoretical, the practical and knowledge by connaturality. These kinds of knowledge focus upon the true, the good, and the beautiful respectively. Now since being is one, good, true, and beautiful we may think that these kinds of knowledge are all one, and that one can mix and match as one pleases, but Maritain disagrees. Unless one is God, the transcendentals do not appear united. Similarly, the good is not necessarily the true, and vice-versa.[6] The implications are enormous. While operating in the world, the different faculties of man grasp being differently. Our "will... does not of itself tend to the true, but solely and jealously to the good of man."[7] The intellect by itself desires the truth, which of itself does not inspire but "only illumines."[8] In fact, nothing with a drive toward the infinite—as is the human aspiration for truth or for goodness—is in accord with any other similar drive.[9] Furthermore, he would claim that within the human being there are many knowledge-based aspirations towards the infinite and that they can be even hostile to each other. He writes in the *Situation of Poetry*:

> The fact is that all these energies, insofar as they pertain to the transcendental universe, aspire like poetry to surpass their nature and to infinitise themselves.... Art, poetry, metaphysics, prayer, contemplation, each one is wounded, struck traitorously in the best of itself, and that is the very condition of its living. Man unites them by force.[10]

We see the resulting conflict being played out in those who, according to Maritain, in the "spirit of Luther, Rousseau, or Tolstoy defend the order of

---

[6] "Wherefore beauty, truth, goodness (especially when it is no longer a question of metaphysical or transcendental good itself, but of moral good) command distinct spheres of human activity, of which it would be foolish to deny *a priori* the possible conflict, on the pretext that the transcendentals are indissolubly bound to one another." Jacques Maritain, *Art and Scholasticism and the Frontiers of Poetry*, trans. Joseph W. Evans (Notre Dame, Indiana: University of Notre Dame Press, 1974), p. 174n68.

[7] *Art and Scholasticism*, p. 7.

[8] Ibid., p. 26.

[9] Jacques Maritain, "Concerning Poetic Knowledge" in Jacques and Raïssa Maritain, *The Situation of Poetry: Four Essays on the Relations Between Poetry, Mysticism, Magic, and Knowledge*, trans. Marshall Suther, (New York: Philosophical Library, 1955; reprint, New York: Kraus Reprint, 1968) p. 56.

[10] Ibid.

the moral good,"[11] while others like Aristotle[12] and Aquinas defend the order of truth. Here are two families that hardly understand each other—here as elsewhere, "the prudent one dreads the contemplative and distrusts him."[13]

Furthermore, even the notion of truth is different for the three kinds of knowledge. Truth for speculative thinking is the adequation or conformity of the intellect to being. Truth for practical knowledge is the conformity of the intellect with the straight appetite; and truth for knowledge by connaturality, associated with poetry, is the conformity of the mind with being but being *as grasped through emotion*.[14] No wonder there are blind spots. If truth is not the same, it follows that to make all of these viewpoints logically coherent would be extremely difficult, if not an impossible, task!

Specifically with regard to the distinction between speculative and practical thinking Maritain illustrates the differences well in his *Peasant of the Garonne*. He has a striking passage concerning the Christian's love-hate relationship with the world. Now we all know about the saint who might talk about hating the world, about the evils of the flesh, and yet we also know of the theologian who claims that both are actually good. Are they contradicting each other? Maritain says no; they are simply speaking different languages. He writes:

> [Reality] does not appear in the same light in both cases. The theologian declares that grace perfects nature and does not destroy it; the saint declares that grace requires us to make nature die to itself. They are both telling the truth. But it would be a shame to reverse their languages by making use in the speculative order, formulas which are true for the practical order, and vice versa.... Let us think of the "contempt for creatures" professed by the saints.... For the philosopher and the theologian it would mean: creatures are worth nothing *in themselves*; for the saint: they are worth nothing *for me*.... The saint sees in practice that creatures are nothing in comparison with the One to whom he has given his heart and of the End he has chosen.[15]

One can only imagine the innumerable other possible applications here. For example, might the relationship between faith and works in the letters of St.

[11] Jacques Maritain, "An Essay on Art" in *Art and Scholasticism*, p. 98.

[12] *Art and Scholasticism*, p. 33.

[13] Jacques Maritain, "The Freedom of Song" in Jacques Maritain, *Art and Poetry*, trans. E. de P. Matthews, (New York: Philosophical Library, 1943), p. 103.

[14] Jacques Maritain, *Creative Intuition in Art and Poetry*, (Princeton, New Jersey: Princeton University Press, 1977), p. 236.

[15] Jacques Maritain, *The Peasant of the Garonne: An Old Layman Questions Himself About the Present Time*, trans. Michael Cuddihy and Elizabeth Hughes (New York: Holt, Rinehart and Winston, 1968), p. 44.

Paul and St. James be clarified? Might one be a practical exhortation and the other a speculative exposition of justification?

Another specific and telling difference is the one between the aesthetic and theoretical viewpoints. While I have dealt with this difference extensively in a previous article "Deconstruction and Artistic Creation: Maritain and the Bad Boys of Philosophy,"[16] we can simplify it here. The theoretical viewpoint wants to use logic, concepts, abstractions, definitions, categories, to understand things discursively and apart from the sensible world, while the aesthetic viewpoint wants none of that, but wants to access the sensible world directly. Maritain writes in the "Frontiers of Poetry":

> The difference is an all-important one, and one that it would be harmful to disregard. Metaphysics snatches at the spiritual in an idea, by the most abstract intellection; poetry reaches it in the flesh, by the very point of the sense sharpened through intelligence. Metaphysics enjoys its possession only in the retreats of the eternal regions, while poetry finds its own at every crossroad in the wanderings of the contingent and the singular.[17]

The last relationship is between the aesthetic and the moral, and Maritain could not be clearer on this issue. Since the practical intellect from which the virtue of art operates differently from the speculative—as seen above—and since the virtue of art and prudence concern to very different goods, one the good of the moral agent and the other the good of the work-to-be-made, art does not concern morality or knowledge. We should not expect it to give an explicit moral lesson. If it does, the work of art suffers an impurity and serves a master beyond itself. It becomes polluted and a form of propaganda.[18]

Now whole philosophies may also exhibit the same tensions. We may begin our exploration with the transcendental of the Good. Thomas Aquinas called Socrates a moral philosopher, and that is most apt, for Socrates, as for his disciple Plato, all of reality is a function of morality. For both, reality is what exists after one has made sense of morality.[19] Reality is what has to exist for morality to make sense. If morality does not make sense in a totally physical and changing world, then a new world must be hypothesized to account for it. And if morality is really about the most important aspects of

---

[16] In *Postmodernism and Christian Philosophy*, ed. Roman T. Ciapolo (Washington, D.C.: American Maritain Association / The Catholic University of America Press, 1997), pp. 118-27.

[17] Jacques Maritain, "The Frontiers of Poetry" in *Art and Scholasticism*, p. 128.

[18] Jacques Maritain, *The Responsibility of the Artist* (New York: Charles Scribner's Sons, 1960), pp. 72-3.

[19] I am indebted here to the lectures on aesthetics given by Fr. Robert O'Connell at Fordham University, Bronx, New York.

our human nature—our soul—what is benefited by justice and corrupted by injustice—then this otherworldly world that provides the foundation for this, must be the most real. Then, of course, as this invisible world of forms becomes the center of reality, the "more real," our physical world ends up relegated to the status of shadows on a cavern wall. On the one hand, the beauty of Platonism is the keen awareness of the special nature of morality and how strange that makes reality. On the other hand, Platonism's blind spots are that it bypasses the "truth" of physical reality and that it cannot tolerate the beauty of embodied existence as expressed through the poets who "know" in an aesthetic way.

The first blind spot is the missing of truth of the material world. Platonism bypasses the body, senses, physical things, and their relationships with each other. All of physical reality goes through the meat grinder of reason alone in Book Five of the *Republic*. The reality of the family and all of its obligations, loyalties, and significances are lost. The truth about the body and the senses are given only lip service. The only purpose for the body, the senses, and the physical world seems to be to enable us to leave them behind. And, perhaps, Augustine, the neo-Platonist, has echoes of this problem as well. The truth of this reality becomes, in a sense, eviscerated, and we are left with shells of symbols.[20]

The second blind spot is that Plato cannot see the value of aesthetic in itself. Those who fear art had their first great spokesman in Plato. He knows that art and poetry do not knock at the front door of reason to get into our souls, but instead, invite themselves right in and play with us. He, in the *Republic*, tells us that "Rhythm and harmony insinuate themselves into the innermost part of the soul and most vigorously lay hold of it"[21] He forbids the craftsman to practice his art so that our youths will not be reared on images of vice, "… and while they are totally unaware of it, are putting together a big bad thing in their souls."[22] Homer's lies are harmful to us who hear them, for if we are not careful, "we will be sympathetic with ourselves when we are bad."[23] Art is powerfully penetrating, it tells lies, and may very likely wreck havoc on our souls. It all boils down to a central moral issue. We are to be good by being rational, but art is, for Plato, irrational. "The unexamined life is not worth living for a human being," but the aesthetic experience of beauty occurs precisely when we seem to be not using reason or examining ourselves.

[20] Ibid.
[21] Plato, *Republic*, 401d
[22] Ibid., 401c.
[23] Ibid., 391e.

In a similar vein, and in the contemporary philosophical era, Kierkegaard reincarnates Socrates and his transcendental preference. Here the good lies in following the commands of Christ and in salvation. In a striking passage from *Works of Love*, Kierkegaard tells us that true love has nothing to do with friendship or romance, for Christ commands us to love our neighbor, and this means we need always to choose to love our neighbor, who is simply anyone. To have a friend or romantic lover means to love out of passion and preference, and, therefore, out of self-interest. When we love out of self-interest we are selfish. As we can see, here again a philosopher has wondered into the moral tunnel and cannot get out. He cannot see his speculative blind spots. He cannot see that it is his human nature and the society of human natures whose interest and preference it is. But here, as in many of his works on Christianity such as *Concerning Unscientific Postscript* and *Philosophical Fragments*, he refuses to make the distinctions of a speculative thinker. He says as much:

> Love to one's neighbor is therefore eternal equality in loving…. This needs no elaborate development. Equality is just this, not to make distinctions, and eternal equality is absolutely not to make the slightest distinction…. Christianity is in itself too profound, in its movements too serious, for dancing and skipping in such free-wheeling frivolity of talk about the higher, the highest, the supremely highest.[24]

Now Aristotle's emphasis on the transcendental of the true, on the theoretical knowledge that is now emergent from its symbiotic relation with practical knowledge in Platonic philosophy, allows him to make distinctions and to glory in them. Not overzealous to be good or pious, Aristotle can reflect upon the physical realities in front of him. Self-love is not egoism or selfishness but rather an expression of an already constituted human nature, already given in experience, before the act of choosing. The preferential loves of friends and family are highly honored by Aristotle.

Aristotle, because he wanted to know the truth about things, understood the necessary reality of the body, senses, and the structures and patterns of things in the physical world. He did not argue that the way to know reality—the true—was to become good first. He did not insist that we have a conversion to fire and sun, but rather thought that to know goodness, one must first know what's true. It is only after I find out what is true about human nature that I can know how humans act well. What is human nature and how does it exist in this physical world? Only by answering these questions first can Aristotle remark about how human nature actually thrives. Ultimately, Aristotle knew that our

---

[24] Søren Kierkegaard, *Works of Love* in *Other Selves: Philosophers on Friendship* (Indianapolis, Indiana: Hackett, 1991), pp. 245-46.

human natures thrived when we acknowledged our bodies, families, and friends, because that is the way we actually find our natures here in this world.

The blind spot for Aristotle was the loss of what might be called the vertical dimension of reality—he could not see the fullness of participation; he could not see any reality higher than an impersonal self-thinking-thought-god and this world. Ultimate human purposes—as seen in the Platonic Form of the Good are lost, our purpose is simply to thrive, to function well, but, alas, we will not function well for anyone or anything more than ourselves in society, and death has the last say.[25] The good is a function of human nature, not vice-versa.

Nietzsche thought that the aesthetic realm—which I correlate to the realm of beauty—was the realm that had the greatest penetration into reality. It was only as an aesthetic reality that the universe could be justified, says Nietzsche in the *Birth of Tragedy*. This is true because only the aesthetic dimension attains to existence. While Plato was interested in moral forms and Aristotle in ontological and theoretical forms, Nietzsche wanted to see inside, around, and between forms, for this was reality too; and often a too overlooked and undervalued reality. As he says of Socratic logic in the *Birth of Tragedy*:

> The voice of the Socratic dream vision is the only sign of any misgivings about the limits of logic: Perhaps—thus he [Socrates] must have asked himself—what is not intelligible to me is not necessarily intelligent? Perhaps there is a realm of wisdom from which the logician is exiled? Perhaps art is even a necessary correlative of, and supplement for science? [26]

Nietzsche wanted to go beyond a logical discussion of good and evil, of an objective text, of a conceptually organized knowledge of things. He perceived well and caused many to take care to notice, (along with his fellow existentialists, existential Thomists, some natural mystics, and Eastern philosophers)[27] that existence itself cannot be conceptually or logically accessed. This is a critical insight and an all-important one. It is through tragedy and literature that one probes the experienced world of contingent and individual beings, their freedom, their actions, motivations, relationships, contexts, interests, and sufferings. Nietzsche is right. A merely theoretical understanding of the world would miss these in its search for forms, universals, the necessary, the permanent, and the caused.

---

[25] There are, of course, discussions on immortality in *De Anima* III and *Nichomachean Ethics*, but they do not amount to a personal immortality.

[26] Friedrich Nietzsche, *The Birth of Tragedy and the Case of Wagner*, trans. Walter Kaufmann (New York: Vintage Books, 1967), p. 93.

[27] I am here indebted to the work of W. Norris Clarke, S.J.

His blind spot is that while he is right about the unique perspective of the aesthetic and right about that fact that it opposes *in its operation* the theoretical and practical perspectives, he was wrong in insisting that if a perspective did not agree with his aesthetic perspective, it did not exist. Perhaps, Nietzsche, in spite of his hatred of system, was the one who was too systematic here, in wanting only the aesthetic view. Maybe he was the one who was exiled, exiled from the theoretical and practical. Now, Maritain wasn't so logical. Maritain did not insist that all human knowings be one system—of one type. He knew their hostile differences. And he urged us—in a very existential and aesthetic way to embrace all of them, even when they didn't match up.

Nietzsche forgot that his whole *Birth of Tragedy* rested upon key distinctions and was parasitic upon theoretical concepts and moral values. After all, it was good—really good for Nietzsche—that we should not miss certain aspects of existential reality. It was really important that we not be rationalists! And it was true, really true, that Socrates was a man who constructed the world through an inquiry into moral concepts. Nietzsche could not but help using a scaffold taken from fragments from the true and the good. It is from this vantage point from which he criticizes the Western Tradition.

Now if we are able to simply allow each philosopher to show us what he can in the line of his transcendental and know in advance that there is going to be problems, then we do not have to be so upset at Nietzsche's nihilism. He almost has to be a nihilist! For nihilism means that nothing exists and that means no forms exist; and that means that the poetic perspective does not see the forms "head on"—and that is true! Poetry, for Maritain, does not concern itself with the forms of things. We can see the existences and the beauty that Nietzsche is trying to protect from the cutting knives of rationalism; however, he too has gone into a tunnel, the tunnel of the aesthetic—the realm of the beautiful—and he cannot get out.

Plato cannot get of the moral tunnel he is in. For if we portray reality as a function of morality, then the natural forms of things which, of course, do not appear in our *a priori* moral concerns, will be missed. And sorely missed! But if we know that, in advance that they will, we can forgive Plato.

Aristotle has difficulty getting out of the speculative tunnel. And the "ought" of morality is never found by examining the true alone. What is his distinction between happiness and blessedness all about? How can one be "happy" when the last act of the play is a bloody one and then they throw dirt over your head?[28]

---

[28] One of the famous Pascal *Penseés*.

However limited may be the viewpoints of philosophers, we must affirm the value of each transcendental appropriation of knowledge. Maritain once claimed that, in spite of the conflict, the human being must affirm all of these kinds of knowing. The trick is not to follow the logic of any particular knowledge to the extreme, but to embrace all of them. The trick is to see in stereo or triphonic! Is this hard? Maritain thought so and, in fact, he thought that Catholicism needed to come to the rescue here. He writes:

> Truthfully I do not believe it is possible outside of Catholicism to reconcile in man, without diminishing or doing violence to them, the rights of morality and the claims of intellectuality, art or science.... How are the children of Adam to keep the balance?[29]

Perhaps it is necessary here to bring in a notion of God as a transcendent source and goal of all of our knowings.

We have examined a number of viewpoints in this paper from the truths of sciences and metaphysics to practical knowledge to aesthetic knowledge. I believe that the failure to affirm any one transcendental will result in some form of ignorance. Something of reality will be lost. We need to beware of becoming imprisoned in and through the perspectives we now have. We are a race that desperately needs to search for the goodness & value in reality, to search for the truth about life, and to search for beauty. And in the recent Encyclical, *Fides et Ratio*, Pope John Paul II is clear about this. And we are a race that cannot do it alone. We need faith and God's "grace to perfect our natures." Perhaps this is one small reason why we need Jesus, the one who reflects the Trinity, and the one who calls Himself "the way, the truth, and the life."

[29] "An Essay on Art", p. 98.

Transcendental Thomist Methodology and Maritain's "Critical Realism"

John F. X. Knasas

Among students of Neo-Thomism, it is standard practice to draw an epistemological divide between Maritain and Gilson, on the one hand, and the Transcendental Thomists (e.g., Joseph Maréchal, Karl Rahner, and Bernard Lonergan), on the other. Both parties profess realism. By "realism" I mean the claim that our basic concepts are valid for a non-mind dependent world. But this espousal takes two forms. For Maritain and Gilson, we are confident in the validity of our basic concepts because one appreciates them as abstracted from real things given in sensation.[1] Concepts are not self-vali-

---

[1] Speaking of classical realism, Gilson asks, "Is it so difficult, then, to understand that the concept of being is presented to knowledge as an intuitive perception since the being conceived is that of a sensible intuitively perceived? The existential acts which affect and impregnate the intellect through the senses are raised to the level of consciousness, and realist knowledge flows forth from this immediate contact between object and knowing subject." Étienne Gilson, *Thomist Realism and the Critique of Knowledge*, trans. Mark A. Wauck (San Francisco: Ignatius Press, 1986), p. 206. Also, "The apprehension of being by the intellect consists of directly seeing the concept of being in some sensible datum." Ibid., p. 197. Again, "When the concept of being is abstracted from a concrete existence perceived with the senses the judgment which predicates of this existent attributes being to it . . . as 'seen' in the sensible datum from which [the concept of being] was abstracted." Ibid., p. 205. See also Jacques Maritain, *The Degrees of Knowledge*, trans. Gerald B. Phelan (Notre Dame, Indiana: University of Notre Dame Press, 1995), p. 98n50, 108n125 and *The Peasant of the Garrone*, trans. Michael Cuddihy and Elizabeth Hughes (New York: Holt, Rinehart and Winston, 1968), p. 100. For Maritain the "intuition of being" was always engendered *a posteriori* from the intellect's contact with real things given in sensation: "I see [the metaphysician's being] as an intelligible reality which issues from the least thing and in diverse respects belongs to all things." *A Preface to Metaphysics: Seven Lectures on Being* (New York: Sheed & Ward, 1958), p. 63; "We must attain a certain level of intellectual spirituality, such that the impact of reality upon the intellect...gives the objects received through our senses...." Ibid., p. 49. For remarks in *The Degrees of Knowledge*, see: p. 226, "...as if in opening a blade of grass one startled a bird greater than the world;" p. 227 on concept of being making "incomplete abstraction from its analogates;" p. 228 on transcendentals as "realized in the sensible in which we first grasp them" and being as "attained in sensible things by dianoetic intellection." Finally, another

dating and the epistemology is worked out from bottom to top. For the Transcendental Thomist our basic concepts are not *abstracta* but *projecta*. They are an *a priori* of the mind. Far from deriving from sense data, they are dynamically injected into that data, they suffuse that data, and allow the data to stand forth in certain determinate ways.[2]

example from *The Peasant of the Garrone*, p. 136: "...the procedure proper to philosophy, which has its starting point in experience and a prolonged intercourse with the world and with sensible reality."

[2] Joseph Maréchal, Karl Rahner, and Bernard Lonergan all regard the dynamism of the intellect towards Being as a constitutive factor for our consciousness of beings. Maréchal remarks: "As soon as the intellect, meeting an external datum, passes to the second act under the formal motion of this datum and the permanent impulsion of the natural appetite, we have a particular, positive determination subsumed under the universal form of being, which previously was only the framework of and the call for all possible determinations. An 'object' profiles itself before consciousness." Joseph Donceel, *A Maréchal Reader* (New York: Herder and Herder, 1970), p. 170. Also, on judgment: "Considered as a moment in the intellect's ascent towards the final possession of the absolute 'truth,' which is the spirit's 'good,' [affirmation] implicitly (*exercite*) projects the particular data in the perspective of this ultimate End, and by so doing objectivates them before the subject." Ibid., p. 152. "...the 'datum' represented in us was constituted as an 'object' in our mind through the judgment of affirmation." Ibid., p. 161. "For the subject is really knowing as such only to the extent that he formally takes part in the edification of the object." Ibid., p. 118. The same constitutive approach can be noted in Rahner. Speaking of the agent intellect, Rahner says: "Insofar as [the agent intellect] apprehends this material of sensibility within its anticipatory dynamism to *esse*, it 'illumines' this material...." Karl Rahner, *Spirit in the World*, trans. William Dych (New York: Herder & Herder, 1968), p. 225, see also, p. 221. Likewise, "Because it is apprehended in this dynamic tendency of the intellect . . . the particular sensible thing is known as finite, i.e., as incapable in its limitation of filling up the space of this dynamism. Because of this comparing of the particular thing to the absolute and ideal term of knowledge, the particular thing appears as existent (concrete being) in relation to being." Karl Rahner, "Aquinas: The Nature of Truth," *Continuum*, 2 (1964), p. 67. Finally, in Bernard Lonergan, *Insight: A Study of Human Understanding* (New York: Longmans, 1965), Lonergan appears to share the same constitutive approach found in Maréchal and Rahner. In fact at p. xxii, Lonergan expresses his intention to incorporate what Maréchal calls the finality of the intellect. Noteworthy are points found in Lonergan's discussion of the notion of being. First, abstraction is described as a provisional disregarding of the intellect's unrestricted objective of being (ibid., pp. 355-6). This suggests that being is an expanse against which things are initially profiled and from which we temporarily depart as abstraction focuses upon some feature. Likewise, judgment is understood as "an element in the determination of the universal intention of being" (ibid., p. 358). This seems to mean that each judgment is profiled against the notion of being. Such a move enables us to see the judgment as an "increment in a whole named knowledge." The move also sets the stage for wondering to arise once more and to lead to further judgments. In sum, McCool, in my opinion, correctly describes both Rahner and Lonergan as "Maréchalian epistemologists" and "Maréchalian metaphysicians," Gerald McCool,"Twentieth-Century Scholasticism," *The Journal of Religion*, 58 (1978), pp. 218-19. For further description and discussion of Maréchal, Rahner, and Lonergan, see John F. X. Knasas, "Intellectual Dynamism in Transcendental Thomism: A Metaphysical Assessment," *American Catholic Philosophical Quarterly*, 69 (1995), pp. 15-28.

Despite being *a priori*, Transcendental Thomists claim that their *projectum* understanding of our basic concepts avoids Kantian skepticism. The *projecta* are self-validating. The self-validation consists in noticing the ineluctability of the *projecta*. Because real doubt presumes the ability to think things otherwise and because the *a priori* are ineluctable, then no real doubt about the *a priori* is possible. Doubt will occur only within a context that affirms the very things doubted. In short, the doubt destroys itself. This procedure they call: retorsion or performative self-contradiction.[3] The veracity of sense is confirmed by its occurrence within the self-validating context of the mind's *a priori*. Realist epistemology is done from the top down. The crucial and defining moment of the methodology is the application of retorsion.

Transcendental Thomists claim that their validating device of performative self-contradiction simply expresses the "indirect proof" utilized by Aristotle and Aquinas to defend the non-contradiction principle at *Metaphysics, IV*. In dealing with deniers of the principle, Aquinas, commenting on Aristotle, says:

> but it is necessary to take as a starting point that a term signifies something both to the one who utters it, inasmuch as he himself understands what he is saying, and to someone else who hears him. But if such a person does not admit this, he will not say anything meaningful either for himself or for someone else, and it will then be idle to dispute with him. But when he has admitted this, a demonstration will at once be possible against him; for there is straightway found to be something definite and determinate which is signified by the term distinct from its contradictory.[4]

Despite the absence of the Transcendental Thomist phraseologies of "retorsion," "performative self-contradiction," "implicit to explicit," and "subjective to objective necessity," Aquinas's thinking, at least at first glance, appears similar to these things. The passage seems to say that because thought to be thought must be definite, then reality is definite. Everything is not its contradictory.

But the identity is an illusion. Only by anachronistically construing Aquinas's opponents as the Kantian opponents of the Transcendental Thomists does the identity appear. But Aquinas's opponents are all realists, a label

---

[3] For Maréchal's key exercise of retorsion, see *A Maréchal Reader*, pp. 215-17, 227-28; for Rahner, "Aquinas: The Notion of Truth," p. 69; for Lonergan, *Insight*, p. 352 on being as unrestricted. In sum, "Yet the absolute validity of [metaphysics'] truths can be established, since it can be shown that the affirmation of these truths is a condition of the possibility of all human knowledge. . . . This explains the great importance of 'retorsion' in Transcendental Thomism. 'Retorsion' is a technical term which refers to the method of demonstrating an assertion by showing that he who denies this assertion affirms it in his very denial." Joseph Donceel, "Transcendental Thomism," *The Monist*, 58 (1974), p. 81.

[4] St. Thomas Aquinas, *Commentary on Aristotle's Metaphysics*, trans. John P. Rowan (Notre Dame, Indiana: Dumb Ox Books, 1995), p. 227 (IV.7.611).

from which a Kantian-type of thinker would scrupulously divorce himself. Unlike a Kantian, none of Aquinas's opponents entrenches himself in a skepticism that maintains that the First Principle might be only subjectively true. Rather, all make reality claims. They say that the First Principle is not true of reality; contradiction is true of reality. To a Thomist, this position may be monstrous, but it is a realist one. Correctly understood, the opponents are not in thought but out in reality.

Closer scrutiny of Aquinas's *Commentary on Aristotle's Metaphysics* validates this realist characterization. Aquinas divides his opponents into two groups. The first is comprised of Heraclitus, Protagoras, Empedocles, Democritus, and Anaxagoras.[5] They were lead to affirm that reality is contradictory because of difficulties. These difficulties included the fact that contraries are generated from the same thing and that contrary opinions appear equally true.[6] Note that in both cases a presumed realism is driving the thinkers to deny the First Principle. Unlike the Kantian, whom the Transcendental Thomist is trying to move from thought to reality, Aquinas's opponents are already in reality, for they are using what they think that they know of reality to deny the First Principle.

Aquinas's second group of opponents are those who deny the First Principle because it cannot be demonstrated. A study of Aquinas's treatment of them reveals some pertinent observations. They can save their own thought and not suffer a reduction to the level of plants only by affirming that what exists is what is perceived. But that result is unacceptable "...because many things are and come to be of which there is neither opinion nor knowledge, for example things which exist in the depths of the sea or in the bowels of the earth."[7] These thinkers likewise cannot be Kantian-style thinkers that begin in subjectivity, for subjectivism is used as a threat against them and their position. In other words, subjectivism is not where these thinkers are but where they will end up. Moreover, when it comes time to criticize subjectivism, Aquinas does not initiate retorsion. Rather, Aquinas simply makes the *a posteriori* remark that we know that things exist unobserved.

If the realist nature of Aquinas's opponents is acknowledged, then one understands how Aquinas's above quoted defense of the First Principle differs from the retorsion interpretation of the same. Despite *prima facie* similarities, Aquinas's defense differs by including a suppressed premise: "Thought is about the real." This residual realism enables Aquinas to catch

---

[5] Ibid., pp. 253 (IV.12.683), 235 (IV.8.637), 250 (IV.12.675), 247 (IV.11.670) and 245 (IV.10.666).

[6] Ibid., pp. 245 (IV.10.665) and 247-48 (IV.11.669-70).

[7] Ibid., pp. 265 (IV.15.716).

the deniers in self-contradiction. All that is required is that the deniers say something meaningful. In other words, if thinking is determined by the real, then to employ words to say something definite is to admit that something definite exists. Everything is not its opposite, and so the principle is affirmed. On the other hand, if the real is the contradictory, it is not definite and so thinking itself should not be.

The Kantian denies this realism consisting in the conformity of thought to reality. The Kantian admits only that thinking is determined by thought itself. As a result performative self-contradictions in thinking point to what may be exigencies in thought alone. There is no manifest way to go beyond thought to the real. Aquinas's indirect approach would leave a Kantian cold. But it was never meant to deal with a Kantian. The approach is at home in realism. Taken out of that context, it losses all efficacy.

The anachronism point continues to hold of Transcendental Thomists who cite the *Summa Theologiae*.[8] In his reply Aquinas concedes the following portion of the objection:

> For whoever denies the existence of truth grants that truth does not exist: and, if truth does not exist, then the proposition *Truth does not exist* is true: and if there is anything true, there must be truth.[9]

In sum, one cannot deny truth under pain of contradiction. So, the argument presumes that the non-contradiction principle is more than a rule of thought. What is the basis for that presumption? It should be Aristotle's *Metaphysics*, (Book IV) in which, as noted, the opponent is not a Kantian but an *a posteriori* realist. For the Kantian, all the above *Summa* text would prove is that if you are to think, you have to think as if there is truth.

The anachronisms are to the good because philosophically the nagging suspicion remains that ineluctability is just what you would expect if the *a priori* are simply ways you have to think rather than ways reality has to be. The screeching of performative self-contradiction could quite well indicate a grinding of merely mental gears and not any manhandling of reality. A familiarity with less encompassing contexts acquaints us with the ideas of something standing outside a context and the context placing the thing in a different light. Contexts can be limited and distortive. One, naturally and correctly in my opinion, wonders if such is the case with the ineluctable *a priori*. Why may they not be actually limited too?[10]

---

[8] *A Maréchal Reader*, pp. 89-91 and "Transcendental Thomism," p. 81.

[9] St. Thomas Aquinas, *Summa Theologiae*, I q. 2, a. 1, obj. 3.

[10] For more on this criticism, see Knasas, "Intellectual Dynamism," pp. 23-26. I understand my criticism to echo generally Gilson's criticism of Maréchal, "It would then be

As mentioned, in the popular mind Maritain is considered an *a posteriori* thinker and an opponent of the transcendental turn in Thomism. And it is true that throughout his writings, Maritain maintained an *a posteriori* source in sensation for our concepts and that his intuition of being thesis, so central for his metaphysics, is no exception to this.[11] Consequently, Maritain says "in the final reckoning, the primary basis for the veracity of our knowledge" is the "resolving of the sense's knowledge into the thing itself and actual existence."[12] Nevertheless, it is this paper's contention that in his *Degrees of Knowledge* elaboration of "critical realism," Maritain effects an out-of-character liaison with the archetypal method of Transcendental Thomism—retorsion.

The thesis of Maritain's critical realism (*"le réalisme critique"*) is that apart from the issue of the source of our concepts, there exists on the intellectual level a philosophically expressible nexus of thought with reality at least as possible. In other words, from our thought alone, we do not know if anything is actual. Our thought does distance itself from reality as actual. Nevertheless, from our thought alone, we do know how reality has to be if it is to be. In short, thought cannot divorce itself from reality as possible.[13] In particular, we do know simply on the level of thought that the principle of identity is more than a rule of thought. It expresses more than what something has to be to be thought of. It expresses what something has to be even when it is not thought of. In sum, for Maritain a point exists at which thought is self-validating. It is not self-validating of reality as actual as the ontological argument for our thought of God. Rather, for Maritain, thought is self-validating of the real at least as possible. This point confounds what Maritain understands to be the modern project of going from thought to real-

easy to show that nonintuitive thought like ours requires and posits, by the finality of its dynamism, 'the independent reality of the ends its pursues.' But, as Fr. Maréchal himself immediately adds, 'from a strictly critical point of view a dynamic necessity, no matter how ineluctable, can of itself only be the basis for a subjective certitude.' What resources does the Kantian method place at our disposal in order to objectify that certitude? Absolutely none. To get around this difficulty Fr. Maréchal quickly adds that, if one could show that the reality of the ends of thought is not only a dynamic necessity but also a logical necessity, the task would be successfully completed. But this is not so, for, outside of relying unduly upon the data of the metaphysical critique, such a demonstration would lead only to an abstract necessity of thought which, no matter how absolute, does not guarantee the real existence of its object. In short, critical thought has imprisoned itself and can find no way to be reunited with reality." *Thomist Realism*, pp. 141-42.

[11] *The Degrees of Knowledge*, pp. 226-28; *A Preface to Metaphysics*, pp. 49, 63.
[12] *The Degrees of Knowledge*, p. 108n125.
[13] Ibid., p. 98n50.

ity. Thought for the moderns is one step further back than thought for Maritain. For the moderns thought succeeds in divorcing itself even from the real as possible. Certainly from that point any contact with the real seems impossible to achieve.[14]

Here is a listing of passages from *The Degrees of Knowledge* that express Maritain's critical realism position.

> In fact, the intellect, *in virtue of its own* proper *activity*, perceives that *necessary* law of all *possible* being in an *actual* (and contingent) existent grasped by it *through* the sense…. But for critical reflection it is well to give distinct consideration to the primary datum (revealed by psychological and logical analysis) of the intellectual perception as such. And this is why we…say with R. Garrigou-Lagrange that awareness of the irrefutable certitude of the principle of identity as the law of all possible being is part of the first conscious (philosophical) grasp that constitutes the starting point of critique.[15]

Maritain acknowledges the sense origin of the principle of identity. But then notice the shift. It is not by an appeal to the principle's sense origin that critique validates the principle. Rather for purposes of initiating a critique of knowledge, this abstractive origin can be placed aside. Now the "intellectual perception *as such*" of the principle validates it at least of the possible real. Later we will note just what is seen in the intellectual perception. Again,

> …our intellect, in simple apprehension, abstracts from existence in act and in its judgments it does not only judge of that which exists but also of a thing that can or cannot exist and of the *de jure* necessities contained in those essences. Thus, it is primarily with reference to the possible real that the value of intellectual knowledge "is justified," or better, confirmed or made explicit reflexively, and it is in reference to this that the critique of knowledge should primarily proceed.[16]

Maritain concedes that thought does succeed in abstracting its object from actual existence. Nevertheless, having gone that far, thought should acknowledge that its object cannot tear itself from possible real existence. Just in the *abstracta* themselves are contained necessities bearing upon the requirements

---

[14] "And as for the possibility of being in general, it is certified for us—even independently (*de jure*) of any perception of actual existence—by the very first judicative intuition of our intellect, for it affirms precisely that being is not non-being. But in a philosophy which starts only with thought, a philosophy according to which the mind attains at first only itself, how can we be sure that all our objects of thought are not beings of reason? That is where the Evil Genius plants his barb. That problem was crucial for Descartes (and for Leibniz, too). By the force of that violent splitting in two, that lived contradiction which is at the heart of idealism, must we not at last ask ourselves if being itself . . . is not a being of reason?" Ibid., pp. 142-43.

[15] Ibid., p. 98n50.

[16] Ibid., p. 98.

for the possibility or impossibility of actual existence. Critique primarily proceeds from these.

Especially strong expressions of the epistemologically autonomous validity of thought are found in these remarks:

> And as for the possibility of being in general, it is certified, for us—even independently (*de jure*) of any perception of actual existence—by the very first judicative intuition of our intellect, for it affirms precisely that being is not non-being.[17]

And at this point citing Garrigou-Lagrange:

> We see at once that it is not only inconceivable, but really impossible, for a thing at once to be and not be. And we thus affirm already the objective and ontological value of the principle of contradiction before any judgment of existence, before reflecting that this primary affirmation presupposes ideas, and before verifying the fact that these ideas come to us by abstraction, from sensible things grasped by our senses.[18]

Maritain's choice of this remark makes clear the relation between his "critical realism" project and the validation of ideas through sense. There is no relation. As mentioned, intellectual perception as such suffices to achieve validation.

---

[17] Ibid., pp. 142-43.

[18] It appears to be in this light that Maritain explains verification in metaphysics: "Metaphysics, however, does not verify its conclusions in sense data, nor like mathematics, in imagination. Nevertheless it too refers to the corruptible existence which can be attained by sensation. But it does so not to establish scientifically what are the realities it studies—those namely which constitute the subject matter of metaphysics, the being 'common to the ten predicaments,' created and material being taken as being—nor in order to know their essence." *A Preface to Metaphysics*, pp. 22-3. Also, "Unlike the Philosophy of Nature, [metaphysics] has no need to find its terminus in the verifications of the sense in order to establish those truths which are superior to time." *The Degrees of Knowledge*, p. 232. Garrigou-Lagrange appears to indulge in retorsion in these words, "Moreover, the intellect sees not only that idealism has not in fact found other evident principles which agree among themselves and with experience, but it sees also that idealism is not able to find others. Why? Because the principle of contradiction is immediately founded on our wholly first notion of being or of the real, presupposed by all other notions, . . ." "Le Réalisme Thomiste et le Mystère de la Connaissance," *Revue de Philosophie*, 38 (1931), p. 76 (translation is the author's). He makes the viability of idealism dependent upon getting outside the notion of being. Realism appears to be critically justified by ineluctability. If not the persons of Maritain and Garrigou-Lagrange, then their positions is what Gilson appears to have in mind when Gilson says, "If you feel that abstraction should not presuppose its object, it would be far better to stop treating it as an abstraction, since there is no longer anything from which it could be abstracted. Make it the idea of some Cartesian thought, but do not try to play two tables at one time." *Thomist Realism*, p. 193.

In fact in a manner similar to the top-down epistemology of Transcendental Thomism, Maritain employs intellectual critique to validate sense, not vice versa.

> *Starting from that certainty*, [the intellect] reflexively confirms for itself ("justifies" to itself) the veracity of sense and its own certitude of the existence of the sensible world. Thus, it is nonsense ["*non-sens*"] to posit (as is constantly done) the problem of the import of intellectual knowledge by bringing into question, as real being other than the ego, not, first of all, possible extramental being, but only the existence or non-existence (in act) of the sensible world.[19]

Maritain leaves unelaborated the intellect's reflexive confirmation of the veracity of sense. My best bet as to what he was thinking is this. The objectivity of the data of sense is no difficult matter, because we already know that our idea of being is true of all possible being. But we can grasp something true for all possible being only by taking it from some actual being. Now, being is taken from the object of sensation. Hence, the object of sensation is an actual. Whatever, noteworthy is how Maritain is using the unity of thing and object on the intellectual level to confirm unity of thing and object on the sense level.[20] Again, Maritain's realism *qua* critical is done top-down.

Obviously, the heart of Maritain's "critical realism" is the autonomous "intellectual perception as such." Just what is it about such a perception that provides critique with the validation it seeks? Two texts give the answer. Following a paragraph that cites Aristotle's *Metaphysics*, (Book IV) the first text reads:

> Through the performing of this task fundamental truths, especially the general validity of knowledge and first principles, are humbly confirmed—by reason of the impossibility of their contradictories.[21]

And why is it impossible to affirm the contradictories of the first principles? The second text reads:

> All anyone has to do is to take counsel with himself and experience within himself the absolute impossibility in which the intellect finds itself: how can it think the principle of identity without positing the extramental being (as at least possible) whose behavior this first-of-all-axioms expresses? A prime object, intelligible extramental being without which nothing is intelligible: that is the irrefutable

---

[19] *The Degrees of Knowledge*, p. 109n75.

[20] Maritain's procedure is top-down but still different from the top-down approach of Transcendental Thomists. In Maritain's approach being remains related to sense as an *abstractum*; it never assumes the guise of a *projectum*, or constitutive *a priori*.

[21] *The Degrees of Knowledge*, p. 79.

factual datum that is thrust upon the intellect in the heart of its reflection wherein it becomes aware of its own movement towards its object.[22]

The mentioned "impossibility of the contradictory" is based on the intelligible primacy of being, such that being is implied in all other intellectual apprehensions. In other words, being is validated by its ineluctability. Because I cannot get beyond it in thought, there is nothing beyond it in thought. A being of reason is conceivable only in reference to something else. Because being cannot undergo a similar reference, it is known not to be a being of reason.

I find this foundation for Maritain's "critical realism" strikingly similar to the retorsion foundation for Transcendental Thomism. Likewise does Gerald McCool, dean of the Neo-Thomist narrative. In his *From Unity to Pluralism: The Internal Evolution of Thomism*, McCool summarizes Maritain's critical realism this way:

> By validating the principle of identity through the technique of retortion and by rooting the objective judgment in extra-mental being at the outset of his philosophical reflection, Maritain provided a reflexive vindication of metaphysics as a necessary science of being.[23]

This talk of Maritain reflexively vindicating metaphysics by the technique of retorsion is guaranteed to warm the cockles of a Transcendental Thomist's heart. Along with McCool's claim that Gilson's lifelong labors in medieval philosophy actually undercut the program of *Aeterni patris*,[24] McCool's locating Maritain within the Transcendental Thomist orbit is one of the outrageous coups of the volume. But sadly I must admit that Maritain has given his kidnapper the rope. For both Maritain and the Transcendental Thomists, being validates itself by its ineluctability. Simply because we cannot think beyond being, i.e., simply in virtue of the intellectual perception as such, we can be fully confident that there is nothing beyond being; we can know that we are not trapped in an inside locked from an outside. Anything we attempt to use to question the validity of being turns out to be something that presupposes being. Hence, idealism is, Maritain says, "an absolute impossibility—impossible *in itself*."[25]

I can only say that I wish it were so. As I said *contra* the Transcendental Thomists, ineluctability is just what you would expect from a mere thought

---

[22] Ibid., p. 100.

[23] Gerald McCool, *From Unity to Pluralism: The Internal Evolution of Thomism* (New York: Fordham University Press, 1992), pp. 120-21.

[24] Ibid., p. 196.

[25] *The Degrees of Knowledge*, p. 77.

context that happens to be fundamental. If that is what you are dealing with, then you will also have the retorsion phenomenon. So the phenomenon by itself is indecisive between realism and idealism. I admit that I sympathize both with Maritain's critical realism and Transcendental Thomism. The *a posteriori*, or abstractive approach to validate our concepts is a messy and laborious affair. The plethora of sense vagaries, e.g., the hallucination and dream possibilities, the relativity in perception, after-images, bright spots during migraines, the distorting effect of social and cultural biases, etc. must be analyzed one after another. The amount of work does leave one pining for a silver bullet, and the ineluctability of intelligible being seems to be that missile. But just as Aquinas for truth's sake forfeited the ease of Anselm's *Proslogion* argument for the tedious affair of Aristotle's proof from motion, I likewise must balk at the retorsion methodology to defend realism and insist on the trek through the jungle of sense perception.

To conclude, I want to note that retorsion methodology is less of a problem for Maritain than for the Transcendental Thomist. For the latter retorsion is the sole way to secure realism, for the *a posteriori* approach from sense is dogmatic and naïve. But Maritain's critical realism included an admission that being was abstracted from sense. I noted Maritain's acknowledgement of the admission along with his insistence that for purposes of critique critical realism can dispense with it. But even in the "Critical Realism" chapter Maritain's insistence is ambiguous. Despite emphasizing the "primacy" of the "intellectual perception as such" for critique and that "intellectual perception" is the "starting point" of critique, Maritain just as explicitly says, "in the final reckoning, the primary basis for the veracity of our knowledge" is the "resolving of the sense's knowledge into the thing itself and actual existence."[26] The epistemological primacy of sensation is another current, though a minor one, in a chapter that appears to say the opposite, viz., in the final analysis the primary basis for the veracity of our knowledge is the unbreakable unity on the intellectual level of thing as at least really possible and object. Hence, in the wake of criticisms of retorsion, Maritain can retreat to this other current and defend the validity of knowledge on an abstractive basis. In fact that is my suggestion. Retorsion is an alien graft that compromises Maritain's otherwise straight forward *a posteriori* epistemology. Cut it off. And an indication exists that Maritain did so. In his *The Peasant of the Garrone*, Maritain avows that sensed actual existence is "the absolutely basic foundation of philosophical knowledge."[27] Nowhere is any

---

[26] Ibid., p. 125n108.
[27] *The Peasant of the Garonne*, p. 100.

talk *à la* critical realism about the "nonsense" of tying the import of intellectual knowledge with the existence of the sensible world. Rather, this "nonsense" appears to be in what the preceding remark indulges. Moreover, *contra* Husserl, Maritian's continued expression of the inseparability of thought and thing thesis[28] makes no mention of the "actual or possible" disjunction omnipresent in *The Degrees of Knowledge*. Finally, *The Peasant* characterizes Aquinas's philosophical realism as an "integral realism" ("*un realisme intégral*").[29] Though this language still differs from Gilson's language of "methodic realism," it also differs from Maritain's own "critical realism" terminology that he so labored to defend in Chapter Three of *The Degrees of Knowledge*.

---

[28] Ibid., p. 106.
[29] Ibid., p. 131.

Ways of Knowing Metaphysical Being
Aquinas and Heidegger

Matthew S. Pugh

The most serious twentieth century challenge to Thomistic meta-physics comes from the work of Martin Heidegger. There are two versions of this challenge: the first appears in such early works as *Being and Time*[1] and the *Basic Problems of Phenomenology*,[2] while the second appears in such later works as the *Nietzsche* volumes,[3] *Identity and Difference*,[4] and *The Principle of Ground*.[5] Both versions of the critique center on the notion of the ontological difference (the differ-ence between Being and beings). Heidegger claims in his early works that Aquinas obscured the real difference between Being and beings by repeatedly conceiving Being, first in terms of the *essentia/existentia* distinction, and secondly as *actualitas*, or static presence. He claims in his later works that Thomas's metaphysics fails to think the *ereignis*, the event of appropriation, as that which gives Being to thinking in each historical age. Thomas's metaphysics fails, in other words, to grasp the *austrag* (dif-ference) between Being and beings—the differing in the difference that makes the ontological distinction possible. Conse-quently, Aquinas's Being is mistakenly thought after the manner of a being; in this case, a Maker, or Uncaused Cause.

[1] Martin Heidegger, *Being and Time*, trans. John Macquarrie and Edward Robinson (New York: Harper and Row, 1962).

[2] Martin Heidegger, *The Basic Problems of Phenomenology*, trans. Albert Hofstadter (Bloomington, Indiana: Indiana University Press, 1982).

[3] Martin Heidegger, *Nieitszche* Vol. I-IV, trans. David Farrell Krell (San Francisco: Harper Collins, 1991).

[4] Martin Heidegger, *Identity and Difference*, trans. Joan Stambaugh (New York: Harper and Row, 1969).

[5] Martin Heidegger, *The Principle of Reason*, trans. Reginald Lilly (Bloomington, Indiana: Indiana University Press, 1996).

Heidegger's Critique of Aquinas

The *Basic Problems of Phenomenology* represents Heidegger's first extended critique of Aquinas's metaphysics. In that work, the basic problem of phenomenology is that of determining how to think the ontological difference, the difference between Being and beings, between Being understood transcendentally as the *a priori* structures of consciousness that make experience possible, and being understood entitatively as objective presence.[6] Any articulation of Being that fails to recognize this distinction, that fails to recognize the constituting role that consciousness plays in the determination of Being, necessarily obscures the true meaning of Being.

Now the medieval thesis which articulates Being into *essentia* and *existentia* is inadequate precisely because it fails to take into account the way in which *essentia* and *existentia* originate in experience. Its proponents fail to see, in other words, that the origin of the *meaning* of these terms lies in consciousness. That the origin of their meaning does lie in consciousness becomes obvious once one deconstructs the medieval thesis by tracing the philosophical genealogy of its key concepts.[7]

Aquinas, for example, typically takes existence to mean *actualitas*, that which makes a thing be real. Heidegger notes, however, that *"actualitas"* is derived from *"agere"* and *"actum,"* whose meanings refer to the action of some human doer. Though *actualitas* appears to mean that which is purely objective, its more fundamental meaning is that which has its origin in some type of human activity. *Actualitas* thus makes a veiled reference to some productive agent; in this case, a human productive agent. The deeper meaning of "that which exists" or is actual, then, is "that which has been brought forth by some productive agent." In short, Thomas's understanding of the meaning of Being as *actualitas* is grounded in a meaning of Being originally projected in terms of making and producing. The same consideration applies to the original meaning of essence.[8]

The Greeks, for example, whose philosophy Thomas for the most part simply takes over, clearly understood essence in terms of making and producing. For the Greeks, the *eidos* of the artisan's work is the result of its having been impressed with a certain *morphe*; the form is in effect a function of the intended look (*eidos*) of the product. The Greek thinks of form in terms of what is to be made or brought forth, rather than what is to be made in

---

[6] See *The Basic Problems of Phenomenology*, pp. 11-23.
[7] Ibid.
[8] Ibid., pp. 100-05.

terms of form. The *eidos* is thus that from which the work, or thing, is descended (its kin or kind); any other thing descended from the same *eidos* belongs to the same kind. *Phusis*, or nature, comes to mean that which produces its own kind—a nature is simply a self-producing essence. Obviously, then, if *phusis* is reality, and reality is made up of self-producing essences, then nature is something produced.[9]

Yet to produce also means "to put" or "to place" something "here." But when so placed, the produced being takes on the appearance of "standing for itself," and so becomes discoverable, first as that which is ready-to-hand in the equipmental context, then as disposable presence (that which is merely present-at-hand) and finally as static presence, as mere thing. The discovery of static presence is occasioned by a shift in awareness from that of circumspective concern, to mere on-looking. The present-at-hand becomes object, while the on-looker becomes subject. In short, for Heidegger the origin of the objective or speculative outlook lies in consciousness.[10]

Since Thomas's understanding of the meaning of the essence/existence distinction is derived from Greek ontology, his metaphysics belongs to the same horizon of "bringing forth" and "producing." However, because it fails to take account of the producer, it is incomplete. When Thomas considers human being, for instance, he considers human being from the standpoint of the merely present, entitatively, as something present; but since the meanings of essence and existence are themselves produced or constituted by consciousness, they cannot be used to account for consciousness. Neither, then, can they account for the meaning of Being in general. Though essence and existence are perhaps adequate as an articulation of the meaning of the Being of entities, they are not adequate as an articulation of the meaning of the Being of human beings. Aquinas simply failed to articulate, to think, their difference.[11]

With the *Nietzsche Lectures* of 1941, however, Heidegger's assessment of Thomas's metaphysics changes. Whereas he maintained in *The Basic Problems of Phenomenology* that Thomas's version of the ontological difference was essentially a continuation of Greek ontology, he maintains in the *Nietzsche Lectures* that Thomas's understanding of the essence/existence distinction in fact marked a radical break with the Greek understanding of that distinction.

Now the *Nietzsche Lectures* reflect the so-called "turn" in Heidegger's thinking, wherein he shifts the emphasis of his ontology away from the con-

---

[9] Ibid., pp. 106-11.
[10] Ibid., pp. 112-17.
[11] Ibid.

stituting role of consciousness, to the way in which Being claims man historically. Consequently Heidegger had to re-think the problem of the origin of the ontological difference in light of his new approach.

For the Heidegger of 1941, the origin of the ontological difference still lies in the Greek philosophical experience, but whereas before the difference lay in the making activity of the human doer, now the origin of the difference lies in presencing.[12]

According to Heidegger, Being first came to light in the thinking of the pre-Socratics. But for those ancient philosophers the primary revelation of Being was as pure presencing, the upsurge of beings into Being, and of Being in and through beings. Being was understood to be an emergent process fluctuating between coming-to-be and passing away. But that which fluctuates between coming-to-be and passing away of the presencing process was soon viewed as that which stands between coming-to-be and passing away; in effect as enduring presence. The Being of a being came to be viewed, in other words, as something "set out," or completed, as something "gathered into completion." In that sense, of course, a being could still be called a work, for a work is simply a gathering into permanent presence of that which comes to be and passes away. Yet the work was not taken to be something made; rather it was understood to be something set out in its manifestness. Beings were viewed, then, not as the product of some making activity, but as what is unveiled through a disclosing revelation. The later Greek understanding of Being as *ousia* is grounded, claims Heidegger, in this pre-Socratic understanding of Being as presencing.

Specifically, this new revelation of the pre-Socratic experience of Being grounds the essence/existence distinction in *ousia,* or enduring presence, in the following way. That which is present primarily and immediately before us is the singular, the "*tode ti,*" while that which is present secondarily is the "look" of the thing, its outward appearance as something of a certain kind, its *eidos.* These two kinds of presence divide Being into the "that" *(existentia)* and the "what" *(essentia),* and the history of metaphysics is just the history of their interrelations; which of the two is emphasized is of little importance since both have their origin in the Being of static presence (presentness).

The problem with Aquinas's metaphysics is that it overlooks the Greek understanding of *ousia* as crystallized *energeia* (the process of setting something into a work in regard to its look—the emergent process whereby beings emerge into Being, and subsequently "congeal" into permanence), and in-

---

[12] Martin Heidegger, *The End of Philosophy*, trans. Joan Stambaugh (New York: Harper and Row, 1973), pp. 1-9.

stead transforms it into *actualitas*, into that which is made. For Thomas, the Being of a being no longer means a working which discloses itself through presence, but something causally made. Existence no longer means *ekstasis*, "stepping out of" into presence, but that which stands outside of its causes. A being, which for the Greeks had been a self-showing disclosing, becomes for Thomas something present as a product. And Being itself becomes that which is causally responsible for beings, for that which is present.[13]

This causal way of thinking about Being, of course, culminates in Thomas's highest theology. There God is the fullness of Being, pure act, that Being whose essence is its existence, who as such is absolutely permanent. Now since the goodness of a thing is defined in terms of its coming to be in accordance with its end, and since what God is is pure act, God is necessarily pure goodness. And from this it follows that God is the ultimate Cause who is himself uncaused. God, then, is the maker of things—things real in virtue of the fact that they stand outside of their Ultimate Cause.[14]

In sum, Heidegger's 1941 assessment of Thomas's version of the ontological difference deepens, and in some respects overturns, the critique of 1928. *The Basic Problems of Phenomenology* showed how the medieval thesis is grounded in the ancient Greek experience of artistic creation, and the productive comportment of consciousness. The *Nietzsche Lectures* of 1941, however, establish (in light of Heidegger's "turn") that Thomas's version of the ontological distinction is ultimately grounded, not in any kind of making activity, as Thomas had thought, but in the process of presencing by which beings rise up into manifestness.

Before we turn to our response to Heidegger's critique, however, a further refinement of it must be mentioned which centers on the notion of the *austrag*, or dif-ference,[15] and *ereignis*, the event of appropriation.[16]

With these two notions, Heidegger intensifies his attack on Aquinas, and indeed on all of metaphysics, for he claims that Thomas not only distorts the original Greek experience of Being as presencing, and thereby the ontological difference, but also (like all metaphysicians) fails to recognize that which makes the ontological difference possible. Thomas's thought, in other words, remains focused on *what* is opened up by the ontological difference (Being and beings) rather than on the differing process itself.

But what exactly is the differing in the ontological difference? According to Heidegger, the distinction between Being and beings, what he calls

---

[13] Ibid., pp. 10-19.
[14] Ibid.
[15] See *Identity and Difference*, pp. 62-74.
[16] Ibid., pp. 23-41.

their *differenz*,[17] originates in that process whereby Being and beings are carried outside each other while simultaneously coming to birth in each other. The *way* in which Being and beings are carried outside of each other while being simultaneously born in each other, identifies the differing in their *differenz*, that is, their dif-ference, or *austrag*. Every metaphysics recognizes a *differenz* between Being and beings, but no metaphysics recognizes the *austrag*, the dif-ference, between Being and beings, the differing in their *differenz*. This is no less true of Aquinas's metaphysics.

It must be understood, of course, that this refinement of the ontological difference is a direct result of Heidegger's philosophical "turn" away from the attempt to conceptually frame Being, toward letting Being be. After the turn, he no longer views the history of metaphysics as something made by man through his thinking activity, but rather as something given by Being to man's thinking in such a way as to completely claim that thinking. *What* is given in each historical epoch is the *differenz* between Being and beings, but *that which gives* the *differenz* to thinking, that which claims it in the way that it is claimed in each historical epoch, is the *austrag*.

How the *austrag* gives the *differenz* between Being and beings is fully described in *The Onto-Theo-Logical Constitution of Metaphysics*.[18] Traditional metaphysics, says Heidegger, has a threefold focus: Being, God, and Reason. Metaphysics studies what is, but it also studies that which unifies and grounds Being. Thus it is a science, or logic, since it attempts to ground the ground, namely Being, through reason. Being then comes to mean the ground that gives itself ground through reason. In this way, Being claims thinking as the ground that grounds. Metaphysics is simply the science that gives account of the ground. Being is thought in terms of ground, and ground is provided for by thinking. And, since metaphysics attempts to give Being the ultimate, or highest ground, it is not only an onto-logic, but a theo-logic as well.

This means, in effect, that Being and beings hold each other in a kind of mutual embrace. Since Being is always the Being of beings, Being comes to birth, or reveals itself, only in and through beings. At the same time, beings appear only in and through the "coming-over" of Being to beings.[19] Being unveils or discloses itself at the same time that beings arrive in Being as beings. Nevertheless, though the "coming-over" of Being to beings allows beings to appear in Being, their arrival in Being simultaneously has the ef-

[17] Ibid., pp. 62-74.
[18] Ibid., pp. 42-60.
[19] Ibid., pp. 69-71.

fect of concealing Being. Thus the extent to which beings are revealed in Being is also the extent to which Being is concealed in beings. This process of the mutual "coming-over/disclosing" of Being to beings, and the subsequent concealing of Being through their arrival in Being, is the *austrag*, a term taken from the Latin *dif-fere*, meaning "to carry away from." *Austrag* simply identifies the differing in the *differenz* between Being and beings.

Now when Being comes over into beings, it does so as their ground, as that *in* which they arrive; in this way Being is called the ground of beings. But in so far as beings conceal Being in their very arrival, or appearing, beings determine and define Being. In other words, beings ground Being at the same time that Being grounds beings. As Heideggger says, Being and beings circle round each other in a kind of perduring dance.

Thomas, of course, thinks what circles in that dance, namely *esse* and *ens*, but he does not think the *austrag*, the dif-ference in the *differenz*, for the *austrag*, the dif-ference, is neither Being nor beings. The *austrag*, rather, is that which gives the ontological difference as the *esse/ens* distinction.

Yet because giving is an event, what is given in the ontological distinction is given in terms of time. As we have seen, Heidegger explains Being in terms of presence. But presence is a temporal notion, for presence signifies the constancy of what passes away, and this in turn signifies the present, or that which remains constant.[20]

Thomas, however, does not see Being in terms of historical presencing, as a temporal giving, as a process. And this means, then, that he misses the absencing, or the withdrawal, implicit in every presencing, for every sending or giving is at once a revealing disclosure and a concealing withdrawal. Every revealing of Being in beings is at once a withdrawing/concealing of Being, for in the present of presence is the absence of "having been," and the futural "not-yet." Presence itself, however, extends to include both the "having-been" of the past and the "not-yet" of the future—the "not-yet" of the future being framed in the context of the past, and the "having-been" of the past revealing itself in the light of future possibilities. The present, therefore, is just the time-space that presence (the mutual embrace of "having-been" and "not-yet") opens up for us. In effect, temporality grounds Being when understood as presence. But in so far as the overeaching of presence into past and future makes the time-space of the present possible, Being grounds time. Time and Being are thus mutually given over to each other. In effect, each appropriates the other for itself, and this event is the *ereignis*, the event of appropriation.

---

[20] Martin Heidegger, *On Time and Being*, trans. Joan Stambaugh (New York: Harper Colophon Books, 1972), pp. 1-25.

Time claims Being as presence, while Being claims time as time-space, as the opening that "lets presence"—that is, the space wherein presence becomes the present.

Together, then, the *austrag* (the differing in the *differenz* between Being and beings) and the event of appropriation, are the preconditions which make the ontological difference possible.

The Thomistic Response to Heidegger

Thomists have typically responded to the Heideggerian challenge by mounting three basic defenses: the Gilsonian, the Maritainian, and the Transcendentalist. The Gilsonians maintain that Aquinas's philosophy is the one philosophy in the history of philosophy able to escape Heidegger's critique of metaphysics, for Thomas's metaphysics is built on the understanding that Being primarily means *esse*, or existence, a being's act of existing, but not essence.[21] As such, *esse* cannot be grasped *via* simple apprehension, and so cannot be known through a concept. *Esse*, rather, can only be captured, or "known" in judgments of existence.[22] In order to be thought conceptually and raised to the metaphysical level, *esse* must be rejoined to essence and then brought under the operations of 1) abstraction (without precision)[23] and 2) separation in the form of a special negative judgment.[24] But here, however, it is precisely *ens*, not *esse,* that is the object of the abstraction/separation. The *esse* component of Being (*ens*) completely eludes conceptualization. For Gilson, rather, our ability to "know" *esse* is completely dependent on, and grounded in, pre-conceptual sensory experience.[25]

The Maritainians, on the other hand, agree that *esse* means existence in the sense of a being's act of existing, not essence, and that *esse* can only be grasped directly in judgment—or more specifically for metaphysical Being, in a specially heightened judgmental appreciation of existence—but nevertheless maintain that the *esse* component of Being can become, if only indirectly, the object of a concept, which must then become (in order to be

---

[21] Étienne Gilson, *Being and Some Philosophers* (Toronto: Pontifical Institute of Mediaeval Studies, 1949).

[22] Ibid., pp. 190-217.

[23] Joseph Owens, *An Elementary Christian Metaphysics* (Milwaukee: Bruce Publishing Co., 1963).

[24] John F. Wippel, "Metaphysics and *Separatio* in Thomas Aquinas" in *Metaphysical Themes in Thomas Aquinas* (Washington, D.C.: The Catholic University of America Press, 1984)

[25] Étienne Gilson, *Thomist Realism and the Critique of Knowledge* (San Francisco: Ignatius Press, 1986), pp. 23-87.

raised to the metaphysical level) the object of an eidetic intuition or visualization grasped at the third degree of formal abstraction/separation. Far from being a universal, the resulting residuum is a transcendental whose mode of predication is that of the analogy of proper proportionality.[26]

The Transcendentalists, of course, take a different approach, for they believe that Thomas's epistemology can be appropriated along Kantian lines, and that metaphysical Being must ultimately be apprehended through the inner dynamism of the intellect.[27]

None of these defenses, however, fully answer Heidegger's charges. In short, in spite of the Gilsonian and Maritainian emphasis on thinking Being primarily in terms of *esse,* or existence, their understanding never overcomes Aquinas's conception of *esse* as *actualitas,* or hardened presence. Hence, like Thomas, they think Being after the manner of that which is made, or caused to be, rather than that which is revealed, or unconcealed. Being itself, pure act, is conceived as Ultimate Maker, Ultimate Cause. Furthermore, that which is fundamental to presencing, namely, absencing—that which withdraws in the revealing of beings (and thereby of Being) to consciousness—is lost sight of in their view. Thus not only have Thomists failed to articulate a real distinction between Being and beings, they have also lost sight of that which gives this distinction in the first place.

The Transcendentalists, for their part, grant Heidegger his starting point and recognize the difference between the ontological (the Being of human beings) and the ontic (the being of entities), and understand that the latter (in an ontological sense) is derived from the former. They nevertheless make the mistake of confining human Being to the subject (specifically the Kantian subject), and so undermine the *a priori* nature of the existential structures of consciousness, which are revealed to be already-in-the-world. For the Transcendentalist, Being is just the necessary guarantor of the unity of consciousness.

Nevertheless, in spite of these failures there is another possible defense of Aquinas that has yet to be tried. This defense is grounded in a reconsideration of the ontological distinction that Aquinas does make, establishing that it is, when rightly understood, the real ontological distinction that does not obscure the difference between Being and beings by misconceiving the former in the manner of the latter.

[26] Jacques Maritain, *A Preface to Metaphysics: Seven Lectures on Being* (New York: Sheed and Ward, 1948), pp. 62-90.

[27] Joseph Maréchal, *Le Point de depart de la métaphysique: Leçons sur le développement historique et théorique du problème de la connaissance* (Paris: Desclée De Brouwer, 1944-1949), chap. V.

Now there appear to be five viable interpretations of Thomas's ontological distinction. Historical and textual cases, of course, can be made for each of these interpretations, but only the fifth escapes Heidegger's critique.

The first version of Thomas's distinction defines the difference in terms of *esse/essentia*, or *existentia/essentia*, where *esse/existentia* means a being's act of existing, or existence, and *essentia* means essence, or that which makes a being be what it is. The second version defines the ontological distinction in terms of *ens commune/ens*, or to be more exact, *ens commune seu universale in universali/ens particulare*, where *ens commune* means common, universal being, or being in general (a universal notion formed via abstraction without precision, from beings understood generally), and *ens* means the particular being. The third version defines the distinction in terms of *esse commune seu universale/esse proprium seu particulatum seu determinatum*, which again, means common or universal being (a universal notion formed by abstracting from individual acts of existing), and *esse proprium seu particulatum seu determinatum* means the determined or particular act of existing. The fourth way defines the distinction in terms of *esse/ens*, understood to mean either a) a being's act of existing, and a being, or b) Being and beings, where Being is pure act, or God, and beings are God's creations.

Now it is the second interpretation of the fourth way that comes the closest to Heidegger's notion of the ontological difference between Being and beings, whereas the first three view the distinction either in terms of metaphysical co-principles applicable to beings, or in terms of a common abstraction based either on the composite being, or the existence component of the composite being. But, even in the fourth way, Being is ultimately just that Being whose essence is its existence—which is the same as to say pure, or unlimited existence, or that Being in whom the existence/essence distinction collapses.

Yet, in all of these interpretations of Thomas's ontological difference, the primary term is taken to mean existence, or act of existing—either a being's act of existing, the act of existing in general, or pure, unlimited act of existing. Here *esse* always means *actualitas*, and *actualitas* always means *existere*, to be, to be actual as that which stands outside of its causes. But we must ask at this point, must *esse* be thought strictly in terms of existence?

We should note, first of all, that *esse* and *existere* do not necessarily mean the same thing, for *esse* means "to be," while *existere* means "to exist." Though both words are verbs, they seem to function in rather different ways. For instance, we can say "Would that she might be more generous!" However, we cannot say "Would that she might exist more generously!" We also note that in Latin *esse* and *essentia* are linguistically related, though essence and existence are not so related. *Esse* means "to be" or "to be real," but *existere* means "to be actual" or "to be outside of its causes." If existence is made synonymous with *esse,* then when placed back into the ontological distinction, the "to be" of *esse* is displaced in favor of *existere*'s nounal sense of *existentia,* or existence, thereby simply identifying a being as that which stands outside of its causes. *Esse* properly understood, however, retains its fundamental verbal sense. *Esse* means being, not existence, for even when conceived as "act of existence," *existere*'s verbal sense defers to the nounal sense of "act" understood as enduring, or hardened presence

Heidegger, it seems, has failed to see this possibility in Thomas. He claims that Thomas does not make a true ontological distinction because he views Being in terms of act and hence in terms of beings that are simply present. But if Thomas in fact distinguishes Being and existence, *esse* and *existentia,* then he at least escapes the first part of Heidegger's critique. Existence must then have the sense of "coming out of," or when accompanied by a noun or adjective, mean "to show itself," a meaning immediately bringing to mind Heidegger's notion of Being as presencing. A being may be said to come into existence by coming out of Being, i.e. by showing itself. Only after a being comes to stand on its own, outside of its causes, can it be viewed in the lesser existential sense of "that which is," the hardened actuality. Existence, then, becomes a derivative of Being (*esse*). In other words, by differentiating *esse* and *existere/existentia,* and then showing how the latter is related to the former, the deeper sense of Being as presencing can be recovered in Thomas's thought.

Unfortunately, the Neo-Scholastics confused or collapsed the two meanings, and so severed their unique relation. Consequently, *esse* came to take on both a copulative *and* an existential function—positing a being as that which stands outside of its causes. But if Thomas is to be retrieved, then the function of *esse* must not be primarily to posit the existence of something in a "yes" or "no" fashion.

Nevertheless, if *esse* does not mean existence, what does it mean? When beings come into existence by coming out of Being, that is, by showing or disclosing themselves, there is always necessarily something that withdraws in the process. In so far as beings show themselves, they ultimately come into Being as existence, as hardened presence, but this showing presupposes, and so is made possible by, that which withdraws. In other words, it is the sending withdrawal of Being, or *esse,* that allows beings to stand forth in hardened presence, or existence. This "letting presence" is not a making, but a revealing through absenting. In so far as *esse* overwhelms or arrives in beings, *esse* reveals part of itself, but in so far as beings arrive in their Being through the unconcealing of Being, something withdraws.

For Thomas, then, Being and beings circle round each other in perduring difference. The one grounds the other, and through their differing, we arrive at a *differenz,* the essence/existence distinction. Yet that which sends the *differenz,* withdraws. Absencing withdrawal is the differing in the *differenz* which opens up, or makes possible, the essence/existence distinction. Being as existence stands forth presently in beings, while Being as *esse* withdraws. Existence then comes to the fore, taking the place of *esse.* Yet the existence which comes to the fore is not something made, or caused to be, but rather that which is revealed through presencing. Neither, then, is that which presences by withdrawing a maker; it is rather, that which unconceals through absencing. Thus, the differing in the *differenz* which gives the ontological distinction, its origin or source, is revealed to be no-thing, nothing other than a withdrawl of Being.

The fifth interpretation of Thomas's ontological distinction thus defines that difference in terms of *esse* and *ens,* but refuses to view *esse* as existence. By so doing, we allow Thomas to recapture the primordial sense of Being as presencing/revealing/withdrawal, while at the same time allowing him to not only make a genuine ontological distinction, but also to think that which makes or gives the ontological distinction in the first place.

Finally, we must ask what all of this means for traditional Thomistic epistemology. Well, as what is present, the completed presence can become the object of an abstraction, either with or without precision. But *what* is captured in that case is either the whole essence of the thing, or its form, either man or humanity, either animal or animality. What is left out of the abstracting process, however, is the Being of the being. Thomists normally say that *esse* is grasped in the judgment; but what is grasped in the judgment when *esse* is re-thought as Being rather than existence, is not a being's act of existing so much as the how of its Being. In other words, when *esse* is re-thought as *Being,* the copulative function of judgment, rather the existential function of judgment, takes priority. If we say, for example, "Mahler's eighth symphony is beautiful," we are saying something about how it is, how its being is; in effect, we are saying something about its degree of perfection, or Being. But this is not the same as saying, "The symphony's existence is beautiful," or simply "The symphony exists."

What presents itself to us in the hardened presence, then, can become the object of an abstraction—and this accounts for Aquinas saying that metaphysics studies the formal being of all things as its subject matter. However, that Being is the Being distributed among the ten categories, and is to be distinguished from transcendental Being, or Being itself. Transcendental Being can be known only through an act of separation, a negative judgment which says that that which makes a being be, need not be identified with that which makes it be a being of a given kind. In a sense, then, what is grasped in the negative judgment is indeed Being.

But there is also something that eludes the metaphysical judgment, for something withdraws with every presencing. As such, this "something" cannot become the object of an abstraction, and cannot be captured in a concept, because as no-thing, as a withdrawal, it is unconditioned. Hence, when viewed in the light of our fifth interpretation of Thomas's ontological distinction, the metaphysical separation of the negative judgment opens the way for thinking to enter into the event of appropriation in a conscious way, by letting Being be. Simply stated, the negative judgment of metaphysics must be viewed as separating not existence but Being—the fullness of perfection—that cannot be identified with any kind of being that would limit it. Yet, because the metaphysical separation necessarily takes the form of a negative judgment, the object of the judgment, pure *esse*, withdraws. *Esse* thus partly reveals itself in predicative judgments and in *essentia*, but ultimately withdraws from conscious appropriation.

Knowing Subjectivity
Jacques Maritain & John Crosby

James G. Hanink

Commonsense can be hard to come by. Consider, for example, the vexed question of self-knowledge.

In Dostoevski's *Crime and Punishment*, Razumihin urges us to "talk nonsense, but talk your own nonsense," and we applaud. How can we suffer another to speak for us, when we alone know ourselves? But what about Bobby Burns's plea (in "To a Louse") "O wad some Pow'r the giftie gie us to see oursels as others see us?" Why, once again we applaud—and just as heartily. For how can we hope to see, and thus to know, ourselves aright when others manifestly cannot see themselves as they are?

Enter Dame Philosophy. Socrates, her liege, enjoins us: "Know thyself." But what are we to make of his injunction? After all, it might seem, *either* we, and we alone, already know ourselves *or*, alternatively, we cannot even hope to know ourselves—not as we really are. How, then, can we follow such counsel? Can philosophy, Fair Mistress that she is, ease our puzzlement? However mixed her past ministrations, let's explore the prospects at hand.

The quest for self-knowledge is vexing, in part, because its proper object is as elusive as it is intriguing. Suppose, for a start, that we understand the *self* of self-knowledge as subjectivity. Fair enough. But what's this subjectivity? With John Crosby, we can profitably understand subjectivity as "self-presence."[1] Note: if we make this start, we can't, without elaboration, simultaneously understand *self* as substance or, as Jacques Maritain sometimes has in mind, "the substantial totality" of the person.[2]

Suppose, too, that we understand knowledge, broadly construed, as grasping the existence of what one knows—as object—in what Maritain calls its "particular field of intelligibility."[3] One last clarification is in order: only

---

[1] John Crosby, *The Selfhood of the Human Person* (Washington, D.C.: The Catholic University of America Press, 1996), p. 94.

[2] Jacques Maritain, *Creative Intuition in Art and Poetry* (New York: Meridian, 1974), p. 82.

[3] Jacques Maritain, *Existence and the Existent* (New York: Pantheon, 1948), p. 11.

subjects can know, and they do so by forming an immaterial, and objective, notion of this or that existent. Knowledge, so construed, calls to mind the adage "*anima est quodammodo omnia.*"

Now, then, the question at issue: can we have self-knowledge in the sense of knowing our own subjectivity?

Herein lies the dispute between Maritain and Crosby. It is instructive, and Crosby—a phenomenological personalist—has recently drawn our attention to it. We cannot, says Maritain, have philosophical knowledge of our own subjectivity, because philosophy knows subjects only as objects. But we cannot form an objective notion of, we cannot objectify, our own subjectivity. To suppose otherwise distorts the nature of subjectivity. In addition, one might infer, though Maritain does not, that if to know the other is, in a way, to become the other, then self-knowledge implies an act by which I come to be myself. But I already *am* myself.

Nonetheless Crosby contests Maritain's analysis. Crosby holds that we can rightly "affirm...the subjectivity of self-presence" even when "objectivized...in philosophical reflection."[4] To suppose otherwise overlooks the obvious: we do philosophize about subjectivity—without reducing it to, or mistaking it for, an objectifying consciousness. Maritain's own practice demonstrates as much. And, of course, we are already ourselves; but this doesn't keep us from gaining knowledge about ourselves, indeed, of our own subjectivity. Such knowledge, it's fair to say, enriches our ways of being.[5]

Another dispute between philosophers, about something so basic as self-knowledge, might seem to be of little help to commonsense. And when the dispute is both plausible and persistent, we're in no position to scold the skeptics. On the other hand, if we can negotiate this dispute, we might be able to silence them. We might even be able to minister to commonsense. As it happens, the prospects for both are promising, or so I will argue. An initial point: if we look closely at key texts, we find that Maritain and Crosby qualify (and complicate) their positions. Given this maneuvering, we can make headway in overcoming their impasse by a careful framing of their remarks.

Maritain: A Closer Look

Granted, the core of Maritain's position seems uncompromising. "Subjectivity as *subjectivity* is inconceptualisable," he insists.[6] But for every core

---

[4] *The Selfhood of the Human Person*, p. 96.
[5] For an acute analysis of this see point, see Yves R. Simon, *Philosopher at Work*, ed., Anthony O. Simon (Lanham, Maryland: Rowman & Littlefield, 1999), p. 183.
[6] *Existence and the Existent*, p. 69.

there's a context. To fill in the context of his position, we can turn to a pair of equally striking, and related, claims that he affirms.

First, Maritain agrees with the sober thesis that we never know everything about anything. But why not? Because each subject is "an inexhaustible well of knowability."[7] We know subjects only as objects and, thus, only in certain of their "intelligible aspects," or rather *"inspects..."*[8] Epistemically, we've always only just begun. But doesn't this sobriety encourage a fresh question? If knowledge of existing subjects is always limited, precisely because they are subjects, why can't there be knowledge, albeit limited, of one's own subjectivity as well? Yes, such knowing involves conceptualizing, and it takes a subject as its object. But it does not, cannot, exhaust the reality of the subject. Neither need it diminish the subjectivity of the knower.

Second, Maritain distinguishes between the self-knowledge of "psychological" analysis and a richer "ontological" self-knowledge.[9] The former introduces us to the ego, not the self. The latter, however, is revelatory; its vehicle is a metaphysical generosity. Maritain relishes the achieving of an ontological self-knowledge in self-donation. But this same dynamic, it seems, could open the way for a philosophical knowledge of self-presence. Given this dynamic, mightn't one also grasp—conceptually—one's self-presence? In self-bestowal, it seems, one can grasp the presence of one's self even as one informs one's character. To be sure, Maritain distinguishes between intellect and will. He writes that "as substantial totality,"

> Subjectivity both receives and gives. It receives through the intellect, by superexisting in knowledge. It gives through the will, by superexisting in love; that is, by having within itself other beings as inner attractions directed towards them and giving oneself to them, and by spiritually existing in the manner of a gift.[10]

Yet intellect and will, however we distinguish them, are powers of the integrated human person. It is I who know, I who will.

Again, Maritain's own analysis raises the fresh question. Why can't we have conceptual knowledge of our ontological self-knowledge? Why can't we have a philosophical knowledge of the subjectivity that becomes open to us (yet inexhaustible) in authentic acts of self-donation? We can know, for example, that such a subjectivity is expressive of both intellect and will. Taken together, our fresh questions suggest that Maritain's epistemology might be

[7] Ibid., p. 66.
[8] Ibid., p. 67.
[9] Ibid., p. 83.
[10] Ibid.

more capacious than some suppose. Perhaps it does allow for a distinctive self-knowledge of the subjectivity of self-presence. The context of this knowledge must be rightly framed. Nonetheless, while sharply limited, it is indeed knowledge; it is a conceptual grasp of self-presence in the act of self-donation. Because, for Maritain, all our objectifying (and thus philosophical) knowledge is of subjects as they present themselves, the grasping of one's self-presence reflects his affirmation of "the basic generosity of existence."[11]

Crosby: Another Closer Look

The core of Crosby's position on knowing one's subjectivity looks as uncompromising as Maritain's. We can, he insists, "put subjectivity in front of us an object, yet understand it precisely as subjectivity."[12] But this core, too, has its context. To fill in this context, we can turn to a sampler of striking—and, again, related—claims that Crosby advances.

There is, first, a temporal qualification. He admits that perhaps "elements [of my subjectivity] are unavailable to me...*as long as* I have the experience, but not *before or after* having the experience."[13] This qualification doesn't make all of one's subjectivity inaccessible. But the limits are worth noting. He reminds us how quickly awkward introspection can spoil the fleeting moment. But his qualification does raise its own fresh question. For when one reflects on the subjectivity of the past, even one's immediate past, isn't one reflecting—to be exact—in the manner of memory? But knowing in the manner of memory, while often conceptual, is not the same as knowing through the contemporaneous grasp of self-presence.

Second, Crosby sometimes shifts from speaking of the knowledge of subjectivity, as an experience, to knowledge of "subjectivity in principle."[14] Fair enough, but doing so leads to another question. Isn't there a difference, on the one hand, between philosophical knowledge of the structure of subjectivity (what subjectivity "essentially" is) and, on the other hand, and understanding it from the inside of one's experience?[15] Even a systematic knowledge of structure might prove less elusive than an episodic, but conceptual, insight into the immediacy of self-presence. In any case, Maritain, for his part, insists that subjectivity has an "intelligible structure."[16]

[11] Ibid.
[12] *The Selfhood of the Human Person*, p. 96.
[13] Ibid. p. 97.
[14] Ibid.
[15] Ibid.
[16] *Existence and the Existent*, p. 81.

Taken together, these new questions suggest that Crosby's account of self-knowledge is, after all, perhaps not so very different from Maritain's. For Crosby, we can know the structure of subjectivity as self-presence. Yet a conceptual grasp of the immediate phenomenon of self-presence is limited. It must be so, because the immediacy of subjectivity is partly opaque. It must be so, as well, for another reason. The selfhood of the person, as the full subjectivity of the person, is incommunicable—that is, it is proper to itself alone. (Nor would Maritain say otherwise.) As incommunicable, moreover, one's subjectivity is conceptually inexhaustible. This incommunicability at once restricts the range of one's knowledge of one's self-presence and points to the mystery of the human person.

Compatibilism and a Pair of Analogies

Despite their official dispute about the knowledge of subjectivity, I propose, then, that Maritain and Crosby share a deeper compatibility with respect to self-knowledge. Let's turn now to a pair of analogies that further support a compatibilist reading.

Consider, first, an analogy between love and knowledge. We can begin with the love of the *other*. As it happens, we can borrow a text here from John Crosby. In discussing Maritain's view of conscience, he reminds us of Montaigne's engaging reply to the question of why he loved so-and-so. "If I am entreated to say why I loved him, I feel that this cannot be expressed except by answering 'Because it was he, because it was I.'"[17] For Montaigne, love is not reductive: its object is simultaneously a subject, and uniquely so.

On this point, Montaigne finds no argument from Maritain. As Crosby knows, Maritain equally insists on the uniqueness of the beloved. In *The Person and the Common Good* he writes:

> Love is not concerned with qualities. They are not the object of our love. We love the deepest most substantial and hidden, the most *existing* reality of the beloved being. This is a metaphysical center deeper than all the qualities and essences which we can find and enumerate in the beloved.[18]

Such a love, Maritain tells us, is inexhaustible; the beloved transcends any inventory. Yet our love brings us a distinctive knowledge of the other. It is,

---

[17] *The Selfhood of the Human Person*, p. 77.

[18] Jacques Maritain, *The Person and the Common Good* (Notre Dame, Indiana: University of Notre Dame Press, 1966), p. 39.

moreover, one that we can, in part, conceptualize. To the extent that we can, it is philosophical.

But consider, now, the love of self. It, too, directs one to a "most *existing* reality." In light of this trajectory, one achieves a distinctive knowledge of one's self. Again, it is one which we can, in part, conceptualize. To the extent that we can, it is philosophical. Herein we can make a fresh inference: if self-love is possible, and it is, then analogously self-knowledge is possible. Note, too, a critical interchange. Self-love both draws on, and gives rise to, a species of self-knowledge.

There is, as well, a second analogy to explore. Consider the analogy between moral self-examination, as the discerning of one's conscience, and self-knowledge, as the knowing of one's subjectivity. Crosby readily affirms universal moral norms. They are indicative of, and keyed to, our shared human nature. This nature of ours is communicable in the sense that we share it. Yet each of us has, beyond a share in human nature, an *in*communicable self and a unique self-presence. Moral scrutiny requires an awareness of one's subjectivity in relation to value and duty. But we can, in part, conceptualize this relationship, even with its subjective pole. This discernment is a moral knowing. In achieving it, we deepen a self-understanding that extends to our subjectivity.

Again, as Crosby appreciates, Maritain insists on a comparable point. We see this in his account of discerning one's most far-reaching moral options. In this discernment, Maritain writes, we meet an "inscrutable" and disconcerting subjectivity. "How can it be otherwise, if it is true that the judgment of the subject's conscience is obliged, at the moment when judgment is freely made, to take account also of the whole of the unknown reality within him...?"[19] Even so, we must press on. This discernment is more than possible; it is an imperative. But it could be neither if it required us to apply moral norms to an altogether unknowable subjectivity. While our subjectivity encloses much that is unknown, we can have some cognitive access to that subjectivity. At the same time, we cannot fully articulate the process of discernment. We cannot exhaust the subjectivity of the self who responds to objective moral norms.

Our second analogy, then, suggests the following. If moral discernment is possible, and it is, we can enjoy—as a form of self-knowledge—a real, if limited, access to our own subjectivity. It is a knowledge that admits, too, of some conceptual articulation. As such, it is philosophical. Note, too, another critical interchange. Moral discernment both draws on, and gives rise to, a species of self-knowledge.

---

[19] *Existence and the Existent*, pp. 53-54.

But there's also a further connection. Self-knowledge is necessary for moral discernment. But moral discernment, with regard to one's own actions or another's, is impoverished without love of self and love of the other. Experience, too, underscores the reciprocity between love of self and love of the other. Without love for self, how can I love another? And if I hold others in contempt, won't I come to feel contempt for self? A reciprocal love of self and others, by contrast, constitutes the horizon of moral discernment and the horizon of the knowledge of persons *as subjects* with their own self-presence.

Maritain himself identifies love's role in the knowledge of subjectivity, whether one's own or that of the other. He writes

> To the degree that we truly love…we acquire an obscure knowledge of the being we love, similar to that which we possess of ourselves; we know that being in his very subjectivity (at least in a certain measure) by this experience of union.[20]

In affirming this dynamism, Maritain reiterates a qualification. The knowledge of subjectivity remains "obscure." Granted. But such obscurity as this, the poets show us, can be eloquent. Why cannot it be philosophical as well?

In any case, Maritain points to an ethical corollary that follows from even the knowledge of an obscure subjectivity. Only insofar as I grasp my subjectivity, he argues, can I judge my actions. For what my actions are depends, in part, on the subjectivity which I express through them. Equally, only insofar as I grasp the subjectivity of another can I judge another's actions. For what the actions of another are depend, in part, on the subjectivity which another expresses through them.

This ethical corollary suggests a theological corollary. Because we know both our own subjectivity and our neighbor's only in part, God alone is a just judge. "The more I know of my subjectivity," Maritain observes, "the more it remains obscure to me. If I were not known to God, no one would know me."[21] Yet nothing in this confession gainsays that I can have some knowledge of my subjectivity. I am enjoined, for example, to discern the beam in my own eye. After this discernment St. Augustine, no stranger to evil times, notes that there may be cause to look to my neighbor. Although Augustine agrees that subjective intention can be elusive, he recalls the Apostle's words in First Timothy 5:24, "The sins of some people are conspicuous and precede them to judgment…." In such cases, Augustine comments, "if judgment fol-

---

[20] Ibid., p. 84.
[21] Ibid., p. 77.

lows them at once, it will not be rash," though our reproof should never make a change of heart more difficult."[22]

Skeptical Challenges

But perhaps my compatibilist analysis comes too easily. A skeptic might ask why one would even try to reconcile Maritain and Crosby. Hasn't Hume, among others, collapsed the ground on which they invite us to stand? And why reckon the prospects of knowing one's subjectivity if there is no self and, hence, no self-presence it manifests? The psychologist, too, if he is William James, seconds such complaints. Why try to parse our grasp of such a self-presence, if only a naïve commonsense misleads us into believing that a unitary self exists?

Recall Hume on knowing the self. "All ideas are borrow'd from preceding perceptions," he writes, so "[w]hen I turn my reflexion on *myself,* I never can perceive this *self* without one or more perceptions; nor can I ever perceive any thing but the perceptions. 'Tis the composition of these, therefore, which forms the self."[23] But if there is no unitary self, no substantial self, an inquiry into its self-presence is futile. There's only this perception (or that) to identify, this (or that) bundle of perceptions to inventory.

James, too, dismisses the "hypothesis" of a unified self. Surveying his own consciousness, he finds that his *"Self of selves"* consists *"mainly of...peculiar motions in the head or between the head and throat,"* these "cephalic motions" being "the portions of...innermost activity" of which, he says, he is *"most distinctly aware."*[24]

David Hume and William James, of course, have their differences. But both would agree that Maritain and Crosby are trafficking in chimeras. Such philosophical self-knowledge is impossible, because neither a self nor a distinct presence of self to self exists. To their credit, however, both Hume and James admit that someone else *might* have an experience that affords a different testimony about the reality of the self and a distinctive self-presence. Such a testimony, we might suppose, could renew—and even accelerate—an inquiry into the knowledge of subjectivity.

But where are we to find this fresh testimony? Could you or I, for example, provide it? We might, I guess, take a quick break to "check out" our

---

[22] Augustine, *Commentary on the Lord's Sermon on the Mount,* in *The Works of St. Augustine* (New York: Fathers of the Church, Inc., 1951) Book II, Ch. 19, No. 60, p. 170.

[23] David Hume, *A Treatise of Human Nature* (Oxford: Oxford University Press, 1978), p. 634.

[24] William James, *Principles of Psychology* (Cambridge: Harvard University Press, 1981), Vol. 1, chap. 10, p. 288. Emphasis in the original.

experiences. But having tried such an experiment in the classroom, with scant success, I'll not attempt it here.

Yet neither will I settle for the reports of Hume and James. So I introduce, as counterbalance, quite another testimony. It comes from a keen observer of particularity. Gerard Manley Hopkins, poet of inscape, offers us the following reflection. Because his remarks are less familiar than Hume's or James', I cite them more fully. When Hopkins searches, he finds

> my self being, my consciousness and feeling of myself, that taste of myself, of *I* and *me* above and in all things, which is more distinctive than the taste of ale or alum, more distinctive than the smell of walnutlead or camphor, and is incommunicable by any means to another man (as when I was a child I used to ask myself: What must it be to be someone else?). Nothing else in nature comes near this unspeakable stress of pitch, distinctiveness, and selving, this selfbeing of my own. Nothing explains it or resembles it, except so far as this, that other men to themselves have the same feeling. But this only multiplies the phenomena to be explained so far as the cases are like and do resemble. But to me there is no resemblance...I taste *self* but at one tankard, that of my own being.[25]

Hopkins's "taste" of self is not of anything else; it is not, for example, the taste of any combination of tastes. Rather, it is the taste of his "selving." This "selving" I understand to be, or at least include, his self's presence to self. Neither does Hopkins experience anything marginal or ambiguous. What he experiences, he reports, is more distinctive than the taste of Guinness.

Suppose, we accept Hopkins's testimony on the taste of self and its selving. Suppose we credit his claim that there's nothing extraordinary in his having such an experience, only that the taste he encounters is extraordinary. What we experience, then, will be extraordinary, too—but in its own extraordinary way. If we grant such suppositions, we can return, with new insight, to the original dispute between Maritain and Crosby. A pair of questions at once arises. First, does Hopkins's contribution better the prospects for either disputant? Second, given his contribution, how stand the prospects for bridging their positions?

The first answer, I think, is that Hopkins betters the prospects for both disputants. The second answer is that in doing so he betters the chances for bridging their positions. On Maritain's side, we can only in part describe an experience so immediate as a taste. Hopkins's taste of "selving," moreover, scarcely exhausts the experience of self-presence, much less does it exhaust his very self. On Crosby's side, Hopkins does describe, if only in part, his

---

[25] Gerard Manley Hopkins, *Gerard Manley Hopkins* (Oxford: Oxford University Press, 1986), p. 282.

experience of his own unique selving. He does so eloquently...and conceptually. We might add that he does so "in retrospect," rather than by breaking into the immediacy of self-identification.

Yet if Hopkins's testimony supports both Maritain and Crosby, it does so in a way that equally supports their deeper compatibility. Let me be more specific, and on two counts.

First, I noted an analogy between self-love and self-knowledge. Self-love calls for a personal agency that, in effect, both Hume and James disavow. But Hopkins, for his part, celebrates the self—more so than Whitman!—chiefly as a lover, a person who loves. Authentic self-love equally calls for the recognition of the selfhood of the beloved. Such recognition is impossible for Hume and James, if we take them on their word. In contrast, Maritain and Crosby insist, and this point is central for them, on the reality of personal agency. It is uniquely the source and worthy object of love.

Second, I noted a corollary that Maritain draws from the reciprocity of love of self and knowledge of self. It is an ethical corollary. We judge ourselves rightly only insofar as we know ourselves, and we can know ourselves only if we love ourselves. If the judging of ourselves is thus limited, *a fortiori* so is the judging of others. Now comes Hopkins's testimony. It recognizes a distinctive human dignity in the experience of his "selving." This experience of self-presence is decisive. If we honor it, we ground a self-knowledge that encourages a love of self. With this love, we become able to judge ourselves. But the experience of "selving" is a human experience. Hence, if we honor the parallel experience of others, we recognize their dignity; in this moral knowledge we can come to love them as they are. And with this love, we become able to judge them, as brothers and sisters. Hopkins's support for Maritain's corollary, to be sure, hardly counts against Crosby, since he would accept the same corollary. He holds that the "interpersonal" is integral to personal existence, especially in the awareness of self that we experience before the tribunal of conscience. He suggests, too, that the experience of the authority of conscience as absolute points us to the infinitely personal.[26]

Envoi

The bridge between Maritain and Crosby, to my mind, is a sturdy one. But we cannot end our reflections without returning to the skeptics, whether notorious or otherwise. Nor can we forget the puzzlement of commonsense with which we began.

---

[26] *The Selfhood of the Human Person,* p. 213.

The skeptics cannot, I submit, match the insight of Hopkins. His inscape reproaches their reductionism. Still, from skeptics the most we can hope for is silence.

I would say more to the friends of commonsense, among whom I count myself. We should, indeed, talk our own nonsense. No one else can, and it's not without some measure of truth. But what, then, of the Scot's wish that "some Pow'r the giftie gie us to see oursels as others see us?" It depends on how well they see us. If they do not love us, they do not see *us* very well—however expert they are in gauging our gaucherie.

Yet there is one who loves us, and loves us best. If we could see ourselves as God sees us, we would see the whole of ourselves and be wholly present to ourselves. In the beatific vision, St. Thomas teaches, we see ourselves as God sees us.[27] Then we will love in a way that we cannot now. Then we could judge, and forgive, in a way that we cannot now. In the vision of God, Maritain reflects, one "knows not only himself and all his life...but also the other creatures whom in God he knows at last as subjects in the unveiled depth of their being."[28] To be sure, such knowledge would be intuitive rather than conceptual.

Still, even now, we are to both forgive and repent. We can do neither without judging. Nor can we repent unless we judge our very selves. To do so, we must act on the self-knowledge we have—even when obscured and conceptual. Confessing our limits, we can yet know, right now, that we both need and have God's forgiveness[29]

---

[27] St. Thomas Aquinas, *Summa Contra Gentiles* , III, chap. 59, n. 6.
[28] *Existence and the Existent*, p. 80.
[29] With collegial grace, Carroll C. Kearley commented on an earlier draft of this essay.

Thomist or Relativist?
MacIntyre's Interpretation of adaequatio intellectus et rei

W. Matthews Grant

A central concern of Alasdair MacIntyre's on-going philosophical project has been to show the compatibility between the following two claims. The first claim has to do with the nature of reason, both theoretical and practical. The claim is that, although observance of the law of non-contradiction and other such formal principles is a necessary condition of rationality, sufficient resources for rational adjudication between competing ethical positions are to be found only by reference to the substantive commitments and presuppositions of some particular tradition. MacIntyre, therefore, urges us to abandon what he characterizes as the Enlightenment belief in universal, ahistorical, tradition-transcendent canons of reason, canons available to and undeniable by any rational person, regardless of place and time. To the contrary, MacIntyre maintains that there is no such thing as rationality as such. Since the canons of rational justification are always immanent to a particular tradition, there are as many rationalities as there are traditions.[1]

MacIntyre's second thesis, which he hopes to show compatible with the first, is the claim that, despite the tradition-constituted nature of rationality, it is possible for one tradition to show itself rationally superior to another.[2] In short, MacIntyre wants to argue that his first claim does not entail the relativism it might seem to imply. And it is not difficult to understand why it might so seem. For if each tradition carries with it its own standards of rationality, it is hard to imagine how one tradition could show itself rationally superior to another. Won't the contradictory claims of two traditions, A and B, always be vindicated each by the peculiar standards of its own tradition?

---

[1] Alasdair MacIntyre, *Whose Justice? Which Rationality?* (Notre Dame, Indiana: University of Notre Dame Press, 1988), chap. 1.
[2] Ibid., pp. 365-66.

Yet won't these same claims appear to lack justification when seen from the standpoint of its rival?

MacIntyre's response to these questions involves developing accounts of intra and inter-traditional rational justification given his views on the tradition-constituted nature of rationality outlined above. According to MacIntyre, a tradition is comprised not only of a set of substantive commitments by reference to which particular moral claims are justified, but also by a set of problems and disputed questions, which form the basis of an ongoing program of research and enquiry within that tradition. Such problems can emerge for a variety of reasons. Perhaps the teachings of the acknowledged authorities of a tradition contain or imply seeming inconsistencies. Or maybe certain experiences of the community raise new questions that challenge traditional assumptions. Whatever the case may be, it is important to note that it is by virtue of its own standards that a tradition recognizes its problems. According to MacIntyre, rational progress occurs within such a tradition when, whether through conceptual innovation or the reinterpretation of authoritative teaching, solutions to such problems can be found without abandoning the fundamental claims and authorities which make the tradition what it is. The theoretical products of such innovation and reinterpretation are justified, and constitute a measure of rational progress, precisely because of their ability to resolve disputed questions while retaining the tradition's basic commitments.[3]

But it may happen that solutions to such problems are not forthcoming, that intra-traditional rational progress does not occur. It is only at this point, according to MacIntyre, that inter-traditional rational progress becomes a possibility. A tradition has reached what MacIntyre calls an "epistemological crisis" when it is able to recognize by its own standards that it has problems, but is repeatedly unable to solve those problems. According to MacIntyre, it is possible for a tradition that has reached this crisis stage to find in some other tradition the resources needed both to diagnose its problems and to solve them. For this discovery to occur, the proponents of the crisis tradition will have to learn the other tradition from the inside out—so that they are able not only to understand that tradition as it understands itself, but also, so that they can see their own tradition from the perspective of the other. Under these circumstances, the proponents of the crisis tradition will discover the rational superiority of its rival if the following conditions are met. First, the rival tradition must afford them resources for seeing why their own tradition is limited in such a way as to generate the problems which it could not resolve given its own beliefs, categories and methods. Second, the rival tradition must be able to over-

[3]Ibid., chap. 18.

come those problems either by virtue of its superior conceptual resources, or by dispensing with the flawed assumptions which generated the problems in the first place. Finally, the rival tradition must not be plagued by an epistemological crisis of its own. When such conditions have been met, the proponents of the crisis tradition are justified in abandoning that tradition in favor of its rival. Notice that the rational conversion from one tradition to the other does not require a set of neutral standards, independent of both traditions; for it is by the standards of the former tradition that its problems were recognized, and it is by the standards of the latter that those problems were explained and overcome.[4]

My purpose in this paper is not to evaluate MacIntyre's success in overcoming relativism given his commitment to the tradition-constituted nature of rationality. I will simply assume for the sake of argument that MacIntyre succeeds,[5] and focus, instead, on his understanding of truth. In particular, I want to ask whether MacIntyre holds a Thomistic conception of truth and, if so, how he might defend that conception. The first question is of interest, not only because MacIntyre increasingly identifies himself as a Thomist-Aristotelian, but also because he does so while defending an ostensibly un-Thomistic,[6] historicist account of rationality. The latter question is of interest, because, insofar as MacIntyre does want to defend a conception of truth as an adequacy or conformity or correspondence between mind and thing, he will immediately be confronted by two sorts of objections, one from the anti-realist, and one from the realist. The anti-realist will regard as unwarranted any attempt to claim truth as a relationship between the mind and a reality independent of the mind. The realist, on the other hand, will embrace the Thomistic conception of truth, but will deny that that conception is compatible with MacIntyre's understanding of rationality as constituted by traditions. In what follows, I consider how MacIntyre responds to the first objection and suggest how he might respond to the second. I argue that the Thomistic conception of truth can be defended against the standard anti-realist objection, and that it can be defended even if MacIntyre is right about the tradition-constituted nature of rationality.

[4]Ibid.

[5]I find MacIntyre's efforts in this regard to be promising, although some have argued otherwise. See Alicia Juarrero Roque, "Language Competence and Tradition-constituted Rationality," *Philosophy and Phenomenological Research* 51:3 (September 1991), pp. 611-17. For criticisms of MacIntyre from a Thomistic perspective see Robert George, "Moral Particularism, Thomism, and Traditions," *The Review of Metaphysics* 42 (March 1989), pp. 593-605; and John Haldane, "MacIntyre's Thomist Revival: What Next?," in *After MacIntyre,* eds. John Horton and Susan Mendus (Notre Dame, Indiana: University of Notre Dame Press, 1994), pp. 91-107.

[6] See especially "Moral Particularism, Thomism, and Traditions," pp. 599-600. See also Janet Coleman, "MacIntyre and Aquinas," in *After MacIntyre,* pp. 65-90.

How Thomistic is MacIntyre's Conception of Truth?

At the very end of *Whose Justice? Which Rationality?*, after four hundred pages devoted to an examination of the rationality of traditions, and after having declared the person allied to no tradition to be in a state of moral and intellectual destitution, MacIntyre finally proclaims his own allegiance to the tradition of Aquinas.[7] Already, in chapter ten of the same book, MacIntyre speaks favorably of Aquinas's conception of truth.[8] And though he doesn't offer an explicit exegesis of the texts in which Aquinas defines truth as *"adaequatio intellectus et rei,"* he does use some form of the English cognate "adequate" over twenty-five times in chapter eighteen, when discussing the notion of truth which accompanies his account of rationality. Hence, even before he reveals his allegiance at the end of the book, the reader can't help but feel that MacIntyre sees himself as giving what is in substance a Thomistic account of truth, freed of scholastic jargon, and ready for consideration by contemporary philosophers.

I suspect most Thomists would heartily welcome the following sorts of passages:

> What is it precisely that corresponds or fails to correspond to what? Assertions in speech or writing, certainly, but these as secondary expressions of intelligent thought which is or is not adequate in its dealings with its objects, the realities of the social and rational world.[9]

> The concept of truth is timeless. To claim that some thesis is true is not only to claim that for all possible times and places that it cannot be shown to fail to correspond to reality ... but also that the mind which expresses its thought in that thesis is in fact adequate to its object.[10]

> One of the great originating insights of tradition constituted enquiries is that false beliefs and false judgments represent a failure of the mind, and not of its objects. It is the mind which stands in need of correction.[11]

Nor does MacIntyre fail to note and to reject the pragmatist alternative to the Thomistic conception of truth. He explicitly criticizes Hilary Putnam's reduction of truth to an idealization of the concept of warranted assertibility.[12]

[7] *Whose Justice? Which Rationality?*, pp. 401-03.
[8] Ibid., pp. 168, 171.
[9] Ibid., p. 356.
[10] Ibid., p. 363.
[11] Ibid., p. 357.
[12] Ibid., p. 169.

All of the above suggests that in *Whose Justice? Which Rationality?* MacIntyre unequivocally holds to a Thomistic account of truth. Nevertheless, there are other passages that might seem to resist this conclusion. MacIntyre denies, for instance, that there are "two distinguishable items, a judgment on the one hand, and that portrayed in the judgment on the other, between which a relationship of correspondence can hold or fail to hold,"[13] and he maintains that it is a large error to read a correspondence theory of truth into such older formulations as *"adaequatio mentis ad rem."*[14] Indeed, in some passages, what seem to correspond are not the mind and reality, but two sets of beliefs. Thus MacIntyre tells us that the correspondence theory of truth originates as a correspondence theory of falsity. We perceive that our former beliefs about the world fail to correspond to "reality as now perceived, classified and understood," and it is by virtue of this failure to correspond to our current beliefs that we judge those former beliefs to be false.[15] Finally, in discussing the truth of our images and concepts, MacIntyre declares that "their adequacy or inadequacy is always relative to some purpose of the mind,"[16] and he states "the mind is adequate to its objects insofar as the expectations which it frames on the basis of its activities are not liable to disappointment."[17] Such passages have led John Haldane to worry that MacIntyre characterizes truth in "ways that suggest a pragmatist version of anti-realism." Haldane, in fact, likens MacIntyre's account to those very proposals of Putnam, which MacIntyre explicitly rejects.[18] What are we to make of all this?

The best interpretation of these passages, which takes into consideration their context, reads them as not so inimical to a Thomistic conception of truth as they might at first appear. Closer examination, for example, reveals that MacIntyre wants to distance *adaequatio mentis ad rem*, not from anything which might be called a correspondence theory, but from a peculiarly modern version of it, which invents pseudo-realities called "facts" to correspond to "propositions," which function as "truth-bearers." According to MacIntyre, "this kind of correspondence theory of truth arrived on the philosophical

---

[13]Ibid., p. 357.
[14]Ibid., p. 358.
[15]Ibid., p. 356.
[16]Ibid., p. 357.
[17]Ibid., p. 356.
[18]"MacIntyre's Thomist Revival: What Next?," p. 105. It is interesting that the English "adequate," unlike the Latin *"adaequatio,"* lends itself to a pragmatist construal. Hence, we perhaps most often use "adequate" in situations where we want to say that someone or something is "adequate to the task."

scene only comparatively recently and has been as conclusively refuted as any theory can be."[19] Nor does MacIntyre's account of the *genesis* of the traditional correspondence theory of truth as a correspondence theory of falsity entail that he believes truth to be a correspondence between two sets of beliefs. For, the passage in which MacIntyre engages in this bit of conceptual genealogy is followed immediately by the first of the passages quoted three paragraphs above, where MacIntyre identifies the correspondence to hold between "intelligent thought" and the "realities of the social and intellectual world." We must distinguish between MacIntyre's account of the *origin* of the concept of truth, and his understanding of the *nature* of truth. More threatening than these passages, perhaps, are the pragmatist sounding passages that trouble Haldane. Yet can we not understand MacIntyre's claim that "the mind is adequate to its objects insofar as the expectations which it frames on the basis of its activities are not liable to disappointment" to be stating a criterion, rather than a definition, of truth? And when MacIntyre states that "adequacy or inadequacy is always relative to some purpose of the mind," should not this be read in light of MacIntyre's corrective to a Cartesian conception of mind as a static container of ideas?[20]

Those who have followed MacIntyre's career from *After Virtue* forward have witnessed his steady development in the direction of Aquinas, and I think that any ambiguity in the *Whose Justice? Which Rationality?* account, if there be any, can be explained, at least in part, as evidence of that development in progress.[21] In a more recent essay, entitled "Moral Relativism, Truth, and Justification," MacIntyre offers an unequivocally Thomistic account. "Truth," MacIntyre tells us, is "the adequacy of the intellect to its *res*." When a "person's intellect is adequate to some particular subject-matter with which

[19] *Whose Justice? Which Rationality?*, p. 358. For a critique of this kind of correspondence theory, MacIntyre refers us to P. F. Strawson's "Truth" in P. F. Strawson, *Logico-Linguistic Papers* (London: Methuen & Co., 1971), pp. 190-213.

[20] Ibid., p. 356. MacIntyre writes: "It is important to remember that the presupposed conception of mind is not Cartesian. It is rather of mind as activity, of mind as engaging with the natural and social world in such activities as identification, reidentification, collecting, separating, classifying, and naming and all this by touching, grasping, pointing, breaking down, building up, calling to, answering to, and so on."

[21] In *After Virtue* (Notre Dame, Indiana: University of Notre Dame Press, 1981), MacIntyre rejected Aristotle's metaphysical biology, and relegated Aquinas to a marginal figure in the history of ethics (pp. 162, 178). By the time of *Whose Justice? Which Rationality?* (1988), Aquinas had become the hero, and even more so in *Three Rival Versions of Moral Enquiry* (Notre Dame, Indiana: University of Notre Dame Press, 1990). In his most recent book, *Dependent Rational Animals: Why Human Beings Need the Virtues* (Chicago: Open Court, 1999), MacIntyre, now, denies that it is possible to do ethics without biology, and manifests an increasing appreciation for those things which make Aquinas different from Aristotle (pp. x-xi).

it is engaged in its thinking, it is what the objects of that thinking in fact are which makes it the case that that person's thoughts about those objects are what they are ... the mind has become formally what the object is."[22] This passage certainly clears up any ambiguity there might be between Thomist and pragmatist characterizations of truth in the pages of *Whose Justice? Which Rationality?*. What the later essay provides, however, is not simply an unequivocal commitment to a Thomistic account of truth, but a more developed set of arguments for rejecting the pragmatist alternative. In the following section, we will consider what role these arguments play in MacIntyre's response to the anti-realist objection.

The Anti-Realist Objection

MacIntyre's sensitivity to the anti-realist objection manifests itself already in *Whose Justice? Which Rationality?*. No sooner has he introduced Aquinas's understanding of truth than he considers why some philosophers have rejected it:

> How can it be, such writers have asked, that our whole web of beliefs and concepts could be judged true or false, adequate or inadequate, in virtue of its and their relationship to some reality quite external to that web? For in order for us to compare our beliefs and concepts to that reality we should have to already have beliefs about it and have understood certain of our concepts as having application to it. So, they conclude, an understanding of any reality, in relation to which truth and falsity, adequacy and inadequacy are judged, must be internal to our web of concepts and beliefs; there can be no reference beyond that web to anything genuinely external to it.[23]

Two contemporary advocates of this objection are Michael Dummett and Hilary Putnam. Dummett, for example, argues that there is a "major conceptual leap" involved when the criterion of truth requires that, over and above a claim's being justified, it relate to "some state of affairs obtaining independently of our knowledge." Dummett suspects that "any formulation of such a condition begs the question whether it is coherent to attribute to anyone a grasp of such a condition."[24] Similarly, Hilary Putnam rejects the correspon-

---

[22]*Moral Truth and Moral Tradition: Essays in Honour of Peter Geach and Elizabeth Anscombe*, ed. Luke Gormally (Dublin: Four Courts Press, 1994), p. 18.

[23]*Whose Justice? Which Rationality?*, pp. 168-69.

[24]Michael Dummett, "The source of the concept of truth," in *Meaning and method: Essays in Honor of Hilary Putnam*, ed. George Boolos (Cambridge: Cambridge University Press, 1990), pp. 12, 14.

dence theory of truth since "to single out a correspondence between two domains one needs some independent access to both domains."[25]

Both Putnam and Dummett would agree with Putnam's demand that "what is supposed to be 'true' be warrantable ... for creatures with a rational and sensible nature."[26] It is precisely because they don't think we can warrant claims that our beliefs correspond to a mind-independent reality that they propose a revision in our understanding of truth. Accordingly, both argue that truth be defined in terms of justification, Dummett sometimes simply identifying truth with justification,[27] and Putnam preferring to define truth as an idealization of the concept of justification.[28] Such proposals entail severe consequences for logic and metaphysics, consequences that neither philosopher hesitates to recognize. Dummett, for example, rejects the law of the excluded middle, since it assumes that the truth-value of an assertion depends on the way things are, and not on whether we have the ability to provide a justification for that assertion.[29] And Putnam, appealing to the theory-dependent character of justification, embraces the possibility that incompatible ontologies could both be true, relative to the different theories on which they are justified.[30]

MacIntyre's strategy for dealing with the anti-realist objection is not to address the argument directly, but to challenge the conception of truth that proponents of the argument propose as an alternative to the correspondence theory. Such may appear a weak strategy on MacIntyre's part, for it may appear that instead of answering the charges against the Thomistic theory, he simply avoids those charges by waging a counter-attack against his opponent's proposal. But I think MacIntyre's approach deserves more credit than that. For, if as MacIntyre seems to believe, the only or most obvious alternative to the Thomistic conception of truth is one which assimilates truth to justification,[31] and if this alternative can be

[25]Hilary Putnam, *Reason, Truth and History* (Cambridge: Cambridge University Press, 1981), p. 74.

[26] Putnam, *Realism with a Human Face* (Cambridge: Harvard University Press, 1990), p. 41. See Dummett, *Truth and Other Enigmas* (Cambridge: Harvard University Press, 1978), pp. 16-17.

[27]"The only legitimate notion of truth is one that is to be explained in terms of what justifies an assertion: a sentence is true if an assertion made by means of it would be justified." Michael Dummett, "What does the Appeal to Use Do for the Theory of Meaning?," in *Meaning and Use*, ed. Avishai Margalit (Dordrecht: D. Reidel, 1979), p. 129.

[28]*Realism with a Human Face*, pp. 114-15. See also Putnam's *Realism and Reason: Philosophical Papers*, vol. 3 (Cambridge: Cambridge University Press, 1983), pp. 49-50, 84.

[29]*Truth and Other Enigmas*, pp. 16-17. See also Dummett's *The Logical Basis of Metaphysics* (Cambridge: Harvard University Press, 1991), p. 9.

[30]*Realism with a Human Face*, p. 40.

[31]For example, MacIntyre states that "it is characteristic of those who adopt this view [the critique of the correspondence theory] that almost always in practice and often enough in

shown to be fatally flawed, then this gives us some reason, at least, to stick with the Thomistic conception and to believe that there must be some problem with any argument purporting to refute it. Furthermore, exposing the difficulties with the alternative conception of truth may provide the clues needed for identifying the problem with the anti-realist argument, which drives some to that alternative conception.

What, then, are MacIntyre's objections to defining truth in terms of justification? I want to focus on three. First, simply to identify truth with justification, as Michael Dummett has sometimes done, is to flout the commonplace that a person can be justified in making a claim which turns out to be false.[32] Even Putnam has argued that "truth cannot simply *be* justification," for "truth is supposed to be a property of a statement that cannot be lost, whereas justification can be lost; justification is a matter of degree, whereas truth is not." Hence, Putnam rejects Dummett's identification of truth with justification in favor of an understanding of truth as an "idealization of justification."[33] It is unclear, however, what difference Putnam's amendment makes, for as MacIntyre observes, "the notion of idealization invoked has never been given adequate content."[34] Indeed, the theory's most notable advocate doesn't seem to think that such content could be given. Thus, Putnam denies that "we can even sketch a theory of actual warrant, let alone a theory of idealized warrant."[35] And though he maintains that a statement is true if it would be justified under epistemically ideal conditions, he confesses that "we cannot really attain epistemically ideal conditions, or even be absolutely certain that we have come sufficiently close to them."[36] These concessions appear disastrous not only for Putnam's conception of truth, but

avowed theory they treat the concept of truth as nothing more than an idealization of the concept of warranted assertibility. For on this view [the anti-correspondence view] we can have no criterion of truth beyond the best warrants that we can offer for our assertions." *Whose Justice? Which Rationality?*, p. 169.

[32]"Moral Relativism, Truth and Justification," p. 10.

[33]*Realism and Reason*, p. 84. In a more recent essay, Dummett backs off from a straightforward identification of truth and justification, but he does not explain precisely how the one is supposed to be defined in terms of the other: "The concept which corresponds to the full-fledged realist notion of truth, but which, on this view, is the most we are entitled to, is indeed more refined than the straightforward concept of justifiability; but it will still be one that can be explained, even if in a complex and subtle way, in terms of justifiability." See "The source of the concept of truth," p. 15.

[34]"Moral Relativism, Truth and Justification," p. 10.

[35]*Realism with a Human Face*, p. 42. See also p. 114, "I do not [believe] that one can specify in an effective way what the justification conditions for the sentences of a natural language are."

[36]*Reason, Truth and History*, p. 55.

also for the anti-realist's case against the correspondence theory. With re-spect to the former, if the concept of truth is defined as justification under ideal conditions, but if no "sketch" of those conditions has or can be given, then the concept of truth is rendered vacuous. With respect to the latter, if the anti-realist's objection to the correspondence theory is that its criterion of truth is one that could never be recognized, and hence that we could never know when to make truth claims or be justified in making them, this objec-tion turns out to apply equally to a theory of truth as idealized justification. For given that there is no account of what the ideal conditions are (not to mention Putnam's claim that we can never attain them), we could no more recognize when the criterion of truth has been met on this theory than on the correspondence theory.

Let us turn, then, to a second objection. If one of the goals of a philosophic account of truth is to explain what we mean and how we use that concept in ordinary moral and scientific enquiry, the account of truth that reduces truth to some form of justification fails miserably. We saw above that contemporary anti-realists are often forced to deny the law of excluded middle, or to affirm that incompatible ontologies could both be true, which is, in effect, to deny also the principle of non-contradiction. But certainly MacIntyre is right when he observes that, almost universally, those making fundamental moral claims are com-mitted to the falsehood of claims incompatible with their own.[37] Moralists never see themselves in emotivist or relativist terms, even if moral phi-losophers do. And, certainly, a presupposition that incompatible ontologies cannot both be true is what motivates the quest for a unified theory in the sciences. Hence, a reduction of the concept of truth to justification, insofar as it denies the law of excluded middle and the principle of non-contradiction, appears at odds with how we ordinarily understand and use that concept. What's more, as MacIntyre argues drawing off the work of Peter Geach, any interpretation of sentences of a natural language involving the most basic logical connectives requires a notion of meaning to be explained in terms of truth conditions, not merely justification conditions.[38] This point can be seen most clearly with respect to conditionals. Take the following example, "If God does not exist, all is permitted." The truth or justification (if you like) of this conditional assertion depends not on whether or not the antecedent can

[37]"Moral Relativism, Truth and Justification," p. 8.
[38]Ibid., p. 15. The works of Geach to which MacIntyre appeals are "Assertion," *Philosophical Review* 74 (1965), pp. 449-65 and "Verdad o Assercion Justificada?" *Annuario filosofico* 15: 2 (1982).

or cannot be *justified*, but on whether or not assuming the *truth* of the antecedent, the consequent follows. The truth or falsehood of Dostoevsky's claim depends not in the least on whether we have good arguments for the existence of God.[39] Such considerations have led Michael Dummett to concede that "although there is a way of understanding conditionals that can be explained in terms of justifiability, rather than of truth, it does not yield even a plausible approximation to the actual use of conditionals in natural language."[40]

A third objection to the alternative conception of truth is that "it has the unfortunate effect of distorting our understanding not only of truth, but also of rational justification."[41] According to MacIntyre, the anti-realist has the cart before the horse. He tries to define truth in terms of the supposedly prior and more basic notion of justification, when it should, in fact, be the other way around: "Practices of rational justification are devised and are only fully intelligible as parts of all those human activities which aim at truth."[42] MacIntyre compares the anti-realist's attempt to reduce truth to justification with other attempts at reductionism: they all fail for the same reason. Thus the concept of a physical object cannot be reduced to or constructed out of that of sense-data, for sense-data have to be already understood in terms of physical objects. The concept of pain cannot be reduced to or constructed out of bodily expressions of pain, for bodily expressions of pain already have to be understood in terms of pain. So also the concept of truth cannot be reduced to or constructed out of the concept of justifiability, for justifiability has to be already understood in terms of truth.[43] Physical objects, pain, and truth are the logically prior concepts. The anti-realist believes that there is an unwarranted "conceptual leap" involved in the move from the concept of justification to that of truth only because he begins with the concept of justification, failing to notice that justification cannot be understood independently of truth, but only as that activity which has knowledge, understanding, and truth as its telos.[44]

---

[39] Notice that this argument against reducing the concept of truth to justification holds even if we are concerned only with the justification (and not the truth or falsehood) of the conditional assertion. For we are justified in asserting "If God does not exist, all is permitted" if, assuming the truth of the antecedent, we have good reasons for believing the consequent. Whether or not we are also justified in believing the antecedent is entirely irrelevant to justifying the conditional as a whole.

[40]"The source of the concept of truth," p. 9.

[41]"Moral Relativism, Truth and Justification," p. 11.

[42]Ibid.

[43]Ibid., p. 17.

[44]Ibid.

In this third objection, we are given what amounts to more than a reason for rejecting the reduction of truth to justification. We are also offered resources for a direct response to the argument against the correspondence theory. For if MacIntyre is right, that an adequate account of justification must presuppose the concepts of knowledge and truth as its telos, then epistemology, understood as the normative science of justification, presupposes the metaphysics of knowledge, understood as that science which tells us what knowledge and truth are. The metaphysics of knowledge is the higher science, providing epistemology with its principles and assumptions. From this standpoint, we can discern both why the anti-realist's challenge to the correspondence theory appears so insuperable, and yet why rejecting that theory leads to serious difficulties of the sort we have been discussing. For the anti-realist is asking the impossible, namely, that a lower science demonstrate the conclusions of a higher science, conclusions which, properly understood, provide that lower science with its basic assumptions. Hence, the anti-realist demands an epistemological justification not just for the truth of this or that conclusion, but for there being any such thing as truth. The problem with this demand is that the whole activity of justifying, giving arguments, and drawing conclusions already tacitly assumes that we can attain knowledge and truth, a point which explains, also, why most skeptical arguments are vulnerable to the charge that they are self-refuting. For even that argument that would justify a denial of truth aims to give us a conclusion about how things are. I conclude, therefore, that a proper understanding of the relationship between truth and justification may be the key to overcoming certain anti-realist arguments.

The Realist Objection

Let us turn, then, to the realist's objection. As will be recalled, the realist has no quarrel with MacIntyre's Thomistic account of truth, but denies, instead, that that account is compatible with an understanding of rationality as tradition-constituted. Consider a passage from John Haldane:

> Given the conceptual connections between rationality and truth, and the claim that the former is immanent within, and constituted by, traditions of enquiry, it is difficult to see how truth itself can be tradition-transcendent, which is what metaphysical realism requires.[45]

---

[45]"MacIntyre's Thomist Revival: What Next?," p. 105.

Haldane's suggestion appears to be that truth cannot transcend traditions unless rationality does also. But this seems wrong. Truth is transcendent not by virtue of any property of rationality or justification, but because it is a relationship between the mind and a reality independent of the mind. It is not the tradition-transcendence of rationality that makes truth transcendent, but the transcendence of the objects of knowledge. Indeed, someone might easily, *pace* Kant, affirm the universality and tradition-transcendence of reason, but deny that the objects of knowledge are transcendent, and thereby deny metaphysical realism.

Surprisingly enough, however, MacIntyre seems to agree with Haldane on an intimate connection between truth and tradition-transcendent rationality. According to MacIntyre,

> Those who claim truth for the central theses of their own moral standpoint are thereby also committed to a set of theses about rational justification. For they are bound to hold that the arguments in support of rival and incompatible sets of theses are unsound, not merely that they fail relative to this or that set of standards, but that either their premises are false or their inferences invalid. But insofar as the claim to truth also involves this further claim, it commits those who uphold it to a non-relativist conception of rational justification, to a belief that there must somehow or other be adequate standards of rational justification, which are not the standards internal to this or that standpoint, but are the standards of rational justification as such.[46]

To be sure, the relationship between rationality and truth here is not precisely the one suggested by Haldane. MacIntyre does not claim that the tradition-transcendence of truth depends on rationality's being tradition-transcendent. Nevertheless, he does maintain that those who make truth claims are committed to the view that there are standards of rational justification that are not just the standards internal to this or that standpoint. One might have expected MacIntyre to argue just the opposite—to argue for the coherence of making truth claims even if there are no standards of rationality as such. Instead, though he endorses a Thomistic account of truth, MacIntyre would seem to require of anyone claiming to reach such truth an understanding of rationality that he himself rejects. Has MacIntyre contradicted himself?

The apparent contradiction results only from a misleading use of language. By "the standards of rationality as such," MacIntyre does not mean to require that those making truth claims believe what he has always argued against—that there are sufficient standards of rational justification available to all persons, regardless of tradition. Rather, he wants to point out that inso-

---

[46] "Moral Relativism, Truth and Justification," p. 8.

far as the truth of an assertion entails the falsehood of incompatible claims, it also entails the falsehood of at least some of the premises or principles on which those claims are justified. To claim that a belief is false, therefore, is to claim, in addition, that the standards which rationally justify that belief are false. By contrast, to claim for one's own beliefs that they are true is to claim truth for the standards that support them. Such standards are not *simply* "the standards internal to this or that standpoint," for they are the "adequate" or true standards. What MacIntyre points out is that those claiming truth for their beliefs must also believe that theirs are the true standards of rationality. But this requirement does not entail their denying that such standards are internal to their tradition, or their believing that they are equally available to all persons.

For MacIntyre, then, even the true standards of rationality are tradition-constituted—a claim which invites a further challenge to his realism. I will follow Haldane's definition of realism as consisting in an ontological and an epistemological thesis. The ontological thesis is that the world exists and has whatever structure it has independently of the mind. The epistemological thesis is that we can come to know and speak truly of this world.[47] I argued against Haldane's suggestion that the transcendence of truth depends on the transcendence of rationality, because it seems to me that truth is transcendent, not by virtue of some property of reason, but because the objects of knowledge are transcendent. Nevertheless, to know these transcendent objects presupposes that our means of knowing are adequate to the task. Now, for MacIntyre, the central means by which we know is the activity of rational justification, for it is this activity that has knowledge and truth as its telos. If we come to know through the process of rational justification, however, there needs to be some explanation of why true beliefs are vindicated and false beliefs discredited. And it is on account of this requirement that many realists balk at MacIntyre's suggestion that rationality is tradition-constituted. For if the true standards of rational justification were available to all persons, then these standards could account for the fact that true beliefs are vindicated and false beliefs discredited, and hence for the fact that we come to know truth through the process of justification. But if the standards of rational justification vary from one tradition to another, then contradictory claims might very well be justified from the standpoint of two different traditions. Since contradictory claims cannot both

[47] John Haldane, "Mind-World Identity Theory and the Anti-Realist Challenge," in *Reality, Representation, and Projection*, eds. John Haldane and Crispin Wright (Oxford: Oxford University Press, 1993), pp. 15-16. Haldane distinguishes strong and weak versions of both ontological and epistemological realism. The definition I adopt accords with the stronger versions of both, the versions which Haldane wants to defend.

be true, the process of justification, far from being that which leads to truth, would be for at least one of these traditions, precisely that which leads to error. The claim that rationality is tradition-constituted, coupled with the claim that we come to know through the process of rational justification, would seem to doom realism's epistemological thesis. For on this view, at most some human beings—those inhabiting the right tradition—would be able to know mind-independent reality.

I think, however, that MacIntyre might be able to answer the foregoing objection. What is needed is an explanation of how all persons can potentially know through the process of rational justification, even if some initially inhabit traditions whose standards of justification support false beliefs. The answer has two parts. MacIntyre provides the first part in his account of how one tradition can show itself rationally superior to another. Recall from the introduction, that such superiority is shown without appeal to independent standards of rationality. For it is by its own standards that a crisis tradition recognizes its problems, and it is by the standards of the superior tradition that those problems are diagnosed and overcome. When the inhabitants of the crisis tradition abandon that tradition in favor of its rival, they adopt the rival's superior standards of rational justification. On MacIntyre's account, then, there is no reason why someone who initially inhabits a tradition whose standards of justification support false beliefs cannot move to a superior tradition with superior standards.

An unsatisfactory aspect of MacIntyre's account of how one tradition can show itself rationally superior to another, however, is that he never gives a good explanation of why a tradition should ever fall into an epistemological crisis. Why should a tradition ever turn up defective according to its own standards? Won't a sufficiently developed tradition interpret experience in such a way as always to confirm its own fundamental claims? It would seem that, on MacIntyre's account, most traditions should devolve into closed systems of mutually supporting beliefs, such that they would never fall into an epistemological crisis, regardless of how badly they conformed to reality.[48] The second part of a response to our objection, therefore, must provide some explanation of why traditions of false belief enter into epistemological crises and why it is the traditions which better conform to reality which show themselves to be rationally superior.

[48] MacIntyre seems to think that the more fully developed a tradition of enquiry, the more liable it is to meet an epistemological crisis. But why shouldn't it be the other way around? In any event, MacIntyre admits that incompatible traditions can coexist side by side for long periods of time without either of them entering an epistemological crisis. See *Whose Justice? Which Rationality?*, p. 366.

Resources for this explanation can be found in the inquiries of Aquinas and his followers into the metaphysics of knowledge. A central conclusion of these inquiries is the thesis that reality measures the mind, for when the mind knows, the reality known is in an important sense the cause of that knowledge.[49] In particular, reality informs the mind, which is a capacity for being so informed, and which is compared to reality as potency to act.[50] Knowledge has been achieved precisely to the extent that this potency has been actualized and the mind has become formally what reality is. Hence, it is not just that truth is a correspondence between two *relata*, mind and thing. One of these *relata*, the thing, is in large part the cause of the conformity that the other, the mind, has to it. What resources do these insights afford for explaining why and giving us reason to expect that traditions of false belief will end in epistemological crises and be supplanted by traditions whose beliefs better conform to reality? Instead of explaining this by appeal to standards of rationality available to all persons from the outset, we can now simply appeal to reality. Since reality measures the mind, which is a capacity to be so measured, it is the formal structure of reality, acting on the mind, which ultimately insures that beliefs that don't conform to that formal structure will turn up defective. On MacIntyre's account, when one set of claims proves itself rationally superior to another, this rational progress can be explained as the thing under consideration exerting its formal causality on the mind whose potential to become informed by reality has become more fully actualized.

These two claims, first, that one set of standards and beliefs can show itself rationally superior to another, and second, that reality influences this process so that those beliefs which better conform to reality will ultimately be vindicated, enable us to explain how all persons have the potential to know through the activity of rational justification, even if some initially inhabit traditions whose standards of justification support false beliefs. Hence, it is shown how realism's epistemological thesis is compatible with the claim that rationality is constituted by traditions.

In conclusion, let me make clear what the foregoing argument has assumed about MacIntyre's thesis that rationality is tradition-constituted. I have interpreted this thesis to mean that the resources sufficient to provide rational justification for and to resolve disagreements about competing scientific, metaphysical, and moral claims are to be found only by appeal to the substantive commitments of particular traditions. So interpreted, this thesis is perfectly compatible with holding that human beings, regardless of tradition,

---

[49] Thomas Aquinas, *De Veritate* 1.a. 2.
[50] Thomas Aquinas, *Summa Theologiae* I, q. 79, a. 2.

share certain cognitive faculties or capacities to know. Otherwise, we could not address the realist's challenge by appeal to a common human potency to be informed by reality. In characterizing my proposal, it is useful to distinguish an internalist theory of justification from an externalist theory of knowledge.[51] An internalist theory of justification holds that rational justification is grounded and makes reference to what is internal and introspectively accessible to the knower.[52] An externalist theory of knowledge, by contrast, holds that knowledge is constituted by certain states or processes that are external and not introspectively accessible to the knower. I assume that MacIntyre holds an internalist theory of justification, but suggest that he needs to combine this theory with an externalist theory of knowledge.[53] According to his theory of justification, the introspectively accessible resources by reference to which justifications are made vary from person to person, depending on their tradition. The kind of externalist theory of knowledge that MacIntyre needs would consist in at least three claims. First, he would need to claim with most externalists that the reason knowledge, unlike justification, is not something introspectively accessible is that knowledge presupposes truth, which, being a conformity between the mind and a reality independent of the mind, is not something to which we have introspective access. Second, he would need to claim that knowledge is made possible by the fact that the mind is capable of being informed by reality, a capacity that, likewise, cannot be verified introspectively.[54] Finally, he would need to claim that the activity of justification is under the informing influence of reality, an influence to which we have no introspective access, but which accounts for the fact that systems of belief are not closed systems and that our activities of

---

[51] For a discussion of this distinction see Robert Audi, *Belief, Justification, and Knowledge* (Belmont, California: Wadsworth Publishing Company, 1988), pp. 113-15.

[52] As used here, "internalism" should of course not be understood solipsistically or as involving commitment to private languages.

[53] Eleonore Stump suggests that Aquinas' theory of knowledge should be understood as a species of externalism. See her "Aquinas on the Foundations of Knowledge," in *Aristotle and his Medieval Interpreters*, ed. Richard Bosley and Martin Tweedale, *Canadian Journal of Philosophy*, supplementary volume 17 (1991), pp. 125-58. See also Norman Kretzmann's endorsement of Stump's suggestion in his article of the same volume: "Infallibility, Error, and Ignorance," pp. 159-94.

[54] Notice that MacIntyre appears to make this claim in the passage quoted earlier where he states that a "person's intellect is adequate to some particular subject matter with which it is engaged in its thinking [when] it is what the objects of that thinking in fact are which makes it the case that that person's thoughts about those objects are what they are ... So the activity of the mind in respect of that particular subject matter is informed and conformed to what its objects are; the mind has become formally what the object is." See "Moral Relativism, Truth and Justification," p. 18.

enquiry and justification – through which we come to know and to which we do have introspective access—yield truth, even if slowly and with much difficulty. On the assumption that the activity of justification is under the informing influence of reality, we are warranted in claiming truth for our beliefs insofar as those beliefs have been rationally vindicated throughout the course of enquiry. But there is no introspectively available feature of justification that guarantees that a set of beliefs is true, and hence, we must be ready to abandon those beliefs if they can no longer be rationally sustained.[55] The proposed solution is realist, but fallibilist.

Admittedly, this non-introspectively-verifiable influence of reality on the contents of introspective consciousness through which we come to know is very mysterious and difficult to explain – which is one reason why philosophers such as Putnam and Dummett have rejected realism. Yet postulating some such influence appears unavoidable for the realist, and whether or not we agree with MacIntyre's claim that rationality is tradition-constituted makes it no less mysterious.[56]

---

[55] Cf. *Whose Justice? Which Rationality?*, pp. 360-61.

[56] To say that something is mysterious is, of course, not to deny that we have may have good reasons for affirming it, take the existence of God or the immateriality of the intellect, for instance. Rather, it is to acknowledge that such things will be difficult to understand for minds that, as Aquinas has pointed out, are primarily equipped for knowing the intelligible structures of material things.

Gilson and Maritain on the Principle of Sufficient Reason

Desmond FitzGerald

Our first principles are said to be so fundamental to our thinking as to be "quasi innate." That is, while not being innate, after our first encounter with being, we understand in an implicit way the difference between to be and not to be. The principle of noncontradiction, more usually referred to as the principle of contradiction, is said to underline our first judgment whatever it is. If we assert "x is y" we are excluding at that moment the thought "x is not y," and so in some form, the first principles of contradiction, identity and excluded middle are always part of our thinking.

Before Leibniz, reference to first principles would ordinarily include along with the principle of contradiction, what later would be called axioms of geometry: "things equal to the same thing are equal to each other" or "the whole is greater than its part." These principles are indemonstrable in their primacy, and are assented to as soon as the meaning of their terms is understood. These principles are the basis of our thinking and to attempt to prove them would involve the fallacy of "begging the question," that is, using in your premises what you are trying to establish in your conclusion. Approaching it from another angle, Aristotle showed that anyone who would try to counter the principle of contradiction with a serious argument would commit the absurdity of having to use what he is attacking as soon as he began to make a statement of his belief.

So too Leibniz in his *Principles of Nature and Grace Founded on Reason* arguing to establish the monad as the fundamental unit of reality asserts:

> Up till now we have spoken as *physicists* merely; now we must rise to *metaphysics*, making use of the great principle, commonly but little employed, which holds that *nothing takes place without sufficient reason*, that is to say nothing happens without its being possible for one who has enough knowledge of things to give a reason sufficient to determine why it is thus and not otherwise.[1]

---

[1] Gottfried Leibniz, *Leibniz: Philosophical Writings*, trans. Mary Morris (London: J.M. Dent & Sons, 1961), pp. 25-26.

120

It is interesting that in the following sentence Leibniz asks that basic question said to be at the foundation of philosophic speculation: "Why is there something rather than nothing?"

The Principles of Nature is dated 1714. Before he died two years later, Leibniz also wrote the classic *Monadology*. Here he affirmed his "reasonings are based on two great principles: the principle of contradiction, by virtue of which we judge to be false that which involves a contradiction, and true that which is opposed or contradicting to the false; and the *principle of sufficient reason*, by virtue of which we consider that no fact can be real or existing and no proposition can be true unless there is a sufficient reason why it should be thus and not otherwise, even though in most cases these reasons cannot be known to us."[2]

John Edwin Gurr, S.J., in his most valuable study *The Principle of Sufficient Reason in Some Scholastic Systems, 1750-1900*,[3] shows how this principle of Leibniz was taken up by the great German systematizer of philosophic teaching, Christian Wolff (1679-1754), and through Wolff became part of the German textbooks of the eighteenth century. Gurr's is a most thorough and excellent study of how the Catholic textbook writers of the late eighteenth and then nineteenth centuries took up the principle of sufficient reason in their ontological textbooks, and for the most part, but not universally, made it part of what might be considered the Catholic philosophic tradition before the gradual re-discovery of St. Thomas in the mid-19th century. By that time it came to be a toss up as to whether or not Leibniz's principle would be included in the scholastic manuals that were being written for seminary students *ad mentum sanctae Aquinatis*. Here it should be said that Gurr's study is something of an exposé in which he has indicted many authors for believing they were authentic Thomists while really they were the victims of an essentialist tradition going back beyond Wolff and Leibniz to Suarez and Avicenna. Gilson's *Being and Some Philosophers* is quoted as part of this indictment of early modern Catholic textbook authors.

In the pre-Vatican II era and well into the 1960's when one was assigned to teach the "natural theology" class, while the students might be using as a course textbook something like Fr. Henri Renard's *Philosophy of God*, as teachers we made use of the notable work by the great Dominican theologian Réginald Garrigou-Lagrange. His two-volume work *God: His Existence and*

---

[2] Ibid., p. 9.
[3] John Edwin Gurr, *The Principle of Sufficient Reason in Some Scholastic Systems, 1750-1900* (Milwaukee: Marquette University Press, 1959).

Nature[4] was a background work that helped a teacher give depth to his preparation. After some 240 pages he did get around to give what he called an "exposé of proofs for the existence of God" but he invested hundreds of pages of refuting objections from Idealists and Agnostics, explaining the Vatican I dictum that God's existence was knowable by natural reason, and reflecting on the metaphysical basis of St. Thomas's famous *viae*. Amongst the foundational items he examined was the principle of sufficient reason.

> The principle of sufficient reason may be expressed by the following formula: "Everything which is, has a sufficient reason for existing" or "Every being has a sufficient reason;" consequently, "everything is intelligible."[5]

Garrigou-Lagrange asserts, of course, that this principle is self-evident; it cannot be demonstrated, but is open to an indirect demonstration by way of a *reductio ad absurdum* were it to be denied. Since Garrigou-Lagrange is not the object of this paper I shall pass over his complicated argument simply noting that he serves as an example of a leading Thomist of the pre-Vatican II era who used Leibniz's principle and gave support to it. He recognized there are various difficulties contemporary critics of the demonstration of God's existence might bring up but since the time of Hume and Kant the issue of causality was an especially sensitive one. My point is how much a part of mainstream Thomism sufficient reason was mid-20th century.

I was actually searching for another book when I stumbled on a Ph.D. dissertation[6] published in 1941 by Sister Rose Emmanuella Brennan, of the Sisters of the Holy Names of Jesus and Mary, based here in the Bay Area. I never got to know Sr. Brennan personally, but I had made use of her translation, the first into English as far as I know, of St. Thomas's *De Unitate Intellectus contra Averroistas*. Her dissertation done at The Catholic University of America under the direction (I infer from the acknowledgment of her introduction) of the Reverend Ignatius Smith, long time Dean of the School of Philosophy. The dissertation was a study of the intellectual virtues according to the philosophy of St. Thomas, and as she comes to the first of the speculative virtues, understanding or the habit of first principles she includes a long quotation from John Henry Cardinal Newman's *An Essay in Aid of a Grammar of Assent*.[7]

---

[4] Réginald Garrigou-Lagrange, *God: His Existence and Nature*, trans. Dom Bede Rose, O.S.B. (St. Louis, Missouri: Herder, 1939), vol. I.

[5] Ibid., p.181.

[6] Rose Emmanuella Brennan, *The Intellectual Virtues According to the Philosophy of St. Thomas* (Ph.D. diss, The Catholic University of America, 1941).

[7] John Henry Cardinal Newman, *An Essay in Aid of a Grammar of Assent* (New York: Catholic Publication Society, 1870), pp.167-69.

Now Newman had no special Thomistic background as far as I know, but he had a brilliant mind that could be very original. Thus he affirms a number of principles that he recognizes as not demonstrable yet serve as a basis for our thinking. Without quoting his pages, he begins with the recognition of our own existence, the existence of other things; that we have a sense of good and evil, a knowledge of our consciousness and a memory for past events; that we are mortal and are part of history, and that the future is affected by the past. It is an interesting list and it would include most of what we would judge to be our "common sense" observations and amongst these is the judgment that there is an order in nature or as he puts it "a universe carried on by laws." I mention this because after Brennan reviews the ordinary lineup of first principles: i.e., identity, noncontradiction, excluded middle, sufficient reason and causality, she adds: "The principle of uniformity," which is introduced as a refinement of the principle of causality as applied to the experimental sciences. Thus our knowledge that the future will be like the past is offered as a basic insight in her exposition of St. Thomas's habit of first principles.

Whereas I had suspected that Garrigou-Lagrange was an influence on Maritain, the convert, when he was learning his Thomism, as it were, in the period of World War I and the early 1920s, this was confirmed by his reference to Garrigou-Lagrange in *A Preface to Metaphysics*.[8] In the fifth lecture of this work whose subtitle is "Seven Lectures on Being," Maritain begins with a consideration of the principle of identity; it is in this context he quotes Garrigou-Lagrange's formulation from *Le Sens Common et la Philosophie de l'Être*: "Every being is of a determinate nature which constitutes what it is."[9] Maritain, however, having quoted him goes on to differ with his friend on the issue of grasping the transcendentals such as being (*ens*) and thing (*res*). Maritain sees it as the same insight viewed under two different aspects: being as existing, and being as something essential, stressing the perfection "a particular essential determination."[10]

Also favorably quoted is my former teacher at Toronto, Gerald B. Phelan. His version of the principle of identity is "being is being." Maritain takes this version from his friend, Phelan, and anticipating the objections of the positivists and the analytic philosophers that it is a tautology, Maritain shows

[8] Jacques Maritain, *A Preface to Metaphysics: Seven Lectures on Being* (London: Sheed & Ward, 1945).
[9] Ibid., p. 92.
[10] Ibid., p. 93.

how other famous phrases such as "What is done is done" and Pilate's "What I have written I have written" are loaded with meaning and thus are not a simple repetition of the subject in the predicate.

In contrast to the attitude of Fr. John Edwin Gurr in his study of sufficient reason's use amongst the German and scholastic philosophers of the eighteenth and nineteenth centuries, Maritain accepts it simply as among the first principles. Gurr regards the principle as a product of the essentialism and rationalism stemming from Suarez, Leibniz and Wolff into the textbooks of the later scholastic philosophers. However Maritain has no trouble affirming it and giving it his Thomistic blessing.

Instead Maritain approaches sufficient reason in the context of the transcendental *Truth*. As he says the intellect faces reality, as it were, and confronts its essential aim intuiting that "being must be the sufficient good of intellect." The follow through on this insight leads ultimately to God, as the ground or ultimate reason for all being. Maritain is concerned to stress the universal character of sufficient reason; its scope embraces all being, created and uncreated. He says:

> This principle has a far more general scope and significance than the principle of causality. For the principle of sufficient reason is exemplified in cases in which the efficient cause plays no part. For instance, man's rationality is the ground, the sufficient reason of his *risibilitas* and *docilitas*. Similarly the essence of the triangle is the ground of its properties, and there is no difference of being, no real distinction the properties of a triangle and its essence. Again God's essence is the ground of his existence, He exists *a se*, He is Himself the sufficient reason of His *esse*, the ground of His existence, since His essence is precisely to exist.[11]

Thus we find Maritain being perfectly comfortable with the principle of sufficient reason: "Everything which is, insofar as it is, has a sufficient reason for being." God explains himself and as far as creatures are concerned they have their sufficient reason from another. This would be the place to go on to a discussion of the principle of causality should he choose but Maritain instead proceeds next to a discussion of the principle of finality.

Gilson wrote a great deal on topics in metaphysics and epistemology, but I failed to find passages that would parallel the treatment Maritain gave sto first principles in *A Preface to Metaphysics*. Where Gilson discusses the beginning of human knowledge he closely follows St. Thomas and speaks of the grasp of being, and then there will be a reference to the principle of noncontradiction. In his *Thomist Realism and the Critique of Knowledge*, speaking of the beginning of our knowledge, he says:

[11] Ibid., p. 99.

This much is certain, then, from the beginning of this new inquiry: the apprehension of being by the intellect consists of directly seeing the concept of being in some sensible datum. For the moment, let us try to clarify the nature of what that is the intellect apprehends when it conceives the first principle. To begin with, we must distinguish two operations of the intellect. The first, which is simple, is the means by which the intellect conceives the essence of things; the other, which is complex, affirms or denies these essences of one another and is called judgment. In each of these two orders there is a first principle: being, in the order of apprehension of essences, the principle of contradiction in the order of judgments. Moreover, these two orders are arranged hierarchically, for the principle of contradiction presupposes the understanding of being. [Here Gilson quotes in Latin a statement of the principle of contradiction from Aquinas's *Commentary on Aristotle's Metaphysics*, Book IV, lect. 6. #605] "Hoc principium, impossible est esse et non esse simul, dependet ex intellectu entis" Thus, the principle which is first in the order of simple apprehension is also absolutely first, since it is presupposed by the principle of contradiction itself. In short, the first principle, in the fullest sense, is being.[12]

Hence we notice that in a discussion of first principles Gilson stays close to the text of St. Thomas. Aquinas, of course, while benefiting from the writings of Aristotle in the principle of contradiction could not anticipate that Leibniz would go beyond the Stagirite and affirm a principle of sufficient reason. Where does that leave Gilson?

It happens that in 1970 when he was a visiting professor at the University of California, Berkeley, I came several times to chat with him in his appointed office hour in which, incidentally he was usually sitting alone. I had earlier presented a paper on "The Principles of Sufficient Reason and the Existence of a Necessary Being," and that provided the occasion for our talking about sufficient reason.

First, Gilson did not reject the principle. How could one reject "Being is Intelligible"? But because of its Leibnizian context he was reluctant to affirm it as a first principle after the principle of contradiction, of course. The background of this is developed in *Being and Some Philosophers*, chap. IV.[13]

To my claim that the principle could be divorced from its essentialist setting in Leibniz and Wolff and given an existential interpretation, he did not reply; he did not counter that this was impossible; it simply seemed that he was reluctant to agree. At the time I was unaware that he had taken a position in an 1952 article in the *Revue Thomiste*, where he wrote: in "Les

---

[12] *Thomist Realism and the Critique of Knowledge*, trans. Mark Wauk (San Francisco: Ignatius Press, 1986), p. 197.

[13] Étienne Gilson, *Being and Some Philosophers* (Toronto: Pontifical Institute of Mediaeval Studies, 1952).

Principes et Les Causes"

Here arises a reversal due to the vicissitudes of history. A philosopher whom St. Thomas could not have foreseen, Leibniz, later affirmed that there are two first principles, one for necessary truths–the principle of contradiction–and the other for contingent truths–the principle of sufficient reason. For Thomists, what is one to do with this second first principle? Some suggest formulating it as follows: "Nothing exists without sufficient reason." In that case it means this: for something to exist in the world rather than not exist, and for it to exist in a given manner rather than in some other manner, there must be a cause that determines whether it exists or does not exist, and exists in this way rather than otherwise. Two reflections now suggest themselves. First of all, this principle cannot be held to be an absolutely first principle. Indeed if nothing determines that something exist rather than not exist, or be as it is rather than otherwise, then it is possible for that thing both to be and not to be, or to be at the same time that which it is and something else.

Since this would be contradictory, one can say that the formula of the principle of sufficient reason leads back to the principle of contradiction. Secondly, and for the same reason, this principle is valid for necessary truths not less than for contingent truths. Thus it is not necessary that man exist, but if he does exist it is held to be necessary the he be endowed with reason and, consequently, since God is infinitely wise everything has been ordered by His thought, and wherever there is order there is reason. This means that there are sufficient reasons for things necessary just as there are for things contingent. Hence the conclusion: "The principle of sufficient reason is true, and it is valid not only for contingent truths but also for necessary truths, so that it must be held to be their principle, but not their first principle."[14]

This last quotation within the Gilson selection is from a text written by Cajeton Sanseverino,[15] a Jesuit from Naples whose seminary textbooks were in use in 1879 when Pope Leo XIII's *Aeterni Patris* served as the Magna Carta for the revival of Thomism. Sanseverino was not a trained Thomist; his early writings were eclectic, reflecting a Cartesian bias but in the latter half of the nineteenth century, he, like other Catholic philosophy professors were making the attempt to write their philosophy according to the mind of St. Thomas Aquinas in the name of Christian philosophy.

This brief study on a small point in the philosophies of Gilson and Maritain is intended as a window to examine their differences. This examination serves to underline two varieties of Thomism: the open innovative character of Maritain and the more traditional approach, even historical approach of

---

[14] Étienne Gilson, "Les Principes et les causes," *Revue Thomiste* 52: 1, pp. 47-48.

[15] Cajeton Sanseverino, *Philosophiae Christianae cum antiqua et Nova Comparatae*, (Naples, 1900, 10th edition) t. II, pp. 4-12.

Gilson. It seems to me not to be too much to say of Gilson's metaphysics that if there is not a textual basis in the writings of St. Thomas, he won't affirm it. But there it is, while well aware of sufficient reason, Gilson ignores it and makes no mention of it in his later editions of *Le Thomisme*, nor in his text-book *Elements of Christian Philosophy*[16] written especially for Catholic schools at the urging of his friend and disciple Anton C. Pegis (who had left teaching temporarily in the 1950's to become an editor of the Catholic text-book division of Doubleday & Company). Thus while not rejecting the principle of sufficient reason Gilson tends to shy away from it as Gurr also does in his study of the principle. Given its origin in Leibniz and its central role in the writings of the rationalists and essentialists of the eighteenth and nineteenth century, there is a hesitation to believe it can be given an existentialist interpretation.

However, speaking for myself as a teacher attempting to make Aquinas's third way, the argument from "possible being" to a necessary being, understandable to undergraduates, I was grateful that the principle of sufficient reason was available for use.

---

[16] Étienne Gilson, *Elements of Christian Philosophy* (Garden City, New York: Doubleday & Company, 1960).

The Loss Of the Knowing Subject In Contemporary Epistemology

> There is something puzzling about demanding an argument to show that the
> world exists independently of our representations of it.
> —John Searle[1]

I argue in this paper that the inability of contemporary American theories of knowledge to validate the central claim of realist epistemology—that some of our concepts refer to corresponding entities in the external world—is inextricably bound up with a failure to grasp the essential contribution of the knowing-self in the subject-object relation that constitutes knowledge. To be sure, much attention is given to the knower and to mental functions, as is clear from the literature on the philosophy of mind.[2] What I am saying is that too many epistemologists take too much for granted by failing to see that the knower contributes more to knowing than just forming beliefs, having memories and mental states, and imposing prejudices, feelings, and expectations on, or acting as a receptacle for, epistemological data.

This neglect results in a representationalist epistemology: the object of knowledge is not the extramental thing but *our concept of the thing.* This third thing between the knower and the known makes realism impossible to justify since, then, the object of knowledge is the concept within me, whereas realism, on the contrary, claims that assertions about the external world must have corresponding extramental entities. For if my representation of things constitutes a screen that blocks my direct knowledge of anything but the representation, then my assertions about the external world can refer only to *putative* external objects. That is why representationalists are inevitably prag-

---

[1] *The Social Construction of Reality* (New York: Free Press, 1995).

[2] See, for example, Jerry Fodor, *The Elm and the Expert: Mentalese and Its Semantics* (Cambridge, Massachusetts: MIT Press, 1994) and John R. Searle's two books, *Intentionality* (Cambridge: Cambridge University Press, 1983) and *The Rediscovery of the Mind* (Cambridge, Massachusetts: MIT Press, 1992).

matists.[3] For I have no alternative, when it comes to deciding whether my representations mirror external reality but to act on the premise that they do and see if I obtain the kind of results associated with the assumption that the representations have corresponding external entities.

Paradoxically, the movement from representationalism to pragmatism must finally rely on a coherentist criterion of truth that reduces "realism" to an epistemology indistinguishable from idealism. Consider: By what standard do we decide that any of our representations have corresponding external entities? The pragmatic criterion cannot be the final court of appeal since trying to justify the results of our actions as desirable or validating by appealing to the results of acting on the assumption that the previous results are valid only strings the question out and never gets to confronting the question of corresponding external entities. Besides, appealing to results to justify results can fall into the pit of circular reasoning. The answer must be an appeal to the coherentist criterion, which, as one of its advocates puts it, "has to be our ultimate criterion of truth."[4] An assertion is true if it is coherent with all the other assertions that comprise my universe of discourse. The pragmatist's assertion that a particular result is desirable or good or valid or true must ultimately find its validation in the coherence of that assertion with all the other assertions that compose his universe of discourse. But this is exactly what idealism holds, namely, that all we know are our ideas and ourselves. A strange realism that ends up indistinguishable from idealism! Despairing of breaking free of the immanentism of representationalism, some epistemologists, chiefly Quine,[5] propose that philosophy surrender epistemology to the field of psychology. Despite the objections that this proposal generated,[6] representationalism logically leads to the conclusion that epistemology is a branch of psychology because the latter is the discipline that studies intramental phenomena.

In contrast, the tradition of Aristotelian-Thomistic realism, which I shall defend in this paper, maintains that in order to know anything, I must enter into a subject-object relationship; for when I know, *I know something*. Know-

---

[3] Consider the dicta of a classic American representationalist: "Ideas become beliefs only when by precipitating tendencies to action, they persuade me that they are signs of things"; "Existence...not being included in any immediate datum, is a fact always open to doubt"; George Santayana, *Scepticism and Animal Faith* (New York: Dover Publications, 1955), p. 16.

[4] Richard H. Schlagel, *Contextual Realism* (New York: Paragon House Publishers, 1986), p. 242.

[5] W. V. Quine, "Epistemology Naturalized," *Ontological Relativity and Other Essays* (New York: Columbia University Press, 1969).

[6] See, for example, Jaegwon Kim, "What is 'Naturalized Epistemology'?," *Contemporary Readings in Epistemology*, ed. Michael F. Goodman and Robert A. Snyder (Englewood Cliffs, New Jersey: Prentice Hall, 1993), pp. 323-35.

ing, then, has two components: an object that is known and a subject who knows. But it is a relationship in which, as I shall argue later, the knowing subject a) *becomes* the object, the thing known; and b) *dominates* and *possesses* the object. If either of these components were lacking, knowledge would be impossible. Ironically, the loss of the knowing subject is the price that is exacted for starting to philosophize within the knowing subject, a methodological blunder that ultimately originates in a refusal to accept the mind's immediate and certain knowledge of extramental things.

Brains and Vats

My first task in this section will be preliminary to explaining what I mean by saying that contemporary American epistemology has lost sight of the knowing subject and how that leads to representationalism and idealism. In unfolding this section, I refer to three authors, Richard Rorty, Hilary Putnam, and John Searle. I limit my critique of Rorty to the task of clarifying how I am using the word "representationalism" in this paper. My critique of Putnam and Searle attempts to show the link between representationalism and idealism. I am conscious of what might seem to be a glaring omission of authors more commonly identified with epistemology nowadays, such as Alvin I. Goldman, Kieth Lehrer, and Laurence Bonjour, to name just a few. My decision to omit them was made in the interests of simplicity and thus a hoped-for clear view of the problem. The fact is that the validation of our knowledge of the external world has either become a question so moot to mainstream epistemology as to warrant scant attention or become practically lost from sight by a jungle-growth of arguments on belief, justification, and warranted assertability,[7] not to mention formulas of escape from representational incarceration by remedies such as semantic externalism.[8] To make my argument, I have chosen Putnam and Searle for their direct and unencumbered approaches to the problem of our knowledge of the external world.

It might be supposed that the "brain in a vat" literature refutes my claim that today's epistemologists are either disinterested in, or guilty of obscur-

---

[7] "I have made no attempt to answer skeptical problems. My analysis gives no answer to the skeptic who asks that I start from the content of my own experience and then prove that I know there is a material world, a past, etc. I do not take this to be one of the jobs of giving truth conditions for 'S knows that p.'." Alvin I. Goldman, "A Causal Theory of Knowing," *The Journal of Philosophy*, LXIV, 12 (1967), p. 372.

[8] See, for example, Anthony Brueckner, "Semantic Answers to Skepticism," *Skepticism: A Contemporary Reader*, ed. Keith DeRose and Ted Warfield (New York: Oxford University Press, 1999), pp. 43-60.

ing, the question of our knowledge of the external world. Admittedly, it cannot be charged with disinterest in the question. When presented in a theory of knowledge lecture, the brain in a vat example aims, we are told, "...to raise the classical problem of scepticism with respect to the external world in a modern way. (*How do you know you aren't in this predicament?*)"[9] But it skews the whole question by gratuitously going over to the idealist camp by embracing Descartes's premise that we are minds in a vacuum: a brain in a vat, no matter how ingenious its hook-ups with the external world, can hardly know in the same way the knowing subject of classical realism knows things. Classical realism operates on the premise of moderate dualism: the knowing subject is an integral composite of matter and spirit; in Aristotelian terms, it is a rational animal for whom all knowledge comes through the senses and for whom there is no sensation without intellection and no intellection without sensation. The brain in the vat proponents have surely kept their eye on the problem of how we know the external world, only they have traded the embodied knower of realism for the disembodied knower of Descartes.

Richard Rorty

Above, I described representationalism as the position that the concept is what we know rather than the thing to which the concept is supposed to refer. But that description needs parsing, at least in terms of its applications. For example, Richard Rorty calls himself an anti-representationalist, arguing that his pragmatism eliminates the need for intentional states of mind.[10] But there are, at least, three difficulties with his claim.

First, it is one thing for him to say that feelings are not intentional states, but quite another to say that beliefs and propositions and, indeed, perceptions of external reality do not result in representations. All these express themselves in mental states and concepts, so unless Rorty affirms the immaterial nature of mental states and concepts, which he does not,[11] then these mental states and concepts must *represent* the things of which they are the mental states and concepts.

Second, the denomination, "anti-representationalist," does not seem to square with his pragmatism. If a pragmatist is to avoid the charge of callousness or recklessness, he cannot, without giving pertinent reasons, offer "the

---

[9] Hilary Putnam, "Brains in a Vat," *Skepticism: A Contemporary Reader*, p. 31.

[10] Richard Rorty, *Philosophy and the Mirror of Nature* (Princeton, New Jersey: Princeton University Press, 1979), pp. 11, 371; *Objectivity, Relativism, and Truth; Philosophical Papers*, Vol. 1 (Cambridge: Cambridge University Press, 1991), pp. 1-12.

[11] *Philosophy and the Mirror of Nature*, chap. 1, esp. p. 20.

best results" as the primary justification for his pragmatism. Not only is there the problem, which I shall address below, of determining which results are "the best," there is also the problem of doing harm to individual human beings and institutions in the name of an overall smudgy criterion of the best result. On the contrary, the primary justification for pragmatism can only be representationalism: because it is impossible to know extramental things except as we represent them to ourselves and because we have no way of telling if our representations truly mirror the things that they are supposed to represent, our only recourse is to act on the premise that a given representation is true or good and see if it produces desirable results.

Third, Rorty looks very much the representationalist when he argues for "the priority of democracy to philosophy." The foundation of democracy must, he insists, be public consensus, which is possible only if the members of society are willing to compromise their most cherished principles.[12] This is so because he maintains that we cannot obtain objective knowledge of things (*pace*, the Enlightenment thinkers and their progeny, the Founding Fathers of democracy) for the simple reason that we are each trapped in our own ethnocentric prisons and can thus know things only from the standpoint of culturally conditioned perspectives. More recently he has identified himself with that group of philosophers who "…deny that the search for objective truth is a search for correspondence to reality and urge that it can be seen instead as a search for the widest possible intersubjective agreement."[13] Borrowing a phrase from Hilary Putnam, Rorty says that objective knowledge would require a "Gods-eye view" of things that we do not have.[14]

I may be rash to brand Rorty's doctrine of ethno-cultural relativism as an instance of full-blown representationalism without establishing whether he means that our ethnocentrism is incorrigible or simply a historically conditioned way of looking at the world that can be overcome by broader experience, reflection, and intellectual and moral discipline. My hesitation is increased because, thanks to John Searle's critique of antirealism (see below), I must now ask myself exactly how Rorty's ethno-cultural conditioning of our knowledge works. Does it distort things to such an extent that there is no way of telling if our representations of them are true or are these representations simply aspectual views of them, so that any distortion would result not from the representations themselves but from our interpretation of them?

---

[12] Richard Rorty, "The Priority of Democracy to Philosophy," *Objectivity, Relativism, and Truth* , p. 190.

[13] "John Searle on Realism and Relativism," *Truth and Progress: Philosophical Papers*, Vol. 3 (Cambridge: Cambridge University Press, 1998), p. 63.

[14] "The Priority of Democracy to Philosophy," p. 202.

At all events, I think that my first two points show that no thinker who clings to a materialist conception of knowing—not even an avowed "anti-representationalist" like Richard Rorty—can escape the clutches of representationalism.

Hilary Putnam

Hilary Putnam is a semantical externalist[15], but he also advances an epistemology that he calls "internal realism."[16] By this term, he means that "...at bottom...realism is *not* incompatible with conceptual relativity. One can be *both* a realist *and* a conceptual relativist."[17] He chooses a lower case "r" for realism, despite the fact that it is part of the title of his theory, to emphasize his point that realism with a capital "R" bedevils commonsense realism. What we need is a theory that accommodates "the many faces of realism."[18] What Putnam hopes to accomplish with his theory is to overcome the dichotomies spawned by conflicting interpretations of experience, such as those between science and commonsense experience. For example, I put, what seem to me, pink ice cubes in my iced tea, but physics tells me that those objects in my glass that seem pink, solid, rectangular, cold, and hard are, in fact, simply groups of atoms and electrons and indeterminate mass particles whirling about devoid of solidity, shape, tactility and color. Which is the reality, the pink ice cubes or the submicroscopic particles? Putnam's answer is that it all depends on your conceptual scheme. If you are drinking iced tea, they are pink ice cubes; if you are doing submicroscopic physics, they are submicroscopic particles. This is the "conceptual relativism" to which he refers.

You might suppose that this dichotomy causes serious problems for realism. Putnam thinks not. "How," he asks, "can one propound this relativistic doctrine and still claim to believe that there is anything to the idea of 'externality', anything to the idea that there is something 'out there' independent of language and the mind?"[19] For Internal realism the answer is simple. Putnam invites us to consider the following example: Imagine a world of three individuals: x1, x2, and x3. How many *objects* are there? According to the logical system of Rudolph Carnap, there are

---

[15] "Brains in a Vat," pp. 27-42.
[16] Hilary Putnam, *The Many Faces of Realism* (LaSalle, Illinois: Open Court, 1987), p. 17.
[17] Ibid.
[18] Ibid.
[19] Ibid., p. 32.

three objects. But some Polish logicians hold that for every two particulars there is an object that is their sum. So, instead of three objects, we have seven. Thus:

World 1 (Carnap's world)   World 2 (Polish logicians's world)
    x1, x2, x3   x1, x2, x3, x1+x2,
                                           x1+x3, x2 +x3,
                                           x1+x2+x3

The answer to the question, "How many objects are there?," turns out to be a matter of choice. If I choose Carnap's language, there are three objects *"because that is how many objects there are"*; if I choose the Polish logicians's language, there are seven *"because that is how many objects there are"* (in the Polish logicians's sense of 'object'). Considerations such as this one lead Putnam to the conclusion that realism (with a small "r") is defensible only if we sign on to his conceptual relativism: "There are 'external facts's and we can say *what they are*. What we *cannot* say—because it makes no sense—is what the facts are *independent of all conceptual choices*."[20] (Putnam's emphases.)

This is a clear case of representationalism, for what we know about the external world depends on the way we choose to represent it, what conceptual scheme we wish to employ. But it is not a simple matter of choice, for, as noted above, Putnam thinks it unintelligible to ask for facts that are independent of all conceptual choices. That Putnam's next step is to embrace pragmatism should come as no surprise, then. The choice of one conceptual scheme over another has to be based, if it is a reasonable choice, on the probability that it will fulfill one's expectations more fully. His agreement with Quine and others that we should abandon the spectator viewpoint in metaphysics and epistemology in favor of the pragmatist view makes sense, given his conclusion that we cannot know external reality "independent of all conceptual choices." We are thus to accept the "reality" of abstract entities not because they are known to be real but because they are indispensable in mathematics; we are to accept the "reality" of microparticles and space-time points not because they are known to be real but because they are indispensable in physics; we are to accept the "reality" of tables and chairs not because they are known to be real but because they are indispensable in daily living.

[20] Ibid., pp. 33-34.

John Searle

I referred earlier to Searle's critique of epistemologies that deny our ability to know external reality. If any philosopher around today can remind us of the importance of linguistic hygiene, he is the one. Searle is suspicious of denials about our ability to know external reality. Like Putnam, but for quite different reasons, he holds that the affirmation of an independent external reality is compatible with alternative vocabularies. For example, depending on which system of weight is used, Searle weighs either 160 pounds or 73 kilograms. But he claims that any inconsistency between the two differing weights is merely apparent: "External realism [the affirmation of an independent external reality] allows for an infinite number of true descriptions of the same reality made relative to different conceptual schemes."[21] It is nonsensical to say that conceptual relativism leads to antirealism and equally so to say that one cannot at the same time weigh 160 pounds and 73 kilograms. Indeed, rather than posing an argument against realism, conceptual relativity presupposes realism "because it presupposes a language dependent reality that can be carved up or divided up in different ways, by different vocabularies."[22] Accordingly, Putnam's two worlds of logical discourse, the Carnapian and the Polish, presuppose something already there to be viewed as either three objects or seven.

The problem with Searle's critique of conceptual relativity is that it stops where it should have begun. Unless I know which, if any, of the alternative vocabularies or conceptual schemes accurately and truly mirrors external reality, how do I know that there is a reality independent of my representations at all? Searle admits that he cannot show that the statement, "The external world exists independently of our representations of it," is true. Here I would ask for a clarification. There is a logical difference between the statements, "I cannot show that the statement, 'The external world exists independently of our representations of it,'is true" and "It is impossible to show that the statement, 'The external world exists independently of our representations of it,'is true." First, does Searle mean simply that so far he has not found a way to prove external reality or does he mean that it cannot be proved at all? Second, regardless of his answer to the first question, does he hold that we nevertheless *know* to be true the statement, "The external world exists independently of our representations of it"? Although I do not know the answer

---

[21] John R. Searle, *The Construction of Social Reality* (New York: The Free Press, 1995), p. 165.
[22] Ibid.

to these questions, it seems a safe bet that Searle would say that unless we can prove that the external world exists independently of our representations of it, we cannot *know* that it exists independently of our representations of it. He does, as mentioned above, argue that "our ordinary linguistic practices presuppose external realism."[23] But, as I shall show below, that approach just as easily presupposes idealism. The difficulty here is that, if I do not know that an external world exists, I surely cannot know that there is any external reality that is "carved up or divided up" by our alternative vocabularies and conceptual schemes, no matter how alluring "our ordinary linguistic practices" make the presupposition of external realism. Given the premise of conceptual relativity, how do I know for sure that there is an external reality?

Although Searle correctly points out that the claim that there is an external reality is an ontological rather than epistemological claim, he has accomplished no more than showing that it is an ontological *concept*, as the following passage makes clear.

> A public language presupposes a public world in the sense that many (not all) utterances of a public language purport to make references to phenomena that are ontologically objective, and they ascribe such and such features to these phenomena. Now, in order that we should understand these utterances as having these truth conditions—the existence of these phenomena and the possession of these features—we have to take for granted that there is a way that the world is that is independent of our representations. But that requirement is precisely the requirement of external realism. And the consequence of this point for the present discussion is that efforts to communicate in a public language require that we presuppose a public world. And the sense of "public" in question requires that the public reality exists independently of *representations* of that reality.
>
> The point is not that in understanding the utterance we have to presuppose the existence of specific objects of reference, such as Mt. Everest, hydrogen atoms, or dogs. No, the conditions of intelligibility are still preserved even if it should turn out that none of these ever existed. The existence of Mr. Everest is one of the truth conditions of the statement; but the existence of a way that things are in the world independently of our representations of them is not a truth condition but rather a condition of the form of intelligibility that such statements have.
>
> The point is not epistemic. It is about conditions of intelligibility and not conditions of knowledge, because the point applies whether or not our statements are known or unknown, and whether they are true or false, and even whether the objects purportedly referred to exist or not. The

---

[23] Ibid., p. 194.

point is simply that when we understand an utterance of the sorts we have been considering, we understand it as presupposing a publicly accessible reality.[24]

I have quoted Searle at length here to show the full force of his argument. The above text shows no more than a conceptual or logical difference between external reality and our representations of it. His argument for realism establishes just this: if there is no external reality, then our public language is odd because it bespeaks an external reality that is independent of our representations of it. Well, so much the worse for our public language!

In fairness to Searle, it must be noted that, at he outset of his discussion, "Does the Real World Exist," he states that "a thorough discussion of these problems [representationalism vs. realism] would require at least another book."[25] Nevertheless, given the direction of his argument thus far, it is hard to see how even a whole other book could save him from idealism. For his argument for external reality does not differ, in principle, from Putnam's. Both justify their realism by an ultimate appeal to a coherence theory of one sort or another. For Putnam, the task is to depict external reality in a way that harmonizes, which is to say, is *coherent* with, one's chosen conceptual scheme; for Searle, the task is to show that our public language is conceptually coherent only if there is an external reality; but, since by his own admission, he cannot prove there is such a reality, the coherence is really between our public language and our *concept* of external reality, not external reality itself. Further than that, Searle cannot proceed since going from concept to reality is an illegitimate transition.

Putnam does, to be sure, advocate a pragmatic epistemology, for he says we should forsake a spectator epistemology in favor of an activist one. In this he is like Rorty, who also advocates pragmatism, but, in the end, the coherentist criterion must prevail. It is one thing for a pragmatist to say that our judgments and theories are verified by successful action and quite another to say what the standard of successful action is. That standard is this: *an action that is successful is one that is coherent with all the other propositions that compose my universe of discourse.* This in no way differs from the idealist's position: *All I know to exist are my ideas and myself.*

Note that the knowing subject plays a silent role in the "realism" of both Putnam and Searle. From Putnam's discourse, we detect an implicit subject who is both an observer and a designer: the subject takes a look at the mind's representations and decides how they can be used to further a plan of action,

---

[24] Ibid., pp. 186-87.
[25] Ibid., p. 150.

whether it is to do submicroscopic physics, mathematics, or Polish logic. From Searle's discourse, we detect the subject as an observer who verifies the mind's representations according to linguistic imperatives. In both instances, the subject's relationship to the known is, first, that of a detached observer "taking a look"; and second, a facilitator: "Does representation A or B or C best suit my objectives (whether those objectives be a plan of action or conformity to a set of linguistic rules)?" Their entire epistemological enterprise reminds one of a motivational expert, playing various videos to decide which one would most effectively motivate the corporation's sales representatives.

Rather than reach so far as to call Searle and Putnam idealists, I shall content myself by concluding this section with the observation that Searle and Putnam are *not realists of fact* but *realists of intention.* I make no attempt to classify Rorty in this regard, for, as I mentioned above, my point in addressing his "anti-representationalism" was to clarify my use of the word "representationalism."

I said above that Quine's proposal that epistemology be handed over to psychology made sense. Indeed, it was predictable, as is clear from the writings of Thomas Aquinas who, centuries ago, emphasized the absurd consequences of holding that the concept is what the intellect knows rather than that *by which* it knows. One of those consequences is the reduction of all the sciences to the discipline that we know today as psychology: "...the things we know are also the objects of science. Therefore, if what we understand is merely the intelligible species in the soul, it would follow that every science would be concerned, not with things outside the soul, but only with intelligible species within the soul."[26]

But what does it mean to say that the object of our knowledge is not the concept but rather what is known *by means of the concept?* The answer is found in an understanding of epistemological realism in its classic form, as espoused by Aristotle and Thomas Aquinas and their twentieth century heirs, such as Jacques Maritain,[27] Étienne Gilson,[28] Yves R. Simon, [29] and Josef Pieper.[30]

[26] Thomas Aquinas, *Summa Theologiae*, I, q. 85, a. 2.

[27] Jacques Maritain, *The Degrees of Knowledge*, trans. Gerald B. Phelan (Notre Dame, Indiana: University of Notre Dame Press, 1995).

[28] Etienne Gilson, *Thomist Realism and the Critique of Knowledge*, trans. Mark A. Wauck (San Francisco: Ignatius Press, 1986).

[29] Yves R. Simon, *An Introduction to Metaphysics of Knowledge*, trans. Vukan Kuic and Richard J. Thompson (New York: Fordham University Press, 1990).

[30] Josef Pieper, *Reality and the Good,* trans. Stella Lange (Chicago: Henry Regnery Co., 1967).

Classical Realism

The principle of classical realism is *things are the measure of mind; mind is not the measure of things.* This principle follows from the premise that *we know extramental things spontaneously and certainly.* This accounts for the impossibility of demonstrating the existence of extramental reality. For one thing, nothing is more evident than the existence of things outside the mind. Searle is quite correct in his observation that "there is something puzzling about demanding an argument to show that the world exists independently of our representations of it."[31] Indeed, the very project of trying to find out what and how we know—which is what epistemology is all about—seems comically sadistic without the presupposition of extramental reality.[32] The classical thinkers would say that the existence of extramental reality is self-evident. That being so, then it is absurd to try to demonstrate what is directly evident to the senses by appealing to what is indirectly evident.[33] We know extramental things as real because we directly grasp them as real as a result of a primary intuition of actual being. This cannot be defended, however, if what we know are our representations of things rather than the things themselves. How did the classical epistemologists avoid representationalism? Thomas Aquinas, for example, rejected the claim that the concept is the object of knowledge, arguing instead that the concept is *that by which we know the thing*, so that the thing itself is the object of knowledge. But how can this be accomplished?

It is worth repeating that classical realism begins with the spontaneous knowledge of extramental things. (This confidence in our initial, spontaneous act of knowledge was shattered when Descartes cast doubt on common sense knowledge by employing his "methodical doubt.") Given this premise, the question is how is this possible? It was clear to Aristotle that the mind's direct knowledge of reality would be impossible if some third thing interposed itself between the knower and the thing known. That is why he says, "mind is, in a way, all things."[34] The alternative to representationalism is, in other words, the proposition that knowing consists of the mind becoming the other *as other*. As curious as that pronouncement may seem, that is the only way of accounting for the claim that we know extramental things directly and certainly. For, as noted above, if the object of my knowledge

---

[31] *The Construction of Social Reality*, p. 177.
[32] *Introduction to Metaphysics of Knowledge*, pp. 1-10.
[33] Thomas Aquinas, *Commentary on Aristotle's Physics*, II, lect. 1, 8.
[34] Aristotle, *De Anima*, III, 8, 431 B20.

consisted of some third thing between knower and extramental thing, I could never know if there were, in fact, any extramental thing, let alone what its characteristics were.

When I say that contemporary epistemologists take the knower and his cognitive operations for granted. I mean that they talk about knowing as if it were nothing more than "taking a look." But what is involved in taking a look? Do plants and beetles and dogs take the kind of look that we call "knowing?" It skirts the issue to say that knowing is true belief and then spend all one's epistemological capital on the evidence for the belief, because that leaves us with the movie screen but no audience to view it. Knowledge requires not only an object that is known, not only evidence for believing that the assertion about the object is true, but also a knowing subject who is more than just one who is taking a look.

That the knower must know himself as the *subject* in order to know a thing *as object* is clear insofar as there is no knowing without a subject. It is *I*, the unique self-being that I am, who knows *x* to be true and *y* to be false." Knowing without a subject who is aware of himself as the *I* who does the knowing is as absurd as cinema in a universe without viewers. The self-awareness here cannot be an awareness of my observing myself, for that is simply to take a step backwards and not explain anything. All that accomplishes is to make the knower the *object* of knowledge, leaving the *subject*, for whom it is the object, unexplained.

Approached from another angle, consider the statement: "I thought I was aware of myself, but it turned out to be some other self I was aware of rather than myself." This is an absurd statement, is it not? Not necessarily. If self-awareness is construed only as a subject-object relation where *myself* is the *object* of my awareness, if it is construed only in the sense that I am aware of myself in the way I am aware of other people and things, then why could I not mistake some other self for myself? After all, I do, from time to time, mistake one person for another, believe that Mary is the one I met at the lecture when it was, in fact, Louise. But the above statement is surely absurd when "self-awareness" refers to myself as an *I* and not a *me*, when it refers to myself as a subject rather than an object. For then we are talking about a perfect act of reflection, so perfect that there is no subject-object distinction, no object that the knowing subject can mistakenly identify. Even a lunatic who thinks he is Napoleon Bonapart cannot be mistaken in his self-awareness. His error lies in believing that his *I* is identical to the being known as Napoleon Bonapart, not in self-identifying knowledge. That is logically impossible.

This shows that there are two importantly different senses of the term, "self-awareness." The first and common usage refers to *explicit* self-awareness. That is the awareness that I have when I am introspective or self-conscious, as when I am aware of myself while performing certain tasks, like writing this sentence. But this very act requires a subject who is aware of himself not as an object but as a subject: not "I know me," but "I know I." This second usage of "self-awareness" refers not to an *explicit* self-awareness but to a *concomitant* self-awareness. So it is not mere self-awareness that allows knowledge but awareness of self *as subject*. Otherwise there could be no objectification. Objectification requires that the thing known be known *as other*. If it is not known *as other*, then all knowledge, so-called, would be subjective: everything I perceived would be *a-thing-for-me*. When a dog perceives its master, it perceives a thing other than itself, but there is no evidence that the dog thereby *conceptualizes* its master. Canine behavior can be explained, if not by a stimulus-response relation with the sensuous image of its master, then to a merely perceptual inference based on an association of images.[35] But if I do not know myself as subject, I cannot know anything *as other* since things known *as other* have meaning only in relation to a self. It is the knowledge of oneself as subject, not as object, that allows the relation to the *other-than-I*, the other *as other*.

An Historical Incident

The debate between Thomas Aquinas and the Averroists illuminates, in a singular way, the indispensable role of the self in knowing. And in doing so, it reinforces my example above about the impossibility, even for a lunatic who believes he is Napoleon Bonapart, of mistaking oneself for someone else.

Averroes argued that the correct interpretation of Aristotle's treatise on the soul was that human beings had material souls. His reasoning, based on a close reading of the text, was as follows: (1) all sensible beings are composed of the co-principles, matter (potency) and form (act); (2) living sensible beings have the soul as their form; it is their *entelechy* or principle of living organization; (3) the soul of a human being is the principle of his organization; it must therefore be a material soul, since it is the principle a material being. But to explain how Aristotle can, at the same time, hold that knowing requires an immaterial intellect, Averroes offered his theory of the *continuatio*. According to this theory, an individual human is able to know by using his material intellectual faculty and phantasm as a kind of plug-in to the one, transcendent agent intellect, which is immaterial.

---

[35] See Mortimer J. Adler, *The Difference of Man and the Difference It Makes* (New York: Fordham University Press, 1993), pp. 136-37.

Thomas Aquinas's criticism of the *continuatio* has its roots in the Aristotelian formula that difference is caused by form. Because the human being differs from other beings by virtue of his rationality, the intellectual principle must be his substantial form.[36] Averroes was hardly ignorant of the need for personal identity in knowing. He was persuaded that his *continuatio* explained how this particular human can be said to know when there is only one intellect for all humans. Using the Aristotelian principle that proper operation comes from form, Averroes held that, since knowing is man's proper operation, the separate intellect must somehow be a form in him. Although the intellect is not a power of the human soul, it is apparently always at his disposal. He is able to know whatever his wishes[37].

But all this would be impossible, on Averroes's view, if the human soul were not especially adapted to the use of the separate intellect. Indeed, without the human soul, with its own enmattered cogitative powers, the separate intellect could not operate.[38] Despite this attribution of mutual dependence, Averroes nevertheless draws a sharp distinction between the soul of the individual human and the separate intellect. He maintains that the intellect is neither the soul nor a part of the soul. The soul is the first act of a physical, organic body, but the intellect is superior to the soul.[39]

As stated above, it is at this point of the intellect's separation from the soul that Aquinas directs his criticism. If the intellect is not a power of the individual soul, then the individual human simply is not the one who knows. This seems a fatal objection to the *continuatio*. This criticism can only originate in the proposition I have been arguing, to wit, that in order to know an object, the intellect must first know itself as the subject who is doing the knowing. One can find further support for it in other of Aquinas's texts.[40] This line of attack devastates the Averroist position, since the one intellect would always know itself as the knower, regardless of the individual humans who might share in its operations.

---

[36] Thomas Aquinas, *Summa Theologiae*, I, q. 76, a. 1.

[37] Averroes, *In De Anima*, III, t.c. 36, (lines 518-598).

[38] "*Iste igitur intellectus passibilis necessarius est in formatione...Idest virtue imaginativa et cogitativa nichil intelligit intellectus qui dicitur materialis; hee enim virtutes sunt quasi res que preparant materiam artificii ad recipiendum actionem artificii.*" *In De Anima*, III, 36, 518-598.

[39] *In De Anima*, III, t.c. 5, (lines 27-38); t.c. 32; see Beatrice Zedler, "Averroes and Immortality," *The New Scholasticism*, 28 (1958), p. 437.

[40] Thomas Aquinas, *De Veritate*, X, 8, *De Unitate Intellectus* III, IV, and *De Spiritualibus Creaturis* IX; see also, Gerad Verbecke, "L'unite de l'homme: Saint Thomas contre Averroes," in *Revue Philosophique de Louvain*, 58 (1960), pp. 220-49.

While the textual evidence cited shows that Averroes and Aquinas both recognize the necessity of the subject knowing himself *as subject* in order to know, Aquinas rejection of the *continuatio* reveals a deeper insight into the role of personal identity. If the individual did not know himself as the knower, how could there be any such thing as knowledge at all? How could we say that Plato knows if Plato does not know himself as the subject who knows? As noted in the previous section of this essay, the self-knowledge in question here is not psychological awareness (knowledge of the self *as object*) but rather an ontological awareness: we are not consciously aware of knowing ourselves as subject, but when we analyze the act of knowing, we see that knowing would be impossible without it.

Knowing Things

I believe that the eclipse of the knowing subject in contemporary episte-mology started with Descartes's method of suspending in doubt everything that cannot be demonstrated as necessarily true or apprehended as clear and distinct. This dichotomized reason and common sense; for some truths enter-tained by common sense defy demonstration, as, for example, the claim that things exist outside and independently of the mind. Subsequently, the episte-mological emphasis was invested in the project of trying to prove the unprovable. If, on the contrary, we begin epistemology with the premise that, although it is impossible to demonstrate, we know extramental things spon-taneously and certainty, then the first question to be answered is: What is knowing and how does it work? The attempt to find an answer directs our attention to the knowing subject. How?

On the premise that we do know extramental things, it follows that the object of knowledge and the thing must be identical. To reiterate, that means that there cannot be any third thing between the object of knowledge and the thing. For then what we would know would not be the thing but rather our representation of the thing. In fact, we would have no conclusive knowledge that there was any thing other than our representation. But since we do know extramental things, we must accept the conclusion that the knowing subject becomes the thing it knows.

If what we know are *things, extramental entities, existents*, it follows that, because there can be no third thing between knower and known, the knower must become the known. There are three possibilities, at least in terms of a logical division, for explaining how this happens. First, the knower becomes the known thing in the latter's physical nature. That will not work because it would violate the principles of identity and contradiction: knowledge of an oak tree would then require that the knower be the knower and the physical tree at the same time. Second, we could revisit the principle espoused by Empedocles, "Like knows like"; the faculty that knows the real must be the same as the real—not entitatively the same, but of the same stuff—as the real: in order to know fire, the intellect must be fire, to know matter, it must be matter, to know movement, it must be movement, etc. The trouble with this demand for a direct apprehension of reality without any conceptual likeness of the object, formed according to the subject's mode of being, is that it reduces knowledge to an identification of the subject and object, but according to the object's mode of being. Objective knowledge would thus be impossible because the subject-object relationship on which objective knowledge depends would be destroyed, as the object absorbed the subject.[41] But knowledge of an object, *as object*, requires that the knowing subject retain possession of itself; know itself as the subject who knows the object. In other words, the knowing subject dominates the object.

This leaves the third possibility as the only viable candidate. The object known is in the subject according to the mode of the subject, which is to say, the knower becomes the known on the intentional level according to the immateriality of the intellect. From the metaphysical standpoint, this amounts to two entities, the thing known and the immaterial likeness that the knowing subject has become. From the epistemological standpoint, however, there is only one entity, the intellect having become the immaterial likeness of the thing known. In the words of Yves R. Simon:

> When one thing is united to another, the usual result is a third thing made of the first two. When the soul is joined to a body, the result is man. When man is joined to virtue, the result is the virtuous man. When the wax is to the impression of the seal, the result is stamped wax. But when an object of knowledge is joined to a knowing subject, no composite results from that union. We think of the union of a physical form with its matter, and we come up with a whole, composed of form and matter. But when we consider the union of an object of knowledge with a knowing subject, we come up with an entirely different kind of whole. Here there is no fusion of two realities into a third reality. If this whole possesses unity, it is because the subject has become the object, and this unity, in the famous phrase of Averroes, so often repeated by Latin Aristotelians, is the most intimate of all.[42]

---

[41] Jacques Maritain, *Bergsonian Philosophy and Thomism*, trans. Mabelle L. and J. Gordon Andison (New York: Philosophical Library, 1955), pp. 107-08.

[42] Yves R. Simon, *An Introduction to Metaphysics of Knowledge*, p. 10.

The primary and fundamental premise of epistemological realism—things exist independently of our minds and we can know some of these things certainly and truly—demands this perfect entitative unity. It is explainable in no other way.

Admittedly, the explanation of how this union between knower and known takes place is every bit as marvelous as the above explanation of intentionality. Because we do know things and because knowing consists in the knower and the known becoming one, it follows that the intellect must somehow create an exact likeness of the thing known. Aristotle provided us with the solution. Through the external senses—sight, hearing, smell, taste, and touch—we form a phantasm, a sensuous image, of the external thing. This requires a process of reconstruction. Since the senses are immersed in matter and matter is the principle of specification, each of the aforesaid senses has its own special object: sight, color; hearing, sound; etc. Coming into the subject separately, they must be reunited into a single, unified image. This is not knowing, but rather its precondition. We are safe in assuming that even the higher animals possess the capacity to form phantasms. As an image, it is completely material, having size, shape, and if it were possible to extend its sensible properties, taste and smell as well.

Knowing occurs when the intellect is able to "define" the object to itself, when it is able to grasp *deskness*, say, in the image of a desk. But this cannot occur as long as the object remains enmattered, for matter is the enemy of knowledge. That is why neither science nor philosophy can address the individual as such. Physics can predict the behavior of electrons but only of electrons as a group, about which it can make statistical correlations; it cannot predict the behavior any one electron as an *individual*. Philosophy can define man as a type but not as an individual. If George is a man, I can define him as *rational animal*, but I cannot define him, *genus et differentia*, as individual. I can only define an individual, whether electron or human being, ostensively; that is to say, by pointing him out. The reason individuals cannot be defined *as such* is the same reason that prevents them from being known *as such*: they are individuated by reason of being immersed in matter and matter resists knowledge. As Thomas Aquinas notes, matter contracts the object when, on the contrary, intelligibility requires universality.[43] For example, I recognize the polygon on the poster as a triangle because I grasp in it the form of *triangularity*. If I could not manage that abstraction, I would only be able to grasp the particular polygon's specific characteristics; I would not be able to grasp its intelligible structure. Now triangularity is a universal

---

[43] Thomas Aquinas, *Summa Theologiae*, I, q. 86, a. 1.

and, as such, it applies to all polygons whose interior angles equal the sum of two right angles, but to no such polygon in particular. We do not, after all, say of a particular triangle, "*X* is triangularity," but rather, "*X* is a triangle." Plato was the first thinker, at least in the West, to distinguish between sensation and knowledge. [44] So clearly did he see the difference that he had no recourse but to dichotomize them: sensation pertained exclusively to sensible objects while intellection pertained exclusively to the immaterial world of pure Forms. His pupil, Aristotle, took the Forms from their ethereal habitat and placed them in material things. Reversing the order of Plato, he insisted that the Forms were "secondary substance" and things were "primary substance." What existed were individual horses, not horsiness. But, now, he had to explain how we traveled from the perception of individual, material things to abstract, universal ideas. To account for our knowledge of things, Aristotle was faced with the task of showing how we freed their intelligible structures from their enmattered state.

This he accomplished by coming up with the theory of abstraction. The intellect focuses on the intelligible structure embedded in the sensible phantasm and, in that way, abstracts the former, thereby freeing it from the contractions of matter. It then makes an immaterial likeness of the intelligible species (known as the *impressed species*) and becomes it (known as the *expressed species*). Then, and not before then, the subject knows the thing. And that is what Aristotle means by saying that "intellect is, in a way, all things."

What is clear from the above account is that knowing is not "taking a look" but a way of being, a becoming of the other *as other*. In the tradition that Aristotle thus fathered, knowing is seen as a way of enriching the ontological status of the knower. Whereas subrational beings are enclosed in, and limited by, their own forms, rational beings overcome the limitation of their forms by becoming the forms of other things without losing their own.

Knowing oneself as a subject rather than an object, as an *I* rather than a *me*, is possible only in a being whose intellect is an immaterial substance, for no material substance can perform the act of perfect self-reflection that such self-awareness is. Physical things can bend back on themselves (self-reflect), but not perfectly. When, for example, I fold a sheet of paper in half, the result is an imperfect reflection, for what I have done is bend the top half of the paper over onto the bottom half. The intellect's immateriality is also evinced by the knowing operation itself. The ability to free the intelligible form from the material constraints of the phantasm and to become it while remaining

---

[44] Plato, *Theaetetus*, 184b-186e.

itself cannot be accomplished by a purely material being. *Per impossibile*, if a donkey could become a lion, it could do so only by destroying itself as a donkey since it would be impossible for it to be a donkey and a lion at the same time and in the same respect. In knowing, on the contrary, the knower fashions an identical replication of the form in the extramental thing and becomes it while remaining its unique self. Whereas a material substance cannot be in two places at the same time, its immaterial form can. And having become the form of the other, the subject, by knowing himself as subject, knows the thing.

To dismiss this explanation on account of its appeal to immateriality betrays a failure to appreciate our direct experiential knowledge of the world around us. We do know, and what we know are things. Any theory of knowledge that loses sight of that primary truth is bound to embrace representationalism and, finally, idealism. The materialization of the intellect and the self eliminates the possibility of objective knowledge from the very start. Objectivity requires a formal causality whereby the intellect replicates an identical copy of the intelligible form of the thing known. Such replication can occur only through the active agency of an immaterial entity. I say "active" because knowing is an act, a reaching out of the self to the non-self. To reiterate, knowing is a becoming, a way of being, an activity by which the self overcomes its limitations by becoming the other, *as other*, while retaining its own unique selfhood.

The materialization of the intellect replaces the subject with an *object*, for matter is passive.[45] Consider, again, the claim that the objectivity of knowledge requires that the concept of the thing known be its identical copy, so that, metaphysically speaking, the concept and the thing of which it is the concept are two entities; but, epistemologically, they are one insofar as, from the standpoint of intelligible structure, there is no difference between them. To effect this, the intellect must *act* on the phantasm by focusing on its intelligible content and, by formal causality, replicating it. But if the intellect is material, formal causality is replaced by efficient causality, and, because a thing is passive to the extent that it is material, the thing known acts upon the knower. That the knower may act on the thing known as well is an irrelevant consideration with regard to objective knowledge. Efficient causality produces an effect that, although containing, in some sense, the likeness of the causal agent, remains importantly different from it. If, for example, I photograph my family, I make an impression on film that is of their likeness. But the impression is hardly

---

[45]*Introduction to Metaphysics of Knowledge*, pp. 39-42.

identical to them. This disparity results from the limitations of the film: it can reproduce my family only to the extent that photographic film can. What we have here, therefore, is not an identical replication but a third thing, different from both my actual family and the film.[46]

Representationalism is the child of a materialist conception of the knowing self. The concept or representation is an *effect* of an efficient cause and, as such, can only represent the thing of which it is the putative representation according to the ability of a materialized self to do so. Above, I said that Descartes's "methodical doubt" burdened philosophy with an impossible task. By casting the shadow of doubt over what the intellect knows spontaneously and certainly to be true, to wit, that things exist outside and independently of the mind, he condemned epistemologists to an reenactment of the sentence the gods imposed on Sisyphus: no matter how industriously and brilliantly they work to establish what the human mind can know, their approach to the answer is always asymptotic; close enough to be tantalizing, yet doomed to veer away, back to the starting point. Had subsequent epistemology not followed his lead by trying to demonstrate the existence of things outside the mind and contented itself instead to finding out how our knowledge of extramental things took place, it is quite possible that the role of the knowing subject in knowledge would not have been eclipsed.

Conclusion

There is an irony in all this. Descartes started his philosophy as if the self existed in a vacuum and could thus know itself directly and purely before any experiences of external reality. After pronouncing his "*Cogito, ergo sum,*" he then proceeded to demonstrate the existence of things outside his mind by appealing to the absolute perfection and goodness of God who surely could not have created in us faculties that mislead us into concluding that things existed when they, in fact, did not[47]. But this triumph was bound to evaporate. He failed and he did so for two reasons. First, he flouted the correct order of knowing. As Gilson noted, if you start your philosophizing inside your mind, you will never get outside it.[48] It is extramental things that we know first; then we reflect on the knowing operation itself; and finally we are

---

[46] Raymond Dennehy, "The Ontological Basis of Human Rights," *The Thomist* 42 (1978) pp. 434-63, esp. p. 440 or Raymond Dennehy, *Reason and Dignity* (Washington, D.C.: University Press of America, 1981), p. 44.

[47] René Descartes, *Meditations on First Philosophy*, Meditation V.

[48] Étienne Gilson, "Vade Mecum of a Young Realist" in *Philosophy of Knowledge,* eds. Roland Houde and Joseph P. Mullally (Chicago: J.B. Lippincott Co., 1960), p. 387.

aware of ourselves as the knowing subject.[49] The second reason is exemplified in Duns Scotus's reply to Henry of Ghent's claim that it is impossible to attain "certain and unadulterated truth" naturally in this life without divine illumination. Scotus pointed out that if our natural knowledge of things is uncertain, it is impossible to make it certain by divine illumination: "...no certitude is possible where something incompatible with certitude concurs. For just as we can infer only a contingent proposition from a necessary and contingent proposition combined, so also a concurrence of what is certain and what is not uncertain does not produce certain knowledge."[50]

Our failures should teach us, but their lessons often go unheeded. Even those most critical of Cartesianism and the rationalist tradition find irresistible the temptation to start their philosophy in the mind rather than with things. Consider the following passage from John Locke's *Essay Concerning Human Understanding*: "...I thought that the first step towards satisfying several inquiries the mind of man was very apt to run into, was to take a survey of our own understanding, examine our own powers, and see to what things they were adapted. Till that was done, I suspected we began at the wrong end...."[51] Is it not curious that an empiricist, bent on showing that the rationalism of Descartes and his followers was profoundly mistaken in supposing that human knowledge originated in any other way than through the senses, should have begun his philosphical labors by paying attention to the phenomena within the mind rather than on what the mind knows about the world? And no one can ever accuse Immanuel Kant of ignoring the knowing subject. He must be given the credit for returning modern philosophy's attention to the knowing subject's contribution to our knowledge of the external world. Only, he seems to have confused the first and second orders of intentionality, thereby assigning to the mind the wrong role in our knowledge of the world. Locke's efforts led to Hume's phenomenalism, while Kant's attempt to save the objectivity of knowledge ushered in German idealism. The irony is that by starting with the knowing subject instead of with extramental things, modern philosophy soon found that not only was it increasingly difficult to justify claims of an external reality, it had also lost the knowing subject.

---

[49] Thomas Aquinas, *Summa Theologiae*, I, q. 14, a. 2; q. 87, a. 1.

[50] Duns Scotus, *Philosophical Writings*, trans. Allan Wolter, (Indianapolis, Indiana: The Bobbs Merrill Co., 1964), p. 112.

[51] John Locke, *Essay Concerning Human Understanding* ed. Alexander Campbell Frazier (New York: Dover Publications, 1959), Vol. 1, p. 31.

Combating the Iron-Gloved Angel

Swift and Maritain v. Descartes

Thomas F. Woods

At first glance, Jonathan Swift and Jacques Maritain seem to have little in common. The former was a staunch Protestant, Anglo-Irish, and a satirist who flourished in the eighteenth century. The latter was decidedly Catholic, French, and a philosopher who flourished in the twentieth century. A second glance should remind us of some telling similarities—Swift's satire has a philosophical vein, and Maritain observes that when "dealing with the great idols of the day,...it is one's duty toward what is highest in the world to use the knife."[1] A third glance, or perhaps extended look, reveals a deep point of kinship: each was a lifelong antagonist of René Descartes. Swift attacked Descartes in *A Tale of the Tub* (the earliest important work of his youth), in the crowning work of his maturity, *Gulliver's Travels*, and in *A Modest Proposal,* his last important work.[2] Maritain caused something of a scandal by attacking Cartesianism in *Three Reformers*, at the beginning of his career; he sustained the attack in the mature essays of *The Dream of Descartes*; and it has a decisive if muted presence in his other writings including his final major work, *The Peasant of the Garonne.*[3] Indeed, the resemblance in their

---

[1] Jacques Maritain, *The Peasant of the Garonne: An Old Layman Questions Himself about the Present Time,* trans. Michael Cuddihy and Elizabeth Hughes (New York: Holt, Rinehart and Winston, 1968), p. 98.

[2] Jonathan Swift, *Tale of a Tub,* in *A Tale of a Tub, with other Early Works: 1696,* ed. Herbert Davis (Oxford: Basil Blackwell, 1957); *Gulliver's Travels, 1726,* ed. Herbert Davis, (Oxford: Basil Blackwell, 1959); *A Modest Proposal for Preventing the Children of Poor People in Ireland from Being a Burden to Their Parents or Country, and for Making Them Beneficial to the Public,* in *Gulliver's Travels and Other Writings,* ed. Louis A. Landa (Boston: Houghton Mifflin Co.; The Riverside Press, 1960), pp. 439-46.

[3] Jacques Maritain, *Three Reformers: Luther, Descartes, Rousseau* (New York: Charles Scribner's Sons, 1955); *The Dream of Descartes, together with Some Other Essays,* trans. Mabelle L. Andison (New York: Philosophical Library, 1944); on the responses to *Three Reformers,* see Richard Farfara, "Angelism and Culture," in *Understanding Maritain: Philosopher and Friend,* ed. Deal Hudson and Matthew Mancini (Macon, Georgia: Mercer University Press, 1987), p. 175n10.

attitudes toward Descartes goes very deep indeed, each of them making quite similar accusations against Cartesian thought: they associate it with irrationality and with self-absorption; they accuse it of distorting the functions of the intellect; of leading to violence and tyranny; of anxious pride.

Madness

We begin with the most startling accusation—that Cartesian "rationalism" is irrational. At first blush, the charge sounds like the sort of ad hominem mounted by those who themselves have no rational arguments available. But Maritain grounds the charge of irrationality in Descartes's own diary as reported by Adrien Baillet, Descartes's seventeenth-century biographer. In this account, Descartes himself claims that the great inspiration for the line of thought that occurred to him while famously isolated in the stove-heated room during a snowstorm was a series of dreams. His diary for 10 November 1619 records, according to Maritain, that "he was filled with Enthusiasm, he discovered the foundations of the Admirable Science, and at the same time his vocation was revealed to him in a dream." Actually, he records a series of three dreams, notable for violent winds, loud bursts of noise, sparks, and oracular advice.[4]

Descartes thought the oracular dream to be a revelation about the future. He interpreted it (in Baillet's words) to mean that the Spirit of Truth wanted "to open for him…the treasure of all the sciences." Descartes reported that he had a forecast of these dreams from the "genius" (spirit) that had been intensified in him, the "enthusiasm which had been burning in him for the past several days." The next day Descartes vowed to make a pilgrimage to Loretto, a shrine of the Virgin Mary—a vow he is said to have fulfilled five years later. Maritain observes with quiet irony that to the next few generations of Cartesians, the founding of modern rationalism upon the "inspiration" and "enthusiasm" of a series of dreams was an embarrassment, as was Descartes's religious pilgrimage.[5]

Two centuries earlier, Swift anticipated Maritain's accusations, satirizing Cartesian irrationality in language and imagery similar to those in Descartes's dreams: *inspiration, enthusiasm, wind and spirit, violence, burning within.*[6] For example, in Section 9 of the *Tale of a Tub* (A Digression on

---

[4] Adrien Baillet, *Vie de monsieur des Cartes* (1691), passages summarized and quoted by Maritain in *Dream of Descartes,* pp.14-15.

[5] Ibid., pp. 13-15.

[6] I know of no direct evidence that Swift read Adrien Baillet's biography of Descartes, though it was published in French in 1691, five years before the composition and nine years before the publication of *Tale of a Tub*, and in an English translation, which I have not seen, in 1693: *The Life of Monsieur Des Cartes* (London, 1693).

. . . Madness), a Modern Hack, the ostensible author, makes a bizarre argument against denigrating Jack's "sect," the Presbyterians. Simply because it was founded by a person such as Jack (John Calvin or John Knox), "whose Intellectuals were overturned, and his Brain shaken out of its natural position, which we commonly suppose to be a distemper, and call by the name of *Madness* or *Phrenzy*" is no basis for disdain, says the Hack.[7] After all, he argues, the initiators of great novelties have generally been mad for one reason or another: he goes on to instance founders of new empires, new systems in philosophy, and new religions. His discussion of novelties in philosophy is calculated to bring Descartes to mind: along with Epicurus, Diogenes, and others, Descartes is one who advances "*new* Systems with such an eager Zeal, in things agreed on all hands impossible to be known." Such men are locked up in madhouses in our time—"mistaken" to be crazy by all except their followers, for the innovators

> generally proceeded...by a *Method* very different from the vulgar Dictates of *unrefined* Reason.... For what Man in the Natural State, or Course of Thinking, did ever conceive it in his Power to reduce the Notions of all Mankind, exactly to the same *Length, and Breadth, and Heighth* of his own? Yet this is the first humble and civil Design of all *Innovators* in the Empire of Reason.[8]

This talk of *method* that reduces all learning to novelties issuing from the geometry of the lone, mad philosopher's mind is almost explicitly Cartesian.[9]

Such remarks allusively accusing Descartes of irrationality are not the limit of Swift's attack on him in *Tale of a Tub*. In Section 8, the Hack discusses the Aeolists—all those of whatever discipline or task who rely on inspiration, including preachers and philosophers—in details and language reminiscent of Descartes. As in Descartes's principle that all learning can be had by starting from intuition and his method, the Aeolists believe that all arts and sciences are refinements upon a grain of wind, "enlarged by certain *Methods* in Education," which should be "freely communicated to mankind." In images reminiscent of one of Descartes's dreams, the Aeolists conclude that "Learning is nothing but Wind"; their learning is communicated "by Eructation," which, when the "Winds and Vapors" issue forth, "distorted the Mouth, bloated the Cheeks, and gave the Eyes a terrible kind of *Relievo*."[10] (Unlike the one in Descartes's dream, this "wind" is internal, not external.)

---

[7] *Tale of a Tub*, sect. 9, p. 102.

[8] Ibid., sect. 9, pp. 104-05; some emphases added.

[9] Michael R. G. Spiller, "The Idol of the Stove: the background to Swift's Criticism of Descartes," *Review of English Studies*, 25 (1974), p. 16.

[10] *Tale of a Tub*, sect. 8, pp. 96-97.

Other passages accusing Descartes of irrationality occur, as we shall see, in *Gulliver's Travels*, Part III, and in *A Modest Proposal*.

Self-Absorption

These accusations that Cartesianism is rooted in irrationality are linked in the minds of Swift and Maritain to their second line of attack, which is, as might be expected, upon the famous Cartesian turn to the self as the source of authority, the turn that is at the heart of much modern thought. Both accusers point out that Descartes's turn causes a neglect of nature, of external reality. Both accusers appear to have in mind the famous story of Descartes's discovery of the truth within himself, a discovery made at night, during a snowstorm, in a warm room—alone.[11]

In Part III of *Gulliver's Travels*, self-absorption is a hallmark of the governing class on the flying island of Laputa, who are, as Gulliver says, quite "singular in their Shapes, Habits, and Countenances. Their Heads were all reclined either to the Right or the Left; one of their Eyes turned inward, and the other directly up to the Zenith." These folks are "so taken up with intense Speculations, that they neither can speak, nor attend to the Discourses of others, without being roused by some external Taction upon the Organs of Speech and Hearing...." The Laputans's upward-turned eye signifies that they look to the stars and planets, imitating Galileo and Descartes in their astronomy; their inward-looking eye signifies that, after the manner of Descartes, they look inward for the truth.[12] There they find triangles and other geometric figures, which they impose upon their food. What they cannot see, unless aroused by their flappers (who bat them on the eyes and ears with balloons made of pigs's bladders), are the plain things in front of them: each Laputan nobleman is "in manifest Danger of falling down every Precipice, and bouncing his Head against every Post." Most importantly, Laputan nobles do not easily register the presence of other people: the King of Laputa is so absorbed in a mathematical problem that he does not see Gulliver standing before him for an hour or more; one noble Laputan wife would rather be

---

[11] Descartes, *Discourse on the Method of Rightly Conducting One's Reason and Seeking the Truth in the Sciences, in The Philosophical Writings of Descartes*, trans. John Cottingham, Robert Stoothoff, and Dugald Murdoch (New York: Cambridge University Press, 1985), vol. 1, p. 116

[12] For the influence of Galileo upon Descartes, see "Idol of the Stove," pp. 22-23, and Peter Redpath, *Cartesian Nightmare: An Introduction to Transcendental Sophistry* (Atlanta: Rodopi, 1997), pp. 29-30. Redpath's book, which came to hand after I had completed most of this essay, outlines in more extensive detail than I many of the same points about Descartes.

beaten daily by the footman with whom she runs off than stay with her husband, who scarcely knows she is there.[13]

Maritain's accusation turns on the same axis as Swift's: Descartes ignores external reality to seek the truth within the self. In striking concert with the quasi-religious themes that Swift associates with Cartesianism in *Tale of a Tub*, Maritain points out that, in order to proceed with philosophic inquiry, Descartes uses the strategies of mental prayer: he "'closes his eyes,' 'stops up his ears,' 'shuts off all his senses,' 'even effaces all images of corporal things from his thought.'" Descartes's practice is the opposite of one who seeks to apprehend being through the senses first and then to grasp it by intellectually processing the evidence presented by them:

> Descartes, making use of the artificial and violent procedure of voluntary doubt, introductory to the revelation of the *Cogito,* has the pretension, in a flight of pure intellect, of rising to the plane of the intellect without passing through the gate of the senses, the way fixed for us by nature.[14]

One consequence of discounting the evidence of the senses is to seal off "thought as thought" in an "impenetrable world, shut in and fixed upon itself." The knower can be sure that the external world has any correspondence to the world of thought only because God guarantees the relationship. "This turning toward the inner self and the mind...fixes this gaze upon the intellect itself and it denies to that perception we have of the world through our senses any validity in knowledge."[15] The resemblance to Swift's Laputans is remarkable.

Misunderstanding How the Intellect Works

The turn to the self is, according to both Maritain and Swift, a dimension of Descartes's confusion about how the intellect works. The set of issues bound up with this question comes readily into view if we follow Maritain's exposition of the differences between the pre-modern and the Cartesian understanding of man, of how learning occurs, and of intellectual power.

According to the traditional view, man is a creature whose soul, integral to his being, is the form of his body; because of the integration of body with an intellectual soul, man is, on the scale of creatures, "the transitional form between the corporeal world and the spiritual world."[16] Descartes, as is widely

[13] *Gulliver's Travels,* pt. III, chap. 2, pp. 127-28, 133.
[14] *Dream of Descartes*, p. 39.
[15] Ibid., pp. 39-40.
[16] *Three Reformers*, p. 55.

acknowledged, views man as a duality, his soul inhabiting his body, using it as a tool, "an angel inhabiting a machine and directing it by means of the pineal gland."[17] Furthermore, the tradition looks upon man as one creature in a complex of beings, diverse in kind, some above and some below him on a hierarchical scale. Descartes looks upon man as a spiritual creature inhabiting (not informing) a body, which in turn inhabits a physical domain characterized by extension only.[18]

Finally, the tradition looks upon human learning as an activity in which, humbling itself before the external, the mind begins with the evidence of the senses, then gradually comes to know the world through experience, abstraction, and discursive reasoning—activities best carried out in a community of learners, both predecessors and contemporaries—who can correct and encourage one another.[19] In contrast, Descartes looks upon human learning as intuitive and mathematical, the learner gazing into his own "autonomous and self-sufficing" mind, which is only tenuously connected to the body and not reliably informed by its senses. Gazing into his mind, Descartes finds "the pure type…of those innate and self-evident ideas" that he believes to be the seeds of science. Then, working alone, he combines and recombines these ideas in different patterns, a kind of addition and subtraction, a process Maritain terms "those series of coupled evidences to which he reduces reasoning." This mathematical process substitutes for discursive thought, for the syllogism.[20] Maritain characterizes this view of the human intellect as itself an intellectual sin, the "sin of *angelism*."[21]

In Maritain's judgment, this view of the relationship among human nature, nature, and the mind has, contrary to Cartesian expectations, the effect of *reducing* the power of the intellect in three ways. First, instead of a diversity of sciences required by the interplay of the intellect with a diversity of creatures and by the intellect's work upon the variety of evidence acquired through the senses, Cartesian science, says Maritain, "finds *in itself* a plurality of ideas, ready made, irreducible, irresolvable, each clear by itself, each the object of primary intuition, intelligible elements to which everything that knowledge has to do with must be reduced."[22] Thus, as Maritain observes

[17] *Dream of Descartes,* p. 179; see *Three Reformers,* pp. 63-64.

[18] *Three Reformers,* pp. 74-75.

[19] *Dream of Descartes,* pp. 48-49; *Three Reformers,* p. 62.

[20] *Dream of Descartes,* p. 52. For Descartes on intuition, see Rule Three in *Rules for the Direction of the Mind,* in *Philosophical Writings,* vol. 1: pp. 13-14; on mathematics as the most powerful mode of understanding, see his Rule Four in *Philosophical Writings,* vol. 1: pp.19-20; on the duality of human nature, see René Descartes, *Discourse on Method,* Part Four, in *Philosophical Writings,* vol. 1: p. 127.

[21] *Three Reformers,* p. 54.

[22] Ibid., p. 72; emphasis added.

rather fiercely, in the Cartesian view, "human science must be *one*, with the oneness of the understanding; there can be no specific diversity of sciences."[23] The second way in which Descartes reduces the power of the intellect results from his insistence on clear and distinct ideas and his mathematization of thought, positions that have the have the effect of making him antipathetic to theology and metaphysics. This antipathy manifests itself in two ways: (1) he dismisses of all that is mysterious, including metaphysics and theology, from the claim to be worthy of attention, thereby reducing the range of what the mind can explore, cutting it off from important dimensions of Being; (2) Descartes imposes mathematics, "the law of an inferior discipline," on metaphysics.[24] Yet another way in which Descartes reduces the power of the intellect, says Maritain, is to make "human reason and its ideological content the measure of what is," with the result that reason "lose[s] its hold on reality," for it cannot take its measure by anything outside itself.[25]

Jonathan Swift mocks the same characteristics of the Cartesian intellect—intuitionism and, as we shall see later, mathematization—by bringing into view the ease with which such an intellect comes to conclusions and the inability of such an intellect to come to terms with external reality. This mockery is a central theme in his portrayal of the Houyhnhnms, the talking horses in *Gulliver's Travels* Part IV, whose "grand maxim is, to cultivate *Reason*, and to be wholly governed by it."[26] But the Houyhnhnm concept of reason is neither Classical nor Thomistic, as this formulation might lead one to believe. Rather, Houyhnhnm reason has the core feature of Cartesian reason: intuition. As Gulliver reports, reason is not in the Houyhnhnms's experience "a Point problematical as with us, where Men can argue with Plausibility on both Sides of a Question." That is so because their reason does not assimilate evidence from the senses and then work syllogistically toward understanding; nor does it make errors that can be corrected by testing against the experience and logic of others. Instead, Houyhnhnms's reason is intuitive, striking them "with immediate Conviction,"

---

[23] *Three Reformers*, p. 64; emphases in original. Cf. *Rules for the Direction of Mind*, Rules Three and Four, in *Philosophical Writings*, vol. 1: pp. 113-20.

[24] *Dream of Descartes*, p. 92; see pp. 72-79, 175. Descartes agrees that geometry and arithmetic provide at least an easy place to start: see Rule Four in *Rules for the Direction of the Mind*, in *Philosophical Writings*, vol. 1, pp. 15-20.

[25] *Three Reformers*, p. 85.

[26] *Gulliver's Travels*, pt. IV, chap. 8: p. 267. The Houyhnhnms appear to fit the textbook definition of human beings: "rational animals." For a review of the controversy over these creatures and over Swift's view of human nature, see James L. Clifford, "Gulliver's Fourth Voyage: 'Hard' and 'Soft' Schools of Interpretation," in *Quick Springs of Sense: Studies in the Eighteenth Century*, ed. Larry S. Champion (Athens, Georgia: University of Georgia Press, 1974), pp. 33-47.

in part because they, unlike Europeans, are not troubled by passions. Dispassionate and relying on ready-made categories, the Houyhnhnms have difficulty grasping the concept of "*Opinion*, or how a Point could be disputable; because *Reason* taught us to affirm or deny only where we are certain."[27] Learning is, as in Maritain's description, easy for the Houyhnhnms.

The Houyhnhnms, accordingly, have no philosophy, a lack that Swift might almost have designed into them to illustrate Maritain's point about Descartes's antipathy to metaphysics. Gulliver's Houyhnhnm master laughs when told of European disputes in natural philosophy. Why, he asks, should a rational creature be concerned about the conjectures of others? Moreover, the master adds in an appropriately Cartesian manner, even if true, such "Knowledge, if it were certain, could be of no Use."[28] A life of pure reason, life without controversy, appeals greatly to Gulliver, who strives mightily to become a Houyhnhnm, even to the point of imitating a horse's gait.

Gulliver himself, however, suffers the consequences of the Houyhnhnms's inability (the negative term is necessary) to think philosophically. The Houyhnhnms, unable to deal with the mystery of human nature, cannot puzzle out what he is. He looks like a Yahoo, one of the despicable creatures whose every physical feature is human but whose behavior is altogether governed by appetite. And he is, on his own testimony, a European, one of those creatures about whom Gulliver has told his master stories illustrating the worst features of human wickedness. The Europeans are clearly and distinctly Yahoos to the Houyhnhnm master's mind, for they exhibit behavior analogous to the anarchic behavior of the appetitive Yahoos. Consequently, the Master places both creatures in the same category: Yahoo. On the other hand, Gulliver has the power of speech, a modicum of rationality, courteous behavior, and cleanly habits. Confronted with a creature that does not meet any of their ready-made, either/or categories ("rational animal" or "Yahoo"), the Houyhnhnms are unable to assimilate information from the evidence before them (Gulliver's appearance and behavior). Nor can they deal with it logically in such a way as to develop a fresh definition for a creature new to their experience.

As a result of their puzzlement, they force Gulliver to leave their island, which he considers paradise.[29] He must return to the miseries of

---

[27] *Gulliver's Travels*, pt. IV, chap. 8: p. 267. Cf. Descartes' disparagement of philosophical opinions in Rule Three, in *Rules for the Direction of Mind*, in *Philosophical Writings*, vol. 1, pp. 13-14.

[28] *Gulliver's Travels*, pt. IV, chap. 8: p. 268. Descartes does insist that philosophy be useful: *Discourse on Method*, Part Six, in *Philosophical Writings*, vol. 1: pp. 142-43.

[29] Changes may be on hand for the Houyhnhnms, however. Although, as noted, the Houyhnhnm Master disparages "opinion," the Grand Assembly of the Houyhnhnms engages

life among Europeans, whom he considers Yahoos, because he has absorbed the categorical thinking of the Houyhnhnms. As in the Cartesian
Science Maritain describes, Houyhnhnm reason is reduced in power; it
cannot deal with a mystery, the mystery of human nature: better to elimi-
nate it from experience.[30]

Mathematics, Extension, and Violence

In the criticisms leveled by Swift and Maritain, the independence of the
Cartesian mind from external reality is linked, through the doctrine of intuition, to Descartes's tendency to reduce the degrees of certitude to
one—mathematical certitude. As presented by both Maritain and Swift, this
adherence to mathematical certitude, combined with Descartes's conviction
that external reality is mere extension, leads to another accusation against
him: the violent consequences, both upon thought and upon external reality,
to which Cartesianism gives rise.

In Maritain's view, such intellectual violence occurs because, "drunk
with mathematics," the Cartesian mind performs "Cartesian analysis." That
is, such a mind engages in "cutting up and leveling down," thereby ignoring and destroying "the originality and diversity of natures, and violently
bring[ing] everything back to...simple principles."[31] Moreover,
Cartesianism views external nature (including the human body), reductively,
as "perfectly clear to our human perception, being nothing but geometrical
extension, perfectly subject to our spirit in cognition before being perfectly
subject to in practice."[32]

As a result, Maritain finds, the Cartesian intellect seeks not to understand but to conquer nature, for, having received all its knowledge by infusion
from God, it can have no other posture toward the external world. The good
of the soul is thereby reduced from contemplation of the divine "to the domi-

in its first genuine debate over the question of what to do about Gulliver and about the Yahoos;
they experience wonder and disagreement, both evidently for the first time. Moreover, the
Houyhnhnm Master conceals the whole truth about the Grand Assembly's decision from Gulliver
for a while, an omission in tension with the Houyhnhnms' supposed ignorance of the concept
of lying (Swift, *Gulliver's Travels*, pt. IV, chap. 9: pp. 271-73; chap. 10: pp. 279-80). Perhaps
they are on their way toward a more complete rationality than they have exhibited heretofore.

[30]Cf. the first paragraph of Descartes' Rule Two in *Rules for the Direction of Mind*, in
Philosophical Writings, vol. 1: pp. 10-11.

[31] *Three Reformers*, p. 73. See the extensive discussion of how external reality is to be
approached: Rule Fourteen, in *Rules for the Direction of Mind*, in *Philosophical Writings*, vol.
1: pp. 56-65.

[32] *Three Reformers*, pp. 74-75.

nation of the physical universe." The "Cartesian angel," the intellect, wearing its own mechanical body, is, in Maritain's evocative phrasing, "iron-gloved, and extends its sovereign action over the corporeal world by the innumerable arms of Machinery!"[33]

Cartesian science, then, is not concerned to grasp the substance and causes of the physical world, but to "spread over the physical world...an immense network of quantitative relations and of theories which save sensible appearances," all in order to subject nature by hard work to our pleasure and safety. The Cartesian angel, the intellect, in collusion with the occultism of the Renaissance, is guilty, says Maritain, of "spiritual concupiscence," a "mystical covetousness of the earth."[34] The desire to possess and control the earth leads to tyranny over it.

Swift depicts the violent effects of Cartesian mathematization in his treatment of the Laputans in *Gulliver's Travels*, Part III. Their intellects—like one of their eyes, turned inward—contemplate geometric patterns and music. They impose these patterns upon external objects. They reshape food, for instance: at one dinner, they present Gulliver with "a Shoulder of Mutton, cut into an Æquilateral Triangle, a Piece of Beef into a Rhomboides, and a Pudding into a Cycloid. The second Course was two Ducks, trussed up into the Form of Fiddles." Bread is cut "into Cones, Cylinders, Parallelograms." When fitting Gulliver for a suit of clothes, the tailor takes his customer's height with "a Quadrant, and then, with Rule and Compasses, described the Dimensions and Out-Lines of [his] whole body." The clothes do not fit at all, but that does not matter, for, gazing inwardly upon mathematical forms, no one notices anyway.[35]

This habit of imposing their self-absorbed will upon the external world takes a tyrannical, indeed violent, turn in their dealings with the people who live below the flying island, which can move over a limited set of islands below. The Laputans support their kingdom by extorting taxes from the peoples who live below. If a city rebels or refuses to pay, the Laputans cause the island to hover over the landscape, cutting off the sun and rain, causing dearth and disease; and they sometimes throw down "great Stones." Faced with the loss of their crops and with destruction, the earthbound folks usually submit or pay up. If they do not, the Laputan King lets "the Island drop directly upon their Heads, which makes a universal Destruction both of Houses and Men."[36]

---

[33] Ibid., pp. 63-64.
[34] *Dream of Descartes*, pp. 101-02. For Descartes's relationship with Rosicrucianism, see ibid., pp. 17-19.
[35] *Gulliver's Travels*, pt. III, chap. 2, pp. 161-62.
[36] Ibid., pt. III, chap. 3, p. 138.

The Cartesian soul, gazing only upon itself to find truth and value, resorts to tyrannical violence, crushing human communities when its will is opposed.

Swift presents the most telling illustration of the violence resulting from the mathematical Cartesian soul in *A Modest Proposal*. The putative author is Swift's most famous Projector, i.e., someone with a grand plan to rescue humanity from danger and pain. In this case, the Projector's proclaimed motivation is pity for the Irish. "[M]elancholy" at the sight of destitute children and mothers—beggars, many of them resorting to prostitution—he wishes to save the children from abortion and infanticide and the mothers from the shame of illegitimate pregnancy, "which would move tears and pity in the most savage and inhuman breast."[37]

These pity-laden phrases drop from view, however, in the Projector's discussion of the elements of his scheme. In the same early paragraphs, the pitiable child and mother are recast into farm animals, "a child just dropped from its dam." The Projector seeks a "fair, cheap, and easy method" of making the children "sound and useful members of the commonwealth." He finds the "other projectors" to have been "grossly mistaken in the computation."[38] The Cartesian analytical method—which turns logic into a version of addition and subtraction,[39] which works, Maritain says, by ignoring the nature of the subject and by breaking it down into its parts—then emerges sharply into focus:

> The *number* of souls in Ireland being usually *reckoned one million and a half*, of these I *calculate* there may be about *two hundred thousand* couples whose wives are *breeders*, from which *number* I *subtract thirty thousand* couples who are able to maintain their own children, although I apprehend there cannot be so many under the present distresses of the kingdom, but this being granted, there will *remain an hundred and seventy thousand breeders*. I again *subtract fifty thousand* for those women who miscarry, or whose children die by accident or disease within the year.[40]

I have emphasized the mathematical and dehumanizing diction in order to highlight Swift's implication that the supposedly compassionate Projector is a madman whose pity, working through mathematical analysis, treats the Irish poor as though they were animals—units of production and sale—on what we would now term an industrial farm. And what do we do with such animals? Why, eat them of course: "I have been assured by a very knowing

---

[37] *Modest Proposal*, in *Gulliver's Travels and Other Writings*, pp. 440.

[38] Ibid., pp. 439-40.

[39] Rule Eighteen, in *Rules for the Direction of Mind, in Philosophical Writings*, vol. 1, pp. 71-76.

[40] *Modest Proposal*, p. 440.

American of my acquaintance...that a young healthy child well nursed is at a year old a most delicious, nourishing and wholesome food, whether stewed, roasted, baked, or boiled, and I make no doubt that it will equally serve in a fricassee, or a ragout."[41] The Projector goes on in this vein, amply illustrating Swift's and Maritain's view that Cartesian Science, treating the external world as extension, issues in violence.

Pride, Progress, and Anxiety

Such violence toward nature and toward their fellow human beings seems to arise from a fifth characteristic criticized by both Maritain and Swift. What would make one believe that reshaping natural objects according to formulas in one's head or that treating peasants and their children as farm animals is morally acceptable? The answer, from both Maritain and Swift, is Pride, the vice Maritain discerns at the center of Descartes's character: "The pride of human knowledge appears thus as the very substance, solid and resistant, of rationalist hopes. Pride, a dense pride without frivolity or distraction, as stable as virtue, as vast as geometric extension, bitter and restless as the ocean, takes possession of Descartes to such an extent that it would seem the universal form of his interior workings and the principle of all his suffering."[42] Both writers claim that Descartes's procedures put him, and those influenced by him, *above and outside* of nature, including the rest of the human race. As noted, Maritain calls this "flight of pure intellect" *angelism*, a term he uses throughout his writings to indicate Descartes's prideful attempt to make human thought independent of intercourse with men and things.[43]

The episode by the German stove is representative, according to Maritain, of Descartes's belief that the "first condition of an intellectual amongst men...is to flee them."[44] In the same vein, Descartes is a "savage ravager of the past," that is of his intellectual heritage. He disparages all learning prior to him—all science, all philosophy, all theology, all poetry—because he wants to be an independent mind in every sense of the word and because he does not perceive that intellectual progress is made by deepening and extending the understanding of previous generations through dialog with them: "he does not understand the essential function of time in bringing human cognition to

---

[41] Ibid., p. 441.
[42] *Dream of Descartes,* p. 56.
[43] *Three Reformers*, pp. 54-55.
[44] Ibid., p. 53.

maturity."[45] Outside of time, outside of the community of learning, Descartes, as we have seen, also places himself outside of nature. His understanding hangs "immediately upon God, *rising above* and measuring all material nature without receiving anything from it."[46] His rationalist followers seem to agree with Descartes's self-assessment, promoting the image of him as outside of time and space, a savior-hero, overthrowing the past. They "delight in picturing him as the breaker of fetters suddenly come down from heaven[,] to sunder the chains of dogma[,] and to set reason free; one who[,] confronting as a demigod an age still under the yoke of authority[,] derives all his strength from himself alone."[47]

Similarly accusing them of pride, Swift too presents Descartes, and those influenced by him, as self-consciously and willfully above their fellow human beings and above or outside of nature. Rejoicing like the Laputans in being above his fellow creatures, the Spider in *The Battle of the Books* builds its geometric web, which, like Descartes, he spins out of himself, "in the highest Corner of a large Window."[48] The Battle in the story breaks out because the Moderns want the Ancients to lower their peak on Mt. Parnassus so that the Moderns's peak will be higher.

Along the same lines, in *The Tale of a Tub*, the Grubstreet Hack muses upon the need to be above the audience, "in a *superior Position of Place*" (emphasis in original). He reflects upon three traditional means—the pulpit, the ladder, and the stage-itinerant—associated respectively with Presbyterian preachers, orators (such as politicians or those condemned to hang), and mountebanks. Why must the speaker gain such a position of superiority? Because, the Hack speculates in full Cartesian (and Hobbist) mode, words are made of air and are therefore "Bodies of much Weight and Gravity." It follows that they "must be delivered from a due Altitude," or else they cannot be aimed well and will not fall hard enough upon the hearers. In order to assure that listeners will receive these weighty words, "Nature...hath instructed the Hearers to stand with their Mouths open, and erected parallel to the Horizon, so as they may be intersected by a perpendicular Line from the Zenith to the Center of the Earth." If "the Audience be well Compact," ev-

---

[45] Ibid., p. 62.
[46] Ibid. Emphasis added.
[47] *Dream of Descartes*, p. 33.
[48] Swift, "A Full and True Account of the Battle Fought Last Friday between the Ancient and Modern Books in St. James's Library, attached to The Tale of a Tub," in *A Tale of a Tub and Other Early Works, 1696-1707*, pp. 147, 142-43. The episode of the Spider and the Bee in *Battle of the Books* is an almost perfect allegory of the contrast between Cartesianism and traditional thought.

eryone will catch a share of something in his open mouth.[49] Given the Hack's talk about eructation (noted earlier), we can have little doubt as to what these people are ingesting.

The sort of pride spoken of to this point is self-regarding. Governed by an inflated vision of his own worth, the Cartesian seeks to be alone or above other men and nature because he believes his mind places him there. But, as Swift and Maritain see it, Cartesian pride has another dimension: even while seeking to flee men, the Cartesian seeks their applause, seeks glory. The Projector in *A Modest Proposal* puts forward his scheme with a view to helping Ireland. He lists at length the advantages of the proposal that will accrue both to the nation and to the poor in the future. He has in view another prospective event, however—his own glorification: "…whoever could find out a fair, cheap, and easy method of making these children sound and useful members of the commonwealth would deserve so well of the public as to have his statue set up for a preserver of the nation."[50] Here we come upon the sixth feature of Cartesianism criticized by both Swift and Maritain: that in the Cartesian soul, pride and aspiration for personal glory are commingled with two other characteristics: progressivism and anxiety for the future.

As perceived by both Swift and of Maritain, Cartesianism is willing to betray or violate the permanent good, the essential good—human nature itself, justice, the peaceful round of ordinary life—in order to strive for a future practical good that will supposedly preserve safety or increase comfort, and bring glory to the prideful Cartesian. In *Tale of a Tub*, for example, the Grubstreet Hack is in a state of frantic desperation about the place of the moderns, principally himself, in relation to the ancients. He writes a Dedication to Prince Posterity, pleading with Posterity to value the works of the moderns over those of the ancients, even though the writings of the moderns—his fellow Grubstreet hacks—are so ephemeral that he cannot find any of them to read. As a result, the Hack can offer no "Particulars" about the books to justify the honors he is sure they deserve from Posterity, who, it should be noted, does not yet exist.[51]

Later, in Section 5 ("A Digression in the Modern Kind"), the Hack sounds a different note than in his earlier concern about the reputations of the Moderns in posterity. Worried about his own reputation in the present, not the future, he deploys a variation of the Baconian paradox, claiming it "fit to lay hold on that great and honourable Privilege of being the Last Writer. I claim an absolute Authority in Right, as the freshest Modern,

---

[49] *Tale of a Tub,* sect. 1, p. 36.
[50] *Modest Proposal,* p. 439.
[51] *Tale of a Tub,* p. 21.

which gives me a Despotick Power over all Authors before me."[52] The most recent writer is perforce the best writer *because* he is the most recent writer: as in his worry about the evanescent reputations of the Moderns, the inherent quality of his work is not an issue. The Hack is so desperate for recognition and despotic power that he lays claim to them based on temporal occurrence, freshness. He does not seem to notice that any writer who publishes a day, or even an hour, after he does will be able to usurp his throne. Fifteen minutes of fame indeed.

The Hack's willingness to sacrifice consideration of inherent literary value for the sake of future recognition has a parallel, though not an exact one, in the practical life of Balnibarbi, an island nation subject to Laputa in *Gulliver's Travels,* Part III, where anxiety about the future arises from faith in technological progress that sets aside the traditional good.[53] Lord Munodi, one of the few sane Balnibarbians, guides Gulliver through his nation and Lagado, its principal city, including the Grand Academy, Swift's parody of a research institution. Melancholy over what is happening to his nation, Munodi explains to Gulliver that, influenced by a stay in Laputa, the Cartesian flying island, certain Balnibarbians began to dislike the traditional way of life to which they were returning. They "fell into Schemes of putting all Arts, Sciences, Languages, and Mechanics upon a new Foot." To that end, they established the Grand Academy, in which Projectors can "contrive new Rules and Methods of Agriculture and Building, and new Instruments and Tools for all Trades and Manufactures."[54] Their aim is technological progress that will bring about a material paradise, in which one person can do the work of many, in which structures will last forever, and in which crops will bloom all year round.

These novel techniques do not bring about the material prosperity anticipated, however. On his way through Lagado, Gulliver notices that the houses are "very strangely built, and most of them out of Repair" and that the countryside bears no crops, despite the busy activities of the populace, "whose Countenances and Habit expressed so much Misery and Want." Misery and want are accompanied in the population by anxiety, the psychological damage consequent upon excessive concern about the future: "The People in the Streets walked fast, looked wild, their Eyes fixed, and were generally in Rags."[55]

[52] Ibid., Sect. 5, p. 81.
[53] *Gulliver's Travels*, pt. III, chap. 4, pp. 172-78.
[54] Ibid., pp. 176-77.
[55] Ibid., pp. 174-75.

Jacques Maritain sounds similar notes about Cartesian self-glorification, emphasis on the future, and bustle, though less pervasively than Swift.[56] Pride, as we have seen, at the core of rationalism, according to Maritain, who observes that Cartesian Science, because it springs from the God-infused knowledge within us, would soon, in Descartes's view, be able to "exhaust" reality. And, according to Maritain, Descartes *is* proud, not only because he provides the source and theoretical power of Science, but also because of the practical effects of his work, effects to be seen in the future. His work will eventually provide human happiness, after two or three centuries—an earthly, not a heavenly, bliss but conditions of life much better than those of the seventeenth century.[57] The originator of Science, like the Balnibarbians, "has no time to lose, he is a man in a hurry (like all moderns). If he can only snatch some tens of years from death, the great work on which the happiness and perfection of humanity depend will be done."[58]

This outline of the charges Swift and Maritain level at Descartes—irrationality, self-absorbed intuitionism, a violent posture toward nature and human nature, pride mingled with anxiety—should not mislead us into thinking that the two critics are alike in all their thoughts. Swift, to take one important example, thoroughly dislikes St. Thomas Aquinas, placing him on the side of the Moderns in *The Battle of the Books*. Nevertheless, that two thinkers of such magnitude—one flourishing at the beginnings of the Cartesian triumph over Western thought, the other flourishing in our time, when the incoherencies of modernism are becoming increasingly apparent—that two such disparately placed and culturally formed thinkers arrive at strikingly similar criticisms, expressed in such cogent arguments and images, should give our pervasively Cartesian culture pause.

---

[56] Maritain's rather tendentious description of Descartes indicates the former's belief in the latter's pride: "the head superbly heavy and vehement, the low forehead, the discreet, stubborn, fanciful eye, the mouth proud and earthly": *Three Reformers*, p. 53.

[57] *Dream of Descartes*, pp. 56-57.

[58] *Three Reformers*, p. 62.

The Politics of Realism
Locke, Maritain, and Hallowell on Liberalism and Knowledge

Douglas A. Ollivant

The rapid spread of liberal regimes in the developed world has been the most notable of the positive political stories of the twentieth century. Throughout the West—and increasingly in other parts of the world—constitutional governments dedicated to protecting, or at least obligated to protect, the rights of their citizens have become the norm. The rise of these states has resulted in an increase in the official recognition of human dignity unthinkable only two hundred years ago. Across the world, the wealthiest and most powerful nations are, for the most part, measured and regularly called to account, through their own constitutional mechanisms, based on how they treat their citizens as human beings—as persons. In fact, it appears that despite continuing pockets of nationalism and tribalism, liberalism has created an ideological hegemony within the developed world. Despite the myriad of political problems we continue to face, the positive effects of this achievement cannot be denied. As John Paul II has himself said, reflecting on the new human rights regimes, "it is impossible for the Christian conscience not to be moved by this."[1]

Yet, this achievement, beginning in the eighteenth century and continuing to the present day, seems to have come about almost solely due to the rise of liberal philosophy—and concurrent decline of Christianity—in the West. This philosophy—expounded by Constant, Kant, and Mill, but ultimately rooted in Locke[2]—maintains that all human beings are autonomous, and must be free to exercise their personal liberty, or freedom.

Locke maintains that persons must be free to pursue their own happiness, which Locke defines as the pursuit of pleasure and the avoidance of pain. This

---

[1] Charles Taylor, "A Catholic Modernity" in *A Catholic Modernity? Charles Taylor's Marianist Award Lecture*, ed. James L. Heft, (New York: Oxford University Press, 1999), p. 18.

[2] "...to the extent that modern liberalism can be said to be inspired by any one writer, Locke is undoubtedly the leading candidate." Sheldon Wolin, *Politics and Vision: Continuity and Innovation in Western Political Thought* (Boston: Little, Brown, and Company, 1960), p. 293.

pursuit of happiness is grounded in Locke's own epistemology and philosophical anthropology[3]—largely outlined in his *Essay Concerning Human Understanding*. In the *Essay*, Locke makes a series of epistemological claims. First, men have no innate ideas. Second, all knowledge comes via sensation; the interaction of our sensory organs with external objects. Third, our complex ideas that are constructed from these sensations fall "short of the reality of things."[4] These tenets are a radical departure from the epistemology of moderate realism in the Western philosophical tradition.[5] The promulgation of these ideas are at least correlated with—if they are not the cause of—the "emotivism" and lack of "unassailable criteria" that dominate public life in the West.[6]

This exposition of Lockean epistemology presents the Christian reader with a dilemma. Despite its dark underside, liberalism has undeniably resulted in a vast expansion of human dignity unparalleled in human history.[7] The expansions of civil rights, of the franchise, and of access to education promoted by liberal regimes (albeit often spurred by Christian groups and/or movements) have all promoted a general increase in personal autonomy. This development should be welcomed and cherished by Christians of all stripes.

Yet this liberal philosophy rests on an epistemology that can only be described as skeptical, or neo-sophistic, denying the ability of the person truly to know the world in which he or she lives.[8] This is disturbing, as the Protestant political theorist John Hallowell convincingly linked this epistemological doubt

---

[3] And ultimately, his implicit metaphysics.

[4] John Locke, *An Essay Concerning Human Understanding*, ed. Peter H. Nidditch (Oxford: Oxford University, 1975), p. 539.

[5] I will use the following as a working definition of "moderate realism": "These basic beliefs of mankind are also the three basic doctrines of realistic philosophy: (1) There is a world of real existence which men have not made or constructed; (2) this real existence can be known by the human mind; and (3) such knowledge is the only reliable guide to human conduct, individual and social." John Wild, *Introduction to Realistic Philosophy* (New York: Harper and Brothers Publishers, 1948), p. 6.

[6] Alasdair MacIntyre, *After Virtue* (Notre Dame, Indiana: University of Notre Dame Press, 1984), pp. 6-17.

[7] This is not the venue in which to discuss liberalism's "dark underside." For recent explications see Francis Canavan, *The Pluralist Game: Pluralism, Liberalism, and the Moral Conscience* (Lanham, Maryland: Rowman and Littlefield Publishers, 1995) on the "dissolving of norms;" Paul Edward Gottfried, *After Liberalism: Mass Democracy in the Managerial State* (Princeton, New Jersey: Princeton University Press, 1999) on contemporary liberalism as a "managerial state" and John Gray, *Enlightenment's Wake: Politics and Culture at the Close of the Modern Age* (New York: Routledge, 1995) on liberalism's "implausibility and strangeness."

[8] Peter A. Redpath, *Masquerade of the Dream Walkers: Prophetic Theology from the Cartesians to Hegel* (Atlanta: Rodopi, 1998), pp. 33-36.

with the rise of totalitarianism in Nazi Germany. Hallowell's argument runs as follows. Liberalism espouses responsible freedom under the law, which is discoverable by reason. We must note, however, "only conscience bids the individual to follow the dictates of reason rather than those of interest."[9] It is not always "rational," from an economic or purely self-interested perspective, to "do the right thing." But it then follows that if the positive law can be restructured to promote one's interest (whether that of an individual, a vocal minority, or a tyrannical majority), rather than the demands of reason—which are, in Locke's account, vague, largely constructs and presumably manipulable—then this limitation can be overcome. Compliance with the new positive law (counter to the old demands of both reason and conscience) will sooth the conscience—as the much-observed phenomenon of the "good Germans" effectively demonstrated. And so long as there exists a mass belief in the relativism of truth, there is no check against such an occurrence. In fact, given our observations of human nature, one should regard such an outcome as at least likely, if not inevitable.

So the mass acceptance of Lockean epistemology, as Hallowell writes, makes a belief in natural law untenable, and thereby frees the State from any limitations other than its own enacted laws, placing the actions of the State beyond good and evil. Once the state rejects ethical limitations, it then "becomes completely irresponsible, ready to turn the control of its organs over to the group with the greatest power for ends which it selects."[10] In short, the adoption of Lockean epistemology, carried to its logical end, has proven itself to be a great enemy to that same recognition of human dignity and freedom that finds its basis in Locke's political teachings. How can these two seemingly incompatible observations be reconciled?

I will deal with this puzzle in three steps. First, I will explicate Locke's epistemology. Second, I examine the tensions between Locke's epistemology and his political theory. Finally, I then use the writings of Hallowell and the Catholic philosopher Jacques Maritain—two mid twentieth century writers who recognized serious difficulties with liberal thought—as a corrective to put forth a more "integral" version of liberalism. This modified liberalism should be able to avoid the excesses and errors—including widespread relativism and nihilism, "possessive individualism" (both economic and sexual), and the "culture of death"—of the current Lockean regimes.[11]

---

[9] John Hallowell, *The Decline of Liberalism as an Ideology: With Particular Reference to German Politico-Legal Thought* (New York: Howard Fertig, rpr., 1971), pp. 7-8.

[10] Ibid., p. 106.

[11] See *The Decline of Liberalism as an Ideology* and Jacques Maritain, *Integral Humanism* in *The Collected Works of Jacques Maritain*, Vol. 11, ed. Otto Bird (Notre Dame, Indiana: University of Notre Dame Press, 1996) on the terms "Integral Liberalism" and "Integral Humanism."

Lockean Epistemology

In his opening chapters, Locke quickly sets out the assumptions underlying his theory of knowledge he will present in his *Essay Concerning Human Understanding*. Locke maintains that men have "no innate principles in the mind" and that all knowledge is a product of sense impressions, both defensible assumptions.

However, as we progress through the text, we discover that Locke is not concerned with the objects of sensation themselves, but instead (turning from the object to the subject) the data which they convey to the mind through the senses. Locke labels the impressions conveyed upon the senses by the mysterious external object "simple ideas." These are the features an object causes us to experience—blueness, largeness, sweetness—that the Aristotelian tradition would call "qualities." From these simple ideas the mind, through the faculty of reflection, assembles complex ideas, or notions. These notions are of two types. There are those that exist only as notions—such as numbers and geometric shapes—and there are those that exist in the material world.

Our complex ideas that have a materially existing referent are labeled as substances. Substances have essences, even for Locke. In fact, they have two. The first essence Locke calls the real essence, that which truly categorizes an object. Locke acknowledges the existence of these real essences. However, he maintains that the real essences are knowable only by God—and perhaps the angels.[12]

Instead, Locke claims we mere mortals deal with nominal essences. As the name implies, these essences are more or less arbitrary categorizations based on our conception of the "powers" or simple ideas in a subject. Therefore, when we categorize by species, or form, or essence, we are not acknowledging the order of the universe, for these "species of Things to us, are nothing but the ranking them under distinct Names, according to the complex ideas in us; and not according to precise distinct real Essences in them."[13] Instead, he says, any glimmer we may have of perceptible order is an individual construct. To maintain that the orderings exist outside our minds is vanity, for:

> we in vain pretend to range Things into sorts, and dispose them into certain Classes, under Names, by their real Essences, that are so far from our discovery or comprehension. A blind man may as soon sort Things by the Colours, and he that has lost his Smell, as well distinguish a Lily and a Rose by their Odors, as by these internal Constitutions which he knows not.[14]

[12] *An Essay Concerning Human Understanding*, p. 440.
[13] Ibid., p. 443.
[14] Ibid., pp. 444-45.

We have neither sensory organ nor cognitive faculty to detect forms or essences—Locke claims—and therefore we cannot know them. God has not empowered his creatures to understand nature. Again, our "idea" of a substance, such as a man, "is only an imperfect Collection of some sensible Qualities and Powers in him."[15] We must, of our own accord, "build a bridge from thought to thing."[16]

Nature and the world around us then have little authority for Locke, since:

> [T]he general Propositions that are made about Substances, if they are certain, are for the most part trifling; and if they are instructive, are uncertain, and such as we can have no knowledge of their real Truth, how much soever constant Observation and Analogy may assist our Judgments in guessing.[17]

Therefore, any real knowledge human beings gain from nature is insignificant, and if humans believe they discern anything of consequence in nature, they are engaging in self-deception. Yet Locke is well known for introducing "natural law" into state of nature theory, essentially taming that Hobbesian condition with the introduction of a more robust natural law. But how, we may ask, do we derive a law of nature from a nature we cannot know?

Locke's answer seems to be that the person constructs a law of nature from the coherence of his or her ideas—simple and complex. The law of nature is "something that we being ignorant of may attain to the knowledge of, by the use and due application of our natural Faculties."[18] Locke is, ultimately, a very tentative metaphysical realist. He does believe that reality is out there, *extra mentem*—he simply thinks that persons perceive reality only in the dimmest sense. Locke maintains that the ideas persons acquire do reflect, however obscurely and with inevitable distortions, the order of the world. Therefore, by use of their reason, human beings can manufacture a reasonable construct—a self-referential system—that will help guide them through the world. While this construct will be imperfect, Locke maintains that men are not to seek happiness or understanding in this world anyway. The imperfection of our understanding should direct individuals towards the enjoyment of God, in whom there is "fullness of joy."[19] Presumably, the inevitable gaps in our merely coherent truth theory will give evidence to our lack of under-

---

[15] Ibid., p. 590.

[16] Jacques Maritain, *The Degrees of Knowledge*, trans. Gerald B. Phelan (Notre Dame, Indiana: University of Notre Dame Press, 1995), p. 75.

[17] *An Essay Concerning Human Understanding*, p. 615.

[18] Ibid., p. 75.

[19] Ibid., p. 130.

standing and point us to God. While this may be a troubling theory for some, it is internally consistent. Locke challenges us to doubt the correspondence between what we perceive and what truly exists.

Political Theory

However, when Locke moves from epistemology to political philosophy, his doubt that we can adequately know nature quickly disappears. For Locke is plain that there is "nothing more evident" than that "Creatures of the same species" should all be equal to each other. This is the key insight and premise necessary for a liberal theory of government. Unfortunately, in his *Essay*, Locke clearly stated that there were neither self-evident principles, nor truly distinguishable species. Therefore, despite its being affirmed in the *Second Treatise*, the equality of persons is implicitly denied by the *Essay*. In short, there appears to be a contradiction between Locke's epistemology and his political philosophy, despite the adamant objections of his defenders.[20]

The key inconsistency between Locke's two theories therefore comes to light. Locke specifically denies that humans can know that they are all of one species—and therefore in their essence—equal. Locke goes so far as to state that persons cannot be certain that all things born of women are humans, or even possessed of souls.[21] The basis of Locke's doctrine of human equality is then, at root, positivistic. Human beings cannot know that they are equal, but it is politically useful for them to believe so.

Locke's assertion that there exists a law of nature is then subject to a similar critique. It is simply that—an assertion—without justification or grounding in his epistemological treatise. Again, this stands in contrast to the classical teaching, in which epistemological realism and moral realism are closely linked.

---

[20] Peter Meyers in *Our Only Star and Compass: Locke and the Struggle for Political Rationality* (Lanham, Maryland: Rowman & Littlefield, 1998) defends this seeming contradiction as part of living in "a manifold state of tension." Meyers proposes Locke as a *via media* between subjectivism and "immoderately rationalist foundationalism"—presumably such as that proposed by Maritain. An alternative—and, I would argue, more probable—reading might claim that Locke's delicate balance between these two positions is a contingent and historical one, which Locke himself was partially responsible for disrupting, and which, at any rate, is no longer tenable.

[21] *An Essay Concerning Human Understanding*, pp. 570-72. It must be acknowledged that this aspect of Locke's thought has the potential to undermine the premise of this project. If the increase in human dignity promoted by liberal states is "purchased" through the denial of human dignity to "weak and defenseless human beings," this may indicate a net reduction, not increase, in the respect for human beings. See John Paul II *Evangelium Vitae [The Gospel of Life]* (Boston: Pauline Books and Media, 1995), especially para. 5.

For example, Aquinas's teaching holds that while what we perceive are the individual things, what is received by the intellect is the general form, as the matter which individuates the form is not transmitted to the intellect. Therefore, contra Locke, Aquinas does *not* hold that the intellect constructs a simulacrum of the species from the individual sense impressions, but instead receives the general form from the individual specimen.[22] The natural law (being those things to which human being naturally incline—whether *qua* substance, *qua* animal, or *qua* rational being) is also known in general terms. Therefore, when the natural law must be put into practice, the general principle is applied to the specific case—the species to the individual—and provided no perversion or evil intervenes, the law will be appropriately applied.[23]

However, Locke's epistemology holds that human beings are not naturally equipped to know nature. The general principles of the natural law, as explicated by Aquinas, are then not known, nor can they be. The reader must conclude that Locke's natural law is at the very least not effectively promulgated (if it exists at all) and therefore not truly law. Thus, the exercise of freedom permitted and encouraged by liberal political theory is almost certain to transgress this unpromulgated law, making a core tenet of Lockean liberalism—that men in the state of nature will observe the natural law and not harm each other—problematic at the very least.

Even if Locke is granted his premise that human beings ought not to harm each other, Locke does not allow us to know the species or form that constitutes a human being. Therefore, "human being" is simply a matter of nominal definition. This nominal definition could be overly inclusive, or (more likely) overly exclusive. History is, of course, rife with examples of the latter. "Barbarians," slaves, "kulaks," Jews, the handicapped, fetuses, the comatose and the elderly have all been deemed unworthy of the appellation "human" at one time or another. So if a society is able to arbitrarily define who must be treated as a human being, the protections of a Lockean natural law may not be extended to all human beings.

This qualification should lead one to question just how much liberty will exist in this liberal state for those left outside the definition. For even if the Lockean "moral relation" between human beings is correctly understood, it will—again—apply only to those who qualify as "human beings" under the nominal definition. For as Locke himself concedes, "all Relation terminates in, and is ultimately founded on those simple Ideas, we have got from Sensa-

---

[22] Thomas Aquinas, *An Aquinas Reader: Selections from the Writings of Thomas Aquinas*, ed. Mary T. Clark (New York: Fordham University Press, 1972), p. 239.

[23] Thomas Aquinas, *Summa Theologiae*, I-II, q. 94, a. 4 .

tion, or Reflection."[24] If our morality is only as reliable as are our senses, would not those with unreliable senses (and whose senses are infallible?) therefore have a deficient understanding of the natural law and be in state of truly invincible ignorance? Can Locke's epistemology co-exist with a belief that there exists a natural law, a law we "can't not know?"[25]

However, despite these disturbing implications, Locke's doctrines still form the core of contemporary liberalism. The "self-evident" equality of individuals has become part of our "secular faith," and this faith has been instrumental in the creation and maintenance of the human rights regimes. Yet these are beliefs without foundations. For example, as Richard Rorty freely concedes, modern philosophy—Locke seemingly included—simply posits these beliefs, the Christian tradition behind them being "...gratefully invoked by freeloading atheists...."[26] This candid admission by perhaps the most famous postmodern apologist of our time gives emphasis to the problem earlier formulated. Modern philosophy cannot defend the principles underlying the natural rights regimes. Developing this point, Robert Kraynak writes that Rorty is "a nonbeliever who demands that all people be treated with dignity and respect but offers no reason why, while thanking the Judeo-Christian tradition for allowing him to live off its teachings about human dignity. Rorty thus concedes Maritain's primary point, that democracy must be grounded on the transcendent dignity of the person as a creature of God."[27] We might follow up on Kraynak's point by asking whether Locke, in seeking another grounding, downplays this same transcendent dignity.

Accepting Aquinas's insight that we have true perceptions of being, or *esse*, we can adequately distinguish the species "man" from the other animals, and know that all human beings are persons.[28] The status of all human beings as persons encapsulates certain characteristics. All persons are spir-

---

[24] *An Essay Concerning Human Understanding*, p. 360.

[25] J. Budziszewski, "Denying What We Can't Not Know" in *Reassessing the Liberal State: Reading Maritain's Man and the State* (Washington, D.C.: American Maritain Assocation / The Catholic University of America Press, 2001).

[26] Richard Rorty, "Postmodern Bourgeois Liberalism", *The Journal of Philosophy* 80 (Oct 1983), pp. 583-89.

[27] Robert P. Kraynak, "Review of *Jacques Maritain: The Philosopher in Society* and *Jacques Maritain (1882-1973): Christian Democrat, and the Quest for a New Commonwealth*" *Journal of Politics* 61:3 (August 1999), pp. 862-64.

[28] "Reality and the knowing mind, then, are not to be conceived as the two separate though somehow interrelated hemispheres of all that is. Instead, reality is the field of reference for the mind, and the mind is the active (more precisely: the actively accepting and receiving) center of the field of reference. All that is, is true." Joseph Pieper, *Living the Truth* (San Francisco: Ignatius Press, 1989), p. 80.

its, or are partially composed of spirit, thereby liberating them from the strict determinism of the material. All persons participate "in the absolute being" and their continued existence is not subject to material utilitarianism. In short, all persons are rooted in the exemplar causality of the Trinity itself and receive an inherent dignity from this created status. In Maritain's formulation:

> To say that a man is a person is to say that in the depths of his being his is more a whole than a part and more independent than servile. It is to say that he is a minute fragment of matter that is at the same time a universe, a beggar who participates in the absolute being, mortal flesh whose value is eternal, and a bit of straw into which heaven enters. It is this metaphysical mystery that religious thought designates when it says that the person is the image of God. The value of the person, his dignity and rights, belong to the order of things naturally sacred which bear the imprint of the Father of Being, and which have in Him the end of their movement.[29]

This status as persons gives men a claim to independence, or liberty— the key ingredient of modern liberalism. However, Maritain argues that certain influential moderns have tragically misunderstood this liberty—here he singles out Rousseau and Kant:

> According to them, man is free *only if he obeys himself alone*, and man is constituted by right of nature in such a state of freedom (which Rousseau considered as lost owing to the corruption involved in social life and which Kant relegated to the noumenal world. In a word, we have here a divinization of the individual, the logical consequences of which are, in the practical and social order: (1) a practical atheism in society (for there is no place for two gods in the world, and if the individual is in practice god, God is no longer God except perhaps in a decorative way and for private use); (2) the theoretical and practical disappearance of the idea of the common good; (3) the theoretical and practical disappearance of the responsible leader, and of the idea of authority falsely considered to be incompatible with freedom.[30]

This misunderstanding is necessitated by modern philosophy, which does not tolerate an equivocal understanding of freedom. Instead, the contemporary definition of freedom denies that the freedom proper to creatures might be only analogous to the freedom of the creator. This dogmatically univocal definition further maintains that "there is neither freedom nor autonomy except insofar as no objective rule or measure is received from a being other than oneself."[31]

---

[29] Jacques Maritain, "The Conquest of Freedom" in *The Education of Man*, ed. Donald and Idella Gallagher (Garden City, New York: Doubleday, 1962), pp. 163-64.

[30] Ibid., p. 170.

[31] Ibid., p. 167.

This view of freedom is also implicit in Locke's epistemology. While Locke will speak at length of the "natural law" in his "state of nature," this law is a law of reason, independently constructed from the various "Ideas" received by the senses and processed by the intellect. Each person is then "free" to create his or her own private universe, governed by laws of his or her interpretation. Despite Locke's attempt to found the polity on consent, only fraud, force or the threat of force can create a political consensus under such a law, unlimited by either innate ideas or an intuition of being.[32] We see the threat of force implicitly in Locke's "golden rule," commanding us not to harm each other as we are—at the core—God's property. The *Second Treatise* reminds us that in the State of Nature, all men being equal, none ought to harm another:

> For Men being all the Workmanship of one Omnipotent, and infinitely wise Maker; All the Servants of one Sovereign Master, sent into the World by his order and about his business, they are his Property, whose Workmanship they are, made to last during his, not one anothers Pleasure.[33]

The threat of Divine retribution is clearly discernible here. Thus the "fear of the Lord"—used in a less than Christian sense—is the mechanism that ensures the counter-Hobbesian character of Locke's state of nature. Locke's consent is made possible only by the threat of God's force.

Locke's glorification of our independent reasoning, based on his highly subjective—and therefore deeply questionable—epistemology, does serve to advance the cause of freedom, albeit in a debased form. However, the idea of freedom, whatever its root, carries with it an imprint, however faint, of the inherent dignity of the person. It is here that we begin to see the unraveling of our modern mystery. The philosophy underlying the modern liberal state carries a powerful truth—the freedom and dignity of the human person—which is not yet totally negated by the "capital error" so closely bound with it. To borrow Maritain's language, the modern democratic movements have not only sought, but also to some extent obtained "true political emancipation under false standards."[34]

But while the freedom gained by such a philosophy is real, the stability of the political consensus underlying it is illusory. For this philosophy of

[32] See also Eugene J. Roesch, *The Totalitarian Threat: The Fruition of Modern Individualism, as Seen in Hobbes and Rousseau* (New York: Philosophical Library Inc., 1963), pp. 147-51.

[33] John Locke, *Two Treatises of Government*, ed. Peter Laslett (Cambridge: Cambridge University Press, 1960), p. 271.

[34] "The Conquest of Freedom," p. 169.

freedom is based on the belief that man is free to posit his own definition of truth. And all good readers of Aquinas and Aristotle know what happens to a *parvus error* in the end.

Hallowell and Maritain

It is at this point that realism, buttressed by Christian belief, calls the reader to a higher understanding of truth. In an age when modern writers such as Vaclav Havel and Aleksandr Solzhenitsyn have clearly shown us the need to live "in light of the truth" and acknowledge the "power of the word," we may have a historic opportunity to clearly articulate such a truth.[35] In short, there is a need to distinguish between theories of liberty which acknowledge the existence and comprehensibility of external truths and those which do not, as well as to demonstrate the dangerous—and ultimately totalitarian—nature of theories which deny our access to truth.

John Hallowell and Jacques Maritain recognized this need, and sought to ground an "Integral Liberalism" (in Hallowell's terms) in a Christian anthropology, known through a moderate realism, resulting in a Christian Realism (in a non-Niebuhrian sense). Both Hallowell and Maritain were unapologetic about this need. Hallowell maintained that, "Only through a return to faith in God, as God revealed Himself to man in Jesus Christ, can modern man and his society find redemption from the tyranny of evil."[36] Similarly, Maritain called fellow Catholics to a "politics intrinsically Christian by its principles, its spirit, its modality, and the claim to proceed in this world to a vitally Christian political action."[37] Why did both Hallowell and Maritain seek a "New Christendom," given the abuses of power by the Old? They both saw a necessity to reform certain principles that were being abused by modern liberalism and were no longer defensible in either theistic or even pragmatic terms. Maritain summed the failure of modern liberalism:

> In modern times an attempt was made to base the life of civilization and the earthly community on the foundation of mere reason—reason separated from religion and the Gospel. This attempt fostered immense hopes in the last two centuries, and rapidly faded. Pure reason appeared more incapable than faith of

[35] Peter Augustine Lawler, *Postmodernism Rightly Understood: The Return to Realism in American Thought* (Lanham, Maryland: Rowman & Littlefield, 1999), pp. 1-13. See also *Living the Truth.*

[36] John Hallowell, *Main Currents in Modern Political Thought* (Lanham, Maryland: University Press of America, rpr., 1984), p. 651.

[37] *Integral Humanism*, p. 319.

insuring the spiritual unity of mankind, and the dream of a "scientific" creed uniting men in peace, and in common convictions about the aims and basic principles of human life and society vanished in contemporary catastrophes. In proportion as the tragic events of the last decades have given the lie to the optimistic rationalism of the eighteenth and nineteenth centuries, we have been confronted with the fact that religion and metaphysics are an essential part of human culture, primary and indispensable incentives in the very life of society.[38]

To once again return to Locke—an architect of the "foundation of mere reason"— his theory of freedom is grounded in the quasi-historical *de facto* freedom of man in a virtually law-less "State of Nature." Since human beings did not relinquish this freedom in the "social contract," they still retain said freedom even upon entering civil society. However, this freedom is unlimited by natural laws, save for a few positivistic ones—namely not to harm another in his person or possessions—given by God. Among men not enlightened by Christian revelation, customs dictate numerous variations on the law. The only law universally known is that of self-preservation.[39] This is entirely consistent with Locke's epistemology in the *Essay*, which maintains that "Things" are "wholly separate and distinct" from both actions which bring happiness, and the signs which order knowledge.[40]

Therefore, Locke's political order, in Dunn's phrasing, relies "for [its] very intelligibility, let alone plausibility, on a series of theological commitments,"—namely those of a heterodox, nominalist Protestantism, probably Socianism.[41] Once these theological commitments are challenged—whether by atheism or orthodoxy—the gaps in Locke's political philosophy quickly surface. If an atheist examines Locke's theory, she will find his "State of Nature" to be indistinguishable from that of Hobbes, therefore requiring an absolute sovereign to save man from his fellow man in the State of Nature. When examined by an orthodox Christian, the very concept of a State of Nature becomes problematic, as does the paucity of Locke's "positivistic" natural law.

But again, the saving grace of Locke's theory is that while the foundation is—at best—shaky, much of the superstructure is sound. This

---

[38] Jacques Maritain, "The Pluralist Principle in Democracy: A Qualified Agreement" in *The Social and Political Philosophy of Jacques Maritain* ed. Joseph W. Evans and Leo R. Ward (New York: Charles Scribner's Sons, 1955), pp. 116-22.

[39] John Locke, *Questions Concerning the Law of Nature*, ed. Robert Horowitz, Jenny Strauss Clay, and Diskin Clay (Ithaca, New York: Cornell University, 1990), pp. 183-93.

[40] *An Essay Concerning Human Understanding*, p. 721.

[41] John Dunn, *The Political Thought of John Locke: A Historical Account of the Argument of the "Two Treatises of Government"* (Cambridge: Cambridge University Press, 1969), p. xi; *Our Only Star and Compass*, p. 23.

superstructure—the regimes of human dignity—provides the basis for the practical "secular faith" of which Maritain speaks—the "practical points of convergence" on which all men of good will can agree.[42]

But—as one earlier reader asked pointedly—if the premises of modernity are false, then how can a sound superstructure, these regimes of dignity, exist? A rotten tree does not bear good fruit, and people do not pick fruit from thorn-bushes. This is indeed a difficult question, but I suggest at least two possible answers. The first borrows from theology, and notes that heretical sects often preserve certain truths better than do the orthodox. For example, a good Catholic must believe the Protestant Reformation to be a rebellion against the true Church. However, in all honesty, the same Catholic must admit that within Protestantism, certain aspects of the faith—particularly a dedication to the study of Holy Scripture and a passion for evangelism—have been more faithfully retained, and perhaps even better developed, than in Catholic practice. A similar effect may be at work in liberal regimes, preserving human dignity in a more complete manner than did "confessional states."

But perhaps a better explanation may be found in Jacques Barzun's most recent work, *From Dawn to Decadence*. Barzun notes that, while modernity assumes that science precedes engineering—that an intellectual must conceptualize the idea before a practical worker can bring it into being—in fact the historical record indicates the converse to often be the case. "Inventors made machines before anybody could explain why they worked…. This sequence of practice before theory has its parallel in literature and the fine arts, which says something important about the workings of the human mind and the essence of culture."[43] In other words, the West may have produced a political culture that still awaits a theory to explain how and why it works. This argument does not discount the insight that "ideas have consequences." However—painful as it may be for academics to admit—not all consequences are the result of philosophical ideas. The oft-maligned common people may be able to work out certain practical solutions and agreements, based on natural reason. Liberal democracy may be perhaps the most notable of these solutions, what Maritain referred to as a "practical conclusion."[44]

Such practical agreements are wonderful things for federal amalgamations, and International Charters. However, the local community—the civil society—should be able to produce something more substantive, rejecting a

---

[42] Jacques Maritain, *Man and the State* (Chicago: The University of Chicago Press, 1951), p. 111.

[43] Jacques Barzun, *From Dawn to Decadence: 500 Years of Western Cultural Life, 1500 to the Present* (New York: HarperCollins, 2000), pp. 205-06.

[44] *Man and the State*, p. 115.

skeptical "overlapping consensus." But again, the problem is that of the *parvus error*, which becomes large in the end. While Lockean liberalism is largely responsible for the expansion of human dignity in the world, it now threatens to degenerate into its logical conclusion—a thoughtless, soft nihilism.[45] It is the task of a Christian philosophy to provide a truthfully grounded liberalism that is not self-consuming.

Maritain clearly posits just what this foundation should be. For Maritain, "the idea of man propounded by the metaphysics of Aristotle and Thomas Aquinas is the rational foundation of democratic philosophy."[46] Rather than principles off which Rortian ironists may "freeload", however, these ideas of man must be foundational to the self-conception of truly free states.

This "idea of man" is a simple one. Contrary to Locke, Maritain maintains—following St. Thomas—that we can know the species of man, for the "quiddity" of a thing "is the first and proper object of the intellect."[47] Truth, then, is not an internally coherent system, but instead a conformity "between the being possessed by the thing and the being affirmed by the mind."[48] The intellect considers not sense ideas and its reflections thereupon, but the form and being of the object[49]—allowing classification of particulars by their essences, not accidental properties.

The implication of this Thomistic insight, philosophically retrieved by Maritain (*inter alia*), is perhaps best expressed politically by John Hallowell:

> When integrally conceived, liberalism postulated as its fundamental premise the absolute value of human personality. Conceiving as the essence of human individuality a God-given soul it espouses individual equality, in a spiritual sense. Each individual is regarded as potentially worthy of salvation, in the sense of fulfilling his destiny or function in the light of his talents and capacity. Hence, individuals are never means but always, as equal moral entities, ends in themselves...
> As its ideal, therefore, liberalism posits freedom under the impersonal rule of law, the law being conceived as filled with certain eternal objective truths and values discoverable by reason. The existence of objective truth and value, of transcendental standards, is presupposed.[50]

Hallowell's integral liberalism then relies on the Thomistic "critical realism" as laid out by Maritain. Just as the false epistemology of modern philosophy

---

[45] *The Pluralist Game*, pp. 125-29; See also Peter Berkowitz, *Virtue and the Making of Modern Liberalism* (Princeton, New Jersey: Princeton University Press, 1999), p. 178.

[46] "The Pluralist Principle in Democracy," p. 121.

[47] *Summa Theologiae*, I, q. 85, a. 5.

[48] *The Degrees of Knowledge*, p. 94.

[49] Though these are transmitted through the sensible species. See *Summa Theologiae*, I, q. 85, a. 2.

[50] *The Decline of Liberalism as an Ideology*, p. 109.

mandates a liberalism that ends in positivism, so a philosophy of critical realism allows for a just and stable integral liberalism. As Hallowell writes elsewhere, "true freedom requires both knowledge of the good and the will to choose the good when known. The denial of either is a denial of freedom."[51]

Locke's doctrines do not allow for knowledge of the good. Since we cannot know the essences of things, but only the ideas we draw from them, Locke's version of freedom allows persons to choose those things whose good is utilitarian, or whose good is pleasurable, but not those things good in themselves—of which the dignity of persons is one. Despite Locke's attempt to preserve as much liberty from the "State of Nature" as possible, his epistemology does not allow the true freedom outlined by Maritain and Hallowell.

The conclusion then seems clear. Liberalism, properly understood, is utterly reliant on a realist theory of knowledge to avoid self-consumption. Without "knowledge of the good," liberalism will inevitably degenerate into a derivative based on deception or force. As the "cultural reservoir" left by earlier realist thinkers begins to decline in America, one must logically expect liberalism to decline as well. The "house we did not build" which is this polity will not survive the erosion of its foundations.

The task before us then becomes equally clear. Political action to repair the polity will likely be futile so long as the public culture rejects or denies its ability to know, discern, and judge the truth. The actions of "Moral Majorities," "Christian Coalitions" or "Catholic Worker" movements, while perhaps instrumental in slowing liberalism's decline, do not attack root causes. One can attempt to preserve the fruits of the Lockean inheritance only through the promotion of a non-Lockean theory of knowledge. Such a theory must demonstrate that human beings are naturally equipped to know the world around them. Universal access to "the truth of all things" is the only hope for political consensus without overt or covert violence. Only such access allows the person to "rule his acts to choose what in fact is good" and participate in a "community of knowers."[52]

Promoting belief in such access will be a difficult task. As Ruth Shively has perceptively written about objectivist (read: realist) truth, while mainstream American political theorists:

> have qualms about the erosion of common ethical moorings...they seem to be even more uneasy about attempts to rebuild ethics on objective moral grounds....
> Among other reasons, they may cite prudential fears about moral truth claims as

---

[51] John Hallowell, *The Moral Foundation of Democracy* (Chicago: The University of Chicago Press, 1954), p. 112.

[52] James V. Schall, *Jacques Maritain: The Philosopher in Society* (Lanham, Maryland: Rowman & Littlefield, 1998), p. 130; *Postmodernism Rightly Understood*, p. 79.

grounds for intolerance and conflict, philosophical qualms about the impossibility or meaninglessness of correspondence theories, or pragmatic concerns with the metaphysical and impractical orientation of objectivist claims. Perhaps most important, however, this unwillingness to consider objectivist alternatives may be linked to the fact that moral contextualism has become an almost axiomatic assumption in political theory today, and this assumption is commonly presumed to stand against belief in objective or supracontextual moral truth.[53]

The political theorist Peter Lawler echoes this warning, cautioning us about "experts" who:

> deny the truth and goodness of traditional accounts of human choice and moral responsibility. The experts are, officially, pro-choice in the sense that they dismiss all accounts of moral limits as reactionary prejudice. They add that, given that there are no limits to choice, we should choose against death and human misery. We should choose against the illusion of personal responsibility or sovereignty. We should trust the experts, not ourselves, for the content and meaning of our experiences. The pro-choice position is anti-life in the sense that it tends to choose against human life as it actually exists. The choice is for a world without choice or virtue.[54]

A re-education of the culture will not be an easy task, and resistance—particularly within the academy—will be strong. However, the age has provided guides and mentors. Realist theories clearly underlie work being done in many disciplines. One may look especially at the practical politics of Vaclav Havel, the novels of the late Walker Percy, and the physics of Stanley Jaki. The calling of the new century must be to build on the work of these realist theorists and actors, Maritain and Hallowell included, in order to communicate to the body politic the necessity of moderate epistemological and moral realism to its continued political well being. A return to Christian realism is not a panacea and does not obviate the need for the study and reform of political institutions. But it is a necessary foundation.

---

[53] Ruth Lessl Shively, *Compromised Goods: A Realist Critique of Constructionist Politics* (Madison, Wisconsin: University of Wisconsin Press, 1997), p. 4.

[54] *Postmodernism Rightly Understood*, p. 181.

The Air We Breathe
The Reality of Our Knowledge and Our Knowledge of Reality

John G. Trapani, Jr.

As a philosopher and a father of two teenage daughters, I regularly find myself reflecting on the kinds of things that influence their developing personalities. And not only their minds, their thinking and their ideas, but their hearts and souls as well—those things that fashion and shape their values and ideals, their passion for life, and the things they come to care for and love.

As parents, we know that what children are taught in the school curriculum has an important influence on their developing minds. So too are the influences of peer pressure and their choice of friends. And yet, equally if not more significant, are the effects from the entire matrix of their cultural environment: music and song lyrics, MTV, the internet, violent video games, chat rooms, and the subjects and images of TV shows, movies, teen magazines, and all the various and sundry forms of advertising, not to mention the seemingly endless hours of telephone. Of course, experts keep telling us that these teen behaviors and pop-culture influences are normal for teens of any generation...that is, until there is tragedy. Enter the Columbine High School tragedy and the parade reverses direction; amid the national soul-searching, society's pundits then ponder, caution, and lament the significance of the influences that so many aspects of popular culture may be having on the minds of these young adults.

Certainly, this national self-reflection and public dialogue is not new to parents who regularly struggle with the tension between allowing for their child's independence for self-growth on the one hand, and providing the necessary structure and restrictions to protect and direct, in a values-oriented way, their child's development and habit-formation on the other hand. As a result, since one frequently encounters parents who themselves embrace popular culture in an *uncritical* way, the task of raising children/adolescents today is especially difficult for those who *are* reflective about the influence that popular culture may be having on them. This is particularly noteworthy since the force of this influence can be detrimental in two ways: first, because of the way that it too easily can alienate young adults from the very people—their parents, teachers, and concerned others—who would seek to cultivate in them a critical mind; and secondly, because of the natural attraction and the immediate, self-gratifying titillation that the thrills of popular culture can provide.

As a way of addressing this problem, I use a metaphor with my own daughters, as a way of helping them to understand the silent, subtle, unassuming, yet pervasive influence of popular culture on their thinking and on the values and beliefs that they otherwise might come to possess uncritically: if you are in a crowded, smoke-filled room, I remind them, you cannot help but come away smelling of smoke—it's *the air you breathe*. Fortunately, they get the point: in this age of awareness about the health risks of smoking, the metaphor reveals to them that it is not only their clothing and their hair that smell of smoke; indeed, they understand that second-hand smoke becomes a part of them too just as an uncritical absorption of popular culture may become a part of them. As parents, we may be glad that they get the point; as philosophers, we grow thoughtful about the epistemological significance of this metaphor and the problem that it raises.

For philosophers of common sense, our reflection upon examples and analogies drawn from nature can provide useful instruction and a reliable starting point. For example, since all living beings have an intrinsic principle of their coming-to-be, there is a unique confluence in them of their formal, efficient, and final causes: what they are (formal cause) also specifies both the means and manner of their growth (efficient cause) and the end toward which the fulfillment of their nature is directed (final cause). The inner dynamism or *energeia*, which operates unerringly for the organism's well-being, will succeed to the extent that the necessary *extrinsic* conditions, specified by the organism's nature, are adequately met and fulfilled. Thus, a tomato plant that has nourishing, balanced soil and adequate rainfall will grow to be a thriving, seemingly healthy plant, yet without the necessary and proper amount of sunlight also required by its nature, this particular plant will not bear fruits: all of the proper external environmental conditions must be satisfactorily met in order for any natural living being to completely fulfill its nature.

This insight becomes more complex, of course, when applied specifically to human beings. As Mortimer Adler points out in his book, *Ten Philosophical Mistakes*,[1] our human nature is properly defined by its spiri-

---

[1] Mortimer J. Adler, *Ten Philosophical Mistakes* (New York: Macmillian Publishing Company, 1985), pp. 156-66.

tual/intellectual powers, and as such, humans are not merely the products of their physical environment alone. Although cultural and individual differences are products of nurture, that does not tell the whole story: our distinctive human activities and operations are but the actualization of our two uniquely human spiritual powers, the intellect and the will. These powers may vary nurturally for both individuals and cultures. Like plants, *though not our bodies only*, all of our innate human powers or potentialities are influenced in their drive toward their fulfillment by all of the various factors that affect the many dimensions of our being. On the lower level of application, for example, few would have difficulty understanding the influence of the effects of the foods we eat and the air we breathe on our physical health; more difficult, however, is the analogous application of this principle (that "we are what we eat") to those myriad factors which influence our emotional, psychological, intellectual, and spiritual health as well. Arrestingly, this is precisely the claim implied by the Thomistic epistemological notion of intentionality: namely, that "the knower becomes one with the object known," or more precisely, *"the knower in the act of knowing is the known itself in the act of being known."*[2]

   If this is correct, as philosophers, we are then led to reflect upon the reality of human knowledge, and consequently, on our knowledge of reality—that is, on the way in which the Thomistic notion of intentionality might shed light on the way in which our cultural environment influences the nurtural outcome of who we—and our children and community—are?

The Reality of Our Knowledge

   One way to understand the reality of human knowledge is to survey the topography of human knowledge; to distinguish and identify the pieces and parts of the epistemological landscape, so to speak. Specifically, there are at least nine important distinctions that Thomistic philosophers of common sense might identify in this regard. Two such philosophers, Jacques Maritain and Mortimer J. Adler, have, at one time or another, written about them all.

   First, if humans are indeed unified, intellectual beings, then, as Maritain has shown in *Creative Intuition in Art and Poetry*,[3] human sense knowledge and, indeed, all of our related human knowing powers are always under the illuminating light of the human intellect. This is especially true of our human

---

   [2] Jacques Maritain, *The Range of Reason* (New York: Charles Scribner's Sons, 1952), p.14.
   [3] Jacques Maritain, *Creative Intuition in Art and Poetry* (Princeton, New Jersey: Princeton University Press, 1977), pp. 106-11.

sense powers which, although nominally the same as their corresponding powers in brute animals, are nonetheless fundamentally different: any notion of
"pure" human sensation is but an abstractive myth, since it is always the distinctive human "I" who has sense experience. "The universe of pure sensation,"
Maritain's pupil and friend, Yves Simon, wrote, "is an inhuman universe that
becomes human only to the extent that sensation is penetrated by thought."[4]
Maritain's own writing on epistemology remained constant concerning this
insight throughout his long career. As early as the second edition of *Art and
Scholasticism* (1926), Maritain identified "intelligentiated-sense;"[5] in *Untrammeled Approaches*, his last book, he refers to it again while adding a reference
to "intelligentiated-imagination."[6] Human intelligence, as a power and act of
our unified human nature, permeates all human knowledge.

The second distinction concerns the word knowledge itself. As opposed to
opinion, Mortimer Adler points out that, strictly or technically speaking, the
term knowledge ought to be reserved for conceptual knowledge—those judgments that are either self-evidently true, experimentally true, or "asserted to be
certainly or probably true as conclusions of valid inference or correct reasoning." All other judgments, he says, "have the status of unsupported opinions."[7]

Despite ordinary-language usage to the contrary, this distinction between
conceptual knowledge and opinion should be clear. The use of the term "experience," however, is not so clear. Throughout his epistemological writings,
Maritain consistently emphasized the important role of "experience/knowl-
edge," (which "is more experience than knowledge"[8]), in the full or complete
understanding of human life. Here, Maritain provides a valuable insight which
reminds us that "knowledge" is an analogous term and as such, he thus expands the legitimate use of the term knowledge beyond the confines of its
otherwise limited, technical reference to conceptual knowledge alone. This
is the third distinction concerning the vast topography of human knowledge
and it addresses the vast topic of connaturality. Beginning with *The Situation of Poetry*[9] (1937), and running through *Redeeming The Time*[10] (1938),

---

[4] Yves R. Simon, *An Introduction to Metaphysics of Knowledge* (New York: Fordham
University Press, 1990), p. 115.

[5] Jacques Maritain, *Art and Scholasticsm* (New York: Charles Scribner's Sons, 1962), p. 164.

[6] Jacques Maritain, *Untrammeled Approaches* (Notre Dame, Indiana: University of Notre
Dame Press, 1997), p. 348.

[7] Mortimer J. Adler, *Intellect* (New York: Macmillian Publishing Company, 1990), p. 155.

[8] Jacques Maritain, *The Situation of Poetry* (New York: Philosophical Library, 1955),
pp. 44-51.

[9] Ibid., pp. 64-66.

[10] cf. Jacques Maritain, *Redeeming the Time* (London: G. Bles, The Centenary Press,
1943), pp. 225-55.

Existence and the Existent[11] (1947), and *The Range of Reason*[12] (1951), Maritain offered many different and over-lapping enumerations of the five various types of connatural or experiential, non-conceptual knowledge.[13]

A discussion of the various kinds of connaturality leads directly to a fourth distinction, which concerns the uses of the term "intuition." Maritain's inventory of the ways in which this term is used divides between Philosophical or Intellectual intuitions (of which there are five[14]) and Non-Philosophical or "Divinatory" intuitions (of which there are four[15]). While Maritain notes that the notion of connaturality is confined to the non-philosophical forms of intuition, the term intuition itself is more universal—so much so, in fact, that it is often confounding. It is, Maritain writes, "one of those [words] which have [sic] provoked ... the most misunderstandings and obscurities."[16] Yet, despite the risks, the value and importance of this notion should not be minimized: in *Untrammeled Approaches*, Maritian writes emphatically that "there is no knowledge without intuitivity."[17]

The fifth distinction concerns the relation between the intellect and the will or affective desire. We ought not forget, Maritain reminds us, that love too has eyes, either by moving the intellect toward what is loved, or by becoming for the intellect, through a "spiritualized emotion" (or "affective resonance") "a determining means or instrumental vehicle through which [what is loved, is] . . . grasped and known obscurely."[18]

In addition to these five distinctions, classical Thomistic epistemology includes at least four more. They concern the distinctions between: 6) the three acts of the mind—apprehension (or conception), judgment, and reasoning; 7) the three degrees or levels of abstraction;[19] 8) the two types of activity of logical reason, induction and deduction; and 9) the five intellectual vir-

---

[11] Cf. Jacques Maritain, *Existence and the Existent* (New York: Pantheon Books, 1948), pp. 70-71.

[12] Cf. *The Range of Reason*, pp. 16-18, 22-29.

[13] Cf., John G. Trapani, Jr., *The Interrelation of Poetry, Beauty, and Contemplation in the Philosophy of Jacques Maritain*, (Ann Arbor, Michigan: University Microfilms International, 1984), pp. 58-77.

[14] Jacques Maritain, *Bergsonian Philosophy and Thomism*, (New York: Philosophical Library, 1955), pp. 149-51; see also *The Interrelation of Poetry, Beauty, and Contemplation*, pp.58-65, 76.

[15] *The Interrelation of Poetry, Beauty, and Contemplation*, pp.58-65, 76.

[16] *Bergsonian Philosophy and Thomism*, p. 148.

[17] *Untrammeled Approaches*, p. 326.

[18] *Creative Intuition*, p. 124.

[19] Cf. Jacques Maritain, *The Degrees of Knowledge* (Notre Dame, Indiana: University of Notre Dame Press, 1995), pp. 37-50.

tues—three speculative (*nous, episteme*, and *sophia*), and two practical (*phronesis* and *techne*).

We might hope to be pardoned for this perhaps tedious epistemological cartography by recalling that, in his essay, "No Knowledge Without Intuitivity," Maritain uses a similar metaphor: epistemological map-making, he says, is an exercise carried out by "cartographers." Yet theirs is a task preceded by the work of a reconnaissance team—those who must first assay the landscape, in order to find the successful route for the explorer to take. In this example (and despite Maritain's own admission of its limitation), we may take the landscape as reality, the journey is the intellect's pursuit of some aspect of truth about reality ("our knowledge of reality"), the explorer is the human mind in search of that truth, the cartographer's work is that of the intellectual, abstractive reason which sets forth its knowledge systematically ("the reality of our knowledge"), while the reconnaissance team represents the intellect's intuitivity—its immediate contact and *experience* with reality, which points the way for the explorer and the cartographer to proceed with veracity and to avoid what is potentially erroneous.[20]

All of this having been said, and despite whatever satisfaction this technical, epistemological analysis might provide for the philosopher in the father, the father in the philosopher is still left wondering: does this systematic mapping of human knowledge have anything to say about the influence of the pop-culture environment, as *the cultural air we breathe*, on the growth and development of society, young and old alike? In other words, if the range of human knowledge and experience is broad, then mustn't the key to a successful cultural critique be equally as broad and comprehensive concerning the impact that our present culture may have upon us, especially if we fail to keep a critical perspective?

Our Knowledge of Reality

In order to answer these questions, we will do well to return to the Thomistic idea of intentionality. Lived-experience suggests that these cultural forces do affect us *and become part of us* just as surely as being in a smoke-filled room affects the stench of our clothing and the purity of the air we breathe. The Thomistic notion of intentionality states that the knower becomes one with the object known in such a way that the abstractive essence of what is known exists in an analogously different way in the knower than its existence in material reality. If this is true, we might then ask: does

---

[20] Cf. *Untrammeled Approaches*, pp. 314-20.

this technical use of the notion of intentional existence also work for things like values and those aspects of our culture that influence us unawares? Does reflection upon all of the various diversities and modes of knowledge previously surveyed permit a *non-technical* extension of this Thomistic notion of intentionality which might shed some light on the cultural conditions under which our many various knowing powers are actuated? In short, is there a way to understand and explain this subtle cultural experience and influence from within the framework of traditional Thomistic epistemology?

Thanks to the insights of Jacques Maritain and Mortimer Adler, I think there is. Although all knowledge *begins* in and through sensation and phantasms,[21] we have seen that knowledge and experience are by no means limited to that of which we have sensation and phantasms; nor is the intellect, in its diverse ways of knowing, restricted to speculative knowledge or conceptual understanding alone. In ordinary lived-experience, the greater percentage of our lives is under the influence of the various kinds and degrees of practical knowledge, some of which are conceptual, and some of which are non-conceptual and affective. And yet, covering all of these diverse kinds and modes of knowledge, is the illuminating light of the human intellect and this notion of intentionality, both technically and non-technically considered. This suggests that the conceptual or experiential union that is the result of intentionality may occur on the physical, emotional, psychological, intellectual, or spiritual levels of our being. From an advertising jingle that one can't get out of one's head, to traumatic or euphoric physical or psychological experiences; from verbal abuse or positive praise to profound poetic intuitions or spiritual ecstasy—all of these experiences, as a "becoming-one-with," have the power to "stay with us," and to affect our thinking, our valuing, our loving,—our being.

Throughout this essay, we have focused on those insights of Jacques Maritain's and Mortimer Adler's epistemology which might be successfully brought to bear on a cultural critique. It is worth noting, however, that, particularly in Maritain's case, his analysis of human nature and knowledge usually focuses on the ideal: on the essence of a human nature striving toward the preordained, supernatural human end which is truth, human perfection, and the unlimited good—an end which ultimately is only completely fulfilled in the Beatific Vision. And while this theoretical analysis correctly addresses the intellectual concerns of professional philosophers

---

[21]"The intellect cannot understand without turning to the phantasms, first and always." cf. Étienne Gilson, *Elements of Christian Philosophy* (Garden City, New York: Doubleday & Company, Inc., 1960), p. 331.

interested in the arts, letters, and faith, it does not provide much direct insight for raising children and young adults, since they are primarily motivated by their desire for social acceptance, peer approval, and sensual delight—not the True, the Good, and the Beautiful.

Fortunately, this problem has a resolution. As philosophers in the Thomist tradition, we understand habits and virtues; we understand that, while "our knowledge of reality" involves the complexity and richness of the universe with which we become unified affectively and intellectually, in the end, we also understand that it is the actualization of our various and diverse knowing powers *through the cultivation of good moral and intellectual habits* that affects the predominance of our ordinary lives. And for as much as the epistemological mapping, categorizing, and explaining might matter to philosophers, it is the critical reflection upon the influence of our environment, inclining us either toward or away from the development of those good moral and intellectual habits or virtues, that matters to parents.

Here at last lies the solution to the problem we have been considering: different people in various places on earth, while the same in their spiritual, intellectual nature, can come to a happy and good fulfillment of their nature (. . . or not), depending upon the nurtural conditions of their cultural environment. Those factors which contribute positively to their physical/biological, emotional/psychological, intellectual/affective, and spiritual well-being are good and healthy; those that do not, are not. Mortimer Adler makes this point perfectly clear: our intellectual powers (both speculative and practical), when exercised in habitually wholesome ways, cultivate in us intellectual and/or moral virtues. The powers themselves are naturally ordered toward truth and goodness.[22] When these intellectual or moral powers are not nurtured or not nurtured in habitually wholesome ways, the corresponding virtue-potential for these powers is not actualized, and their non-use or misuse results in intellectual or moral vice. Moreover, since vice runs counter to the human good which is obtained through the fulfillment of our human spiritual nature, our cultural/social environment, as *the air we breathe*, does matter: it leads us, through the varieties of intentional union, either toward or away from that goodness and fulfillment which our nature naturally desires.

Mortimer Adler points out that good and bad governments and societies may be assessed by the way in which they either contribute toward or away from the fulfillment of natural human needs with all of the real goods to which, being common goods, they have a natural right. He concludes:

[22] Cf. *Intellect*, pp. 143-48.

The only standard we have for judging all of our social, economic, and political institutions and arrangements as just or unjust, as good or bad, as better or worse, derives from our conception of the good life for man on earth, and from our conviction that, *given certain external conditions,* it is possible for men to make good lives for themselves by their own efforts.[23]

As we observed at the outset, when the environmental conditions necessary for the health and well-being of that tomato plant are not adequately met, that plant produces no, or sickly, fruits. Analogously, that basic insight may be applied to a critical understanding of our cultural environment as well: it is an observation that is as simple and as true for tomatoes as it is for ourselves, our children, our loved ones, and for the future well-being of the entire human family. And even though our human nature is not as dependent on our external environment as are tomatoes, the scriptural wisdom that "by the fruit, you shall know the tree," may also be applied analogously here: by society's fruits, we shall know something about our society itself—and something about the environment and culture which has nurtured it as well.

[23]Mortimer J. Adler, *Desires, Right & Wrong: The Ethics of Enough* (New York: Macmillan Publishing Company, 1991), p. 193. [emphasis added.]

Understanding Freedom as a Way of Knowing Social Life

Henk E. S. Woldring

The problem of human freedom is nearly as old as philosophy itself. Human freedom—understood as freedom of the will—was denied by some pre-Socratics (Xenophanes and Democritus) and by the Stoic philosophers. These thinkers maintained that a strict law of material causality prevailed throughout the whole of nature, and that human beings were no exceptions to this law. After the Renaissance, scientific discoveries convinced many scholars that physical laws governed everything in the universe, including the minds of human beings. In particular, both Darwin's theory—in which human beings were considered as a species of mammals and, consequently subject to biological laws—and Freud's theory of an unconscious realm of human mind—with its instincts, passions and repressed motivations which influence human actions—strengthened the idea that free will was either non-existent or irrelevant

Jacques Maritain acknowledges the relevance of these physical, biological and psychological theories of human action. However, he argues that the question of free will exceeds the competence of these disciplines, and that this question is one of philosophy, which must therefore be dealt with in a philosophical frame of reference. According to Maritain, to use scientific arguments to support a philosophical determinism, to conclude that there cannot be a free will or free agents with moral consciousness and intelligence, goes beyond the proper domain of those sciences. Acknowledging that free will presupposes a complex dynamism of instincts, tendencies, psycho-physical dispositions and acquired habits, Maritain still maintains that it is where this dynamism emerges in the world of spirit that freedom of choice is exercised, where and when the person decides to give or withhold decisive efficacy to the inclinations and urges of nature.[1]

[1] Jacques Maritain, "The Conquest of Freedom" in *The Education of Man: The Educational Philosophy of Jacques Maritain*, ed. Donald and Idella Gallagher (Notre Dame, Indiana: University of Notre Dame Press, 1962), p. 161.

Maritain rightly maintains that to use scientific arguments to support philosophical determinism, to conclude that there cannot be a free will, goes beyond the competence of the sciences. He also argues—again, rightly so—that the quest to understand free will is a philosophical quest. He argues that we inherit free will as a form of spiritual energy through our rational nature; "we do not have to achieve it: it appears within us as an initial form of Freedom."[2]

In Maritain's theory, freedom of will and freedom of choice in various fields of action are closely connected. Sometimes he even equates these two: "We maintain then that freedom of choice, freedom in the sense of good will." However, he also distinguishes them when he argues that the free act is "like an instantaneous flash in which the active and dominating indetermination of the will operates."[3] Elsewhere he writes, "the notion of Freedom is very much wider than the notion of Free Will. Free will is indeed the source and spring of the world of Freedom."[4] This then raises the question: What is the nature of the relationship between free will as a form of spiritual energy on the one hand, and freedom of choice in various fields of action on the other?

Freedom of Autonomy

Maritain answers this question by introducing the idea of "freedom of autonomy." He considers the free will to be an indispensable prerequisite to, and preparation for, freedom of autonomy, which he deems much more important. For Maritain, freedom of autonomy means that the free will—or the initial, immature, form of freedom—must develop in a psychological and moral attitude that permits a person to be one "having dominion over our own acts and being to ourselves a rounded and a whole existence."[5] With this true freedom of autonomy, a person can rule his acts, having the power to overcome and to control those impulses and instincts, desires and passions that easily make human beings their slaves.

Maritain further maintains that the psychological and moral development from mere free will to freedom of autonomy does not occur naturally. However, this development is a necessary process, if we are to bring ourselves to maturity as morally responsible agents.

---

[2] Jacques Maritain, *Freedom in the Modern World* (New York: Gordian Press, 1971 [1936]), p. 30.
[3] "The Conquest of Freedom," p. 162.
[4] *Freedom in the Modern World*, pp. 29-30.
[5] Ibid., p. 30.

Discussing freedom of autonomy, Maritain argues that he employs this term "in a Pauline and not Kantian sense."[6] He distinguishes his freedom of autonomy from Kant's, in which the individual human being is considered to be free only if he obeys the law he gives himself. For Kant, freedom of autonomy consists in obedience to the moral law, and this moral law is conceived of as being strictly self-imposed.[7] Ultimately, a human being is not subject to any external rule; his obedience is due solely to himself.

Maritain opposes Kant's position. He agrees with the apostle Paul who posits that freedom of choice in various fields of action consists essentially in obedience to the divine moral law as revealed in the Gospel, which is unequivocally imposed from without. The crucial point is that these moral laws should be obeyed voluntarily because they are acknowledged to be just; they are obeyed out of love for justice, and never through coercion. Because of this commitment to justice, these moral laws will strengthen freedom of autonomy.[8]

James Schall describes freedom of autonomy as "freedom that comes when, through discipline, asceticism, habit and purpose, a person can rule his acts to choose what in fact is true."[9] Since discipline, asceticism and habits differ from one person to another, freedom of autonomy may be achieved in different degrees in different human beings. Moreover, love for a just and true life may (and indeed should) inspire people to achieve their freedom of autonomy more and more.[10]

Again, for Maritain, the free will is a necessary precondition for freedom of autonomy. But this begs the question as to whether the reverse may also be the case in a certain respect; although the free will is the necessary condition of freedom of autonomy, should not the true meaning of free will and freedom of choice in various fields of action be understood when we know what someone's freedom of autonomy is? My provisional answer to this question is that the free will is the essence of freedom of autonomy, and that freedom of autonomy is the cognitive condition for understanding the free will and freedom of choice in various fields of action. I will therefore discuss more extensively the nature of the relationship between free will and freedom of choice.

---

[6] "The Conquest of Freedom," p. 159.

[7] This idea of autonomy is a key term in Kant's *Fundamental Principles of the Metaphysics of Morals* and in his *Critique of Practical Reason.*

[8] "The Conquest of Freedom," p. 168; *Freedom in the Modern World*, p. 36-37. See also *St. Paul's Epistle to the Romans* 8:13-15.

[9] James V. Schall, *Jacques Maritain : The Philosopher in Society*. (Lanham, Maryland: Rowman & Littlefield, 1998), p. 130. See also Charles A. Fecher, *The Philosophy of Jacques Maritain* (Westminster, Maryland: The Newman Press, 1953), p. 182.

[10] "The Conquest of Freedom," pp. 165-68.

Maritain's Theory Reconsidered

As earlier discussed, Maritain argues that free will transcends instincts, tendencies, psychological dispositions, acquired habits and inheritable traits. He acknowledges that certain physical, biological and psychological factors have a determinative efficacy to human actions, while other factors are conditional. Since human beings have no gills or wings they cannot live like fishes or birds. The physical-biological characteristics of human beings, inherited through the human genome, are coercive or determinative factors of human life.

However, not all physical-biological factors are determinative. There are individuals who are deaf or color blind. For a choice of career these factors may be decisive, but not always. Many of these people are looking for compensations or alternative possibilities to overcome their physical-biological restrictions. For these people those factors have a conditional efficacy to their actions. There are people who have unchangeable psychological characteristics that may have a determinative nature. However, there are other psychological traits that have the character of conditional factors that can be changed, however difficult this may be. The same can be said of social factors, most notably education, that have a conditional influence on human life.

Those conditional factors combine to produce *dispositions*: fundamental, stable and dynamic moral attitudes that contain the permanent moral and spiritual achievements (or deprivations) of human beings. These dispositions then underlie human intentions and actions. Morally good dispositions prepare and fortify a person to make right use of her freedom of choice in various fields of action. However, a person who cultivates immoral dispositions will be inclined to misuse this freedom.[11] Dispositions should then be considered as an intermediate stratum or stage between the determinative physical-biological factors and the final human intentions and actions.

An example of a disposition may be what Maritain calls the *adherence of minds* to a *moral charter* of a democratic society. He argues that notwithstanding the diversity of worldviews citizens have a fundamental and stable attitude that contains the achieved acquirement that they should adhere to the following elements: human equality, fraternity, mutual tolerance and respect, social and political rights and liberties of human persons and corresponding responsibilities towards the common good.[12]

---

[11] *Freedom in the Modern World*, pp. 22, 38.

[12] Jacques Maritain, *Man and the State* (Chicago: The University of Chicago Press, 1951), pp. 111-13.

Dispositions are stable factors that regulate conditional human choices in various fields of action. But what motivates people to cultivate dispositions in either a morally good or a depraved manner? There is another factor that gives dispositions their dynamism: this dynamic moral force that drives people may be called *ethos*.

In his discussion of democracy Maritain argues that a genuine democracy requires a fundamental agreement between minds and wills on the basis of life in common. Democratically thinking citizens should have such a common thought or a common human creed, the creed of freedom.[13] This faith is not a religious faith but a *secular* or *civic* one. Maritain employs the conception of a *common ethos* of democracy: the inner energy of the secular democratic faith and moral force people have, and which underlie and vitalize cultivation of their democratic dispositions.[14]

Moreover, there is another conditional factor that gives this ethos its strength: the deepest or *spiritual center* of a person's existence that has the potentiality to transcend the world around. This center of our existence is the "location" of free will, the initial form of freedom that belongs to the "world of spirit." It is the most fundamental and integral idea of freedom because it refers to the direction of life a person wants to choose. It is the "anchor place" of human life in which a religious human being intends to live in communion with God, love and truth.

I come back to the question asked before: What is the nature of the relationship between free will as spiritual energy on the one hand, and freedom of choice in various fields of action on the other? The substructure of determinative physical-biological factors, and conditional factors like dispositions, ethos and the center of spiritual energy culminate in human beings developing their freedom of autonomy and performing their freedom of choice in various fields of action. Both these conditional factors and human actions make a person a morally responsible person.

However, there is another complication. Persons achieve their freedom of choice in concrete social, economic, juridical, and moral actions. These actions are also conditioned by a variety of social communities in which they occur. Will social communities endanger freedom of choice in various fields of action?

Isaiah Berlin answers this question affirmatively. He criticizes all theories of human freedom that distinguish between physical, biological and psychological factors (lower nature) on the one hand and those spiritual and

---

[13] *Man and the State*, p. 109. See also Jacques Maritain, *The Range of Reason* (New York: Charles Scribner's Sons, 1952), pp. 165-71.

[14] *Man and the State*, p. 145.

intellectual factors (higher nature) on the other that master the lower natural factors. He fears the monopolizing of the higher natural factors by embracing social collectives like the church and state. According to him, in history these social collectives have been largely oppressive.[15] If Berlin's criticism has merit, it would imply a serious flaw in Maritain's theory of freedom. I shall discuss this question below.

Freedom and Authority

Since Maritain accepts the idea of heteronomy, he argues that to achieve freedom of autonomy we need authority or some kind of rule. Moreover, freedom of autonomy does not only apply to individuals but also to communities because, according to Maritain, we should acknowledge that communities have their own rights, liberties and moral responsibilities. Authorities in communities do not guide only the individual participants but also these communities as entities. Moreover, these authorities do not consider individual and community-centered liberties and rights independently, but as parts of society. These authorities are bound in conscience to feel responsible toward society at large. On the other hand, the authority of the government has not only to protect the liberties of individual citizens and their private associations but also to guide these liberties toward the common good. In short, if associations are able to show the strength of their own responsibilities and purposes to promote their own good and the common good as well, they are also characterized by having freedom of autonomy.

Maritain argues that freedom and authority are not in fundamental opposition to each other. Although authority is often equated with coercion, and although authority sometimes needs coercion in a legitimate way, we should distinguish these two. A good citizen ought to obey authority and laws not out of compulsion or fear of punishment but of his own free will and love for a just social order.[16] To practice authority or to obey authority is neither irrational nor inhuman. On the contrary, both can be perfectly intelligent acts. If the social order should be an order of freedom it needs authority, not as a guarantee but rather as a necessary condition.[17]

---

[15] Isaiah Berlin, "Two Concepts of Liberty" in *Four Essays on Liberty* (London: Oxford University Press 1969), pp. 132-34.

[16] *Freedom in the Modern World*, p. 79.

[17] "The Conquest of Freedom," p. 171. See also Yves R. Simon, *A General Theory of Authority* (Notre Dame, Indiana: University of Notre Dame Press, 1962), pp. 1-79. See also *Jacques Maritain: The Philosopher in Society*, p. 122.

Maritain argues that this freedom will not be a quiet and easy-going peacefully expanding freedom, but rather one defined by tensions. According to him, we need education for freedom and authority for the sake of the society of the future.[18] However, if freedom of autonomy, both of persons and communities, requires authority, what conditions do we need to prevent that authority from suppressing freedom of autonomy? If freedom of autonomy should be understood as a property of a person or community that enables them to choose one from among several alternative courses of action (positive freedom), what is the area in which they can employ their freedom of autonomy in various fields of action without external constraint beyond their control (negative freedom)?

Social Freedom

Maritain argues that society at large consists of a multitude of social communities that should achieve their freedom of autonomy. Autonomy means that every social community governs itself, and carries out duties according to its own freedom, rights and responsibilities. As such, the true political society is characterized by social pluralism.

While civic associations have an enduring worth, from the standpoint of the communities as well as individuals, oppression within these associations is often overlooked. In fact many associations are undemocratic. Maritain argues that freedom of autonomy of civic associations cannot be achieved without freedom of participants, and, consequently, principles of democracy should also be applied to these communities.[19]

I have already discussed that there is a mutual and indissoluble relationship between freedom and authority. This means, more precisely, that freedom of action of both participants and communities as wholes is conditioned and limited by the authorities of these communities. In this context it may be illuminating to discuss briefly the concept of authority as found in the writings of the Dutch neo-Calvinist philosopher Abraham Kuyper.

Kuyper (1837-1920) was the founding father of neo-Calvinism in the Netherlands. He was the founder of the first Christian political party in the Netherlands (1879), founded the Reformed *Vrije Universiteit* (Free University, 1880) in Amsterdam, and was inspirational in the struggle for free denominational schools. Kuyper argued that parents should have the right to

---

[18] Jacques Maritain, *Education at the Crossroads* (New Haven, Connecticut: Yale University Press, 1943), pp. 98, 102.

[19] *Man and the State*, pp. 9-12.

found their own denominational schools independent from the state. Consequentially, the Dutch constitution contains an article that acknowledges the right of denominational schools, and, moreover, the financial standardization of denominational and public schools by the state.

One of the central ideas in Kuyper's political philosophy is the idea of *sphere sovereignty*. Kuyper argues that each form and level of government ought to be considered as "God's servant," and that it therefore has the obligation to maintain social justice.[20] Because of this religious calling of the government, he rejects the Enlightenment idea of popular sovereignty that underlies the French Revolution. The revolutionaries opposed divine authority, and they refused to recognize any deeper ground of political life than that which is found in the people as an aggregate. Consequently, Kuyper rejects any individualist view of society.[21]

Kuyper then further rejects the unrestricted sovereignty of the state. This conception of sovereignty proposes that everything is subordinate to the will and the goal of the almighty state. There is no other right but the positive law that is codified in the law. The law is right not because its content is in harmony with principles of justice but because it is law. This internal logic of state sovereignty seems to demand centralization of power in the government, regardless of effects on the rights and liberties of its citizens. In this case the government would absorb the responsibilities of its citizens and thereby undermine the vitality of society.[22]

In contrast to both the idea of popular sovereignty and the idea of unrestricted state sovereignty, Kuyper presents his organic view of society. He argues that a nation is an organic whole that not only comprises individual citizens as its parts, but also civic associations. Citizens should not only stand up for their individual rights and liberties but also for the rights and liberties of their civic associations.

Kuyper defends his organic concept of *sphere sovereignty* as follows:

> In a Calvinistic sense we understand hereby that the family, business, science, art, and so forth are all social spheres, which do not owe their existence to the state, and which do not derive the law of their life from the superiority of the state, but obey a high authority within their own bosom; an authority which rules, by the grace of God, just as the sovereignty of the state does.[23]

---

[20] Abraham Kuyper, *Calvinism: Six Stone-lectures* (Amsterdam: Höveker & Wormser, 1899), pp. 105-06.
[21] Ibid., pp. 109-12.
[22] Ibid., pp. 113-14.
[23] Ibid., pp. 116, 123-27.

Kuyper acknowledges that God is the absolute sovereign to whom all other forms of authority are subordinated. Next, he acknowledges that his idea of sphere sovereignty involves a sharp distinction between state and civil society: private associations belonging to each of those social spheres have their own sovereignty, authority and freedom that are not derived from the competence of the state. These private associations should practice their proper competencies and freedoms to promote their private interests. The state should acknowledge these authorities and liberties and not intrude. On the other hand, these private associations contribute to the public policy that they tend to amplify. In contrast to the perception of private associations as special interest groups, Kuyper argues that from their acknowledged special interest they also contribute (optimally) to the public interest.

According to Kuyper, the law has to acknowledge the rights and liberties of citizens and their private associations and protect them from abuse of power by the government and other institutions. Although he discusses the idea of sphere sovereignty of civic associations that are characterized by their own authority, he also speaks of these spheres as a "palladium of our liberties."[24]

Kuyper's ideas on freedom and authority are compatible with those of Maritain. Maritain's idea of the freedom of autonomy of differentiated social communities and Kuyper's idea of sphere sovereignty tend to struggle against both individualist and totalitarian social theories. Berlin's criticism of higher natural factors that are often identified by totalitarian, all-embracing, social collectives cannot be applied to Maritain's and Kuyper's parallel theories. Maritain and Kuyper characterize their theories of freedom as both communal and personal.[25]

This leaves one last difficulty. If freedom of autonomy should be understood as a property of a person and a community that enables them to choose one from among several alternative courses of action (positive freedom), what are the boundaries within which they can employ their freedom of autonomy without external constraint (negative freedom)? For larger social communities also have their own dispositions, ethos, and a core of existence that underlie their actions, and which the freedom of others might endanger. I have already discussed Maritain's idea of a common ethos of a democratic society. Other social communities like families, schools and industries have their own fundamental agreement between minds and wills on the basis of life in common. This idea of a differentiated social ethos underlies social

---

[24] Ibid., p. 141.
[25] *Freedom in the Modern World*, p. 46. *Calvinism*, p. 141.

dispositions within a variety of social communities. They have their own stable socio-moral attitudes (customs of cooperation and communication) which condition and fortify the individual and common activities of the participants. Therefore, the core competencies of social communities are characterized by their proper qualifications. Families, industries, schools, churches, etc. have their own moral, economic, educational or religious qualification. They therefore have their own proper purposes that flow from these qualifications, beyond which their autonomy is limited. These qualifications of social communities and their ethos and dispositions characterize the freedom of autonomy of these communities.

A person's freedom of choice in various fields of action can be achieved only through and within differentiated social communities. Freedom of choice does not belong only to the personal sphere but also to the sphere of social communities. These communities are permanent frameworks of human actions that transmit moral values, norms, discipline, asceticism, habit and purposes of action. They may contribute to the formation of human dispositions and ethos. In short, through and within social communities we learn our freedom of autonomy or how to become morally responsible persons.

In opposition to Berlin who univocally considers every sacrifice of freedom to be a loss, however great the moral need for it may be,[26] I argue that there will nowhere and never be freedom without (at least) authority and (often) constraint, but authority and constraint do not necessarily result in a loss of freedom. On the contrary, the word "authority" comes from a Latin word that means "to grow" or "to cause to grow."[27] In this context this means that citizens need authority to be themselves, to be what they are or, better yet, what they ought to be as morally mature and responsible agents striving toward freedom as autonomy. I shall clarify this thesis below.

Authentic Freedom

Maritain argues that the idea of freedom is dominant in the theories of many political philosophers after the Renaissance. However, he repeatedly asks, what notion of freedom do they employ and in what way do they elaborate it?

A general characteristic of philosophic thought after the Renaissance on the relationship between man and society is, according to Isaiah Berlin, the

---

[26] "Two Concepts of Liberty," p. 125.
[27] *Freedom in the Modern World*, pp. 79-80. See also *Jacques Maritain: The Philosopher in Society*, pp. 123, 128.

idea that "there is no value higher than the individual."[28] Charles Taylor argues that the general characteristic of post-Renaissance philosophy is that a person considers himself as a "self-defining subject."[29] A new conception of man emerged that was characterized a) by a separation and gaining of independence by the "self" in opposition to nature, society and history, and b) by replacing this separation or gain of independence by an alternative: human beings were in search of possibilities of self-determination and self-realization in and through reconsidered relationships to nature, society and history. However, there is a serious tension between a) and b). The "self-defining subject" stood in an oppositional relationship to what he considered to be a contingent world. Post-Renaissance philosophers no longer looked for the meaning of human actions in relationship to a cosmic order. They found their starting-point in the individual human being who defines his "self" in relationship to nature, society and history, and also to God. These ideas underlie many, if not most, liberal social theories.[30]

There are other political theories that do not start from the freedom of individuals but instead turn to the state as the guarantor of freedom for its citizens, for instance Georg W. F. Hegel and Karl Marx. Since in these theories the state is interpreted as the fulfillment of free will and freedom of choice, Maritain characterizes these theories as imperialistic.

I concentrate for the moment on the individualistic ideas that underlie the liberal social theories that are dominant in our time. However, these liberal theories have become far-removed from the authentic meaning of freedom. A fundamental error committed by many contemporary liberal philosophers is that they confuse (in Maritain's terms) free will with freedom of autonomy, and they do not accept the possibility of a chosen moral commitment. Maritain argues:

> This error makes the highest form of freedom consist in freedom of choice; as if the reason for choosing were not to escape having to choose again! Free choice becomes an end in itself, and man, condemned to recurrent acts of choice, without ever being able to bind himself, is launched into a dialectic of freedom which destroys freedom. In order always to be ready to make any fresh choice that the circumstances of the moment may suggest, he refuses to declare for an end which, once chosen, would limit the field of possible choices in the future. In order to enjoy as supreme good the pure exercise of his freedom he refuses to determine it by reference to a rational ground.[31]

---

[28] "Two Concepts of Liberty," p. 137.
[29] Charles Taylor, *Hegel* (Cambridge: Cambridge University Press, 1975), p. 6.
[30] *Freedom in the Modern World*, pp. 39-41.
[31] *Freedom in the Modern World*, pp. 31-32.

Maritain argues that a human being in action makes choices and that these choices reflect his freedom of autonomy or his psychologico-moral attitude. These choices may either affirm or correct former choices but new choices do not damage the continuity of actions. If a person denies this continuity he gets caught in his own self-denials. The essence of freedom of autonomy always implies, according to Maritain, a moral commitment. I shall clarify this essence of freedom by reminding briefly some historic notions of freedom.

From the sixth century B.C. in ancient Greece, freedom (*eleutheria*) of citizens was connected originally with the experience to be "at home," to belong to a people or to live in a concrete social milieu. The original question was not "Who is free?" but "Where is someone free?" In the *polis* the question is not primarily to be free human beings but to be free as citizens. Citizens of a *polis* can exist only if they are associated in a well-ordered society that is ruled by laws (*nomoi*). However, *nomos* does not mean only law but it refers also to moral values: human beings cannot exist as independent individuals but they can exist only within the moral order of a political community.[32]

Certainly, there have always been tensions between freedom and law in the *polis*, but no contrast (except in situations of tyranny). Freedom for the citizens could only be achieved if they accepted and internalized laws by reasonable insight. Freedom was not only endangered by tyranny but also by growing individualism, and the concurrent weakening of the binding force of laws.

Further, in the Jewish and Christian traditions the idea of freedom is a central one. In these traditions freedom means first of all: liberation from slavery (in Egypt). Next, freedom refers to the direction of a new home country, the land of promise. This liberation *from* and liberation *to* arises from a divine act that is characterized by love and justice. Moreover, this divine love implies a call of imitation, to act toward fellow human beings with love and justice. In the Jewish and Christian traditions freedom is a *relational* concept. Freedom will be endangered if a person as an individual breaks away from this relationality and if he does not imitate love and justice.

Both in the ancient Greek tradition and in the Jewish and Christian traditions the essence of freedom had nothing to do with individualistic ideas of freedom. Freedom was considered as a relational concept that has something to do with choice, the fundamental choice of a moral commitment to the state

---

[32] See Dieter Nestle, *Eleutheria. Studien zum Wesen der Freiheit bei den Griechen und im Neuen Testament.* (Tübingen: Mohr, 1967), pp. 26-30, 104-12.

or the people. In our socially differentiated society the essence of freedom, freedom of autonomy or what I call *authentic freedom* is characterized by a moral commitment to a variety of social communities.

Degraded Freedom

After the Renaissance, in particular since John Locke, representatives of liberal mainstream theories employed the concept of freedom in various ways. Most of these representatives acknowledged the individualist basis of their conceptions of freedom. They restricted freedom to individual human beings who are characterized as "self-defining subjects." Moreover, they ascribed to freedom certain civic rights, participatory rights, and economic rights such as property and competition between individuals in free markets. These needs and rights underlie contemporary constitutional states. In particular, market freedoms have had a decisive impact in contemporary Western societies, and not only in the economic sectors.

Freedom of the market is characterized by commerce, competition and contracts between citizens. Everyone is an end in himself, and everyone considers others as potential opponents. Consequently, fellow-men become "counter-men." Many liberals use the market as a model for other sectors of society. However, society at large is not a market. In a socially differentiated society there are also families, groups of friends, religious communities, schools and hospitals. Freedom of the market is essentially different from freedom in those differentiated communities.

Certainly, neo-liberal theories do not want to use the market as a model without restrictions for other sectors of society. They pay attention to ideas such as the responsibility of individuals and industries for society at large, and to social justice. However, these ideas are primarily additive and corrective, and they can only veil the individualist character of the liberal concept of freedom, both in the market and other sectors of society.

From their individualistic perspective, many people stand up for their needs and they claim their fundamental human rights to defend their properties, which gives them a feeling of certainty, at least materialist certainty. To look for such a certainty is not wrong in itself but, according to Maritain, it does not mean that our use of property rights will be good.

Maritain's younger contemporary, Emmanuel Levinas, argues that freedom starts with liberating oneself from possible commitment with pseudo certainties, and to have an eye for other human beings, in particular, for widows, orphans, strangers and other vulnerable people. This means that we should test the authenticity of what we call our freedom: it should be tested by the critique of others who are related to our freedom. Levinas argues that authentic freedom is hardly achievable, and, therefore, he characterizes it as "difficult freedom."[33]

Berlin acknowledges that his concept of negative freedom may be compatible with social injustice. His idea of negative freedom answers the question: "What is the area within which the subject—a person or a group of persons—is or should be left to do or be what he is able to do or be, without interference by other persons."[34] He argues: "Legal liberties are compatible with extremes of exploitation, brutality, and injustice. The case for intervention, by the state or other effective agencies, to secure conditions for both positive, and at least a minimum degree of negative liberty for individuals, is overwhelmingly strong."[35] To avoid widespread misery (lack of income, knowledge or health), Berlin is prepared to sacrifice some, or all, of his freedom for the sake of justice, equality or love of his fellow men. However, he considers a sacrifice of freedom always as a loss, however great the moral need of the compensation of it may be.[36]

There is an important difference between Berlin's and Levinas's ideas of freedom. Berlin's starting point is the liberal conception of individual freedom as the highest value. Next, he is willing to correct any immoral consequences of his starting point and to sacrifice some of his freedoms in so doing. Levinas's starting point is that human freedom is not an individualist but a relational concept that locates people in relationships of responsibility to others. These relationships presuppose acknowledgement of human dignity. This implies that freedom has a normative dimension that becomes visible in a variety of concepts closely connected to it: community, justice, service and care.

Conclusion

Liberal social theories have become far removed from the authentic meaning of freedom as socio-moral commitment. In this respect they degenerate the authentic meaning of freedom that is characterized by freedom of choice in various fields of action, and by a moral commitment to social communities that have their own liberties and responsibilities. These responsibilities imply ideas of public spirit, social justice, service and care.

---

[33] Emmanuel Levinas, *Difficult Freedom: Essays on Judaism* (Baltimore: Johns Hopkins University Press, 1990), pp. 11-26.

[34] "'Two Concepts of Liberty," pp. 121-22.

[35] *Four Essays on Liberty*, p. xlvi.

[36] "Two Concepts of Liberty," p. 125.

Further, these concepts are not simply supplements or amendments to correct individualistic visions of freedom. On the contrary, public spirit, justice, service and care lie at the basis of freedom. These factors give freedom its authenticity and strength, and give rise to critical reflection on its use, and understand it as a way of knowing social life.

r

Known Invincible Ignorance and Moral Responsibility
When We Know That We Don't Know

John F. Morris

In his *Nicomachean Ethics*, Aristotle argues that when a human agent has acted in ignorance of any of the particular circumstances surrounding an action, then the agent is said to have acted *involuntarily*—and so is not "fully" responsible for her or his action.[1] However, what would happen if we *knew* that we did not know all of the relevant moral facts of a given situation? Or, what if it was apparent that there was no way for any human being to know such facts in a given situation—that is, if we faced an *invincible* ignorance? Excluding cases of emergency when there is not sufficient time to deliberate on a proper course of action, could an agent still act while fully aware of such ignorance?

I believe this is an important question for our times. Humanity is in a peculiar place in history today, in which we find that our technological possibilities far outreach our understanding of them. The implications of what we do not know about our technology and its effects are becoming more and more apparent. Consider the following observations from Dr. Jared Goldstein in his 1990 article titled "Desperately Seeking Science: The Creation of Knowledge in Family Practice":

> With uncertainty all around me, I sometimes long for the security that science appears to offer. Unfortunately, science can no longer offer the comfort that I need. Positivism has long since given way to probability. Modern science has discarded traditional notions of certainty, but the applied sciences have failed to fully absorb the message. An ordered, deterministic universe of accurate diagnosis and definitive treatment will always be just beyond my grasp. My patient's fears fall through the cracks of the probabilistic certainty that remains.[2]

---

[1] Aristotle, *Nicomachean Ethics*, trans. W.D. Ross in *The Basic Works of Aristotle*, ed. Richard McKeon (New York: Random House, Inc., 1941), p. 966.

[2] Jared Goldstein, "Desperately Seeking Science: The Creation of Knowledge in Family Practice," *Hastings Center Report*, vol. 20 (Nov/Dec, 1990), p. 28.

The uncertainty involved within the field of medicine is but one of many examples we could reflect upon. All around us, technology offers us the promise and assurance of a better life. But, do we really understand our technology, and the consequences that will follow from its continued development and use? In the arena of research and development, it is openly admitted that we do not really grasp the fullness of what we are doing in something like the Human Genome Project. Does our lack of knowledge here diminish or remove responsibility for what we are doing?

Our present situation is further complicated by the plurality of ethical approaches being used to solve moral dilemmas today. Well-meaning, intelligent, conscientious people are reaching deeply opposed conclusions on issues such as genetic engineering and abortion. As Vernon Bourke noted in the late 1960s, "Ethics has reached a point of crisis, when many of the experts admit that their judgments are no more valid than the opinions of the man in the street."[3] This "crisis" has only intensified in the 30 years since Bourke wrote this statement, and is realized in the inadequacy of contemporary theories of ethics to provide adequate answers for current moral dilemmas. One positive aspect of our contemporary "crisis" has been the renewed interest in the classic ethical texts, such as those of St. Thomas Aquinas, to see how they can illumine our ethical studies today. It is in this spirit that I appeal to the work of Aquinas and examine his position on ignorance and its affects on human responsibility in moral decision making.

First, I will make some preliminary remarks about St. Thomas's epistemology. Central to this will be a discussion of the difference in certitude between *speculative* and *practical* knowledge. I will then explore several key aspects of Thomistic ethics, which, I believe, provide a clear guide for human agents when faced with difficult moral situations involving unknowns. Drawing on Thomistic texts, I will suggest that the most appropriate way for human beings to respond when aware of ignorance or doubt is to base moral decisions upon *the strongest evidence available*. In that way, a human agent can never knowingly and willingly hide behind ignorance. This conclusion flows from the very nature of Aquinas's thought—true "human" action must always be based upon reason. I will conclude my paper by discussing the practical value of the Thomistic position for today. I believe that a Thomistic approach, when fully understood and appreciated, gives valuable insight into managing our growing technology.

---

[3] Vernon J. Bourke, *Ethics in Crisis*, (Milwaukee: The Bruce Publishing Company, 1966), p. xiii.

Preliminary Remarks on Knowledge

For St. Thomas, that which makes humans different from the other animals is our reason. As he notes in the *Summa Theologiae*, Question 76, article 1: "the difference which constitutes man is rational, which is applied to man on account of his intellectual principle."[4] And so, as Vernon Bourke notes in his work, *Ethics*, when a human being, "acts reasonably, he acts in accord with his own formal nature."[5] And yet, Aquinas does not insist that human beings are purely intellectual beings. Rather, Aquinas holds that the human being is a composite of matter (our physical body) and substantial form (our intellectual soul). The soul informs the whole body, not just one organ, and as such it is the substantial form or essence of the whole human person.[6] This view is known as the *hylomorphic* understanding of the human being.[7]

An important characteristic of the *hylomorphic* theory is that the union between the human body and soul is one of harmony and not conflict. In most dualistic theories of the person, there is the suggestion of a tension between the soul and the body. For Aquinas, the case is quite different. St. Thomas holds that the human soul is incomplete when separated from the body, as any form that desires matter is imperfect when separated from materiality.[8] Aquinas will not insist that the soul cannot exist without the body—indeed, it can for the soul is incorruptible.[9] However, this is not a "natural" state for the soul to exist in, because again, the soul finds perfection only in union with the body.[10]

---

[4] Thomas Aquinas, *Summa Theologiae*, I. q. 76, a. 1, *sed contra*.

[5] Vernon J. Bourke, *Ethics: A Textbook in Moral Philosophy*, (New York: The MacMillan Company, 1951), p. 126.

[6] Thomas Aquinas, *Summa Contra Gentiles*, Bk. II, Ch.LXXII: "For the proper act must be in its proper perfectible subject. Now the soul is the act of *an organic body*, not of one organ only. Therefore it is in the whole body, and not only in one part, according to its essence whereby it is the form of the body."

[7] This was first suggested by Aristotle, but developed by Aquinas. Here I am referring to Thomas' recognition of the "act of existence" which stands in relation to a being's essence as "act" to "potency." More could be found on this in Aquinas' short work, *On Being and Essence*.

[8] *Summa Contra Gentiles*, Bk. II, Ch.LXXXIII: "Every part that is separated from its whole is imperfect. Now the soul, since it is a form, as proved above, is a part of the human species. Consequently as long as it exists by itself apart from the body, it is imperfect."

[9] Ibid., Ch.LXXIX: "For it was proved above that every intellectual substance is incorruptible. Now man's soul is an intellectual substance, as we proved. Therefore it follows that the human soul is incorruptible."

[10] Ibid., Ch.LXXXIII.

Thus, for Aquinas, the essential characteristic of humanity is that of an *embodied soul*. Humanity's place is found in material creation. And yet, we are different from the rest of material creation in that we possess an intellect. The notion of *embodied soul* reveals the place of humanity in Creation. God knows all things by the Divine Essence.[11] Angels do not know by their essence, yet they do not require a physical body to acquire knowledge. Though below God, they remain superior to human beings in the order of rationality.[12] Human beings, by virtue of the power of abstraction, have more perfect knowledge than mere sensing creatures. Yet our knowledge is intimately caught up in the composite of our intellectual soul and our physical matter. In the view of St. Thomas, humanity's place in creation is unique:

> Accordingly we may consider something supreme in the genus of bodies, namely the human body equably attempered, which touches the lowest of the higher genus, namely the human soul, and this occupies the last degree in the genus of intellectual substances, as may be seen from its mode of understanding. Hence it is that the intellectual soul is said to be on the *horizon* and *confines* of things corporeal and incorporeal, inasmuch as it is an incorporeal substance, and yet the form of a body.[13]

The human person spans the distance between pure materiality and pure immateriality. We live and move between these two realms of reality.

Embodied soul, then, is an important way of understanding the human person in Aquinas. In any discussion of ethics, it is crucial to keep this understanding in focus. For St. Thomas, who we are as human beings plays a role in determining what is morally good for us to do. As our rationality is what makes us different from the rest of material creation, our power to know and its limitations will bear upon our moral decisions. With these

[11] *Summa Theologiae*, I, q.14, a.4, *sed contra*: "in God to be is the same thing as to understand. But God's existence is His Substance…Therefore the act of God's intellect is His Substance." Also, q.84, a.1, *responsio*: "if there be an intellect which knows all things by its essence, then its essence must needs have all things in itself immaterially…Now this is proper to God, that His Essence comprise all things immaterially, as effects pre-exist virtually in their cause. God alone, therefore, understands all things through His Essence: but neither the human soul nor the angels can do so."

[12] Ibid., q.57, a.2, *responsio*: "as man by his various powers of knowledge knows all classes of things, apprehending universals and immaterial things by his intellect, and things singular and corporeal by the senses, so an angel knows both by his one mental power. For the order of things runs in this way, that the higher a thing is, so much the more is its power unified and far reaching…. Accordingly, since an angel is above man in the order of nature, it is unreasonable to say that a man knows by any one of his powers something which an angel by his one faculty of knowledge, namely the intellect, does not know."

[13] *Summa Contra Gentiles*, Bk. II, Ch. LXVIII.

remarks made, let us turn to consider more fully what human knowledge involves for Aquinas.

Division of Knowledge: Speculative and Practical

Before discussing the issue of ignorance and its implications for human action, it will help to first discover what certitude is for Aquinas. In discussing predestination in Question 6 of his work, *On Truth*, St. Thomas offers these remarks:

> [C]ertitude of knowledge is had when one's knowledge does not deviate in any way from reality, and, consequently when it judges about a thing as it is. But because a judgment which will be certain about a thing is had especially from its causes, the word *certitude* has been transferred to the relation that a cause has to its effect; therefore, the relation of a cause to an effect is said to be certain when the cause infallibly produces its effect.[14]

To have certainty our knowledge must get to the proper causes of things: where they came from, what they are, what their purpose is, how they function, and so forth.

In considering this point it becomes clear that not all human knowing attains complete certitude. Realizing human knowledge was limited in the degrees of certitude it could attain, Aquinas distinguished those forms of knowledge that yielded complete certainty from those that did not. One early formulation of this distinction in human knowledge was laid out in Aquinas's "Foreword" to the *Commentary on the Posterior Analytics of Aristotle*:

> [T]here is one process of reason which involves necessity, where it is not possible to fall short of truth; and by such a process of reasoning the certainty of science is acquired. Again, there is a process of reason in which something true in most cases is concluded but without producing necessity. But the third process of reason is that in which reason fails to reach a truth because some principle which should have been observed in reasoning was defective.[15]

In the mind of St. Thomas, barring any defects in reasoning, human knowledge can always attain some level of certitude.

Now, to the first process of reasoning mentioned, the name of *speculative* knowledge is given. It is called *speculative* because it does not directly engage

    [14] Thomas Aquinas, *On Truth*, Vl., I, q.6, a.3, Questions I-IX, translated by Robert W. Mulligan, (Chicago: Henry Regency Company, 1952), p. 270.
    [15] Thomas Aquinas, *Commentary on the Posterior Analytics of Aristotle*, translated by F. R. Lorcher, (New York: Magi Books, Inc., 1970), p. 2.

the contingency of reality, but only considers those principles of reality that are necessary. Since *speculative* knowledge deals with necessary things precisely as they are necessary, it disengages from the materiality of reality, as it were, and considers reality in its immaterial, necessary components.[16]

The second process of reasoning is that of the *practical* intellect which directs human action. This lacks complete certitude because the objects of this form of knowledge are contingent. In his *Commentary on the Nicomachean Ethics*, Book VI, St. Thomas explains that there are two divisions of contingent things. There are those concerning what should be done, what action should be taken. There are also those things concerning art and making things.[17] It is clear that both of these require some degree of knowledge and reasoning. Ethics falls under the first category of contingent things, as it pertains to what actions should be done.

Now one may ask how there can be any certitude at all with *practical* reasoning? Even though it involves knowledge, that knowledge is caught up intimately in the contingent, undetermined activity of human beings. Although there may not be scientific, demonstrative certitude in ethics, there can indeed be a proper moral certitude, and there are two primary things that help secure our certainty.

First, there is a standard employed in ethics by which actions are judged so as to keep them from being arbitrary. St. Thomas refers to this standard in several places in his writings, such as in his commentary on Book II of the *Nicomachean Ethics*. Aquinas says, "Now the distinctive form of man is that which makes him a rational animal. Hence, man's action must be good precisely because it harmonizes with right reason."[18] When it comes to act-

---

[16] Jacques Maritain, *The Degrees of Knowledge*, (Notre Dame, Indiana: University of Notre Dame Press, 1995), pp. 37-41.

[17] Thomas Aquinas, *Commentary on the Nicomachean Ethics*, Bk. VI, lec. 3, trans. C. I. Litzinger, (Chicago: Henry Regnery Company, 1964), p. 554.

[18] Ibid., Bk. II, lec. 2, p. 257. See also, Bk. IV, lec.1, p. 539: in morality, "there is an object, as it were a mark, on which the man with right reason keeps his eye; and according to this he strives and makes modifications (i.e., he adds or subtracts) or considers by this mark what the limit of the middle course is, how it ought to be ascertained in each virtue. Such a middle course we say is a certain mean between excess and defect, and in accord with right reason." And, lec.2, p. 546: "Choice is the appetitive faculty deliberating inasmuch as the appetitive faculty takes what was preconsidered…. But to counsel is an act of reason…. Since then reason and appetitive faculty concur in choice, if choice ought to be good—this is required for the nature of moral virtue—the reason must be true and the appetitive faculty right, so that the same thing which reason declares or affirms, the appetitive faculty pursues. In order that there be perfection in action it is necessary that none of its principles be imperfect. But this intellect or reason (which harmonizes in this way with the right appetitive faculty) and its truth are practical." Also, lec. 2, p. 547: "the appetitive faculty is called right inasmuch as it pursues the things reason calls true."

ing, then, to be fully human we must follow our reason. Thus, even though as embodied beings we are affected by appetite, emotion, belief, opinion, etc., we should not act according to these *per se*, but rather we should act according to our understanding of the situation and our knowledge of good and bad.

Second, in practical matters our intellect always begins it's reasoning from universal truths and first principles. St. Thomas explains in the *Summa Theologiae*, Ia-IIae, in his discussion of human law, that just as science proceeds from first principles, "so too it is from the precepts of natural law, as from general and indemonstrable principles, that the human reason needs to proceed to the more particular determination of certain matters."[19] Ethics is not arbitrary. In making practical decisions, human beings use their knowledge of the world around them, but they should also appeal to the universal principles of natural law. So, we find proper moral certitude in making moral decisions by following both right reason and the universal principles of the natural law. However, this still does not yield complete certainty in our ethical decisions. Whereas the principles of natural law are universal and do not admit of variance, it must be admitted that in the particular situation actions may vary from individual to individual in some cases, due to the contingency of human activity.[20]

In his *Theory of Knowledge*, R. J. Henle, develops this notion that there are various levels of certitude in human knowing. First, there is simple, subjective certitude.[21] This is exemplified when someone is simply convinced that something is true, regardless of whether or not it actually is true. The person's mind is made up, so to speak, and the agent feels certain about what is being considered. Second, there can be objective certitude.[22] This is the "determination of the intellect to a true judgment."[23] Now this

---

[19] *Summa Theologiae*, I-II, q. 91, a. 3, *responsio*.

[20] Ibid., q. 94, a. 6, *responsio*: "the natural law is altogether unchangeable in its first principles: but in its secondary principles, which…are certain detailed proximate conclusions drawn from the first principles, the natural law is not changed so that what it prescribes be not right in most cases. But it may be changed in some particular cases of rare occurrence, through some special causes hindering the observance of such prescripts…." Also, a. 4, *responsio*: "Thus it is right and true for all to act according to reason: and from this principle it follows as a proper conclusion, that goods entrusted to another should be restored to their owner. Now this is true for the majority of cases: but it may happen in a particular case that it would be injurious, and therefore unreasonable, to restore goods held in trust, for instance if they are claimed for the purpose of fighting against one's country. And this principle will be found to fail the more, according as we descend further into detail…."

[21] R. J. Henle, *A Theory of Knowledge*, (Chicago: Loyola University Press, 1983), p. 262.

[22] Ibid., p. 263.

[23] Ibid.

can be in either of two ways. There is material objective certitude, which is marked by the presence of objective and valid evidence in support of the judgment the mind has committed to.[24] At this level, there is reliable evidence present that we can turn to in support of what we are considering and this gives us certitude. Finally, there can be formal objective certitude, which occurs when there is objective evidence that is fully comprehended as such.[25] That is, when we know something is true, have evidence to support our position, and know why the evidence supports our position, we then have formal objective certitude.

And so, in the Thomistic understanding, human action will involve deliberation over alternative actions that are not determined to any fixed course. In this, certitude is found in beginning from universal principles, and in employing right reason as the standard that guides the intellect in its deliberation towards the good and away from evil. There is a difference, then, between *speculative* and *practical* knowledge. The end of scientific inquiry results in a judgment of knowledge about something that is necessary in the world, and so yields formal objective certitude. Practical reasoning leads to a judgment of action for a particular, contingent situation, and can yield material objective certitude.[26] More could be said regarding the distinctions between *speculative* and *practical* knowledge,[27] but for the purpose of this investigation we draw two conclusions: 1) since morals involve contingent things, human beings cannot make decisions about such matters in purely scientific terms, expecting complete certainty, and so the Thomistic system is not purely dogmatic; 2) but we cannot conclude therefore that morality is arbitrary and has no certitude, for there are guidelines for human action which are universal and certain principles.

Knowledge is therefore crucial in human moral decision-making. So much so, that the lack of knowledge will affect both the truth of our moral judgments, and our responsibility for our actions. However, it is important to emphasize that even though a lack of knowledge can be a factor in moral activity, we find that human agents can indeed attain proper moral certitude.

---

[24] Ibid.

[25] Ibid., p. 264.

[26] *Commentary on the Nicomachean Ethics*, Bk. VI, lec.2, op. cit., p. 547: "the practical intellect has a beginning in a universal consideration and, according to this, is the same in subject with the speculative, but its consideration terminates in an individual operable thing."

[27] I would refer anyone who would like to pursue the distinctions between speculative and practical knowledge to John E. Naus, and his work, *The Nature of the Practical Intellect According to Saint Thomas Aquinas* (Rome: Universita Gregoria, 1959). It was an extremely helpful resource.

Ignorance and Practical Knowledge

Our discussion has led us to the following questions. First, how does ignorance affect the human act in general, by making it more or less voluntary? Second, how does ignorance affect the responsibility for moral action? As to the first, we find St. Thomas examining ignorance in the *Summa Theologiae*, I-II, Question 6, article 8. Here he notes three ways in which ignorance affects human actions: "in one way, *concomitantly*; another, *consequently*, in a third way, *antecedently*."[28] Ignorance is *concomitant* with volition when some ignorance of the circumstances is present, but the agent was so bent on acting that, even had the missing knowledge been present, it would not have made any difference. This type of ignorance has no real bearing on the act itself, but merely accompanies the action. Such ignorance does not make the act involuntary, but more precisely non-voluntary.[29] This is because the will cannot properly choose what is unknown.

Ignorance is *consequent* with volition when an agent purposefully chooses to remain ignorant of a situation so as not to be held responsible. This is the ever-popular "ignorance is bliss" approach to life. This state of ignorance is clearly chosen by the agent, and so is voluntary. In addition, ignorance is *consequent* with willing when an agent could or ought to have the specific knowledge that is lacking—this is the case of negligence. An action performed out of negligence is voluntary, then, because it could and should have been avoided by the agent.

The final type of ignorance is the only one that can cause an involuntary action in a human agent.[30] *Antecedent* ignorance precedes the willing of the action, but the ignorance itself is not willed. Such ignorance primarily involves those things that an agent is not bound to know. In these cases, if the particular missing fact or circumstance were known, then the agent would not have performed the action, but there is no reason why the agent should have that knowledge. And so, *antecedent* ignorance impedes the freedom of the agent's choice.

In regard to human action, then, ignorance can reduce the voluntariness of action. Bourke summarizes this in the following way: "The perfection of the

---

[28] *Summa Theologiae*, I-II, q.6, a.8, *responsio*.

[29] Ibid., "ignorance of this kind, as the Philosopher states (*Ethic*. iii. 1), does not cause involuntariness, since it is not the cause of anything that is repugnant to the will: but it causes *non-voluntariness*, since that which is unknown cannot be actually willed."

[30] Ibid., "Ignorance is *antecedent* to the act of the will, when it is not voluntary, and yet is the cause of man's willing what he would not will otherwise...Such ignorance causes involuntariness simply."

voluntary act is directly dependent on the perfection of the agent's rational knowledge of the end and of the things conducive to the end. Where such knowledge is more or less lacking, the agent is more or less imperfect in his voluntariness."[31] And, since ignorance in some cases detracts from voluntariness, it can also diminish one's moral responsibility. But with this goes a serious charge. Since, for Aquinas, all things long for fulfillment and completion, one goal for human beings will be to act in a fully human way.[32] As rational, then, human beings must seek knowledge of those things we are bound to know prior to making moral decisions. St. Thomas was quite aware of the tendency in human beings to use ignorance as a means of hiding from responsibility.[33] But hiding behind ignorance does not fulfill what it is to be human. Since we are endowed with reason, human beings are obliged to know where we stand in relation to the world. In understanding our place in creation, we recognize that our decisions should not only consider our own, personal good, but the common good and the good of humanity as a species, as well as God's eternal law.[34] Our reason compels us not to move in ignorance of any of these relationships. In the Thomistic view, then, there is a strong commitment to the knowledge that human beings can attain, as that knowledge provides the means of ordering our *practical* actions to their proper ends.

These considerations are important for determining human responsibility for action. For Thomas, only fully human acts merit moral praise or blame:

> [T]hose actions alone are properly called human, of which man is master. Now man is master of his actions through his reason and will; whence, too, the free-will is defined a *faculty of will and reason*. Therefore those actions are properly called human which proceed from a deliberate will. And if any other actions are found in man, they can be called actions *of a man*, but not properly *human* actions, since they are not proper to man as man.[35]

So, how is an agent's responsibility affected when an action is performed in conjunction with these various forms of ignorance? This issue of responsibility

---

[31] *Ethics: A Textbook in Moral Philosophy*, p. 73.

[32] Ibid.

[33] *Summa Theologiae*, I-II, q. 76, a. 4, *responsio*: "it happens sometimes that such like ignorance is directly willed and essentially voluntary, as when a man is purposely ignorant that he may sin more freely, and ignorance of this kind seems rather to make the act more voluntary and more sinful, since it is through the will's intention to sin that he is willing to bear the hurt of ignorance, for the sake of freedom in sinning."

[34] Ibid., a. 2, *responsio*: "all are bound in common to know the articles of faith, and the universal principles of right, and each individual is bound to know matters regarding his duty or state."

[35] Ibid., q. 1, a.1, *responsio*.

is discussed more fully in the *Summa Theologiae*, I-II, Question 76, under the aspect of sin. First, Aquinas clarifies the case of *concomitant* ignorance, which merely accompanies an action. St. Thomas notes that if an agent would have performed a particular action whether there was full knowledge or not, the ignorance has no bearing on the responsibility of the agent, as it merely accompanies the action performed. If a thief breaks into a house no matter what, then not knowing if anyone is at home becomes unimportant, and so does not detract in any way from the responsibility of the thief for the action.

St. Thomas then turns to a more thorough consideration of *consequent* ignorance and how it bears upon moral responsibility. In the second article of Question 76 Aquinas explains that there are some things we are bound to know, such as the things regarding the law and our social and political duties. Ignorance of this type involves negligence, since the agent does not attempt to know all of the particulars of the action being considered. To the degree that an agent fails to seek knowledge when an obligation to do so is present, or avoids it altogether, voluntariness remains and responsibility is not excused. Such an action goes against right reason, and so is a disordered act. However, there are other things human knowers could know but are not bound to know, such as mathematics or science. Certainly any human being has at least the potential to know these things, but the lack of knowledge of them will not be a source of sin because no obligation is present, and so responsibility is lessened.

St. Thomas adds a further distinction to the types of ignorance in this discussion that was not present earlier, namely *invincible* ignorance: "such like ignorance, not being voluntary, since it is not in our power to be rid of it, is not a sin: wherefore it is evident that no invincible ignorance is a sin."[36] It would seem the reason for this is that an agent faced with *invincible* ignorance has no way of gaining the knowledge that is lacking, and so cannot make a voluntary choice. But what constitutes an *invincible* ignorance? St. Thomas does not list what qualifies as *invincible*. However, some light can be shed upon this issue by reference to I, Question 86. Here Aquinas points out two things that the human intellect *cannot* know. First, the human intellect cannot have knowledge of the infinite precisely as it is infinite.[37] Hence, we can never fully understand God, as the Divine Essence is infinite. Second, the human intellect cannot have knowledge of the future in itself.[38]

---

[36] Ibid., q. 76, a. 2, *responsio*.

[37] Ibid., I, q. 86, a. 2, *sed contra*: "It is said (*Phys.* i. 4) that the *infinite, considered as such, is unknown*."

[38] Ibid., a. 4, *sed contra*: "It is written (*Eccles.* viii. 6,7), *There is a great affliction for man, because he is ignorant of things past; and things to come he cannot know by any messenger*."

Now, it would seem that this could open the door for claiming *invincible* ignorance of all human action since every action is future to our deciding upon it and so is fully unknowable. But St. Thomas counters any such claims:

> The future cannot be known in itself save by God alone...but forasmuch as it exists in its causes, the future can be known by us also. And if, indeed, the cause be such as to have a necessary connection with its future result, then the future is known with scientific certitude, just as the astronomer foresees the future eclipse. If, however, the cause be such as to produce a certain result more frequently than not, then can the future be known more or less conjecturally, according as its cause is more or less inclined to produce the effect.[39]

Human beings can indeed have some knowledge of the future because they can acquire knowledge of the proper causes of things discovered in reality. When the causes of necessary things are known, the result is scientific knowledge that is necessarily true. When the causes of things that are *not* necessary are known, certitude is had to the degree that there is some objective evidence to support one's conclusions. If we can understand the causes at work, then we have *some* evidence upon which to base our decisions about future actions. The presence of such evidence allows us to have *some* level of material objective certitude.

And so, we can draw an important conclusion regarding human responsibility when faced with an apparent *invincible* ignorance. If one truly finds some fact wanting or unknowable in a situation, there is still one final recourse, as opposed to acting upon the ignorance as such. "Conjectural knowledge," which admittedly lacks complete certainty, is still more proper grounds to base a moral decision upon than any claim to ignorance of the situation. Such knowledge is not arbitrary, but attains material objective certitude to the extent that the evidence given reasonably supports the conclusions of the agent.

St. Thomas expresses this same point in another way in II-II, Question 70. When discussing the evidence given by witnesses in court cases, he writes:

> [I]n human acts, on which judgments are passed and evidence required, it is impossible to have demonstrative certitude, because they are about things contingent and variable. Hence, the certitude of probability suffices, such as may reach the truth in the greater number of cases, although it fail in the minority.[40]

What the moral agent appeals to is not the mathematical probability of what will be the odds of something happening. Rather, an agent gathers the available evidence to discover what is most probably true in a moral situation.

---

[39] Ibid., *responsio.*
[40] Ibid, II-II, q. 70, a. 2, *responsio.*

Ethical decision-making is not a gamble of odds, but an appeal to the strength of the evidence available as a guide in the face of uncertainty. And so, I do not interpret Aquinas as appealing to probability in the mathematical sense, but rather he is concerned with knowledge and evidence. Even when there may be a situation where we are aware that we do not "know" all of the circumstances, humans are faced with an obligation, which befits our nature, to consider similar situations as well as the evidence given by others to form some type of certitude upon which to act. This position also remains consistent with the recognition of moral absolutes, because moral absolutes serve as part of the evidence to which a moral agent will appeal in making a moral decision.

In the end, I believe the above considerations show that there can never be a case of "known *invincible* ignorance." To truly be faced with an unconquerable ignorance, one could not be aware of such a lack of knowledge prior to acting. If one were aware, then one would be obligated—as time allows—to gather as much knowledge as possible to form some level of material objective certitude. If one cannot achieve a reasonable level of certitude, then one must not perform the action—to do so would be a case of negligence, willingly proceeding in the face of ignorance.

So, we could not say that Adolph Hitler's parents were immoral because they decided to have children and one of their children committed terrible crimes against humanity. They had no way of knowing or predicting what their son would do in the future, and as such were involuntary agents in producing the leader of the Holocaust. For any agent faced with such unconquerable ignorance, no responsibility can be assessed. An agent cannot employ right reason when such ignorance is present. Further, such ignorance would clearly not be discovered until well after the action. However, if one wanted to attempt the cloning of a human being in the name of scientific discovery, without really knowing what consequences will follow—one could not claim this as a case of *invincible* ignorance and shirk responsibility for the outcomes. Rather, one would be obligated on both scientific and moral grounds to act only in reasonable certitude of what will happen, based upon knowledge and evidence already available. If no certitude could be established, then the action must be foregone. Simply put, excluding emergency situations, a human agent should never act without proper knowledge.

Applications

So what applications do these conclusions have for today? Let me use just one illustration—the current debate on abortion. Read almost any editorial page, skim through any journal of ethics, browse over any library shelf—all in search of the topic of abortion—and one will undoubtedly recognize the strongly contrasted approaches to this delicate, but crucial topic. Abortion, of course, is not a wholly new technology. But important advancements in the technology involved with abortion (such as RU486, and "emergency contraception") continue to cloud the ethics of this practice in our country, making it more and more difficult for some to make the important distinctions necessary to understand exactly what abortion involves.

What seems to be the point of divergence between those who strongly oppose abortion and those who equally defend it? It seems too simplistic to say that one group advocates legalized murder, while the other opposes it— indeed, both groups oppose making innocent people suffer. On the one hand, Baruch Brody argues that whereas it is difficult biologically to determine exactly when a fetus becomes human, "it surely is not a human being at the moment of conception, and it surely is one by the end of the third month."[41] Supporters of this position hold that the status of the embryo changes during pregnancy, and hence the morality of abortion also changes. John Noonan describes an opposing view: "Once conceived, the being was recognized as man because he had man's potential. The criterion for humanity, thus, was simple and all-embracing: if you are conceived by human parents, you are human."[42] Finally, there is a third group who would hold that even after birth, a baby is not a human person because it lacks consciousness and the ability to relate to other human beings in a meaningful way, and so is devoid of any right to life.[43]

These conflicting opinions indicate that a crucial issue of the abortion debate (indeed, perhaps *the* crucial issue) involves how the fetus is viewed. The sciences are hesitant to settle the question because of the lack of what most scientists would consider cold, hard facts. Veatch reveals this hesitation when he writes: "It is logically impossible to offer a strictly biological argument for the status of the fetus, although it may be possible to claim that some biological event, such as conception, implantation, or the beginning of breathing, is the factor that ought to be given moral significance."[44] But even

[41] Baruch Brody, *Abortion and the Sanctity of Human Life*, (Cambridge: The MIT Press, 1975), p. 112.

[42] John T. Noonan, Jr. "An Almost Absolute Value in History," in *The Morality of Abortion*, ed. John T. Noonan, Jr., (Cambridge: Harvard University Press, 1970), p. 51.

[43] J. C. Willke and Dave Andrusko, "Personhood Redux," *Hastings Center Report*, vol. 18, (Oct/Nov, 1988), p. 32. One might also think of Peter Singer's 1979 text, *Practical Ethics*, as well as his more recent work.

[44] Robert Veatch, *Case Studies in Medical Ethics* (Cambridge: Harvard University Press, 1977), p. 170.

recognizing the hesitation of the sciences to formulate a decisive position, Lisa Sowle Cahill, in discussing the use of the RU 486 pill, notes that there is still a choice involved which ends the life of the embryo, regardless of its status, the responsibility of which even early abortion cannot, and should not, remove.[45] Even those who will insist the fetus is not a human being and has no rights must admit that abortion is not simply a matter of how a woman wishes to care for her body. Abortion is the choice to terminate (at the very least) a "potential" human being.

What, then, are we to do in the face of such conflicting positions over the status of the fetus? If ethicists and scientists cannot agree on this issue—does this mean we are facing a case of *invincible* ignorance? Consider the following excerpts from the 1989 *Webster v. Reproductive Health Services* case, which came before the United States Supreme Court. In his oral argument for Reproductive Health Services, Frank Susman was insisting for the pro-choice side that abortion was a "fundamental right" of a woman. Susman partly argued that the Constitution supported a woman's right to an abortion. But Susman also recognized the lack of scientific certitude in determining the humanity of the unborn. Since no one knew for sure, a woman should be the sole person to decide when a fetus was a human or not. Justice Scalia objected to this line of reasoning. The record of the discussion between Scalia and Susman portrays the striking divergence of opinion that arises over the uncertainty of the status of the unborn:

JUSTICE SCALIA: Let me inquire. I can see deriving a fundamental right from either a long tradition that this, the right to abort, has always been protected. I don't see that tradition, but I suppose you could also derive a fundamental right just simply from the text of the Constitution, plus the logic of the matter or whatever.

How can—can you derive it that way here without making a determination as to whether the fetus is a human life or not? It is very hard to say it just is a matter of basic principle that it must be a fundamental right unless you make the determination that the organism that is destroyed is not a human life. Can you as a matter of logic or principle make that determination otherwise?

MR. SUSMAN: I think the basic question—and, of course, it goes to one of the specific provisions of the statute as to whether this is a human life or whether human life begins at conception—is not something that is verifiable as a fact. It is a question verifiable only by reliance upon faith.

It is a question of labels. Neither side in this issue and debate would ever disagree on the physiological facts. Both sides would agree as to when a heartbeat can first be detected. Both sides would agree to when brain waves can first be detected. But when you come to try to place the emotional labels on what you call

<hr />

[45] Lisa Sowle Cahill, "'Abortion Pill' RU 486," *Hasting Center Report*, vol. 17, (Oct/Nov, 1987), p. 8.

that collection of physiological facts, that is where people part company.
JUSTICE SCALIA: I agree with you entirely, but what conclusion does that lead you to? That, therefore, there must be a fundamental right on the part of the woman to destroy this thing that we don't know what it is or, rather, that whether there is or isn't is a matter that you vote upon; since we don't know the answer, people have to make up their minds the best they can.
MR. SUSMAN: The conclusion to which it leads me is that, when you have an issue that is so divisive and so emotional and so personal and so intimate, it must be left as a fundamental right to the individual to make that choice under her then attendant circumstances, her religious beliefs, her moral beliefs, and in consultation with her physician.[46]

The uncertainty regarding the humanity of the unborn is openly admitted by both gentlemen in their discussion. How should a moral agent act regarding abortion in the face of such uncertainty? Susman indicates that the very presence of uncertainty on this issue secures the right of the woman as the only one who can make the decision to terminate a fetus. But is this the most appropriate way for human moral agents to act? What we have to ask is whether or not it is reasonable (*right reason*) to base a strong, positive right to control one's body to the extent that certain people can determine the humanity of the unborn upon their personal belief and be both legally and morally justified, all upon an uncertainty—a lack of knowledge? Or, is it reasonable to protect the fetus as human life, regardless of whether it ever achieves its full potential? A woman contemplating an abortion, or a doctor contemplating doing such a procedure cannot simply say they do not know for sure what we are doing. Employing the natural law approach laid out earlier, we need to examine those facts that we do know—even if they only yield material objective certitude—and follow *the strongest evidence at hand.*

In this regard, John Noonan offered the following argument against abortion:

> If a fetus is destroyed, one destroys a being already possessed of the genetic code, organs, and sensitivity to pain, and one which had an 80 percent chance of developing further into a baby outside the womb, who, in time, would reason.... It is this genetic information which determines his characteristics, which is the biological carrier of the possibility of human wisdom, which makes him a self-evolving being. A being with a human genetic code is man.[47]

---

[46] From the "Oral argument of Frank Susman on Behalf of the Appelles," *Webster v. Reproductive Health Services (1989),* in *Landmark Briefs and Arguments of the Supreme Court of the United States: Constitutional Law,* edited by Philip B. Kurland and Gerhard Casper, (Frederick, Maryland: University Publications of America, 1990), pp. 944-45.

[47] "An Almost Absolute Value in History," p. 57.

Noonan first made this argument in 1970. The advances in genetic re-search and the Human Genome Project, however, have clearly added to the strength of this argument today. An appeal to genetic evidence re-veals that an embryo, from conception on, has all that it ever needs to develop as a human being. How, then, can we see it as anything less than human? Yet, the 1975 argument of Baruch Brody, which had objected that the genetic argument was still inconclusive from a scientific per-spective, continues to reign (as we read with Frank Susman and pro-choice advocates). Brody's point was that the mere presence of human genetic information does not "prove" that human "life" is present. And so he pursues other avenues for arguing against abortion.[48] But in the absence of scientific certitude, one must consider the evidence that is available. What Noonan indicates is that every fertilized human egg by possessing its genetic information has the potentiality of full human life. This is an important point. No one denies that once conceived a fetus will become nothing but human if nurtured. However, this is often glossed over as a trivial point. *But this is evidence!* The "collection of physiological facts" that Susman mentions, facts such as the presence of genetic information, represent evidence that a human agent must recognize before making a moral decision. Right reason will direct an agent to recognize that the fertilized egg from conception on contains the full potentiality of a hu-man being—a potentiality that is, and will continue to be, developing. All of the possibilities of that human being in all of its uniqueness are present in those first cells. This is evidence that can guide our moral decisions. This is evidence that can give us moral certitude in recogniz-ing that abortion ends a human life.

Conclusions

A Thomistic approach indicates that the proper way for human agents to act when faced with an uncertain situation is to follow *the strongest evi-dence available*. Although this approach does not yield absolute or scientific certitude, it does give the human agent a proper moral certitude regarding her or his action. To follow the strongest evidence available is the only proper way for a human agent to act in any uncertain situation. That is, basing our moral decisions upon the evidence that we do have is the only way to act properly as rational, responsible moral agents.

---

[48] *Abortion and the Sanctity of Human Life*, p. 91.

An approach like this demands much from people. It calls us into a dynamic of reasoning, understanding, investigating, and judging. However, it does bridge the gap between an overly dogmatic approach, and a loose "do-as-you-will" approach to life. It avoids dogmatism by requiring us to recognize that human activity is not determined to any one course, but must be reasoned out. It avoids emotivism by showing that what humans do must not be arbitrary, but rather must follow right reason to be fully human. The natural law approach of Thomas Aquinas puts a great responsibility upon humanity in moral decision-making.

This investigation clearly does not answer all of the uncertain moral dilemmas that humanity will be faced with. However, I believe that the method of Aquinas sheds light on the confusion of ethics today. By focusing on right reason and the importance of following the strongest evidence when faced with uncertainty, St. Thomas challenges us to be fully human in every action we undertake—even when they involve difficult and controversial cases.

So—when you know that you do not know—find out! If you cannot find out, don't do it!

Maritain and Macintyre on Moral Education

Christopher H. Toner

One of the central themes of the philosophy of Jacques Maritain is his focus upon the person. Following St. Thomas, Maritain writes: "[t]he notion of person signifies what is most perfect in all nature."[1] In us, as corporeal beings subject to change, the center of liberty that is personality "is only manifested by a progressive conquest of the self by the self accomplished in time."[2] This conquest of the self by the self, which gives "a face to the turbulent multiplicity that dwells within him,"[3] can be completed only by grace. But it can and must be begun in the natural order by the acquisition and exercise of the natural virtues, united by the commanding activity of prudence. How are the virtues, and particularly prudence, to be acquired?

As any Aristotelian will remind us, the virtues are acquired through habituation, but not of course through the kind of habituation applied to nonhuman animals through conditioning. Habituation into the virtues must proceed through the eliciting of free responses from the human apprentice, through a kind of education adequate to its human object. Thus Maritain tells us "the prime goal of education is the conquest of internal and spiritual freedom to be achieved by the individual person."[4] Education is to be an art aimed at integrating a "turbulent multiplicity" into a projectile directed toward Heaven. The conquest is to be achieved, or at least well begun, through the instilling of prudence into the soul. But prudence requires experience, practical intuition, and rightly ordered loves, none of which, Maritain reminds us, can be taught in the classroom. "In spite of all that," he continues,

---

[1]Jacques Maritain, *The Degrees of Knowledge*, trans. Gerald B. Phelan (Notre Dame, Indiana: University of Notre Dame Press, 1995), p. 248. Here Maritain cites the *Summa Theologiae*, I q. 27, a. 3.

[2] *The Degrees of Knowledge*, p. 247.

[3] Ibid.

[4]Jacques Maritain, *Education at the Crossroads* (New Haven, Connecticut: Yale University Press, 1943), p. 11.

"education should be primarily concerned with them."[5] Thus, looking forward in 1943 to the hoped-for victory over Axis Powers, he writes that the "task of moral re-education is really a matter of public emergency."[6] Now, not only must students be morally educated: they must be so educated by morally good persons, lest they be corrupted, and indeed by moral persons with a certain kind of intuitive capacity (about which more will be said shortly), who must themselves have undergone a similar education.[7] Thus Maritain sets for himself quite a problem, and I do not think that he provides an adequate solution. He does drop a number of hints for us as to how moral educators might go about this seemingly impossible task of teaching or educating for prudence and practical knowledge, but they are largely suggestive and sketchy.

My purpose is to develop these suggestions by appeal to the work of a later Thomist, Alasdair MacIntyre, and in particular to his account of practices, which Kelvin Knight has called "the schools of the virtues."[8] MacIntyre does not say much under the official heading of "philosophy of education," but he does say much that is eminently relevant to it. Bringing what he does say under a Maritainian architectonic of education as art assisting nature sheds light upon his implicit philosophy of education, and this in turn sheds more light upon Maritain's explicit philosophy of education. Showing the connections between these philosophies of education also provides the materials for a response to the claim made by at least one of MacIntyre's critics, the claim that practices play no important role in a Thomistic account of the virtues.[9] Practices do play an important role, and even if this was largely implicit in Aquinas, it becomes much more explicit in later Thomistic accounts, such as that of Maritain. This excursion into the writings of MacIntyre will be seen (though here only in brief outline) to come full circle, in that MacIntyre's invocation of traditions of moral enquiry and his own metaphysics of the human person point us back, or onward, to Maritain's personalism.[10] I believe that both philosophers are enriched by the revolution.

---

[5] Ibid., p. 23.

[6] Ibid., p. 93.

[7] Ibid., p. 108.

[8] Kelvin Knight, "Introduction" to *The MacIntyre Reader*, ed. Kelvin Knight (Notre Dame, Indiana: University of Notre Dame Press, 1998), p. 10.

[9] See David Miller, "Virtues, Practices and Justice" in *After MacIntyre*, ed. John Horton and Susan Mendus (Notre Dame, Indiana: University of Notre Dame Press, 1994), p. 246. Miller is here speaking of justice in particular.

[10] The affinity of MacIntyre's thought to that of Maritain is of course due in large part to their common master, St. Thomas, and it is important to stress that I do not mean to make the genetic claim that MacIntyre was always consciously and single-mindedly working out

The Degrees of Practical Knowledge

Before turning to what Maritain has to say about practical education, we must see, in outline, what he takes practical knowledge to be. Maritain distinguishes three levels of practical knowledge, in ascending degree of proximity to the concrete action to be done here and now: the speculatively practical, the practically practical, and the prudential. The first of these, the speculatively practical, corresponds to moral philosophy and is largely communicable; it can be taught in a classroom. The latter two, however, depending decreasingly on abstract ideas and increasingly on experience and on uprightness of character, are increasingly incommunicable. These three levels are best distinguished by understanding their objects, modes, and ends.[11] For all three, the object is the operable, human action.[12]

The speculatively practical has as its end "*knowing* as the foundation of *directing*" action "*from afar.*"[13] Its mode is speculative in that it is analytic, breaking actions down into their constituents. Thus St. Thomas in the Ia-IIae treats in separate treatises the will, passions, habits, and so forth. But Maritain hastens to point out that its mode is not purely speculative; moral philosophy is not merely a metaphysics or psychology of the virtues.[14] It considers the operable, human action, as related to its end, and is thus a normative science. In this sense its mode is practical and compositive.

Practically practical science (and it is a science since it still consists in the organization of universal truths), on the other hand, has as its end the

Maritainian ideas in his development of his notions of practices, traditions, and so forth. He owes intellectual debts also to Cardinal Newman, Wittgenstein, Marx, Gadamer, Anscombe, and so on and on, and he is moreover a very creative philosopher in his own right. But MacIntyre is also happy to acknowledge his explicit debts to Maritain. See *After Virtue* (Notre Dame, Indiana: University of Notre Dame Press, 1984), p. 260, where he refers to Maritain as one of the "philosophers for whom I have the greatest respect and from whom I have learned most."

[11] Maritain's discussion of these levels is to be found in chap. VIII and Appendix VII of *The Degrees of Knowledge*. Ralph McInerny offers a helpful discussion and criticism in his essay "The Degrees of Practical Knowledge" in his *Art and Prudence*, (Notre Dame, Indiana: University of Notre Dame Press, 1988), pp. 63-76. McInerny here argues that Maritain's division does not map onto that of Aquinas in the *Summa Theologiae*, I q. 14, a. 16. He is, moreover, skeptical about whether the three levels of practical knowledge really need involve three distinct sorts of *habitus*. This dispute, to the extent that it is a dispute, is not my concern here. Even if the speculatively practical and practically practical did turn out to run together, this would do nothing to undermine Maritain's philosophy of education. It certainly does not worry MacIntyre in his working out of his own related project.

[12] *The Degrees of Knowledge*, p. 484.

[13] Ibid., p. 481.

[14] Ibid., p. 482.

direction of action "from nearby."[15] Thus, e.g., instead of arriving at a general precept to tell the truth to those who have a right to it, practically practical science will arrive at a much more particular precept to tell the truth to such and such a person in such and such a situation. As to its mode, it is practical and compositive through and through. As Maritain writes, "there is no question here of explaining and resolving a truth, even a practical truth, into its reasons and principles. The question is to prepare for action and to assign its proximate rules...knowledge here, instead of analyzing, composes...it gathers together everything that is known."[16] Practically practical science knows in a way close to intuition. The practitioner of this science must imagine a situation described in detail, and try to see what a virtuous person would do in it (or a continent person; advice must of course be tailored to the level of the development of the advisee). As examples of practitioners of the science of morals Maritain puts forward such "deeply intuitive men" as Dostoyevsky, and indeed the novel is a splendid medium for this science.[17] Unfortunately absent from his list (but let me now add her) is Jane Austen. In her novel *Mansfield Park*, Austen portrays a situation in which the heroine, Fanny Price, overcomes a dispute, and thus brings some peace to a very troubled household, by making a gift of a silver knife to one of her sisters.[18] In seeing what she should do in this situation and doing it, Fanny acts virtuously. In presenting this scenario, Austen is so far a practitioner of moral science. She imaginatively places herself in Fanny's situation (and invites us to do the same) and gathers together moral precepts and the thoughts, feelings, and intuitions she takes it that a virtuous person such as Fanny would have, and tells us how she would act. Yet here, it should be pointed out, Austen is not exercising prudence, for though she judges she does not act. And the judgment is still universal, in that, for all its particularity, it applies to anyone of such a type in such a (albeit narrowly circumscribed) situation; Jane Austen is not Fanny Price. Now, Maritain insists that practitioners of this science are not psychologists, but moralists: they educate us; they are teachers.[19] And indeed the possession of the *habitus* of this practical science is the "intuitive capacity" which I said above is required of teachers if they are to be effective moral educators. And, if novelists are practitioners of moral science *par excellence*, there is a more common and humble way of practicing

---

[15] Ibid., p. 484.

[16] Ibid., p. 334.

[17] Ibid., p. 335.

[18] I select this example because MacIntyre discusses it in his "How Moral Agents Became Ghosts," *Synthese*, 53 (1982), p. 311; his discussion, though, focuses upon Price, not upon Austen.

[19] *The Degrees of Knowledge*, p. 335.

this science, by serving as the knowledgeable friend giving practical advice of the form "Well, what I would do is...."[20] We all practice this science, with varying degrees of competence.

In prudence, the "continuous movement of thought inclined toward concrete action to be posited in existence" is completed; its end is "to direct action immediately." Prudence is knowing incarnate in action. It judges and commands what is to be done here and now, and thus presupposes the rectitude of the will. As to its mode, it is practical and compositive "to the highest degree." Indeed Maritain remarks that it is only prudence that is, strictly speaking, practically practical.[21]

A word or two should be said about the relation of these three levels of practical knowing. Speculatively practical science presupposes neither of the other two. A vicious person who is lousy as an advisor could be a fine moral philosopher. Similarly for prudence: a simple person ignorant of moral philosophy can be an outstanding human being; and such a person may be incapable of writing novels, or even of giving good advice in a widely accessible way (Joe Gargery of *Great Expectations* leaps to mind). Practically practical science is different. Maritain tells us that it depends upon speculatively practical science, and also upon prudence: it depends upon the right dispositions of the appetite and upon prudential experience and especially upon prudential judgment.[22] It does not, of course, involve command.

Maritain on the Teaching of Practical Knowledge

We can now turn to what Maritain has to say about the teaching of practical knowledge.[23] He insists that "The only dominating influence in the school...must be that of truth...from the very start the teacher must respect in the child the dignity of the mind;" he continues, "if the one who is being

---

[20]McInerny makes just this point in "The Degrees of Practical Knowledge," p. 70.

[21] *The Degrees of Knowledge*, pp. 333, 481, 483-84.

[22]Ibid., pp. 334, 336, and 487. Importantly, Maritain reminds us that rectitude of the will is "*even more* necessary for prudence" (p. 487n7), since only prudence involves actual command. It seems to me that a merely continent, or even an incontinent person (though not a vicious person) could act as a practitioner of moral science, since practically practical science deals with absent situations, and the incontinent characteristically does have practical knowledge, although he acts against it. Thus Maritain qualifies this dependence, stating that practically practical science depends upon prudence "if not in respect to the experimental material and partial truths it can gather up, at least for its complete truth and scientific certitude" (p. 488). The incontinent practitioner would lack certitude because he is always susceptible to distraction.

[23]I focus on *Education at the Crossroads*, where his concern with practically practical science is largely implicit.

taught is not an angel, neither is he inanimate clay." Although there is of course no innate knowledge, "the vital and active principle of knowledge does exist in each of us." Education, then, is an art that ministers to nature, and in which the student himself is the principal agent and the teacher an effective but only secondary agent.[24]

In the case of speculative truths, which are communicable through the medium of ideas, truths are not simply placed in or imposed upon the mind. Rather, they are set clearly before the student's mind so that it naturally and freely assents to them.[25] Now, just as the mind is fundamentally disposed toward the true, so is it disposed toward the good.[26] So it would seem that the same technique, that of setting the object before the mind and so eliciting a natural movement toward it, should be applicable to moral education. The difficulty, of course, is that it must be set before the mind as good, *sub ratione boni*. The student must be brought to see something, a concrete action to be done here and now, as good. Now we can hold out certain moral standards, and we can teach moral philosophy, at least to those with enough lived experience to understand it, and thus Maritain thinks that we can exert a certain indirect influence upon the will.[27] But as we descend toward the concrete, where particulars loom large and passions can intervene, we must lean on two things that cannot be shared in the classroom, or strictly communicated at all: experience and character. Thus Maritain insists that "that right appreciation of practical cases which the ancients called *prudentia*, and which is an inner vital power of judgment developed in the mind and backed up by well-directed will, cannot be replaced by any learning whatsoever."[28] And this is the problem.

The solution Maritain points us toward involves taking the students out of the classroom and submerging them in the extra-educational sphere of cooperative labor and play in the context of largely self-organized teams. This sphere

---

[24] Ibid., pp. 26, 30-31.

[25] Ibid., p. 31.

[26] See ibid., pp. 36-38, where Maritain quickly enumerates a partial list of fundamental human dispositions: toward the love of truth, and of justice, toward simplicity or openness to the real, toward working well, and toward cooperation with others in common work. Maritain's list is similar to, and perhaps able to be mapped onto, that of St. Thomas in the *Summa Theologiae*, I-II q. 94, a. 2.

[27] *Education at the Crossroads*, p. 27. Aristotle warns us that it is useless to teach ethics to the very young, and Maritain concurs, counseling that ethics and political philosophy not be taught until the fourth year of college. Personal and social morality will have been taught all throughout the students' education, but on the sly, through the reading of history's great humanistic authors (pp. 67-68) (the reading, that is, of practitioners of moral science).

[28] Ibid., p. 23.

embraces "the entire field of human activity, particularly everyday work and pain." The paradox, Maritain tells us, is that "all this extra-educational sphere exerts on man an action which is more important in the achievement of his education than education itself."[29] In his essay entitled "Moral and Spiritual Values in Education," Maritain suggests forming students into self-organized teams "intent upon improving the work and discipline of their own members, as well as their sense of fairness, justice and good fellowship in their mutual relations." Such teams, he thinks, may provide students with the "effective beginnings of a real formation of the will."[30] What forms might such teams take, and what sorts of activities might they embrace?

Maritain accords a great importance to play, taken broadly as activities in which the mind freely expands. In this category he includes games and sports, handicraft work and home economics, gardening, and training in the arts.[31] He also, of course, accords a great importance to common work, and thus to training in common labor, in trades.[32] Thus examples of Maritain's self-organized teams might include chess clubs or dramatic acting associations, baseball teams or reading circles or quilting clubs, electricians's or mechanics's guilds or fishing crews. But how is participation in such activities to do the work set for it? Participants will, of course, acquire much needed practical experience through the activities, but how is it that participation effects the formation of prudence, or at least the beginnings of it? Part of the answer lies in the (suitably circumscribed) moral authority that Maritain recognizes that the educator must possess over the educated, an authority the possession of which will also extend to the coach, to the club advisor.[33] In the extra-educational sphere we will see something along the lines of a master teaching his trade to his apprentice. But this sort of practical teaching, however much it helps us answer the first question, about the teaching of prudence (and more needs to be said), raises a second, for it is just the sort of teaching that most requires in the teacher the habit of practical science, the habit of giving good advice. Was this habit acquired during the master's own apprenticeship, and if so how? Maritain has pointed us in the right direction, but has not led us to the goal.

---

[29] Ibid., p. 25.

[30] Jacques Maritain, "Moral and Spiritual Values in Education," in *The Education of Man*, ed. Donald and Idella Gallagher (Garden City, New York: Doubleday & Company, 1962), p. 110. I do not take Maritain to mean by "self-organized" anything like "completely autonomous;" I assume that such teams will have advisors.

[31] Ibid., p. 55.

[32] Ibid., pp. 45-46

[33] Ibid., p. 33.

Here I turn to MacIntyre, for if we begin to describe Maritain's coop-erative activities in a general way (they are coherent, complex, socially established, cooperative, develop human capacities, etc.) we will see that they are examples of what MacIntyre calls practices. And in his elucida-tion of this notion, MacIntyre offers a more detailed account of the moral development of the participants. Thus I will turn to the subject of practices with two central questions: how can participation in practices (begin to) instill the habit of practical science, and how can it (begin to) instill the habit of prudence?

MacIntyre on the Teaching of Practical Knowledge

These two presuppose a third question: what are practices? MacIntyre defines practices (and we may as well have the greater part of this rather long sentence before us) as:

> any coherent and complex form of socially established cooperative human activity through which goods internal to that form of activity are realized in the course of trying to achieve those standards of excellence which are appropriate to, and partially definitive of, that form of activity, with the result that human powers to achieve excellence, and human conceptions of the ends and goods involved, are systematically extended.[34]

Briefly, we may discern seven characteristics of a practice: it is, first, human activity; second, coherent and complex (MacIntyre excludes tic-tac-toe but includes chess); third, socially established and cooperative (he excludes throw-ing a football with skill but includes football); and it is the sort of activity that, fourth, realizes goods internal to that sort of activity; fifth, is partly constituted by accepted standards of excellence; sixth, extends human pow-ers to achieve excellence; and seventh, extends conceptions of the goods of that activity. A little more needs to be said about the last four characteristics.

Goods internal to a practice are best understood by contrasting them with external goods, goods that, first, can be obtained in many other ways; second, can be specified and appreciated as goods by (nearly) anyone; and third, are competitive. Thus, the prize money won in a chess tourney is an external good: money can be obtained in other ways, its possession can be seen by non-players to be a good, and its possession by the winner prohibits its possession by others. Goods internal to a practice, then, first, can be ob-tained only through participation in that or a similar practice; second, can be

---

[34] *After Virtue*, p. 187.

specified and recognized as goods only by reference to a practice; and third, are typically common goods with respect to all practitioners.[35] The good of confounding the opponent's Stonewall Defense by fianchettoing one's bishops is a good internal to chess: it cannot be obtained outside of chess, it can be specified only in terms of chess, and can be appreciated only by players, and it contributes to the excellence of the game in a way shared by the players and the knowing onlookers, and perhaps also by players of later games. MacIntyre distinguishes two kinds of internal good.[36] First, there is excellence of product. Artistic painting being a practice, an excellent painting (or perhaps better, the excellence of a painting) is an internal good of this type. Second, there is the excellence of character, the excellence of living a certain kind of life, the life of an artist, or of a baseball player or fisherman. I will have more to say about this shortly.

Practices also involve, and are partly defined by, standards of excellence. "To enter a practice," MacIntyre writes, "is to accept the authority of those standards and the inadequacy of my own performance as judged by them."[37] As a beginning pitcher in baseball, I must learn from others (coaches, senior pitchers, or the catcher) when it is best to throw a fastball and when it is best to throw a curveball. If I do not accept the authority of established standards, and of senior practitioners as experts on what those standards require, "I will never learn to appreciate good pitching let alone to pitch."[38] A beginner in a practice, then, in order to excel, must first apprentice himself to recognized masters (coaches, advisors, senior practitioners).

Through this apprenticeship, the participant in a practice extends his powers to achieve excellence in that practice. It is not only that he becomes more technically skilled; he also extends his powers of practical reasoning. The young pitcher at first learns the general rules of pitching, and then, with the acquisition of experience, learns to see each situation, each pitch, in its particularity. Having mastered the basics, he learns to *see* what pitch he should choose. The freshman gets beat up when he shakes off his senior catcher—the sophomore, maybe not. The freshman "knows" that he should always throw a fastball when facing a 3-0 count; the sophomore sees that sometimes, he should throw a curve. Thus, an apprentice gradually emerges from being under the authority of senior practitioners to become more or less self-governing. He becomes what MacIntyre later calls an "independent prac-

---

[35] Ibid., pp. 188-90.
[36] Ibid., pp. 186-90.
[37] Ibid., p. 190.
[38] Ibid.

tical reasoner."[39] The apprentice can become an adept, and can even go beyond the standards established to this point. This points to the final characteristic of practices.

Participation in practices can extend conceptions of the goods of that practice, both of the individual participant and of the practicing community. The individual's conceptions alter drastically, of course: he must first come to see the goods internal to a practice as goods at all, and then move to a greater and greater understanding and appreciation of them. This is a function of education, whereby he must in many ways become like senior practitioners. But, as noted, the participant can surpass previously set standards, and in this way can extend the whole community's conceptions of the goods of that practice. Sticking to baseball, the conceptions of a good power hitter before and after Babe Ruth were very different, because Ruth "broke" all the rules. The four-minute mile that used to be an ideal is now a commonplace. Excellence in chess is raised to a new level when a player develops a new opening or an effective counter to a certain strategy. And so on. What it is to be excellent, to excel, in a given practice, develops over time. Thus MacIntyre writes that practices "never have a goal or goals fixed for all time ... the goals themselves are transmuted by the history of the activity."[40]

Let us look at the example MacIntyre gives of how participation in a practice operates in the ways he says it does, that of the chess-playing child.[41] MacIntyre asks us to imagine an intelligent seven-year-old, Ruth, let us say, whom he wishes to teach chess. Ruth has no desire to play, but MacIntyre bribes her to play with candy, and promises her more candy if she wins, promising further that he will always play so as to make it difficult but possible for her to win. Desiring candy, Ruth plays to win, but, MacIntyre points out, has as yet no motive not to cheat, as her only motive is to win candy. But we may hope, he says, that after a time she will "find in those goods specific to chess, in the achievement of a certain highly particular kind of analytic skill, strategic imagination and competitive intensity, a new set of reasons...for trying to excel in whatever way the game of chess demands. Now if the child cheats, ...she will be defeating not me, but...herself." She comes to value the internal goods of chess more than external goods, or at least some of them. She comes to acquire a new set of motivations. How does this work? For the details, we should ask a child psychologist, but we know that it often

---

[39] See Alasdair MacIntyre, *Dependent Rational Animals* (Chicago: Open Court Publishing Company, 1999), especially chap. 8.
[40] *After Virtue*, pp. 193-94.
[41] Ibid., p. 188.

does: if not with chess for this particular child, then perhaps with skating, or handicraft work, or fishing. However the psychologist cashes out the details for us, I think that we should see this as the operation of the fundamental inclination toward excellence in work (and play) that Maritain attributes to us.[42] Ruth comes to see what is excellent in chess in her struggles to win, even when motivated solely by candy, and the more she sees certain modes of play as excellent, the more she will see them as desirable in their own right. And what holds for chess will hold for baseball, for fishing, for crafts, or for other activities in Maritain's extra-educational sphere, which we saw should be construed as practices.

So it should be clear that Ruth's conceptions of the good are extended through her participation in the practice of chess, and this holds not just for her conception of the good of chess, but for her conception of her good as a person. It is not of course that she sees excellence in chess as her good, but she does come to see it as a real good, and therefore at least potentially as part of her good. We can see also that her "human powers" are extended. Playing chess of course extends her analytic skill and strategic imagination, but it also allows her to begin the development of moral habits, of virtues. It is in the context of his discussion of practices, of course, that MacIntyre offers us his "first, even if partial and tentative definition of a virtue:"

> A virtue is an acquired human quality the possession and exercise of which tends to enable us to achieve those goods which are internal to practices and the lack of which effectively prevents us from achieving any such goods.[43]

This definition does embrace intellectual excellences such as strategic imagination, but it also embraces moral virtues. Thus MacIntyre notes that Ruth came to see fairness in play as a good, and indeed argues in *After Virtue* that at least three moral virtues are necessary for success in any practice: justice, honesty, and courage.[44] We must correctly accord merit to goods and to other practitioners, giving what is due to all. We must tell the truth (I will return later to this very important point). And we must have the courage to risk what is lesser for what is greater. In later writings, MacIntyre explicitly recognizes as well the need across practices for temperance (I must not be diverted from greater internal goods by lesser or external goods) and, of course, for a sort of prudence (obviously, to succeed in a practice, I must be able and inclined to deliberate, judge, and command with respect

---

[42] *Education at the Crossroads*, p. 38.
[43] *After Virtue*, p. 191.
[44] Ibid.

to actions to be done here and now).[45] The development of moral virtues is an example of the second kind of internal good MacIntyre posits, the good of a certain way of life, or, excellence of character (as well as, of course, an extension of human powers).

Now, there is a problem in that MacIntyre's definition at this stage relativizes virtues to practices. It is for this reason that I referred to "a sort of prudence." We might refer to the prudence, and to the other virtues, developed in this way as *practicial* prudence, or practical virtues.[46] I will come back to MacIntyre's response to this problem, but it should be fairly clear how activities in Maritain's extra-educational sphere, seen as practices, can at least begin to instill the virtue of prudence. It is not of course that they stamp out apprentices shaped in a certain mold. Rather, they provide an encouraging environment in which the apprentice's natural inclinations and powers of practical reasoning begin spontaneously (though not without guidance) to develop into virtues.[47] And this is all we should expect from more or less narrowly circumscribed spheres of activity. At this point, I need to come back to practical science: how is this habit developed through participation in practices? The answer to this question will simultaneously shed further light on the development of prudence.

When beginning to participate in a practice, MacIntyre says that we must learn from senior practitioners to make two different kinds of distinction:

> that between what merely seems good to us here now and what really is good relative to us here now, and that between what is good relative to us here now and what is good or best unqualifiedly.[48]

---

[45] See Alasdair MacIntyre, *Whose Justice? Which Rationality?* (Notre Dame, Indiana: University of Notre Dame Press, 1988), pp. 40, 44.

[46] By *practicial* I just mean relative to a practice; saying *practical* prudence seems redundant and, in this context, ambiguous. It is worth noting briefly that St. Thomas seems to recognize this sort of prudence, in his discussion of what is sometimes called regional prudence, which is ordered to business, say, or to sailing, in the *Summa Theologiae*, II-II q. 47, a. 13.

[47] Appeal to natural inclination or internal dynamism here and in the case of the chess-playing child above might seem spooky to some philosophers. It might seem that instead of explaining the learning I am just saying "that's what apprentices do." It seems to me that any explanation must eventually reach such a step. And I might note that this not a "problem" only for Thomists. Addressing the question "How is it that the pupil, given that sparse instruction, goes on to new instances in the right way?" John McDowell writes, "we can say: it is a fact (no doubt a remarkable fact) that, against a background of common human nature and shared forms of life, one's sensitivities to kinds of similarities between situations can be altered and enriched by just this sort of instruction." In other words, acquiring a sensitivity to situations is just the sort of thing human beings do. See John McDowell, "Virtue and Reason," *The Monist*, 62 (1979), p. 341.

[48] *Whose Justice? Whose Rationality?*, p. 30.

It is upon the second distinction that I wish to focus. An example of this distinction is that made between excellent apprentice work and a true masterpiece. It is my contention that the habit of accurately making this distinction between what is best simply and what is best for someone at a certain level of development is partly constitutive of the habit of practical science (it should be obvious that it is also necessary for prudence). How so?

Consider a novice pitcher. He learns the art of pitching largely through observation of, teaching by, and imitation of more expert pitchers. But though he does become better by imitating them, he must constantly keep in mind that he is not yet as good as they are. Thus he may have learned that in a certain situation, say with a 3-2 count with the bases loaded facing a certain kind of hitter, the best thing to do would be to throw a hard curve that nicks the outside corner, thus catching the batter off guard. But he must also remember that his control is not good enough yet to risk throwing a curve; he should throw a fastball down the middle and hope for the best. Now, later on, after hanging up his spikes and becoming a coach, he can keep alive the habit of making this sort of distinction between what is best simply and what is best for someone at a certain level of development. And when he later visits the mound in a similar situation, he will, taking into account his pitcher's skill, be able to give advice tailored to that pitcher's situation, even though he himself is not in that situation. And, when he writes his "How to" book on youth league baseball, he will be able to give advice tailored to narrowly circumscribed situations of this and other sorts. He will be able to do so by composing, by bringing together, the various things he has learned about baseball: the rules of the game, general guidelines, and recollections and imaginings of certain types of situation. He will have acquired, that is to say, the habit of practical science that is required of coaches and advisors of all sorts.

Making this sort of distinction requires taking up the viewpoint of another (a junior or senior practitioner, or a peer). In *Dependent Rational Animals*, MacIntyre gives a more detailed account of how this works. Recall that the goal of the practice of practical science is to regulate action from nearby, to give advice, and thus in some sense to speak for the other. "I learn this [how to speak for others]," MacIntyre writes, "in the course of learning how to speak for myself," in the course of learning, that is, to be an independent practical reasoner.[49] As we have seen, we learn how to do this through participation in shared structured activities, in practices in which we submit ourselves to shared standards and to the authority of senior practitioners: "It is by having our reasoning put to the question by others, by being called to

---

[49] *Dependent Rational Animals*, p. 147.

account for ourselves by others, that we learn...to understand ourselves as they understand us."[50] Indeed, it is often only through this sort of dialogue that we come to understand ourselves at all, for we may have acted unthinkingly, on unconscious motives. Now, if you question my actions or comportment, I make myself intelligible to you, and justify myself, by telling you the relevant part of my history and explaining to you my ends, what individual or common goods I take myself to be pursuing at this time in these ways. But to engage in such a dialogue successfully, I must be able to assume your point of view, at least to the extent that I am able to respond to the concerns that you are actually expressing in questioning me. And to the extent that "we are successful in doing so, we become able to speak with the other's voice.... In achieving accountability we will have learned to speak for the other."[51] An example would be helpful here. Let us stick with our novice pitcher.

Suppose that he has just given up a three-run home run to a powerful hitter. His part in the business had been to shake off his senior catcher's call for a low curveball and to throw a high fastball. The coach approaches the mound, and pointedly asks, "Why did you do that?" Is the coach asking, "Why did you, with your fastball at the stage of development that it is, try to overpower this particular hitter?" Or is he asking, "Why did you, a freshman, shake off your senior catcher?" The pitcher must know his coach, but he is probably asking both questions. Perhaps the pitcher will shame-facedly admit that he let his pride get the better of him. In this case, he will see, or have it pointed out to him, that he had allowed himself to be distracted from the proper goal of helping the team. Or perhaps his answer will take the form of telling a part of his history (he'd been working on his fastball, and thought it was improved; moreover, he did not fully trust his catcher because such and such had happened) and explaining his goals (he thought a fastball would catch this hitter off guard, thus furthering the good of the team). Perhaps the light of day will reveal to the young pitcher the weakness of his reasoning, or perhaps the coach will point it out to him. Perhaps he had seen a better player do it. Here he will see, or have it pointed out to him, that he is not such a player yet (here, of course, is the aforementioned distinction between the best and his best, in explicit form). Through this dialogue (in this admittedly idealized conference on the mound), guided by the coach's questions, he learns to reason better about what to do in such situations. He is also, in the process, beginning to learn how to think about pitching and about baseball as

---

[50] Ibid., p. 148.
[51] Ibid., p. 150.

his coach thinks about them. It is worth remarking here that both this ability to take up the perspective of another, and the disposition to tell the truth to that other, are essential to the submission to standards (and to the senior practitioners who represent the standards) that is itself essential to progress in a practice.

In the case of the coach's questioning, a largely shared framework, and a largely shared history, that of the practice of baseball in the context of a certain team, is presupposed. But now suppose that the hitter's father, ignorant of baseball and just released from a psychiatric hospital, interrupts the summit on the mound, asking the same question: "Why did you do that?" Here it is even more obvious that the pitcher must take up the questioner's point of view in order to respond appropriately to the question, for it is now likely that the question has nothing to do with his behavior described as a pitch in a game of baseball. Perhaps the father saw the action as the throwing of a hard object at his son. The pitcher will be unable to respond appropriately at all, until, probably through questioning of his own, he has come to a greater understanding of his questioner's concerns. This points also to the need for moral education to go beyond what can be acquired in practices.

The point of this example, of course, is to make clear the fact that, to succeed in a practice, to develop what I have called practical prudence, an agent must learn to make his reasoning intelligible to other practitioners, and especially to those who are senior to him and from whom he must learn. And in learning to do this, the agent simultaneously develops the habit of practical science relative to that practice. In learning to take up the viewpoint of another practitioner and address the concerns specific to that viewpoint, he learns to exercise the kind of judgment necessary for the giving of advice. He starts down the road to becoming a coach. To become a good coach, of course, many other qualities will be needed (memory, imagination, articulateness, a sort of charisma, and so on).

Thus, participation in Maritain's extra-educational spheres of activity, seen as participation in MacIntyre's practices, does turn out to be a vehicle for the "teaching" of both practically practical science and of prudence. As Maritain told us, the "teaching" here is very different from the teaching that goes on in a classroom. Much more is required of the student-apprentice. Participation in practices does afford an opportunity for apprentices to acquire the experience necessary for the making of informed practical judgments, and it does provide an arena in which his or her natural inclinations can expand and develop into virtues. But here the apprentice is required to mobilize more of his natural inclinations. In the classroom, the inclination to know the truth is sufficient, provided only that it is not interfered with. In practices, more of the person must be invested to assure success. What Maritain calls the fundamental dispositions to justice, to work well, and to cooperate with others in common work must come into play. I have not focused on this, because my chief concern here is with practical knowledge, but of course, as both Maritain and MacIntyre realize, prudence and, to a lesser extent, practical science, cannot be separated from the moral virtues. We have already seen that MacIntyre thinks that at least the cardinal virtues are required for successful practice. And he sees truthfulness as especially important, as we cannot profit from the advice of others if we are not truthful with them about, e.g., what we were thinking and feeling when we did such and such (throw that fastball, e.g.). We cannot exercise practicial prudence without being truthful to ourselves about our present state of expertise, and we certainly cannot give good advice without being truthful about what we take the other's state of expertise to be. A great deal more should be said about this, but here is not the place.

What I do need to address, if only briefly, is the worry that I have already raised that in practices we can acquire only practicial virtues, virtues relativized to a practice (this same worry, of course, will arise in the context of Maritain's spheres of activity). In presenting in outline form MacIntyre's response to this worry, I will also point out that that here too we see a development of Maritain's thought.

Practices, Politics, and Traditions

The first thing that needs to be said is that, although one does not acquire the virtues, strictly speaking, through participation in practices, one does, in acquiring practicial virtues, acquire the matter of virtue. In baseball, an excellent player can acquire the disposition to "take one for the team," to allow himself to be hit by a pitch. This would be an act of practicial courage commanded by practicial prudence. Although this is not yet true virtue, the disposition to overcome the fear of a lesser evil for what is judged to be a greater good is there, waiting to be further informed by a more adequate conception of the good.

MacIntyre realizes that a human life informed by a conception of the good and of the virtues as relativized to practices would be pervaded by "*too many* conflicts and *too much* arbitrariness.... The claims of one practice may be incompatible with another."[52] There is no place yet for a "*telos* of a

[52] *After Virtue*, p. 201.

whole human life" or for such virtues as constancy.[53] The various practices and their goods, MacIntyre tells us, must be ordered in two ways. They must be ordered within the community, and here MacIntyre appeals to the architectonic practice of politics in an Aristotelian sense.[54] And they must be ordered within the life of the individual person, and here MacIntyre appeals to traditions, which are historically extended rational enquiries into the good human life, and which are socially embodied in institutions, practices, and practitioners.[55] The individual can learn how to order the various practices and their goods through adhering to a tradition and subscribing to the conception of the human good that it professes.[56] For MacIntyre, it is ultimately through adherence to traditions, to include participation in the practices in which they are partly embodied, that we pursue wisdom, practical as well as theoretical, and through traditions that we move toward achieving our good as persons. And it is from traditions that come the resources for the crowning elements of Maritain's vision of liberal education: theoretical and practical philosophy, and ultimately the foundations of wisdom that can unite the many ways of knowing.[57]

The progression of individuals's pursuit of their goods that MacIntyre portrays for us—from our starting point in a family situation forward through practices, civil society, and on to adherence to a tradition—almost exactly mirrors what Maritain calls "a vertical movement of the persons themselves in the midst of social life."[58] Maritain of course singles out just one tradition as adequate to the task, and furthermore sees this vertical movement as metaphysically grounded in a way that the MacIntyre of *After Virtue* would not have liked. But he comes around, to a significant extent. In his essay, "Plain Persons and Moral Philosophy," he begins by describing plain persons as "proto-Aristotelians," noting that through participation in practices they become full-blooded, even if unwitting, Aristotelians, and ends by noting that his account must be situated within a certain metaphysical and theological

---

[53] Ibid., pp. 202-03. *Constancy* is a virtue concept taken from Jane Austen, and which makes sense only in the integrated context of a whole human life. In *After Virtue*, MacIntyre also recognizes the similar standing of such virtues as justice and patience; the later MacIntyre would surely include charity in this list.

[54] See *Whose Justice? Whose Rationality?*, p. 47, 107.

[55] *After Virtue*, pp. 222-23.

[56] My point is not that these two modes of ordering practices must be actually separate; at its best politics itself will be informed by a tradition in good order, and ideally by the same tradition that guides all or most citizens.

[57] *Education at the Crossroads*, pp. 67-68, 71-72.

[58] Jacques Maritain, *The Person and the Common Good*, trans. John J. FitzGerald (Notre Dame, Indiana: University of Notre Dame Press, 1966), pp. 79-80.

context.[59] And by the time he writes *Dependent Rational Animals*, MacIntyre seems ready to sign back on to Aristotle's "metaphysical biology" (albeit minus certain "important elements" of it (which are here unspecified); see the Preface, p. x).

Concluding Remarks

So MacIntyre can be seen improving upon Maritain's philosophy of moral education, for his work on practices, as the schools of the virtues, makes clear, or at any rate clearer, how extra-educational activities perform the moral tasks set for them. By way of a brief summary, they do so by:

1. Lifting the student-apprentice into a cooperative sphere of activity where practical reason operates under a new set of motivations and is engaged in the pursuit of new goods held in common with others.

2. Teaching student-apprentices to make the twin distinctions between real and apparent goods, and between their current best and the best simply—this helps to set fundamental inclinations free to follow their natural course toward virtue, and toward practical science.

3. Instilling the capacity to take up the viewpoint of others, and thus to speak for those others—this is important for developing prudence and for becoming an independent practical reasoner, but is even more central to the capacity to give good moral advice, and thus to the practice of practical science.

But if MacIntyre moves the inquiry forward, he does so in a way that is deeply indebted to Maritain, and that ultimately points back toward him. In the end, both men are engaged—and I think successfully so—in working out a true philosophy of education, which sees that education's real aim is neither to cater to the untutored individual nor to force him into the mold of some cultural type, but is rather "to make a man."[60]

---

[59] Alasdair MacIntyre, "Plain Persons and Moral Philosophy: Rules, Virtues, and Goods," *American Catholic Philosophical Quarterly* 66 (Winter 1992); cited from *The MacIntyre Reader*, pp. 138, 140, 152.

[60] *Education at the Crossroads*, p. 100.

Yves R. Simon on the Nature and Role of Moral Philosophy

Ralph Nelson

In the latter stage of modern philosophy in the nineteenth century, leading thinkers stated their intention to overcome an objectionable antinomy by
somehow combining theory and practice. Hegel remained a notable exception to this trend when he insisted that the philosophic science of right, and
the state, was theoretical. Once those who argued, in opposition, that the task
of philosophers was to change, not merely interpret the world, it was the
theory of practice that was paramount. Of course, there were those who simply would do away with theory altogether and adopt a kind of practicalism,
but usually, as with the utilitarians and positivists, some kind of theory was
still required even if the main direction was practical.

More recently, John Dewey, set out to overcome any dichotomy between
theory and practice, knowing and doing, having discarded the idea of a purely
theoretical philosophy.[1] Richard Rorty's version of pragmatism, free of
Dewey's scientism, simply embraces localized practice.[2] At least one well-
known proponent of the Analytic school has accepted the division of theoretical
and practical knowledge, but then proceeds to deal with ethical concepts in a
completely theoretical fashion.[3] Parallel in many respects to Dewey,
Habermas—searching for the tasks remaining to philosophical thought "after the breakdown of metaphysics"—maintained, "The future of philosophical
thought is a matter of political practice."[4] So the tendency apparent in a num-

---

[1] The best source for Dewey's views on this topic is *The Quest for Certainty: A Study of
the Relation of Knowledge and Action* (New York: G.P. Putnam's Sons, 1960).

[2] Richard Rorty, *Objectivity, Relativism, and Truth; Philosophical Papers* (Cambridge:
Cambridge University Press, 1991), vol. I, pp. 29-30.

[3] P. H. Nowell-Smith, *Ethics* (London: Penguin Books, 1954).

[4] Jürgen Habermas, *Philosophical-Political Profiles*, trans. Frederick G. Lawrence
(Cambridge, Mass.: The MIT Press, 1985) pp. 12, 17. Cf. what Habermas says about "a
theoretically guided praxis of life" in *Theory and Practice* trans. John Vietrel (Boston: Beacon
Press, 1973) p. 253.

ber of philosophers, and John Rawls could be added to the list, has been to reject theoretical philosophy, while retaining an interest in theory as implicated in practice.

The aim of this essay is to examine Yves R. Simon's reflections on the nature and role of moral philosophy beginning with *Critique de la connaissance morale* (1934), hereafter referred to as *A Critique of Moral Knowledge*,[5] or simply *Critique*, and extending right to the end of his days. The primary problem in moral philosophy, as he saw it, concerned the identification of moral philosophy as practical knowledge. Any reader of Simon is aware that he situated himself within the lineage of Aristotle, Aquinas, John Poinsot (John of St. Thomas), and Jacques Maritain. Indeed his first study of moral knowledge may be fittingly described as an elaboration of the germinal appendix in the *Degrees of Knowledge*.[6] But as a student of French sociology, he was influenced as well by the writings of Emile Durkheim and Lucien Lévy-Bruhl and their project of a science of morals, a social theory whose counterpart would be a moral art (applied morality)[7] Even if he rejected their solution, he recognized that there was a real problem and much was to be learned from them.

On the other hand, John Poinsot in his *Ars Logica*[8] had taken moral philosophy to be a purely theoretical inquiry, not basically different from the philosophy of nature or that part of it that dealt with human psychology. Simon's dissent from this position is probably his most notable criticism of Poinsot, who had such an impact on him.

The upshot of both the sociological school and the Thomistic commentator is either that moral philosophy disappears as moral science achieves maturity, or that moral philosophy is not practical knowledge. In the former case, Simon concedes that moral philosophy needs knowledge of social facts. But the central question is whether sociology "is capable of being consti-

---

[5] Yves R. Simon, *Critique de la connaissance morale* (Paris: Desclée de Brouwer, 1934). See the forthcoming English translation entitled *A Critique of Moral Knowledge*, trans. Ralph McInerny (New York: Fordham University Press, 2002).

[6] Jacques Maritain, *The Degrees of Knowledge*, trans. Gerald B. Phelan (Notre Dame, Indiana: University of Notre Dame Press, 1995), Appendix vii, pp. 481-89.

[7] For a valuable collection of Durkheim's writings on morals, accompanied by an introductory essay and useful notes, see W.S.F. Pickering (ed,), *Durkheim: Essays on Morals and Education* (London: Routledge and Kegan Paul, 1979). Since Durkheim never completed his projected *La Morale*, his follower's treatise remains the most systematic account of a Durkheimian moral theory. Lucien Lévy-Bruhl, *La Morale et la science des moeurs*, 15th ed. (Paris: Presses Universitaires de France, 1953).

[8] John of Saint Thomas [John Poinsot], *Ars Logica, Cursus Philosophicus*, vol. I, ed. Beatus Reiser (Turin: Marietti, 1933).

tuted without the illumination of principles formulated by the practical science of human action," that is, moral philosophy.[9] He concludes that the project is impossible because of the very nature of its object. To abstract from what are moral matters would involve falsification of that object, for "in moral matters there are no judgments of reality without value judgments."[10] The presumed independence of sociology is denied; its attachment to moral philosophy affirmed.

No doubt Simon, when he examined what John Poinsot had to say about moral science in his "incomparable" *Ars Logica* was surprised to find that the commentator, "celebrated for his customary fidelity to the teachings of Aristotle and Saint Thomas",[11] had, in fact, set out a position that seems not to square with the indications of his predecessors. For Poinsot, discussing the *Summa theologiae*, maintained that in the *Prima Secundae*, one finds an exposition of moral science alone, and in the *Secunda Secundae*, one finds moral science combined with prudence. However, it then becomes clear that this moral science is purely theoretical, concerned with the nature of the virtues. The conclusion was that there was no practical science properly speaking, hence no bridge between the theoretical sciences and prudential determination.

Now Simon was convinced that there is a kind of continuity beginning with purely theoretical philosophy and descending to prudential determination. He adopts Maritain's distinction between theoretically practical and practically practical in order to provide the intermediary sciences in this descent to action. So in the *Critique* he employs the distinction between the analytic and the synthetic method in philosophy. "Science proceeds by analyses and definitions, the practical by motions and syntheses."[12] To analyze in this context means to resolve effects into causes, or consequences into antecedents, not dissolving a whole into its constituent parts.[13] Theoretical inquiry provides an explanation. Simon wants to argue that moral philosophy, or moral science, uses a synthetic method, though it is theoretical in mode, for it

---

[9] *Critique de la connaissance morale*, p. 129.

[10] Ibid., p. 131.

[11] Ibid., p. 82.

[12] Ibid., p. 83.

[13] Ibid., p. 68n2. The *modo resolutorio* (analysis) and *modo compositivo* (synthesis) distinction was taken up by Thomas Hobbes. "There is therefore no method, by which we find out the causes of things, but is either *compositive* or *resolutive*, or partly *compositive*, and partly *resolutive*. And the resolutive is commonly called *analytical* method, as the compositive is called *synthetical*." *Elements of Philosophy, The English Works of Thomas Hobbes* (London: Scientia Aalen, 1962), vol. I, p. 66. The method employed in his political theory is resolutive-compositive, proceeding from parts to the whole, from matter to the generation of form.

aims at directing action, albeit from afar.[14] If there is a feature that marks practical knowledge from theoretical knowledge, it would be whether or not movement is occurring, a knowledge that moves, instigates, influences, opposed to a knowledge that does not. Of course, Hume is always there to tell us that reason is wholly inactive.[15] Simon's position rests on the assumption that reason moves; it is a moving cause. But it moves according to formal, not efficient, causality. If reason cannot move in any sense, then the position is undermined. If reason moves us it is in a certain direction, so a brief way of describing moral philosophy is to say it involves directive knowledge.

Concerning the issue of fidelity to Aristotle and Aquinas one might rest with the conclusion that Simon's position is more faithful to Aquinas regarding moral philosophy but that is hardly sufficient. He has to convince us that such a practical knowledge exists. The treatment here attempts to avoid those disputes as to whether or not a particular doctrine is that of the master rather than whether or not it is truly tenable. This is especially difficult because one easily enters into that briar patch where controversies go on about the extent to which Aquinas's own position is or is not found in his commentaries on the works of Aristotle and Boethius. Clearly this is an important issue in the search for an authentic Thomism.[16] While in principle most accept the view that the commentaries are just commentaries, Aquinas does not speak in his own name, in practice recourse is made in particular cases to the commentaries for Thomas's own doctrine. This seems to be the case with the use of the *Commentary on the Nicomachean Ethics*. It is often asserted that moral philosophy is to some degree in the business of giving advice. Moreover, recently we have seen the emergence of philosophical therapists. In order to deal with the competence of moral philosophers to give advice, Simon makes a distinction between the moral philosopher and the moralist. To understand the terminology Simon employs, it might be useful to recall a common distinction used in the French language in defining *un moraliste*. Although the main distinction is found in *Le Grand Robert*, the explanation in *Grand Larousse* is more to the point. While a moralist, and the prototype is always

---

[14] *Critique de la connaissance morale*, p. 87, "de loin sans doute, mais efficacement tout de même."

[15] "Since morals, therefore, have an influence on the actions and affections, it follows that they cannot be derived from reason; and that because reason alone as we have already proven, can never have any such influence." David Hume, *A Treatise of Human Nature*, ed. L. A. Selby-Bigge (Oxford: At the Clarendon Press, 1888, 1962), Book III, Part I, Section I, p. 457.

[16] Ralph McInerny deals extensively with the use of commentaries in *Boethius and Aquinas* (Washington, D. C.: The Catholic University of America Press, 1990) and *Aquinas on Human Action: A Theory of Practice* (Washington, D. C.: The Catholic University of America Press, 1992).

Montaigne, describes, analyses, and criticizes mores, the moral philosopher purveys a moral theory. The distinction then seems to be between a moral observer and a systematic moral theorist. A third meaning refers to a person who loves to give moral advice, or what is frequently referred to today as a moral scold. Now Simon wants to compare the first two meanings, but he wants to do it very precisely in view of capacities (and, let us say, competence). Sometimes when he uses the term *un moraliste*, he simply means a moral philosopher. However, in one key passage he speaks of a philosopher-moralist and indicates that such a personage "would be extremely rare."[17] Why? He would have to combine the abstractive intellect of the scientist and the concretive intellect "which finds itself perfectly at ease only in the contingent singular."[18] Here we have a new and quite precise notion of a moralist. Aside from the fact that a moral philosopher may be immoral, it is unlikely that most moral philosophers would be the ones to seek out for advice in particular cases. The advice they can offer, if they are competent, remains at a rather general level. The conjunction of these two capabilities is consequently unlikely, but not impossible.[19]

After about twenty years Simon once again discussed Poinsot's views on moral philosophy in an important note to the translation, *The Material Logic of John of St. Thomas*.[20] There is an extended examination of the difference between what is now called ethical science and prudence.

> In principle the line between ethical science and prudence can always be drawn by the operation of the following criteria: A given proposition is a scientific conclusion if and only if it is deductively connected with the self-evident principles of morality. But a proposition that admits of no deductive connection with ethical axioms derives whatever certainty it enjoys from its agreement with the inclinations of the virtuous will.[21]

He reiterates his judgment that Poinsot's characterization of ethical science "is thoroughly un-Aristotelian and constitutes a paradox never satisfactorily explained."[22] In fact Simon never ceased to wonder and conjecture why Poinsot

---

[17] *Critique de la connaissance morale*, p. 76.

[18] Ibid.

[19] Ibid. Simon believes great minds like Aristotle, Aquinas, and Cajetan possess both talents.

[20] John of St. Thomas, *The Material Logic of John of St. Thomas*, trans. Yves R. Simon, John J. Glanville, and G. Donald Hollenhurst (Chicago: The University of Chicago Press, 1965) p. 592n34. The translation was seven years in the making. A section had already been published in 1949.

[21] Ibid.

[22] Ibid.

had taken the view that he did.[23] The basic distinction between the two methods, analytical and synthetic, the former appropriate for theory, the latter for practice, is again articulated, but with important additions and clarifications. Now he refers to combinations of the two methods in practical thought. The practical sciences "use methods in which analysis and synthesis combine in diverse proportions."[24] This is clearly an addition to his elaboration in *Critique*. Secondly, he now distinguishes between two kinds of explanation: "unqualified explanation, explanation in terms of essential necessity," and practical "explanation in terms of human action" and in response to such questions as what ought to be done.[25] On one hand, in moral philosophy, which is a theoretically practical science, "conceptualization and explanation are governed by a law of exact analysis."[26] On the other, practical knowledge involves "a synthesis totally foreign to the mores of theoretical thought."[27]

Simon now introduces the distinction between nature and use that he will fully exploit in what may be called the third, which turned out to be the final, stage in the development of his conception of moral philosophy. "Theoretical science abstracts from problems of human use."[28] Practical science cannot do this, but recognizes the degrees of practicality implicated in the descent from theoretically practical science, through practically practical science to prudential determination. The notion of a practically practical science is not yet problematic for him.

A remark in the dense note provides a linkage to the third phase found in the compilation, *Practical Knowledge*. "A practical science is necessarily an ambiguous entity, less scientific than a prudential habitus and bearing the mark of a sort of compromise."[29] The comparable passage, in *Practical Knowledge*, reads as follows:

> There is such a significant contrast between thought and action that the notion of practical thought may seem to bear the character of a compromise...Indeed, at a distance from the concrete, as in the case of a universal rule considered as universal, thought falls short of total practicality.[30]

[23] Yves R. Simon, *Practical Knowledge*, ed. Robert J. Mulvaney (New York: Fordham University Press, 1991), p. 101.

[24] *The Material Logic of John of St. Thomas*, p. 592n34.

[25] Ibid. Cf. Yves R. Simon, *Foresight and Knowledge*, eds. Ralph Nelson and Anthony O. Simon (New York: Fordham University Press, 1995), pp. 14-15.

[26] Ibid.

[27] Ibid.

[28] Ibid.

[29] Ibid.

[30] *Practical Knowledge*, p. 4.

In a series of oppositions, some already utilized, at least one quite new, Simon once more explores the contrast between the theoretical and the practical. But here the opposition between analysis and synthesis is treated in greater depth so as to remove certain possible objections, for instance, the idea that synthesis is not completely foreign to theory. Let us keep in mind Maritain's formulation, distinguish in order to unite. In order to clarify the extent to which synthesis might be relevant to theory, it is noted that analysis has two meanings: (1) a process of decomposition, best illustrated by the way in which a whole is broken down into its constituent parts. While this is a popular understanding of the term taken over from certain scientific procedures, many contemporary thinkers, notably the Gestalt psychologists, have opposed the misuse of it. It is, according to Simon, at most a preparatory phase of philosophical inquiry, not its main method. (2) For the proper sense of philosophical analysis is the resolution "of effects and consequences into causes and principles."[31] Perhaps Descartes's use of the clear and distinct criterion to sharply distinguish a thinking substance from an extended one, only to be faced subsequently, in *The Passions of the Soul,* with the apparently intractable problem of accounting for their intercommunication, is one of the best known instances of an analytic-synthetic method in philosophy. In any case, whatever auxiliary role whole-part analysis may play in philosophy, and it is certainly important, Simon argues that it is analysis in the second sense that is characteristic of theoretical method.

The synthesis involved in practical thought is not to be confused with synthesis as employed in theory. To be precise in this regard, Simon now refers to "the *synthesis of realization*" in which "the ultimate practical judgment involves a unique synthesis, namely, the putting together of a certain 'that' and the act of existing."[32]

The second opposition brought forward for the purpose of setting down the specificity of practical as opposed to theoretical thought articulates in a novel way some themes implicit in earlier discussions of explanation. I mean the opposition between explanation and fulfillment, so important for the third phase. This opposition or disjunction becomes particularly relevant in dealing with the so-called practically practical sciences. Let it be remembered that both in the *Critique* and in the long note to *The Material Logic* Simon did not raise any objection to calling this kind of information scientific. Now he does. The problem, as he now sees it, is whether or not this segment of the movement to practical determination really comprised

[31] Ibid., p. 6.
[32] Ibid., p. 5. See also pp. 52, 58.

science if the segment is not explanatory, as are theoretical philosophy and the theoretically practical knowledge of moral philosophy. If it is assumed that a form of knowledge ceased to be explanatory in some sense, by the same token, however significant it might be, it was erroneously named a science, always understanding science in the philosophical sense. But since explanation itself may be theoretical or practical,[33] an additional qualification is that without theoretical explanation, the knowledge at hand is not scientific. There is no doubt that the practically practical knowledge furnished by the writers on morality—Montaigne and Pascal are mentioned—involves practical explanations. Yet, unless the distinction between theoretical and practical explanation is tendentious, indeed superfluous, the knowledge acquired qualifies this sort of discourse as constituting a discipline not a science.[34] It is in this way that Simon parts company with Maritain's contention, reiterated in their correspondence, that these are sciences, and no doubt it is one of the few disagreements he had with his teacher and friend. So the general principle is established that where theoretical explanation is absent, so also is scientific status. Once prudence comes into play we are in the sphere of fulfillment itself. And fulfillment can occur even if explanation cannot be supplied.

In the third opposition used to spell out the specificity of moral philosophy, that between nature and use, there is a more thorough inspection of a distinction mentioned earlier. Practical knowledge "considers not only natures, as theoretical sciences do, but also the human *use* of things placed within the control of man."[35] It is what differentiates ethics from psychology. As a distinct way of differentiating practical knowledge from theoretical, this opposition has the singular advantage of opening up a new approach to the status of the social sciences in relation to ethics, one of Simon's early themes and main preoccupations. Although he now insists that "the primary purpose of moral philosophy is to understand moral essences,"[36] this is balanced when he accentuates the concern of moral philosophy "with problems of right and wrong use."[37] Since moral philosophy is concerned with use, it is, by that fact, concerned with what he has called the synthesis of practical thought. As always the distance between "the last word of philosophy and the work of prudence,"[38] is emphasized. For virtue alone can affect that ulti-

---

[33] Ibid., pp. 84-85.
[34] Ibid., p. 112.
[35] *The Material Logic of John of St. Thomas*, p. 592n34.
[36] *Practical Knowledge*, p. 54.
[37] Ibid., p. 51.
[38] Ibid., p. 55.

mate synthesis; virtue, that in the words of St. Augustine, is "a quality...of which no one makes a wrong use."[39] Virtue implies a good use.

The distinction between nature and use is relevant in dealing with the current issue of gun control in which both the principal and instrumental causes are at stake, those who have access to firearms and the use that is made of them along with the nature of these instruments and the likelihood of their being used for legitimate or illegitimate purposes. Leaving aside the sophistries that becloud the issue, one must say, on one hand, that legitimate arms, those with legitimate purposes, such as self-defence and protection against animal predators, or for sport and hunting, must be kept out of the hands of the criminally inclined and the mentally deranged, and the imma- ture, and, on the other hand, that there are certain kinds of weapons that fulfill no legitimate internal purpose; these are weapons designed for use in military action. As a society we have accepted the notion that a person deemed legally intoxicated cannot make a good use of a motor vehicle. The same logic would lead us to attempt to remove firearms from the hands of those who, it is presumed, cannot or will not make a good use of them. The opposi- tion of nature and use, then, is not meant to be an antinomy, for the moral issue requires both factors to be taken into consideration. Pure theory alone does not deal with use.

Secondly, the nature-use opposition proves to aid in the sorting out of the relation between ethics and the social sciences, an old concern of Simon's. Where formerly he addressed the French or Durkheimian sociologists, he now reacts to Weberian sociology, principally because of its importance in the United States. Very briefly, in place of Max Weber's notion of ethical neutrality (and its accompanying antinomies), Simon states that "facts per- taining to the life of human society seem to be of such a character that a philosophy of man is necessarily at work in the reading of their intelligibil- ity."[40] This entails the rejection of an independent social science, presumably a theoretical discipline. To leave aside the moral perspective would falsify the very object under investigation. On this count Simon quotes with ap- proval the famous essay by Leo Strauss on Max Weber's sociology. The conclusion is that both social philosophy and the social sciences fall under the heading of practical philosophy.[41]

---

[39] Ibid., p. 10.

[40] Ibid., p. 132. I have discussed the relation of the social sciences and moral philosophy in "Yves R. Simon's Philosophy of Science," in Anthony O. Simon, ed. *Acquaintance with the Absolute: The Philosophy of Yves R. Simon* (New York: Fordham University Press, 1998), pp. 64-65, 79-81.

[41] Ibid., pp. 131-32.

Following his elaboration of the three oppositions—analytic/synthetic, explanation/fulfillment, and nature/use—Simon proposes a new definition of moral philosophy. "At the present time, my tendency is rather to view moral philosophy as a system of explanation, which though practical in a proper sense by reason of its consideration of human use, exists primarily for the sake of explaining the things of morality."[42] He recognizes that this involves a shift from *A Critique of Moral Knowledge*, for in the earlier work, he says, "I laid strong emphasis on the function of moral philosophy as science to *direct human action*."[43]

On a number of occasions in his last work on moral philosophy, Simon speaks of moralists. No longer does he propose the earlier, rather eccentric, distinction between the moral philosopher and the moralist in terms of the kind of intellect one might expect from one or the other of these characters. What he now accepts is the rather conventional distinction between the moral philosopher a systematic thinker, as he understands the role, and that group of thinkers known in France as *les moralistes*, a category that would probably include such twentieth century writers as Denis de Rougemont and Albert Camus, who are not systematic. For the most part, Simon has in mind this latter group when he refers to moralists, although there is at least one context in which no distinction is made between a moral philosopher and a moralist.[44] There is no attempt to denigrate the contribution of people like the French *moralistes*. Quite the contrary, for he singles out "the kind of knowledge that we find in this extremely important work of human thought, the work of the moralists."[45] We must not lose sight of the fact that Simon expends considerable effort to define exactly what a moral philosopher is and does. Further, this definition must account for the limitations of the moral philosopher as a scientist. When human action is in question, it would be foolish to ignore the probability that practitioners may be more helpful in confronting particular moral quandaries than philosophers.

In conclusion, I offer the following overview. From his earliest reflections in the 1930s to his final remarks shortly before his death, Yves Simon never ceased to reconsider the situation of practical philosophy. If in the first exposition, Simon was intent on showing that moral philosophy is directive

---

[42] Ibid., p. 106.

[43] Ibid.

[44] Moral philosopher and moralist are identified in *Practical Knowledge*, p. 129, but elsewhere are contrasted (pp. 30-31, 87, 103). The earlier distinction between abstractive and concretitive is still considered valid, even if it is not now used to set out the difference between a moral philosopher and a moralist. See ibid., pp. 35-36.

[45] *Practical Knowledge*, p. 87.

knowledge, his final statements greatly stressed the need to present moral philosophy as involving explanation and understanding. The breakdown of tradition as a moral guide combined with the contemporary demand for a rational account of human affairs convinced him that this explanatory task was actually paramount. Had he basically altered his stance on that status of moral philosophy, for instance, did he revert to a position similar to that of John Poinsot? That he expressly denied. Or was it a matter of emphasis, now on one side of theoretically practical knowledge as formerly on another, direction from afar? That there was a change in emphasis is undeniable. However, Jacques Maritain in response to some of Simon's late reflections argued that no dilemma existed concerning the two tasks, that, in fact, they were complementary, not incompatible. Thus moral philosophy is recognized as having two roles: that of moral explanation and that of moral direction. The former consists in working on the theoretical foundations of practical knowledge. In that respect one might see a resemblance with a recent attempt to construct a firm foundation for contractualist ethics.[46] Though it is a far way from a moral philosophy geared to what we can agree upon to one that concerns what human nature requires.

---

[46] T. M. Scanlon, *What We Owe To Each Other* (Cambridge: Harvard University Press, 1999). In his review of the treatise, Colin McFinn states that Scanlon is "trying to find a philosophical foundation for the traditional absoluteness of moral values." *The New Republic*, 24 May 1999, p. 35.

Mystical Theology in Aquinas and Maritain

Robert A. Delfino

Recently, some Thomists have offered new understandings of "science" (*scientia*) and the relationship between philosophy and theology. John Jenkins, for example, offers a revisionary account of Aquinas's conception of science, and provides us with a new understanding of revealed theology.[1] Despite these developments, however, there remains a rarely challenged view, namely that there are only *two* kinds of theology in Aquinas: natural theology and revealed theology. Is it possible that there is a third and higher kind of theology in St. Thomas Aquinas—a theology of mystical experience?

Prima faciae, the answer seems to be "no" because the Common Doctor only speaks of two kinds of theology: natural and revealed.[2] The first Thomas calls *scientia divina*, taking his lead from Aristotle;[3] it begins in sense knowledge and studies being as being (*ens commune*) using the natural light of reason. God is not the primary subject of this science, but this science studies God because God is the cause of the being of creatures. Thomas engages in natural theology when he proves things about God in the first three parts of the *Summa Contra Gentiles*.[4] The second kind of theology Thomas calls *sacra doctrina*; it begins in faith, proving things about God from principles that have been divinely revealed.

Correspondence to: rob@ded.com.

[1] John I. Jenkins, *Knowledge and Faith in Thomas Aquinas* (Cambridge: Cambridge University Press, 1997).

[2] Aquinas, *Expositio super Librum Boethii de Trinitate*, Q. 2, a. 2, resp., trans. Armand A. Maurer in *Faith, reason and theology* (Toronto: Pontifical Institute of Mediaeval Studies, 1987), p. 41; Aquinas, *Summa Theologiae* I, q. 1, a. 2, ad. 2.

[3] In *Metaphysics*, VI, c. 1 (1026a19), Aristotle uses the term *theology*.

[4] Aquinas, *Summa Contra Gentiles*, I, c. 9, 3 and cf. IV, c.1, 9.

Not only does Thomas not discuss any other type of theological science,[5] he says that revealed theology is the highest science there is[6] and the
highest wisdom.[7] Even God's knowledge, although it is a higher form of
knowledge, does not properly speaking constitute a science because it is
not discursive. Moreover, Thomas says that the principles used in revealed
theology come from God's very own knowledge which He shares with the
blessed;[8] as there is no higher knowledge than God's, what would a higher
theology use as principles?

Despite these difficulties, and by relying on Thomas's own principles, I
argue that another type of theology is implied by Thomas's views. I then
briefly outline the nature of this science, which I propose to call "mystical
theology," and discuss both how it is distinct from other sciences and what
place it has among the other sciences. Jacques Maritain also discussed mystical theology drawing upon Aquinas, St. Teresa of Ávila, and St. John of the
Cross, in his famous work *The Degrees of Knowledge*.[9] Later on I evaluate
Maritain's conception of mystical theology, discussing some of its merits
and deficiencies.[10]

I

The traditional interpretation of Thomas's conception of science is that
he followed Aristotle's lead both in regards to his understanding of the nature of a science and in how the sciences are distinguished from each other.
(This view has been challenged by Jenkins, but his view does not jeopardize
my conclusions.[11]) Aristotle had listed several conditions of a science, some

---

[5] Thomas does mention civil theology (*theologia civilis*) and mythical theology (*theologia fabularis*), when discussing the pagans (*Summa Theologiae* II-II q. 94, a. 1, resp.). He also discusses *theologia mystica* (*Expositio in Librum Dionysii de divinis nominibus*, 1, 3), but this is not considered by him to be a science separate from revealed theology.

[6] *Summa Theologiae* I, q. 5, resp.

[7] *Summa Theologiae* I, q. 6, resp.

[8] *Summa Theologiae* I, q. 2, resp.

[9] Jacques Maritain, *The Degrees of Knowledge*, trans. Gerald B. Phelan (Notre Dame, Indiana: University of Notre Dame Press, 1995).

[10] It is important to note that Maritain discusses two types of mysticism, supernatural and natural, in *The Degrees of Knowledge*. Here I shall discuss his view of supernatural mysticism. For his views concerning natural mysticsm see Curtis L. Hancock, "Maritain on Mystical Contemplation" in *Understanding Maritain: Philosopher and Friend* ed. Deal W. Hudson and Matthew J. Mancini (Macon, Georgia: Mercer University Press, 1987), pp. 257-69. As Hancock notes, Maritain also discussed mysticism in some of his other works; for a list of these see ibid., n. 1.

[11] *Knowledge and Faith in Thomas Aquinas*, chaps. 2-3.

of which are: it must use demonstrative reasoning (i.e., valid, deductive, syllogistic reasoning, where the premises are known to be true); it must be of the universal; it must be knowledge of cause, and it must produce certain knowledge.[12] Thomas did not consider all of these necessary conditions, and considered the first and last to be necessary and sufficient. As a result, Thomas called revealed theology a science because it uses demonstrative reasoning, and because it produces certain knowledge. In the *Commentary on the De Trinitate of Boethius*, he succinctly described the nature of science saying: "The nature of science consists in this, that from things already known conclusions about other matters follow of necessity."[13] This is the sense in which Thomas generally used the term *scientia*, although at times he did use *scientia* to refer to various types of non-scientific knowledge (e.g., the knowledge God has, and one of the Gifts of the Holy Spirit). Both natural and revealed theology are *scientiae* in the first sense, i.e., certain, demonstrative knowledge.

Science, strictly speaking, exists only in the mind of a knower. It is a certain quality of the intellect (*habitus*) that disposes a person to act in a certain way. Thomas separates the different sciences according to the formal objects they study.[14] For example, in regard to the speculative sciences (metaphysics, mathematics, and physics), Thomas says: "Each [of the speculative] science[s] treats of one part of being in a special way distinct from that in which metaphysics treats of being."[15] It is the formal object that gives unity to a science and thus, with respect to revealed theology, Thomas says:

> Holy Teaching [*sacra doctrina*] should be declared a single science. For you gauge the unity of a habit and its training by its object, and this should be taken precisely according to the formal interest engaged and not according to what is materially involved; for instance the object of the sense of sight is a thing as having colour, a formal quality exhibited by men, donkeys, and stones in common. Now since Holy Scripture looks at things in that they are divinely revealed, as already noted, all things whatsoever that can be divinely revealed share in the same formal objective meaning. On that account they are included under holy teaching as under a single science.[16]

Therefore, if we can discover a formal object that is not treated in the other sciences and from which certain knowledge can be acquired, we have another science. This is what I maintain occurs in mystical theology.

---

[12] Aristotle, *Posterior Analytics*, I, cc. 2-14 (71b8-79a33), especially 71b17-73a32.

[13] *Expositio super Librum Boethii De Trinitate*, q. 2, a. 2, resp.

[14] *Summa Theologiae* I-II, q. 54, a. 2, ad 1; cf. *Summa Theologiae* I, q. 1, a. 1, ad. 2.

[15] *Expositio super Librum Boethii De Trinitate*, q. 5, a. 1, ad. 6.

[16] *Summa Theologiae* I, q. 3, resp.

II

In the *Summa Contra Gentiles* Thomas says that a person can know God in three ways:

> There is...in man a threefold knowledge of things divine. Of these, the first is that in which man, by the natural light of reason, ascends to a knowledge of God through creatures. The second is that by which the divine truth—exceeding the human intellect—descends on us in the manner of revelation, not, however, as something made clear to be seen, but as something spoken in words to be believed. The third is by which the human mind will be elevated to gaze perfectly upon the things revealed.[17]

From this it seems that there are only three ways a person can know God, and that only two of them are available in this life. The formal object of the first way of knowing God is God as known through the being of creatures. Thomas is fond of quoting Paul, "[God's] invisible attributes of eternal power and divinity have been able to be understood and perceived in what he has made."[18] The formal object of the second way of knowing God is God as known through a proposition that is known to be divinely revealed.[19] Hence, God as known by reason, arguing from sensible world, constitutes the formal object of *natural theology*, and God as known by faith constitutes the formal object of *revealed theology*. In the third way of knowing God, God is known through the light of glory, which occurs in the next life.[20]

---

[17] *Summa Contra Gentiles* IV, c. 1, 5.

[18] *St. Paul's Epistle to the Romans* 1:20.

[19] In *Summa Theologiae* II-II q. 1, a. 1, Thomas distinguishes between the material object of faith, and the formal object of faith. The material object of faith concerns the content of faith (e.g., that God is triune). Concerning this distinction, Thomas notes that "First, from the perspective of the reality believed in, . . . the [Formal] object of faith is something non-composite, i.e., the very reality about which one has faith [i.e., God]. Second, from the perspective of the one believing, . . . the [Material] object of faith is something composite in the form of a proposition." *Summa Theologiae* II-II, q. 1, a. 2, resp. The formal object of faith is the First Truth (i.e., God), because we assent to an article of the faith "only because it has been revealed by God, and so faith rests upon the divine truth itself as the medium of its assent." *Summa Theologiae* II-II, q. 1, a. 1, resp. For a contemporary discussion concerning the material and formal objects of faith, with some discussion of Thomas, see Avery Dulles, *The Assurance of Things Hoped For: A Theology of Christian Faith* (New York: Oxford University Press, 1994), esp. pp. 187-90.

[20] "Our intellect is not equipped by its nature with the ultimate disposition looking to that form which is truth; otherwise it would be in possession of truth from the beginning. Consequently, when it does finally attain to truth, it must be elevated by some disposition newly conferred on it. And this we call the *light of glory*, whereby our intellect is perfected by

So it seems there are only two kinds of theology, because even though, according to Thomas, we can know God in the Beatific vision, after this life, this is not discursive knowledge; rather it is a simple and immediate apprehension. The blessed in heaven cannot derive anything from this vision because everything they know is known through the simple apprehension of God face to face and not discursively. But science is discursive knowledge, and so it seems that there can only be two kinds of theology: natural and revealed. Thomas does hold, however, that some persons (e.g., prophets such as Moses and St. Paul) have had a partial glimpse of God in this world.[21] Moreover, in the *Commentary on the Sentences of Peter Lombard*, he discusses another way we can know God in this life. There he writes about how the soul can be united to God in this life through the love of the Holy Spirit. He describes this as a kind of experiential knowledge of God (*quasi experimentalis*).[22] Now this is different than knowing God in the three ways

God, who alone by His very nature has this form properly as His own.... Of course, we shall never comprehend Him as He comprehends Himself. This does not mean that we shall be unaware of some part of Him, for He has no parts. It means that we shall not know Him as perfectly as He can be known, since the capacity of our intellect for knowing cannot equal His truth and so cannot exhaust His knowability. God's knowability or truth is infinite, whereas our intellect is finite. But His intellect is infinite, just as His truth is; and so He alone knows Himself to the full extent that He is knowable." Aquinas, *Compendium theologiae*, I, cc. 105-6, trans. Cyril Vollert, *Light of Faith: the Compendium of theology* (Manchester, New Hampshire: Sophia Institute Press, 1993), pp. 118-19; my emphasis.

[21] *Summa Theologiae* II-II, q. 174, a. 4, resp.; cf. *Summa Theologiae* II-II, q. 175, a. 3, ad 3.

[22] "[To the third (objection) it should be said that not any kind of knowledge suffices for the understanding of the mission, but only that which is received from some gift appropriate to the Person (of the Trinity), through which we are joined to God, according to the proper mode of that Person, namely through love, when the Holy Spirit is given (to someone). Whence that knowledge is, as it were, experiential] *Ad tertium dicendum, quod non qualiscumque cognitio sufficit ad rationem missionis, sed solum illa quae accipitur ex aliquo dono appropriato personae, per quod efficitur in nobis conjunctio ad Deum, secundum modum propium illius personae, scilicet per amorem, quando Spiritus sanctus datur. Unde cognitio ista est quasi experimentalis....* [To the fifth (objection) it should be said that although knowledge is appropriate to the Son (i.e., Christ), nevertheless that gift from which experiential knowledge is had, which is necessary for the mission, is not necessarily appropriate to the Son, but sometimes (is appropriate) to the Holy Spirit as love] *Ad quintum dicendum, quod quamvis cognitio approprietur Filio, tamen donum illud ex quo sumitur experimentalis cognitio, quae necessaria est ad missionem, non necessario appropriatur Filio, sed quandoque Spiritui sancto, sicut amor."* Aquinas, *Scriptum super libros Sententiarum Magistri Petri Lombardi*, I, 14, 2, a 2 ad 3 and 15, 2 ad 5, ed. P. Mandonnet and M. F. Moos, vol. 1. (Paris, 1929-1947), pp. 326 and 342; my translations. Like *ratio*, *missio* is difficult to translate by one word for all occasions. I have translated it by "mission" but this needs explanation. "*Missio*" for Aquinas is a rich term capturing several things at once. From one perspective it refers to Christ's being sent (*mitto, mittere*) to us to save us and to speak God the Father's truth to us. From another perspective it

enumerated above. The formal object of such an act of knowing is God as experienced by the person, though it is only a partial experience, as we shall clarify later.[23] This gives us insight into the formal object of a third and higher kind of theology, which I propose to call "mystical theology" because its formal object is God as experienced by the person in mystical union.[24]

refers to the indwelling of the Persons of the Trinity within us through grace. And this is related to the mission of the Church, which is to preach the Gospel. For example, St. Paul was given that grace (that is, *missio*). For more on this see *Summa Theologiae* I, q. 43, and the two questions referred to above. Also note that Thomas uses the term "*cognitio*" above. Scott MacDonald warns us that we should not equate *cognitio* with knowledge since Aquinas says we can have false cognition. See his "Theory of Knowledge" in *The Cambridge Companion to Aquinas* (Cambridge: Cambridge University Press, 1993), pp. 162-63, 188 n13. However, the awareness of the presence of God through the love of the Holy Spirit (or through some other kind of intuition, for that matter) would be *cognitio* of a simple essence and hence not subject to error as Aquinas himself says in *Summa Theologiae* I, q. 17, a. 3, resp.

[23] God as known in mystical experience is a direct, though partial, type of knowledge. For example, when a person is aware of the presence of God in mystical experience this is direct knowledge because God's presence is not known through concepts or sense images. Because we are not aware of God's presence all of the time He must give us a *special light* which allows us to be aware of His presence. (The possibility of such a light is left open in *Summa Theologiae* I, q. 89, a. 1, ad. 3 where Thomas holds that when the soul is separated from the body it knows by sharing in a divine light just as other immaterial substances do, though in an inferior mode. If the soul has this potency in its nature then it is possible that even while it is joined to the body God can grant it that light it has when separated from the body.) Insofar as this light allows us to be aware of God's presence, the knowledge we have is direct; insofar as this light is lesser than the light of glory, which we receive in the Beatific vision, the knowledge we have is partial (cf. n. 20 above). We are also aware of the changes God is effecting in us in mystical experience. And it is from these experiences (along with our awareness of His being present) that we derive the propositions that are used in mystical theology. Hence we have an insight of a different and deeper order into the fact that God is love when we experience the Love that He outpours to us in mystical experience, than when we simply assent to but do not experience that "God is love." This should also prepare us to see that while the Beatific vision may be inarticulable because God is purely simple, discussing the effects God causes in us in mystical experience *are* articulable. That is, they, at the very least, admit of some explanation. This is why it is profitable to study what St. John of the Cross has to say about mystical experience of God— because we can gain some insight; if mystical experience were completely inarticulable such a study of St. John would be in vain.

[24] The term "mystical theology" comes from the title of a work written by the Pseudo-Dionysius. However, what the Pseudo-Dionysius meant by "mystical theology" was not what later Christians came to mean by it, as Paul Rorem explains: "Both *mystical* and *theology* need clarification. The traditional translation of *mustikos* [in the title of the Pseudo-Dionysius' work] as *mystical* can be quite misleading if the connotations of later mysticism are read back into the Dionysian corpus and into this title. In the premedieval usage of Dionysius and other authors, the word does not mean the suprarational or emotional ecstasy of extraordinary and solitary individuals. It carries the simpler, less technical sense of something mysterious, something hidden to others but revealed to those initiated in the mysteries." *Pseudo-*

Thus, just as natural theology differs from revealed theology in formal object, so does mystical theology differ from the other two in regard to formal object. In revealed theology God (and, more generally, the things that belong to Christianity) is considered from propositions known to have been divinely revealed. In mystical theology God (and indirectly His creation) is considered from the experience of God by the mystic.[25]

It is important to understand the differences between reason, faith and mystical experience. For example, in metaphysics, we can know that God exists and that God is one through discursive reasoning. In this case, although the premises may be known to be true by us, the conclusions are inferred from them. In faith, we have some understanding of the articles of the faith and we assent to them—but we do not posses sight (excepting the *revelabilia* or preambles of the faith, which some can "see" mediately through reason).[26] Even in Jenkins's supernatural externalist interpretation of faith, he admits that we do not experience what the articles of the faith refer to, but rather only know that they are revealed by God and we assent to them.[27] But in mystical experience we have more than just assent and understanding of an article of the faith; to borrow an analogy from St. John of the Cross, in

Dionysius: A Commentary on the Texts and an Introduction to their Influence, trans. Paul Rorem (New York: Oxford University Press, 1993), pp. 183-84. An example which illustrates the shift in meaning of "mystical theology" from the time of Pseudo-Dionysius to the later middle ages is that of Jean le Charlier de Gerson (1363-1429), who defined "mystical theology" as: "experiential knowledge of God attained through the union of spiritual affection with Him." *Selections from "A Deo exivit," "Contra curiositatem studentium" and "De mystica theologia speculativa,"* trans. and ed. Steven Ozment (Leiden: E. J. Brill, 1969), pp. 64-65. For a brief history of the word "mysticism" in the West (and some comments on "mystical theology") see Harvey D. Egan, *An Anthology of Christian Mysticism* 2nd ed. (Collegeville, Minnesota: The Liturgical Press, 1991), pp. xx-xxv and 1-16. For more contemporary treatments of mysticism which share, more or less, my understanding of "mystical experience" see: Dennis Tamburello, *Ordinary Mysticism* (New York: Paulist Press, 1996), pp. 5-26; D. L. Carmody and J. T. Carmody, *Mysticism: Holiness East and West* (New York: Oxford University Press, 1996), pp. 3-26; Walter H. Principe, "Thomas Aquinas' Spirituality" in *The Étienne Gilson Series 7* (Toronto: Pontifical Institute of Mediaeval Studies, 1984), pp. 1-29.

[25] Of course we may also ask if the experience of angels falls under the formal object of mystical theology. Insofar as such experience gives insight to the nature of God, the answer seems to be yes. But this is a matter requiring more treatment than can be given here.

[26] Even the preambles of the faith (e.g., God exists) are not known like the first principles of metaphysics. Rather, God can be known to exist from knowledge about the sensible world through demonstration *quia*. But *what* God is remains unknown to us in this knowledge (cf. Aquinas, *Quaestiones disputate de Potentia Dei,* q. 7, a. 2, ad 1, and *Summa Theologiae* II-II, q. 1, a. 2, ad 3).

[27] *Knowledge and Faith in Thomas Aquinas*, pp. 190-97.

mystical experience we "touch" God.[28] Thus we do not just understand and assent to the proposition "God is love"[29]—we experience God loving us in our soul.[30] God acts upon the soul, which passively receives and is aware of His love and presence and through this a person gains some insight into the being of God. This awareness of His love and presence is direct since it is not known through concepts or sense images, but rather through a higher light. Nevertheless, God's being is not fully disclosed in this light, and so this knowledge is indirect insofar as the light is lesser than the light of glory, which in the next life allows us to know God as much as our finite natures can. It is precisely because of this that mystical experience is a higher form of knowledge than faith or reason. Thus God as experienced by the person in mystical union is the formal object of this higher science. For easy comparison, I have outlined all three sciences below:

MYSTICAL THEOLOGY (*Theologia Mystica*)
SUBJECT: God (and indirectly His creation)
FORMAL OBJECT: God as experienced by someone in mystical
                     experience/union
PRINCIPLES: Principles derived from mystical experience
METHOD: Intuitive/Discursive
AIM: Speculative and Practical

REVEALED THEOLOGY (*Sacra Doctrina*)
SUBJECT: God (and, more generally, the things that belong
                     to Christianity)
FORMAL OBJECT: God as known through propositions known to have
                     been divinely revealed
PRINCIPLES: Principles known by faith

---

[28] "The Lord grants these communications directly, [thus] they are wholly divine and sovereign. They are all substantial touches of divine union between God and the soul. In one of these touches, since this is the highest degree of prayer, the soul receives greater good than in all else…. Since a substantial touch is wrought in such close intimacy with God, for which the soul longs with so many yearnings, a person will esteem and covet a touch of the divinity more than all God's other favors." St. John of the Cross, *Dark Night of the Soul*, Book 2, chapter 23, trans. by Kieran Kavanaugh and Otiio Rodriquez in *The Collected Works of St. John of the Cross* (New York: Doubleday & Company, Inc., 1964), pp. 453-54.

[29] *The First Epistle of St. John* 4:8.

[30] It should also be noted that, owing to Thomas' doctrine of proper proportionality, God's love is only *analogous* to human love. Hence, the experience of God's love in someone's soul, even though it is only a partial experience of God's love, is like no other kind of love ever experienced.

| METHOD: | Authoritative/Discursive |
| AIM: | Primarily Speculative, but Practical as well |

NATURAL THEOLOGY (*Scientia Divina*)

SUBJECT:	God[31]
FORMAL OBJECT:	God insofar as He is the cause of the being of creatures[32]
PRINCIPLES:	Principles known by reason
METHOD:	Intuitive/Discursive
AIM:	Speculative

Note, too, that because the formal object of mystical theology is God as partially experienced, there can be no fourth theology. The only other way left to know God is as He is (i.e., in His essence), which occurs in the Beatific vision, and beyond which other knowledge is not possible.

III

I would like to reply briefly to some objections that can be raised against my view, and in doing so I hope to further clarify my position. The first objection is that mystical theology is a part of revealed theology and the latter is not compartmentalized for Thomas into mystical theology and revealed theology. Thomas Gilby voices this objection:

> St. Thomas did not conceive of mystical theology as a special science, the study of rare and miraculous phenomena, but as that part of ordinary Christian theology

---

[31] God, properly speaking, is not the subject of *scientia divina* (i.e., metaphysics) for Thomas. Metaphysics only studies God indirectly, as I have noted earlier. However, for the sake of comparing the three types of theological knowledge, we can limit our focus to the natural theology present in Thomas' metaphysics, which is what I have done diagrammatically above.

[32] "[I]f a science considers a subject-genus, it must investigate the principles of that genus, since science is perfected only through knowledge of principles, as the Philosopher explains in the beginning of the *Physics*" Aquinas, *Expositio super Librum Boethii de Trinitate* Q. 5, a. 4, reply. Thomas then distinguishes between two sorts of principles: "Some are complete natures in themselves and nevertheless they are the principles of other things [e.g., God], ... And for this reason they are considered not only in the science of the beings of which they are the principles, but also in a separate science...some principles, however... are not complete natures in themselves, but only the principles of natures, as unity is the principle of number, point the principle of line.... Principles of this sort, then, are investigated only in the science dealing with the things of which they are principles of all beings." Ibid.

which treats of the fully grown-up condition of the new life that is born in baptism; he countenances no separation of mystical from ascetical theology, no separation of exegetical from moral theology, no separation of moral theology from dogmatic theology, no separation of dogmatic theology from the Scriptures. And so in the first question of the *Summa*, he describes theology as a function of being in love with God and therefore working through sympathy as well as science.[33]

What Gilby says is generally true of Thomas, but in one respect, at least, Thomas's principles dictate otherwise. Since it is the formal object that specifies a science, different formal objects will bring about different sciences. Thus, although Thomas does not explicitly distinguish between mystical theology and revealed theology, his view implies a distinction. Now moral and dogmatic theology can all be treated under revealed theology insofar as moral truths and dogmatic truths can be demonstrated from principles that have been revealed to us by God. But moral and dogmatic theology can also be treated under mystical theology insofar as insofar as moral truths and dogmatic truths can be derived from mystical experience.

Just as the proposition "God loves us" can be known in natural theology, where it is inferred from other knowledge, and in revealed theology, where it is known that it is true and understood analogously through concepts, so too can it be known in a different and higher way in mystical theology, where it is experienced directly in the soul. Moreover, as we shall see below, we can derive other knowledge from the experience of God loving us in our soul. Therefore, to say that "Christian theology is not like mathematics which can be treated like a genus and divided into specifically different parts, e.g., arithmetic, geometry etc.," then, is incorrect.[34]

A second objection points out that Thomas said, "All things whatsoever that can be divinely revealed [*revelabilia*] share in the same formal objective meaning. [And so,] on that account…are included under revealed theology as under a single science."[35] Moreover, it seems we can understand "revelation," in a broad sense, to include both faith and mystical experience; for both share the fact that God reveals something to persons, they differ only in the *way* in which something is revealed. Sometimes God reveals a message, as in the case of the prophets, other times God reveals Himself by allowing the soul to experience Him through His actions. In faith, that which is revealed is not experienced but is assented to and understood to some degree.

---

[33] See Thomas Gilby, "Appendix 6" in *Summa Theologiae*, vol. 1 (New York-London: McGraw-Hill, 1964-1969) p. 86. The exact passage that Gilby is referring to when he mentions the first question of the *Summa Theologiae* is I, q. 1, a. 6, ad. 3.

[34] Thomas Gilby, marginal note in ibid., p. 14 note e.

[35] *Summa Theologiae* I, q. 3, a. 3, resp.

In mystical experience, that which is revealed is partially experienced. But if the formal object is the *revealable*, then perhaps Thomas was correct in holding that there is no separation of mystical theology from revealed theology. Indeed, in his commentary on Paul's *Second Letter to the Corinthians* he declares that prophetic visions (which are generally categorized as mystical experiences) fall under the category of revelation:

> Revelation includes vision and not vice versa; for sometimes some things are seen, the understanding and meaning (*significatio*) of which is hidden from sight, and then it is vision alone, as [in the case of] the vision of the Pharaoh and Nebuchadnezzar...but when [along] with vision is had the meaning and understanding of those things which are seen, then it is revelation.[36]

Hence those visions that are accompanied by understanding and signification—in short those visions accompanied by a message that can be transmitted to people—fall under the category of revelation. Indeed, when the message is lacking only the vision remains, which by itself is nothing more than a private mystical experience. But the experience of God *qua* the experience does not fall under the category of revelation. For revelation is the transmission of a truth or message that is not seen, and an experience *qua* the experience is non-propositional,[37] and thus not a message. Hence the articles of faith and the messages of prophetic visions, as preached and recorded in the canonical books of Holy Scripture, are used as premises in revealed theology. However, the experience of the vision in the prophet's mind is not contained under the formal object of revealed theology. Similarly, the experience of God in the soul of the mystic, is not contained under the formal object of revealed theology, but instead constitutes the formal object of mystical theology. Indeed, Thomas says: "In this life revelation does not tell us what God is, and thus joins us to him as to an unknown."[38] Hence, while revelation can communicate truths about God to us, it is different from an experience of God, which does give us a taste, however limited, of what God is.

---

[36] "*Nam revelatio includit visionem, et non e converso. Nam aliquando videntur aliqua quorum intellectus et significatio est occulta videnti, et tunc est visio solum, sicut fuit visio Pharaonis et Nebuchodonsor, Dan., II, et Genes., XLI. Sed quando cum visione habetur significatio intellectus eorum quae videntur, tunc est revelatio.*" Aquinas, *In Epistolam II ad Corinthios*, XII, 1, in *Opera Omnia* (Paris: Vivès, 1871-1880), vol. 21, p. 451; my translation.

[37] Our experience is always of individual things, and not universals. Therefore our experience of things *qua* experience of them is always non-propositional. It is through the mental acts of abstraction and judgment that we judge things to be members of a certain class of things (e.g., cats).

[38] *Summa Theologiae* I, q. 12, a. 13 ad 1.

The third objection is that mystical experience seems to be simple and non-propositional, thus while it may be a sort of knowledge—it can neither be scientific knowledge nor used as premises in scientific demonstration. There are many different kinds of mystical experience (e.g., visions, ecstasy, etc.), and while all of them as experiences are non-propositional, this does not prevent mystics from reflecting upon their mystical experiences and making judgments about them that will be used as premises in mystical theology. Indeed, many mystics throughout the ages have expressed the insights they have gained from mystical experiences in words and concepts even if words and concepts are only able to convey some understanding of the mystical experiences. Thus, I maintain that by reflecting on some of our mystical experiences we can make judgments that will be used in this science.[39] Such judgments are propositional and can be used in argumentations. Let me provide some examples to make this clear, though the examples are mine and not Thomas'.

Consider the person who has a mystical experience while in deep prayer and meditation. During this experience, the person becomes aware of the presence of God in his soul. The person feels at once joyous and at peace; all of this happens rapidly and is incommensurate to anything that the person could have effected. Yet the person knows that his actions did not merit this gift for he has sinned. From having had this wonderful experience of God loving him in his soul many things can be derived. For one, God is with us and therefore deist theology is wrong. Second, mystical knowledge is higher, clearer, and more certain than faith. This in no way denigrates faith, but means that mystical experience surpasses faith. It is a higher type of knowledge because unlike faith there is more than assent and partial understanding—there is an experience of God. It is clearer insofar as God is more clearly known through partial experience than in faith. It is more certain insofar as a higher experience of God moves the will more strongly than a lower one. Thus the blessed in heaven possess the highest certitude followed by those in mystical union with God, and then those who have faith. Third, it can be derived that the science of mystical experience is higher than revealed theology because it surpasses it both in certitude and in the kind of knowledge obtained. Thomas uses certitude and rank of subject-matter (*dignitas materiae*) to establish the position that revealed theology excels all other sciences.[40] Since the rank of the subject-matter is the same (i.e., God) and since both the certitude and the kind of knowledge obtained in mystical experience is greater, mystical

---

[39] For even if mystical experience is non-propositional we can still make judgments about it. Just as in the intuition (*cognitio*) of sensible things we do not have propositional knowledge but can abstract from and make judgments about that which we intuit, so too in mystical experience can we make judgments about that which we mystically experience.

[40] *Summa Theologiae* I, q. 1, a. 5, resp.

theology is a higher science than revealed theology. Moreover, since the judgement about the certitude of mystical knowledge can only be made by a mystic, the above proof cannot belong to revealed theology.

Finally, I want to point out that those who disagree with my view and hold that mystical theology is merely a part of revealed theology are in danger of embracing a nominalistic view of science. For unless they hold that mystical theology does not have a different formal object than revealed theology, which seems incorrect, or that the formal object is different but absolutely nothing can be derived from mystical experience, which also seems incorrect, they are guilty of nominalism—a view that sees science as an ordered system of concepts and propositions, rather than, as Thomas held, a single *habitus* that gets its unity from its formal object.[41] By embracing such nominalism we are in danger of confusing distinct habits, for example the habit of metaphysics and the habit of revealed theology, with each other. Is this not what Ockham did when he claimed that the habit of demonstrating that God is one is neither theological nor metaphysical?[42] And is there not the same danger, then, of confusing revealed theology with mystical theology? The point is that it does not matter if some of the conclusions of revealed theology and mystical theology are the same; what does matter is that the formal objects are different. For indeed, some of the conclusions of natural theology and revealed theology are the same but they are not one science. Therefore, once we admit that in mystical experience we know God in a different way than through faith, and that from mystical experience at least some knowledge is derivable,[43] we must, at the very least, admit that mysti-

---

[41] For more on the historical difference between Thomas' conception of science and nominalism, see Armand. A. Maurer, "The Unity of a Science: St. Thomas and the Nominalists," in *St. Thomas Aquinas 1224-1274. Commemorative Studies*, ed. Armand A. Maurer (Toronto: Pontifical Institute of Mediaeval Studies, 1974), vol. 2, pp. 269-91. Of course, concerning habits, one could argue that mystical theology cannot be a science because it relies on God's grace, and therefore cannot be a steady habit. Indeed, Thomas himself, in *Summa Theologiae* II-II, q. 171, a. 2, resp, held that mystical experience was not a steady habit: "On the other hand, a steady disposition, *habitus*, is that by which a person acts when he wishes to as Averroes says. Now none can take to prophecy when he wills, as is clear from the story of Elisha.... Thus prophecy is not a lasting disposition." Although Thomas only speaks of prophecy here, what he says should hold for other kinds of mystical experiences; for since such experiences are gifts from God, and thus not in the power of the human agent to elicit, mystical experiences are not stable habits. However, this objection can be answered by pointing out that Thomas does not discuss the fact that God can freely choose to give many such experiences to a person who is willing to accept them, and thereby the *habitus* can be steady and persist over a considerable span of time.

[42] William of Ockham, *Scriptum in Libros Sententiarum*, I, Prol., q. 1.

[43] At the very least it seems some things concerning mystical union and its relation to our spiritual life can be derived.

cal theology is a third type of theology. Whether or not it is higher or subordinate to revealed theology would still be debatable, but I have already advanced arguments for the former conclusion.

Of course we have not covered all the important issues concerning mystical theology that should be covered in order to have a complete understanding of it. For example, we have not covered issues concerning the verification of authentic and inauthentic mystical experience, but these and other issues go beyond our present scope and shall have to be treated elsewhere. For now, we move to Maritain.

IV

While many Thomists in this century have focused upon Thomas's metaphysics, or the theology of the *Summa theologiae*, Jacques Maritain should be commended for doing important work concerning mystical theology. Using his own creative genius and drawing from the wisdom of Aquinas, John of the Cross, and Theresa of Ávila, he discussed the nature of mystical theology in *The Degrees of Knowledge*. In that work, he describes the formal object of this science in the following way:

> Mystical theology...consists in knowing the essentially supernatural object of faith and theology—Deity as such—*according to a mode that is suprahuman and supernatural....* It is no longer a question of merely learning, but rather of suffering divine things. It is a matter of knowing God by experience in the silence of every creature and of any representation, in accordance with a *manner* of knowing, itself proportioned to the object known, insofar as that is possible here below.[44]

He explains that in mystical experience we are elevated by grace to experience God's presence within us.[45] According to him, this is "a *real* and *physical* (ontological) presence of God in the very depths of our being...a fruitful, experimental knowledge and love which puts us in possession of God and unites us to Him not at a distance, but really."[46] Maritain rightly stresses the non-conceptuality of this knowledge, which he says is also a knowledge by connaturality,[47] since by charity, which presupposes sanctifying grace, we are made connatural to God, as far as that is possible.[48]

---

[44] *The Degrees of Knowledge*, p. 270.
[45] Ibid., pp. 273-74.
[46] Ibid., p. 274.
[47] Ibid., p. 276.
[48] Ibid., p. 277.

For Maritain knowing God in mystical union differs from knowing God through faith, since faith relies on concepts and analogy.[49] In contrast to faith, in mystical experience "the inspiration of the Holy Ghost uses the connaturality of charity to make us judge divine things under a higher rule, under a new formal *ratio*."[50] So far much of this is similar to my view of mystical experience and mystical theology.

However, Maritain's view has some inadequacies. First, Maritain remarks that the practical and speculative sides to mystical theology are actually part of the science of revealed theology taken in a general sense.[51] For Maritain, this general sense of revealed theology means "The whole organism of our knowledge of the mysteries, faith itself, the theological discursus and the gifts of the knowledge, understanding, and wisdom."[52] But then he speaks of "speculatively practical mystical theology" (hereafter "SPMT") and "practically practical mystical theology" (hereafter "PPMT"), separating the last, but not the former, from revealed theology taken in a strict sense (i.e., the science of the virtually revealed or what Thomas calls *sacra doctrina*).[53] In fact, Maritain should separate both from revealed theology in the strict sense since he holds that the formal object of both (i.e., SPMT and PPMT) is the same and also differs from the formal object of revealed theology in its strict sense. Yet he says that charity is necessary for the PPMT but is not necessary for SPMT.[54] It is unclear how the SPMT can still be a mystical theology if the connaturality of charity, which is its formal object, is lacking from it. Moreover, Maritain says that the SPMT and the PPMT are distinct but not specifically different habits.[55] But, again, if that's the case, then either both are part of revealed theology or neither is.

Second, just as revealed theology for Thomas is one science involving both speculative and practical aspects, so I claim it is with mystical theology. There are not two mystical sciences born from the experience of God, but rather one science that has both speculative and practical sides. The experience of God has practical benefits for the person, and the person's knowledge is increased by the experience—thus there is both a speculative and practical

---

[49] Ibid., p. 276.

[50] Ibid., p. 279.

[51] Ibid., pp. 337-38. The text does not read "revealed theology in a general sense." First "sacred doctrine" is used and then "theology." Maritain reminds us that "'theology' in the strict sense [is the] . . . science of the virtually revealed [see the chart on p. 269]." The science of the virtually revealed, for Maritain, is what Saint Thomas would call revealed theology.

[52] Ibid., p. 337.

[53] Ibid., p. 335-37.

[54] Ibid., p. 337.

[55] Ibid., p. 338.

side to mystical theology. In short, Maritain's distinction between the speculatively practical mystical theology and the practically practical mystical
theology is a misguided one.

Third, although Maritain did emphasize that mystical experience is the
fruition of faith and the life of grace,[56] and that it is the closest taste we can
have in this life of what is to come in the Beatific vision,[57] he does not emphasize the awesome potential of mystical experience, and the knowledge
we can derive from it, to transcend our current metaphysical and theological
knowledge of God and the creation. Instead, he stresses that "mystical
wisdom…uncovers for us no object of knowledge which faith does not attain."[58] But given the infinitude of God, and the finitude of the deposit of
faith, it seems unreasonable to put limits on the knowledge that lies in wait
for those who are one with God in love. It is my hope that in the years ahead
many more will follow Maritain's example by focusing upon mystical theology, and sharing its fruits with others. This is especially true for Thomists,
for if it is true that mysticism is the maturity of the life of faith and grace,
then any Thomism that excludes the study of mystical theology has not reached
its maturity.[59]

[56] Ibid., pp. 275-76.
[57] Ibid., p. 341.
[58] Ibid., p. 281.
[59] I would like to thank Fr. Armand A. Maurer for his invaluable help and encouragement
in undertaking this project. My gratitude also extends to Jorge J. E. Gracia, who read and
provided very useful comments on an early draft of this paper. I also benefited from the
insightful comments of John F. X. Knasas, William Sweet, James and Tyra Arraj, Curtis
Hancock, Anne and Owen Smith, and Christian Brunelli. Charles Jones should also be
acknowledged for his generous and kind support. *Et Deus meus, laudo te propter immensa
indigno mihi praestita benefica.*

Nonlocality and Maritain's Dream of A Philosophy of Nature

James Arraj

In 1952 Jacques Maritain was living in Princeton at 26 Linden Lane with its walls covered with murals of Parisian street scenes. That spring he had given the A.W. Mellon Lectures on the Fine Arts at the National Gallery in Washington, which were to become his *Creative Intuition in Art and Poetry*.

Not far away a young physicist named David Bohm was teaching at Princeton and had written a textbook on quantum physics which he had sent to Neils Bohr, who did not answer, to Wolfgang Pauli, who was enthusiastic about it, and to Einstein who called him and invited him to visit.

These two events, so close in physical proximity and yet apparently completely unconnected, are a fitting symbol of the dialogue, or better, the failure of dialogue between Thomism and modern physics.

Maritain had long had a deep interest in reviving a Thomist philosophy of nature. He had not only laid down the epistemological principles that would govern and guide such a dialogue in his *The Degrees of Knowledge*, but he had gone to listen to Einstein speak at the Sorbonne some thirty years before and had written an intriguing study of relativity. Later, when these Princeton years were a bitter-sweet memory, he would write in *The Peasant of the Garonne* that this program for a renewed philosophy of nature was "a vanished dream of my youth."[1]

Bohm, for his part, was at the beginning of what looked like a promising career in physics. It must have been deeply gratifying that Einstein wanted to talk to him. Einstein had always resisted the prevailing orthodoxy of the Copenhagen interpretation of quantum physics that had coalesced around Bohr, an approach that Bohm had largely followed in his textbook, and now he urged Bohm to see if he could go beyond it. And Bohm did in two papers that appeared in 1952. But no one, including Einstein and Bohm, himself,

---

[1] Jacques Maritain, *The Peasant of the Garonne*, trans. Michael Cuddihy and Elizabeth Hughes (New York: Holt, Rinehart and Winston, 1968), p.140.

really grasped the full import of what those papers presaged. Soon Bohm was banished from the Princeton scene, another victim of the House Committee on unAmerican Activities, and went off to exile in Brazil.

But let us try to see what could have been, and still can be, in terms of a dialogue between quantum physics and a Thomist philosophy of nature. "Few spectacles," Maritain wrote in *The Degrees of Knowledge,* "are as beautiful and moving for the mind as that of physics...advancing towards its destiny like a huge, throbbing ship."[2] But physics is a very human enterprise, as well. Bohm's 1952 papers were like explosives with a slow burning fuse. They were going to cause distant detonations that would change the landscape of modern physics, or to pursue Maritain's metaphor, the great ship of physics was going to find itself sailing the strange and simmering sea of nonlocality.

In order to understand what is at stake in a dialogue between Thomism and quantum physics we need to take a short tour of quantum theory. The still prevailing Copenhagen interpretation can be best explained in terms of the two-slit experiment. A beam of particles is shot at a screen, and a barrier with two narrow slits is placed between the source of the particles and their target. If one slit is closed, the particles go through the other and form a line on the target, which is just how particles should act, but if both slits are open, instead of there being two lines formed on the target, we see a whole pattern of light and dark lines, an interference pattern that indicates to the physicist that these particles in some way also have the qualities that they attribute to waves.

Now in the Copenhagen interpretation the wave-like distribution of the particles is attributed to a probability wave—that is, the mathematical probability that tells us what the odds are a certain particle will end up in a certain place. There is no way, they tell us, to discover which slit an individual particle goes through, and this indeterminism of the particle is given a philosophical meaning. The physicist, John Gribbin, explains the matter like this: "The electrons not only know whether or not both holes are open, they know whether or not we are watching them, and they adjust their behavior accordingly. There is no clearer example of the interaction of the observer with the experiment. When we try to look at the spread-out electron wave, it collapses into a definite particle, but when we are not looking it keeps its options open. In terms of Born's probabilities, the electron is being forced by our measurement to choose one course of action out of an array of possibilities. There is a certain probability that it could go through one hole, and an equivalent probability that it may go through the other; probability interfer-

---

[2] Jacques Maritain, *The Degrees of Knowledge,* trans. Gerald B. Phelan (Notre Dame, Indiana: University of Notre Dame Press, 1995), p. 165.

ence produces the diffraction pattern at our detector. When we detect the electron, though, it can only be in one place, and that changes the probability pattern for its future behavior—for that electron, it is now certain which hole it went through. But unless someone looks, nature herself does not know which hole the electron is going through."[3]

The Copenhagen interpretation was only reinforced in 1932 when the famous mathematician, John von Neumann, created a proof that showed that there was no way to go beyond the Copenhagen interpretation and arrive at what was going on deeper down and discover some sort of hidden variables. None of this ever sat well with Einstein, as I said, which is why he wanted Bohm to try to go beyond it. Bohm's 1952 papers showed that there was another way to interpret the mathematical formalism of quantum theory and, indeed, in this other way the much-proclaimed quantum weirdness of the Copenhagen interpretation disappears. Bohm proposed that a quantum potential, or quantum wave, was guiding each particle. In the two-slit experiment, then, when one slit is open the particle and its pilot wave go through it and form a line on the screen. But when the two slits are open, each particle goes through one slit or the other, but its attendant pilot wave goes through both and causes the characteristic interference pattern.

While Bohm's 1952 papers made scarcely a ripple in the world of physics, they did interest a young Irish physicist, John Stewart Bell, and by 1964 Bell was ready to seriously think about their implications. At least two things struck him. One was that von Neumann's proof must be wrong because otherwise Bohm could not have written his papers at all because they propose a hidden variable theory. And secondly, Bohm's quantum wave was nonlocal, that is, it had to be instantaneously propagated to distant objects in order to cause the effects that it did. And so Bell took an important step and asked himself whether all quantum theories had be nonlocal. What was at stake was this: let us imagine that two particles interact and go off in different directions. If we measure one, according to the normal law of physics, we assume that this measurement does not affect the other particle unless the first particle can somehow communicate with the second particle at a speed under the speed of light, which physicists set down at the speed limit of the universe. But here is Bell asking himself whether these two particles can somehow communicate faster than the speed of light, although this is not quite how to put it, or better, if one particle somehow instantaneously knows what is happening to its partner. Bell later used the analogy of two identical twins, reared apart, who later, it is discovered, share many characteristics

[3] John Gribbin, *In Search of Schrödinger's Cat*, (New York: Bantam, 1984), p. 171.

with no known means of communication between them, for example, each of them names his dog George.

It was a few years before physicists figured out a way to test Bell's theory, and ever since they have been staging ever more refined experiments to see if nonlocality is actually a feature of the universe, and so far the experiments have demonstrated that it is. Recently, for example, experimenters split a photon and sent the pair through a fiber optic network until they were ten kilometers apart. When they measured the energy of one photon, it instantaneously determined the measurement of the other.

Now that you are up to speed on quantum physics, let us turn to the question of a dialogue between it and Maritain's philosophy of nature. There are two principle issues. First is the problem of quantum weirdness and its implicit or explicit philosophical meaning. The second question is what to do with nonlocality itself.

As far as the first issue is concerned, if physics confronted us with the Copenhagen interpretation with all its philosophical baggage, and said that the experimental evidence demands that we accept it, we would, as Thomist philosophers, face great difficulties. We would have to try to deal with the world in which causality is no longer operative, and this is really a metaphysical impossibility.

Instead, we need to make a fundamental distinction between the mathematical formalism of quantum theory and its philosophical interpretation. There are several ways we can begin to do this. We might say, with Maritain, that the mathematical formalism is one thing, while the underlying physical world that it measures is quite another. Physics measures this world and submits those measurements to the rule of mathematics, and this web of physico-mathematical constructs, while it does, indeed, grasp the real physical world, grasps it blindly as far as its ontological nature is concerned, and we cannot expect that these constructs have a point by point correspondence to the physical world. What seems to be happening in the Copenhagen interpretation is that not only are the physico-mathematical constructs presented as the only thing we can know, and the underlying physical world as unknowable in principle, but the different constructs, for example, the wave aspects of the electron and the particle aspects of the electron, which represent contrasting theories, are paradoxically presumed to be characteristics of the unknowable physical world, itself, and therefore we are told about the quantum weirdness of that world.

This point is brought out well in the mathematician Wolfgang Smith's book *The Quantum Enigma* where he tells us that a distinction must be made between the electron and its observables, or the electron in the corporeal world and how it is grasped by the methods of physics: "...one spuriously projects," he writes, "the results of distinct and interferring measurements upon the electron itself, which consequently seems to combine logically incompatible attributes."[4] Wolfgang Smith has continued this line of thought in his articles, "From Schrödinger's Cat to Thomistic Ontology," and "Bell's Theorem and the Perennial Ontology."[5]

What is at issue here is a series of challenging epistemological questions, but questions for which we can look for the resources to answer them in Maritain's well developed ideas on the epistemological type of modern physics, or in Wolfgang Smith's use of perennial themes of classical Western philosophy, or in an updated Thomistic view of the philosophy of nature that can be found in William Wallace's *The Modeling of Nature,* and his article, "Thomistic Reflections on *The Modeling of Nature.*" Quantum weirdness in the Copenhagen sense vanishes when we take the proper philosophical perspective.

But this does not mean that nonlocality has vanished. Nonlocality has been called one of the greatest scientific discoveries of the past century. Somehow things communicate in the universe in a way that defies the normal models of the physicist and the normal speeds of interaction. We could say that they do not seem to communicate through the normal ways of efficient causality as physics understands them. Bohm has developed some intriguing examples to illuminate what we are up against. Imagine, he tells us, that we have two cameras mounted at 90° to each other facing an aquarium. When we look at the two monitors attached to the cameras, we can elaborate various theories whose purpose is to try to correlate the two different images that we are seeing. But these two dimensional images are aspects of a higher, in this case, three-dimensional reality. If we could somehow take that higher perspective, we would have no problem understanding the two different perspectives that we see on the monitors. This is what Bohm means by an implicate order about which he wrote a great deal.

But just how are we, as philosophers of nature, to begin to deal with the apparent fact of nonlocality? Let me sketch one approach that can find support in Bohm's writings. Modern physics can be said to be focused on efficient causality. But is it not possible that there is an implicate dimension of things, a dimension that is akin to formal causality, and it is this dimension that physics is encountering in nonlocality?

---

[4] Wolfgang Smith, *The Quantum Enigma,* (LaSalle, Illinois: Sherwood Sugden Co., 1995).
[5] Wolfgang Smith, "From Schrödinger's Cat to Thomistic Ontology," *The Thomist,* 61 (1997), pp. 455-67; Wolfgang Smith, "Bell's Theorem and the Perennial Ontology," *Sophia* 3 (1997), pp. 19-38.

Let us take the two particles that have interacted and gone off far apart, and yet know what is happening to each other. Why not say, with Bohm, that the two particles are manifestations of one higher order implicate reality? However strange this might sound from the point of view of physics, it is not really strange to philosophers of nature if we look beyond the surface terminology. Maritain, for example, in a footnote in *The Degrees of Knowledge* wrote: "The problem arises whether the substantial unity of a corporeal individual (for example, like a molecule of a gas, or a living organism) necessarily requires continuity in extension, as the ancients believed. In other words, cannot a substantial form inform a whole of discontinuous parts, whether contiguous (as blood plasma is contiguous to the walls of the blood vessels) or, on the atomic scale, separated by inter-atomic or intermolecular interstices (in the case that, contrary to the hypothesis of Gredt, these interstices would not themselves be informed by the substantial form of the individual whole). In my opinion, such a structural discontinuity is compatible with the substantial unity of the individual whole, and I think that, in that case, the Thomistic theory of individuation by *materia signata quantitate* is verified without special difficulty. The transcendental relation of matter to quantity would then mean, a transcendental relation to a constellation of positions."[6]

Now to turn this remark into a full-fledged philosophical theory of nonlocality would demand, among other things, that we do a fundamental analysis of the notion of formal causality and the way things interact, and along with it, take an equally searching look at the notion of matter in the Aristotelian-Thomistic tradition, and then take these hopefully renewed ideas and apply them to the question of nonlocality. I tried to begin to do this in my book, *The Mystery of Matter,*[7] which touches not only on nonlocality, but Jung's ideas on synchronicity and Rupert Sheldrake's on morphic resonance. The question of the nature of matter is particularly intriguing because it leads us to the very heart of Thomist metaphysics because matter must be brought into intimate relationship not only with form, but also with *esse*. The pioneering work of William Carlo is particularly important in this regard.[8]

A final remark. If a Thomistic philosophy of nature has been and still is mostly moribund even in the aftermath of the great Thomistic metaphysical

---

[6] *The Degrees of Knowledge*, p. 191n72.

[7] James Arraj, *The Mystery of Matter* (Chiloquin, Oregon: Inner Growth Books, 1996).

[8] William Carlo, *The Ultimate Reducibility of Essence to Existence in Existential Metaphysics*, (The Hague: Martinus Nijhoff, 1966).

revival around World War II, it is not because it lacked the philosophical resources to enter into dialogue with the natural sciences, but because it is still asleep, and the most promising way for it to awake and mobilize those resources is to attempt to look at central issues in the sciences, like nonlocality, and try to understand them from its own particular philosophical point of view.

Out Of The Shadow
Henri Bergson and Three French
Philosophers

William J. Fossati

Belle époque France did not have a more productive philosopher than Henri Bergson. Bergson's attempt to bridge the chasm between science and spirituality put him at the center of intellectual ferment during the period. Because of this, he influenced a broad array of political, scientific, and religious thinkers in the first years of the twentieth century. Those whom he influenced were as different as Georges Sorel and Marcel Proust.[1] Beyond the specifically academic dimension to his work, Bergson became an early-day celebrity in the eyes of the literate public. His lectures at the *Collège de France* drew Parisian society ladies as well as students. As a lecturer, he was nearly as much showman as academician.[2] This was true on both sides of the Atlantic.

Thus it is no surprise that Bergson provided inspiration, irritation, and challenge to a generation of French intellectuals. They damned him as often as they venerated him, yet French men and women of letters during the first thirty years of the century could never deny his importance.[3] So it was with three of the most impressive Catholic philosophers of the time: Maurice Blondel, Gabriel Marcel, and Jacques Maritain.

Bergson's epistemology was problematic for all three men and, indeed, was the source of much of their interest in his work. Certainly Bergson's entire approach to knowing was a startling departure from the rationalist tradition. In the Bergsonian world, one did not *know* things; one *intuited* them. Not the least of the striking quality of Bergson's stress on intuition lay in the eloquence with

---

[1] See Jacques Maritain, *Ransoming the Time*, trans. H. L. Binsse, (New York: Charles Scribner's Sons, 1941), p. 53. See also Gabriel Marcel, "Discours sur Bergson," *Bulletin de la Société Française de Philosophie*, 54 : 1, (Jan-Mar), p. 32.

[2] "Discours sur Bergson," p. 27.

[3] See Maurice Blondel, *La Philosophie et l'esprit chrétien*, (Paris: Presses Universitaires Universitaires de France, 1950), Vol. I, p. 78.

which he expressed it. As an animated speaker, Bergson could—and often did—beguile his listeners. The slight cock to his head, the abrupt motion of his right arm while lecturing were captivating to student audiences.[4] One is tempted to suspect that in Bergson's dynamic style, as well as in his personal charm, there was the potential for seduction. Without a doubt, this accounted for much of the persuasiveness in his principle of intuition.

In any case, Bergson's belief in intuition as the vehicle for human knowing was central to his philosophy. Like the trunk of a tree, it supported any number of subordinate principles as though they were branches. His positions on duration, perception, biological evolution, and faith all bore on his treatment of intuition. Like the problem of epistemology itself, these other questions demanded the attention of his contemporaries. It was here that they entered into an intriguing acceptance/rejection posture with regard to Bergson. Unlike Bergson, Blondel, Marcel, and Maritain were Catholic philosophers. Therefore their interests and priorities with regard to epistemological questions took different perspectives.

In Blondel's case, any philosophical exercise had of necessity to lead to an understanding of God's divine plan.[5] Because his career oscillated between philosophical and theological considerations, care must be taken when reading Blondel. The epistemological ground that he staked out in regard to God's existence had a Thomistic starting point. A partial knowledge of God can be gained from the study of philosophy. However, Blondel was dissatisfied with a thoroughly philosophical approach to the knowledge of God.

Though he did not acknowledge Bergsonian influence, he turned to intuition as a means of completing our apprehension of the nature of God. "Prophetic intuition" as Blondel termed it, brought the Holy Spirit into our consciousness.[6] The human mode of apprehending Divine Revelation is driven by intuition. The inherent tension between Thomistic and Bergsonian epistemology seemed not to distress Blondel in the least. In fact, reading Blondel forces one to question whether or not he had the intellectual discipline to appreciate the elegance of St. Thomas's approach to human knowledge.

In tones more reminiscent of Tertullian than Thomas, he goes on the offensive against philosophy in his book, *La philosophie et l'esprit chrétien*. Warning of "the temptations of prideful independence [and] scientific pretension…"[7] he argues that knowledge of God is based on faith, not reason. Continuing his diatribe against philosophical inquiry, he adds that the core of

---

[4] Ibid.
[5] Ibid.
[6] Ibid.
[7] Ibid., p. 115.

Christian belief is neither subject to rational investigation nor open to critical analysis. He cites, as an example, the matter of the Holy Trinity. He begins, "Doubtless there are reasons for the philosopher to pose certain problems which concern the necessary unity of God and His sovereign personality. But it is not legitimate to assume, as do certain Doctors [sic], that a rational 'demonstration' can or ought to be offered in order to clarify our thoughts on the most necessary, the most fundamental of truths."[8] Blondel imposed boundaries on discursive knowledge, which were meant to point up the futility of rational attempts to understand the divine.

Bergson had his own critique of discursive reasoning that he revealed (among other places) in his *Introduction to Metaphysics*. In his criticism of rational investigation, Bergson insisted that our abilities to *know* through reason were limited to the *relative* understanding of a given object.[9] The great inadequacy of discursive reasoning for Bergson was that it confined our knowledge only to a set of simulacrums that could do no more than represent the *absolute*. Using his well-known example of the object moving through space,[10] Bergson demonstrated that the actual flight of the object could only be traced by mathematical or empirical symbols, none of which could capture the real dynamism of a moving, animated object. Points of reference and axis marks are only able to *represent* the movement of Bergson's flying object. They cannot tell us the absolute nature of the thing. They cannot present us with the *thing in itself.*

It is here that we can detect a reason for Blondel's rejection of rational epistemology. The reason was Immanuel Kant and his insistence that the human intellect could not know things in their essence, *der Ding an sich*. Since the end of the eighteenth century and the appearance of Kant's *Critique of Pure Reason*, French thinkers had been forced to contend with the limits that the Königsberger had imposed on epistemology. He proclaimed that we could never know the substance of anything; it was beyond our human abilities. Kant had many adherents in France by the end of the nineteenth century.[11] To Catholic philosophers like Blondel, Marcel, and Maritain, Kantian constraints on human knowing presented serious difficulties with the knowledge of God. The Kantian critique of human knowing set strict limits on what we could discern of the universe and especially the Kingdom of Heaven.

[8] Ibid., p. 214.
[9] See Henri Bergson, *Œuvres*, Textes Annotés par André Robinet, 2ᵐᵉ éd., (Paris: Presses Universitaires de France, 1963), p. 1393.
[10] Ibid.
[11] See A. D. Sertillanges, *Avec Henri Bergson* (Paris: Gallimard, 1911), p. 11.

After 1899, Bergson's was the most insistent voice against Kantian rationalism. Much of Bergson's doctrine of intuition was aimed at making an end run around the imposing critical edifice of Kant's epistemology. Conceding to Kant the limits he placed upon human knowledge, Bergson introduced a new dimension to the realm of cognition. It was his contention that the most profound understanding comes not from reason, but from an affinity with the metaphysical. Here was a development in the theatre of French thinking which was nothing short of dramatic. To grant Bergson his argument regarding the limits of discursive reasoning and the limitless potential of intuitive reasoning was to make all things possible. As Bergson expressed it:

> Symbols and points of reference place me outside of it [the object]; they do not yield to me anything but that which is common to others of its type and not its essence.[12]

Thus Blondel could renounce rational approaches to the knowledge of God. He was at once calling for a reaffirmation of faith and striking a blow at the epistemological constraints of Immanuel Kant. Hence he was able to warn his listeners against the use of "empirical pseudo-sciences" in modes that presume to know and understand Divinity.[13]

Gabriel Marcel was similarly fascinated with Bergsonian intuition. In Marcel's case, his interest in intuitive knowledge rested as much on its didactic qualities as on its investigative attributes. He saw in Bergson's startling approach to knowing a "power of propulsion" capable of having the most profound influence on those who were exposed to it.[14] Specifically, he pointed to two of *fin de siècle* France's most renown authors: Charles Péguy and Marcel Proust. It was Marcel's contention that both these men, having been students of Bergson, came away with his brand of intuitive epistemology. More than this, Marcel contended, Péguy and Proust pursued opposing directions in their work and in their personal convictions.[15] And both of them proceeded to build their ideas on the foundation that they had taken from the master.

In Marcel's eyes, the reason for the greatness of both Péguy and Proust was that they understood what was true and real; not just the empty symbols of the truth.[16] So, Gabriel Marcel recognized Bergsonian epistemology for its teaching and inspirational qualities.

---

[12] Henri Bergson, *Œuvres*, p. 1394.
[13] See Maurice Blondel, *Exigences philosophiques du christianisme*, (Paris: Presses Universitaires de France, 1950), p. 280.
[14] "Discours sur Bergson," p. 32.
[15] Ibid.
[16] Ibid.

At the same time Marcel was put off by what he distinguished as a difference between what he viewed as Bergsonism as a philosophical system and Bergsonism as "a mode of thinking."[17] By way of criticism, Marcel feared that much of Bergson's philosophizing, including the matter of intuitive knowledge, was suffering from intellectual sclerosis. Bergson's disciples had embraced the form, but not the substance of their master's thinking. In Gabriel Marcel's estimation, Bergsonism as a system had completely discounted the role of the intellect in knowing.[18] Latter-day Bergsonians had fallen into the snare of confusing the product of intelligence for intelligence itself. Marcel's critique of Bergsonian epistemology as practiced by his followers points out a tension between intellect and instinct. This, he says, is a tension that ought not to be. Marcel's reading of Bergson shows the dynamics of intellect and instinct as complementary, not as adversaries. Writing in 1932, Marcel mourned the "decaying ideas" which by that time he perceived as having attacked Bergsonism.[19] Apparently, Marcel admired Bergsonian intuition in its pristine form, but was saddened to see its fall from grace as a result of mishandling by Bergson's later adherents.

Jacques Maritain had been one of Bergson's earliest pupils. Both he and his wife, Raissa, had attended Bergson's lectures at the *Collège de France*. Maritain's later career was characterized by a developing critique of Bergsonism. At the heart of Maritain's reproof, was the lack of asperity in Bergson's epistemology. Maritain pointed out that the starting point for Bergsonian intuition was empiricism.[20] As a former mathematician and scientist, Bergson had retained an epistemological procedure that was scientific in its essentials. As Maritain came to embrace Thomism, he also became aware of the lack of logical rigor in Bergson's order of thought.

Maritain was perfectly willing to celebrate Bergson's rebellion against the scientism of nineteenth-century figures such as Herbert Spencer, yet he lamented the Bergsonian tendency to fall in with the existential speculations of someone like Martin Heidegger.[21] Bergson's denial of the efficacy of rational thought in favor of the instinctual posed a major weakness in his epistemology as far as Maritain was concerned. Nonetheless, Maritain main-

[17] See Gabriel Marcel, *Creative Fidelity*, (New York: The Crossroad Publishing Co., 1982), p. 13.

[18] Ibid.

[19] See Gabriel Marcel, "Henri Bergson et le problème de Dieu," *L'Europe Nouvelle*, 142, (30 avril, 1932), pp. 558-59.

[20] See Jacques Maritain, *De Bergson à Thomas d'Aquin: essais de métaphysique et de morale*, (Paris: Paul Hartmann, 1947), p. 34.

[21] Ibid., pp. 33-34.

tained an immense respect for Bergson as a counterweight to nineteenth-century idealism. In Maritain's estimation, it was Bergson who reintroduced the possibility of a *cosmic* universe into European philosophy.[22] Idealist philosophers—once again we meet Kant—had insisted on a universe that could be accommodated within the bounds of the human imagination. Therefore, any notion of the Deity was slave to the limits of human cognition. This, of course, was a serious assault on Christian theology. Bergson had mounted an effective counterstroke against Kantian idealism with his insistence on the metaphysical interpretation of the universe. Celebrating Bergson's metaphysics as the "most profound, penetrating, and daring known to our times,"[23] Maritain had nothing but admiration for "…the master of my youth."[24]

Like Blondel, Maritain rejoiced in Bergsonian intuition for its brilliant opposition to Kant. Unlike the mercurial Blondel, Maritain tempered his gladness with the conviction that for all his heroics, Bergson remained well outside the limits of Aristotelianism.

Bergson's last major publication was *The Two Sources of Morality and Religion*, which appeared in 1932. In that study, he examined the metaphysical differences between what he called "closed" morality and "open" morality.[25] Closed or "static" morality was intellect-driven and designed to provide for human survival. Its major characteristics were stasis, self-centeredness, and intolerance toward different sets of belief. Open morality, on the other hand, featured continual change (evolution), inclusiveness, and an attitude of outreach toward humanity. Open morality, unlike closed, was sparked not by the intellect, but by intuition.

The Two Sources was a distillation of almost all of Bergson's philosophy. He seemed to be pulling all of his earlier statements together in this final testament. Creative evolution was linked to intuition as well as the *élan vital*, and the nature of God. For this reason, his valedictory drew the interest of the intellectual community of France and the entire west.

Marcel saw in the concepts of open and closed morality the central question in religious matters. His reading of open morality described it as providing the psychological impetus for admiration. Admiration served to remove human self-centeredness. In admiration, one was able to escape from self-absorption. For Marcel, the first step toward open morality was to escape from our egotism. Conversely, to partake of closed morality was to

[22] Ibid., p. 72.
[23] Ibid., p. 57.
[24] Ibid., p. 127.
[25] See Henri Bergson, *The Two Sources of Morality and Religion*, trans. R.A. Audra & C. Brereton, (Garden City, New York: Doubleday Anchor, 1954), p. 205.

consign oneself to isolation from the community of man.[26] To the extent that one was in a state of closed morality, he/she was unreceptive to the needs, aspirations, and accomplishments of the rest of humanity.

In the matter of open and closed morality, Marcel found himself closer to Bergson than in any other aspect of Bergson's thinking. Marcel pointed out that closed morality presupposed a closed society. He went on to say, "I belong to" a closed society is to relegate oneself to social as well as spiritual stagnation. When one proclaims, "I belong" in the context of an open society, he/she is making it possible to outgrow self-centeredness and to clear the way for spiritual development.[27] In Marcel's reading of Bergson, open morality was the key to creativity; in fact, without a free and open environment (one of the themes of *The Two Sources*), the phrase "I belong" is rendered meaningless.

In a specifically religious vein, Marcel reflected on the nature of conviction and belief in the context of open and closed morality. He drew a fine, but crucial distinction between the two words by associating "conviction" with the egocentrism of closed morality. To Gabriel Marcel, conviction denoted an uncreative, unresponsive state of mind. At the end of the day, this sort of closed mind would not be able to sustain itself and could not endure.[28] Marcel associated "belief" with open morality. The individual, who was central to his reading of open morality, was open to spiritual growth through belief. Belief called upon the individual to assert all of his/her faculties. The act of belief served as a spiritual exercise designed to draw the individual out and to open to him/her all the possibilities of the active life.[29]

Blondel also saw a vital spark in Bergson's work. In praise of Bergson, he referred to his writing as the "first life of spring, removing the spirit-smothering sediment of twenty-five centuries of science."[30] Blondel had an affinity for Bergson's opinions regarding the nature of life and the importance of action in that life. Because of this, he made an easy transferal of his religious priorities to terms with which Bergson would have agreed. Even as Bergson had spoken of the Christian mystics as personifying open morality, Blondel described Christian theology as being "open and maintain[ing] a flexibility of adaptation by reason of the strength of all its attachments to

---

[26] See Gabriel Marcel, *Creative Fidelity*, p. 48.

[27] Ibid., p. 96.

[28] Ibid., p. 133.

[29] Ibid., p. 134.

[30] Maurice Blondel, *L'itinéraire Philosophique de Maurice Blondel*, ed. Frédéric Lefèvre, (Paris: Editions Spés, 1928), p. 48.

irrevocable and organically plastic decisions like a living being."[31] His version of open morality was frankly Christian, but in this instance, he saw a role for philosophy in guiding the individual believer to true openness. Though he saw philosophy and faith essentially at odds, Blondel also viewed the two as having a "symbiotic relationship" which presents each person with a unique destiny, which he dares not shun.[32] None of which is to say that he was prepared to grant philosophy a blank check in leading humanity to spiritual openness. While he was willing to entertain certain Bergsonian points of view, he was adamant in warning those who would seek open morality away from Descartes. He rejected Cartesianism as both "fruitless" and "barren."[33]

Both Blondel and Marcel were willing to adapt Bergson's open morality in the service of Christian thought. So, indeed, was Maritain. Maritain was gratified by Bergson's treatment of the Christian mystics in *The Two Sources*. By making of mysticism the intelligent manifestation of Christianity,[34] Bergson convinced Maritain that dynamic religion was a mode of knowledge. In this instance, it was a matter of gaining knowledge of God's transcendent nature. Maritain came close to stating that *The Two Sources*, if carefully read, revealed Bergson's actual commitment to Christianity. He advised friends to "read between the lines" in *The Two Sources* for a glimpse of Bergson's cryptic conversion to Catholicism.[35] Maritain identified Christian mysticism as the key to Bergson's coming to the point of belief in Christianity.[36]

So it was that Maritain, Marcel, and Blondel, each in his own way, embraced Bergson. In the case of Maritain it was a rather ginger embrace. Yet, the fact remains that each of these three men wrestled Bergson's influence into some form that accommodated itself to their individual thought.

---

[31] *La Philosophie et l'esprit chrétien*, p. 232.
[32] Ibid., p. 233.
[33] *Exigences philosophiques du christianisme*, p. 284.
[34] See *The Two Sources of Morality and Religion*, p. 213.
[35] *De Bergson à Thomas d'Aquin: essais de métaphysique et de morale*, p. 70.
[36] Ibid., p. 88.

Composing Subjectivity:
Maritain's Poetic Knowledge in Stravinsky and Messiaen

Robert Fallon

Although Jacques Maritain interrogated the nature of poetic knowledge in several studies, scholars have struggled to clarify his views. In focusing their attention on the relationship between morality and poetic knowledge, they have overlooked the fundamental importance that Maritain invested in subjectivity. "The primary requirement of poetry," he wrote, "...is the obscure knowing, by the poet, of his own subjectivity."[1] At the same time, studies of poetic knowledge have maintained a philosophical approach to the concept, even though Maritain claimed that "Poetic knowledge...finds its expression not in conceptual statements, but in the very work made."[2] This study attends to two works made whose subject is truth, Igor Stravinsky's *Oedipus Rex* (1927) and Olivier Messiaen's *La Nativité du Seigneur* (1935). Historical surveys of each composer establish Maritain's influence on their works and demonstrate that the relationship between poetic knowledge and subjectivity is closer than even Maritain asserted.

Though Maritain explored the philosophical components of poetic knowledge (particularly in *Creative Intuition in Art and Poetry*), his attempts to trace the route of artistic creation back to its seed as poetic knowledge do not venture far down the path of art criticism. In explaining a poem by Donne, for example, he reduces the germ of the poem to three words: "He begins with creative emotion, or poetic intuition, and

---

[1] Jacques Maritain, *Creative Intuition in Art and Poetry* (New York: Meridian Books, 1955), p. 83.

[2] Maritain, "Poetic Experience," *The Review of Politics* 6: 4 (October 1944), pp. 387-402, originally published as "Connaissance Poétique," École Libre 4, no. 12 (1943). Maritain's principal treatise on poetic knowledge is *Creative Intuition in Art and Poetry*, though parts of *Art and Scholasticism*, *Art and Faith*, and *The Situation of Poetry* also address the subject.

the argument follows. Donne forcefully and eloquently developed his theme—...poisonous minerals, and me—and by virtue of which the whole poem exists." His reading of a poem by Blake is equally unconvincing: "In an invisible flash of intuitive emotion, which is obscurely conveyed to us—what can we say? Dust of pride and God's glory—and by virtue of which the whole poem exists."[3] Maritain's literary criticism is hardly more illuminating than the "texts without comment" he quotes in *Creative Intuition*. Maritain's critical aims are better served in less laconic terms, especially when the artistic self-consciousness with which *Oedipus Rex* and *La Nativité* treat their themes of truth reveals so much about the poetic knowledge in each work. That a work's subject is truth may seem irrelevant to its poetic knowledge, since the former is a conscious intellectual concept, whereas Maritain's idea of the latter is preconceptual.[4] However, in the works discussed here, musical symbols of truth permeate the score. They constitute the very substance of the works, not an intellectual overlay on the underlying music, and so are identifiable with the poetic knowledge at their core. Maritain described the relationship of poetic knowledge to truth as one of conformity, where an artwork's veracity is proportional to its degree of conformity with the original poetic vision.[5] Though the primordial state of any poetic vision is by nature evanescent and ineffable, the fact that these works concern veracity itself enables a glimpse into their original condition. They can be read, in other words, as statements on the artistic process itself and as evidence for the character of the composers' poetic knowledge. Because there are significant differences between the two composers and their works, the reflection of each composer's view of truth in his composition exemplifies Maritain's claim that subjectivity is at the center of poetic knowledge.

Basing Knowledge on Music

For Maritain, poetic knowledge is an intuitive knowledge gained by an artist during the process of creation.[6] He based his concept of poetic knowl-

---

[3] *Creative Intuition in Art and Poetry,* pp. 258–59.

[4] For more on the relation of concepts to poetic knowledge, see ibid., p. 223.

[5] On truth and poetic knowledge, see ibid., pp. 34, 38, 52, and 174.

[6] See Samuel Hazo, "Maritain and the Poet," *Renascence* 34: 4 (Summer 1982), pp. 229-44; Gerald C. Hay, "Maritain's Theory of Poetic Knowledge: A Critical Study," (Ph.D. diss., The Catholic University of America, 1964); and Francis Fergusson, "Poetic Intuition and Action in Maritain's *Creative Intuition in Art and Poetry,*" in *Jacques Maritain: The*

edge on Thomas Aquinas' distinction between two styles of making moral judgment. Thomas illustrates the first in the figure of the philosopher who, though educated in the moral virtues, may not be virtuous. He locates the second in the uneducated man who cannot discuss the philosophy of the moral virtues, but who exercises them because they are part of his nature, due to his "affective union" with them. The unlettered man has a "connatural" knowledge of virtue, a knowledge by inclination or intuition that is intellectual, but preconceptual.[7]

Maritain applies Thomas' distinction between types of knowledge to art. There are craftsmen, he says, who know how to construct art based on rules and yet fail to express significant artistic sentiment. Real artists, on the other hand, know how to express truth within the realm of artistic value, even if they lack a refined knowledge of their craft. They possess their poetic knowledge through their connatural union with the art object. Maritain defines poetic knowledge in terms of the artist's subjectivity:

> That is poetic experience or poetic knowledge, where subjectivity is not grasped as an object, but as a source.... The more deeply poetry becomes conscious of itself, the more deeply it becomes conscious also of its power to *know*, and of the mysterious movement by which...it draws near to the sources of being.[8]

Maritain thus intimately ties artistic creation to the self-consciousness of the artist. But he also repeatedly emphasizes throughout his works that self-knowledge and awareness of identity result from a consciousness of the outside world. In *The Situation of Poetry*, for example, he writes that "It is in awakening to the world, it is in obscurely grasping some substantial secret in things, that the soul of man obscurely grasps itself." Restated less poetically but more clearly, he writes in *Creative Intuition in Art and Poetry* that "the content of poetic intuition is both the reality of the things of the world and the subjectivity of the poet."[9] Maritain thus acknowledges the influence of the greater world on the poet's subjectivity.

Nevertheless, he focuses on the genesis of the artwork, frequently adopting the metaphor of music to describe poetic knowledge.[10] In *Creative*

Man and His Achievement (New York: Sheed and Ward, 1963), pp. 128–38. Ralph McInerny, "Maritain and Poetic Knowledge," *Renascence* 34: 4 (Summer 1982), pp. 203–14, addresses the relationship between artists and morality rather than poetic knowledge per se.

[7] Thomas Aquinas, *Summa Theologiae*, I, q. 1, a. 6, ad 3m.

[8] "Poetic Experience," p. 387.

[9] *Creative Intuition in Art and Poetry*, p. 90.

[10] Maritain's most extensive writings on music are, in order of interest, "Sur la musique d'Arthur Lourié," *Oeuvres de Jacques Maritain* (Fribourg, Switzerland: Éditions

Intuition in Art and Poetry, he says that music is the first step of artistic creation: "The very first effect, and sign, of poetic knowledge and poetic intuition, as soon as they exist in the soul—and even before the start of any operative exercise—is a kind of musical stir produced in the depths of the living springs in which they are born."[11] In *The Situation of Poetry*, music becomes the original condition and the very soul of art: "Art...always supposes a moment of contemplation, and the work of art a melody, that is to say, a sense animating a form."[12]

Maritain's ideas about music derive in large measure from the Russian composer and critic Arthur Lourié. Lourié admired Maritain and his wife, as seen in his various settings of texts by Raïssa Maritain and in his advocacy of Maritain's neo-Thomism. In turn, Maritain wrote an article on Lourié, calling his music "ontological"—a high honor indeed from a philosopher, meant to indicate how closely connected he found Lourié's music to his initial inspiration.[13] Lourié introduced Maritain's philosophy to Stravinsky. As an émigré in Paris, he served as Stravinsky's amanuensis, reading proofs and preparing piano reductions of his scores in the 1920s and 30s. His own music followed Stravinsky's lead into a neoclassical style of composition. In his Thomistic critique of Stravinsky's ballet *Apollo*, he correlated ethics and aesthetics, and he composed two well-received works for orchestra and chorus, a *Sonata Liturgica* in 1928 and a *Concerto Spirituale* in 1929, that are sometimes regarded as precursors to Stravinsky's *Symphony of Psalms* of 1930. His disapproval of Stravinsky's marriage to his second wife soured their relationship, but by this time Lourié had piqued Stravinsky's interest in Maritain.

Lourié's article "De la mélodie" (1930) is the principal source for Maritain's view of music.[14] For Lourié, melody is the locus of artistic

Universitaires, 1984), vol. 6, pp. 1060–66; "De Quelques Musiciens," *Oeuvres de Jacques Maritain,* vol. 14, pp. 1117–26; "Préface à *Sonata grafica:* Les dessins d'Arthur Lourié," *Oeuvres de Jacques Maritain,* vol. 13, pp. 1244–51, and "[Message]," *Oeuvres de Jacques Maritain,* vol. 6, pp. 1053–54. For an excellent study of Maritain's views on music, see Clare Joseph Martini, *Maritain and Music* (Ph.D. diss., Northwestern University, 1958).

[11] *Creative Intuition in Art and Poetry*, p. 202.

[12] Jacques and Raïssa Maritain, *The Situation of Poetry,* trans. Marshall Suther (New York: Philosophical Library, 1955), p. 50.

[13] "Sur la musique d'Arthur Lourié," p. 1062. In *Creative Intuition and Art and Poetry,* Maritain writes: "These lines, which deal with poetic intution in general, were written in relation to music, and to Arthur Lourié, who to my mind provides us with the greatest example, in contemporary music, of that depth in creative inspiration of which I spoke" (p. 105). In the footnote to this sentence, Maritain cites Frederick Goldbeck's attempt to legitimize Lourié by placing him in a "direct line" of descent from Monteverdi.

[14] Arthur Lourié, "De la mélodie," *La Vie Intellectuelle* (25 December 1936), pp. 491–99.

truth because it reveals the ineffable artistic subject. Unlike harmony and counterpoint, which he regards as "objective," melody for him is "subjective." He situates the meaning of a composition exclusively in melody, for only in the melody do "the depths of existence and of the subject communicate." Following Lourié, Maritain too emphasizes the pre-eminence of melody, as he wrote in his *Situation of Poetry*: "Melody is the very spirit of the music and the realisation of the intimate being of the musician."[15]

Maritain exerted a strong but understated influence on Stravinsky, catalyzing his religious conversion and coloring his aesthetic writings with neo-Thomist austerity. The earliest link between them is Maritain's attack on Stravinsky's music in the first edition of *Art and Scholasticism* (1920). In a chapter entitled "The Purity of Art," Maritain says that both Gregorian chant and Bach employ "no material element from things or the subject except what is absolutely necessary," whereas the "impure" music of Stravinsky and Wagner tend to "dull or 'debauch' the eye, the ear, or the mind."[16] Maritain revised his judgment of Stravinsky in a well-known footnote from the 1923 edition of *Art and Scholasticism*:

> I regret having thus spoken of Stravinsky. All I had heard was *Le Sacre du Printemps*, and I should have perceived then that Stravinsky was turning his back on everything we find distasteful in Wagner. Since then he has shown that genius conserves and increases its strength by renewing it in light. Exuberant with truth, his admirably disciplined work teaches the best lesson of any to-day of grandeur and creative energy, and best answers the strict classical "austerity" here in question. His purity, his authenticity, his glorious spiritual strength, are to the gigantism of *Parsifal* and the Tetrology as a miracle of Moses, to the enchantments of the Egyptians.[17]

Maritain's rescue of Stravinsky from Wagner's debauchery—with an orientalist metaphor that substitutes Stravinsky's Russia for Moses' Canaan—is not surprising in itself, for French musicians had long opposed

---

[15] *The Situation of Poetry*, p. 63. Maritain's use of the word "melody" is vague and poetic. Although Maritain insisted that poetic knowledge is manifested only in works of art, he never successfully demonstrated this in his writings on music, the very art he felt most directly touched the source of artistic creativity. His descriptions of music are never specific and are often naïve and fanciful, as when he wishfully describes Satie's *Socrate* as being written in Gregorian modes, or when he elevates Lourié to the spiritual line of Debussy and de Falla without providing justification. See "De Quelques Musiciens," p. 1124.

[16] Maritain, *Art and Scholasticism*, trans. J. F. Scanlan (London: Sheed and Ward, 1923), p. 60.

[17] Ibid., p. 60n1.

Wagnerian decadence.[18] But the reasons that Maritain gave for it unmask his ignorance of Stravinsky's music. What caused Maritain to reverse his condemnation of Stravinsky? Between 1920 and 1923, Stravinsky showed increasing signs of his so-called neoclassical style with works such as *Symphonies of Wind Instruments* (1920) and *Mavra* (1922). Since Maritain claimed that he did not hear Stravinsky's ballets *Petruschka* or *Les Noces* until after 1923, it is probable that he simply did not know much of Stravinsky's music when he wrote the original critique and the later footnote. In the early 1920s, however, critics like Boris de Schloezer garnered Stravinsky with the epithet "neoclassical"—an adjective surely appealing to Maritain's anti-art-for-art's-sake aesthetics.[19] So it is apparently Stravinsky's changing reputation, rather than his music, that accounts for Maritain's reversed opinion.

Maritain and Stravinsky first met after a concert on 10 June 1926, at the time that Stravinsky was writing his first work with a religious text, a Pater Noster for four-part chorus. That year, Cocteau published his *Lettre à Jacques Maritain* and Maritain his *Réponse à Jean Cocteau*; both volumes are dedicated to Stravinsky. By the end of April 1927, Stravinsky had returned to the Orthodox faith that he had abandoned in his youth. He later wrote that "Jacques Maritain may have exercised an influence on me at this time [1926]."[20] Though Stravinsky denied that Maritain played a role in his conversion, his assistant Robert Craft says that Maritain did exert some influence on his return to the Church.[21] In May 1927, Stravinsky's opera-oratorio *Oedipus Rex*, a collaboration with Cocteau, premiered in Paris. Following *Oedipus Rex*, however, Stravinsky's attitude toward Maritain became ambivalent. In 1928, he wrote to one of his patrons, Victoria Ocampo, that Maritain's entourage nauseated him. In another letter he describes Maritain as:

one of those people of superior intelligence who are lacking in humanity, and if Maritain himself does not deserve this judgment, certainly it applies to a great deal of his work.

---

[18] See Jean Cocteau, *Cock and Harlequin*, trans. Rollo H. Myers (London: Egoist Press, 1921). Saint-Saëns was a still earlier early critic of the excesses of Wagner's followers.

[19] See de Schloezer, "La musique," in *La Revue contemporains* (1 February 1923): pp. 245-48. It is ironic that the word neoclassicism in music came to refer (among other things) to music stripped of extramusical meaning, for in literature and painting it refers to the representational art that Maritain advocated.

[20] Igor Stravinsky and Robert Craft, *Expositions and Developments* (Garden City, New York: Faber and Faber, 1962), pp. 64-65.

[21] Robert Craft, *Stravinsky: Chronicle of a Friendship*, revised ed. (Nashville: Vanderbilt University Press, 1994), p. 15.

Maritain is still attached to the nihilism of his youth, and this can be sensed in all of his books, despite the great value of his work in Christian and Thomist thought.[22]

Stravinsky's famous Norton Lectures of 1941, delivered at Harvard University and later published as *Poétique musicale*, refer several times to Maritain and borrow his neo-Thomistic definition of a composer as a medieval artisan who orders and disciplines his craft.[23] The book's considerable debt to Maritain includes quotations from the very same passages from Baudelaire, Poussin, Bellay, and Montaigne that Maritain had used in *Art et Scholastique* two decades earlier.[24] He also jibes the patrons of art by describing the reluctance with which pompous Parisian society read "the great Saint Thomas Aquinas"—but still they read him, he says, because "*snobisme oblige*." By 1944, both men had emigrated to the United States. Their friendship, if not their mutual respect, ended after Stravinsky consulted with Maritain about a continuing spiritual crisis.

Oedipus Rex

Composed at the time of Maritain's greatest influence on Stravinsky, the Christian overtones of *Oedipus Rex* are so clear that Lourié compared the work to a Bach passion. Cocteau's libretto identifies Oedipus Rex with Jesus Rex: the chorus calls for Oedipus to "save" the city; Oedipus boasts of his ability to deal with the powers of darkness; it is rumored that God speaks to Oedipus and that he is born of a great god; and as an infant, his feet are pierced and he is found by a shepherd—in the Latin of the libretto, "pastor."

Stravinsky did not deny that *Oedipus Rex* was a sort of Christian allegory. "A Christianized *Oedipus*," he wrote, "would require the truth-finding process to resemble an *auto-da-fé*, and I had no interest in attempting that. I can testify, though, that the music was composed during my strictest and most earnest period of Christian Orthodoxy."[25] His stated reason for its not

---

[22] Letter dated 5 November 1936 to Victoria Ocampo, quoted in Vera Stravinsky and Robert Craft, *Stravinsky in Pictures and Documents* (New York: Simon and Schuster, 1978), p. 632.

[23] It is often observed that Stravinsky did not write his *Poetique musicale*, but that Alexis Roland-Manuel and Pierre Souvschinsky were his ghost-writers. However, Maritain's influence is discernable in Stravinsky's own notes for the lectures, as when he declares that "the phenomenon of music is one of speculation." See ibid., p. 511.

[24] Louis Andriessen and Elmer Schönberger, *The Apollonian Clockwork: On Stravinsky,* trans. Jeff Hamburg (Oxford: Clarendon Press, 1989), pp. 81–96.

[25] Igor Stravinsky and Robert Craft, *Dialogues and a Diary* (Garden City, New York: Doubleday and Co., 1963), p. 9.

being Christian, then, is that he did not wish to portray the overwhelming feeling of guilt that Oedipus would display upon learning that he had killed his father and married his mother. The explanation implicitly approves of a Christian interpretation and is plausible in light of Stravinsky's new aesthetic of neoclassical understatement. Stravinsky also connected his opera-oratorio with his conversion in his book *Dialogues and a Diary*. Immediately after attributing *Oedipus Rex* to his "most earnest period of Christian Orthodoxy," he describes his return to the Church, when, in answer to his prayers, his injured finger miraculously healed before playing a concert.[26]

The design of *Oedipus Rex* turns on Oedipus' discovery of his true identity and what he has done with his parents. An article by the English musicologist Wilfred Mellers helps to explain the emergence of Oedipus' identity by showing that the work uses certain keys and key relationships to symbolize the tragedy's ideas.[27] Truthful statements, for instance, are written in D major. Power relations take the idea of the "dominant" key literally: the stronger force is always portrayed in the dominant key relationship. There is no stronger force in the opera than D major, that of truth. Tiresias, the seer who alone knows the truth, sings his obscure condemnation of Oedipus, "Rex peremptor regis est" [The king is the king's murderer], in a stentorian D major. When Oedipus asks rhetorically, "Did Jocasta say crossroads?" he sings a D on the word "trivio," Latin for crossroads. There follows a short duet between Oedipus and a timpani as Oedipus admits to Jocasta, his mother and wife, that he killed an old man (his father) at a crossroads. The duet is in G minor, making his D on the word "trivio" the dominant—the dominating truth—of the murder that Oedipus describes.

Soon the messenger brings the news that Polybus is not Oedipus' real father, but that Polybus had merely adopted Oedipus as a foundling. Responding in the key of G major, the chorus sings "Falsus pater per me!" [He was not Oedipus' real father!]. It is well known that in this chorus, the words "falsus pater" are painted by a "false relation," a conflict between two tones with the same letter name, in this case F and F#. In G major, the F# is the proper note, the F-natural the false one. The F# also distinguishes D major, the key of truth, from D minor. These keys

<hr/>

[26] See Stravinsky and Robert Craft, *Dialogues* (Berkeley: University of California Press, 1982), p. 26. This book is a shortened version of *Dialogues and a Diary*.

[27] Wilfred Mellers, "Stravinsky's Oedipus as 20th-Century Hero," in *Stravinsky: A New Appraisal of His Work*, ed. Paul Henry Lang (New York: Norton, 1963).

become important when Oedipus pompously sings about how he will uncover his true lineage in "Ego exul exsulto" [I, an exile, exult]. Oedipus' long, high notes are F-naturals, making the aria in D minor, not major. The minor key underscores his continued denial of the truth behind his illicit relationships with his parents.

Finally, Oedipus owns up to his guilt and accepts the truth. The chorus' statement that the truth never should have come out is sung in D minor, followed by a low D minor chord in the strings that alternates with a high D major chord in the flutes. In his Octet of 1924, Stravinsky had said that he preferred the rigidity of wind instruments to stringed instruments, which he found "less cold and more vague." The lucidity of the flute chords leads to Oedipus' admission of the truth. When he sings "Lux facta est!" [All is now made clear], he intones the word "Lux" [light] on an F# to signal in D major his acceptance of the truth (Example 1).

Example 1. Stravinsky's "Lux facta est" at rehearsal 169 of *Oedipus Rex* (reduction).

The problem with the F# is that "Lux facta est" is not heard in D major at all. Oedipus' melody is best heard in B minor, the F# being the fifth scale degree, not the third scale degree in D major. The accompanying harmonies, however, strongly suggest D major. The clarinet even adds a famous trill leading to a G-flat, equivalent to an F#, that highlights this tonal ambiguity. The music seems to tell us that Oedipus sees the light (with the F#), but not fully (hence its placement in B minor). He soon blinds himself when he finds that his mother has killed herself from shame, and is then driven from the city by the riotous chorus.

Oedipus Rex's disturbingly ambiguous notion of truth exemplifies Maritain's convictions that an artist expresses his or her subjectivity in the work made, and that knowledge of the artist's intentions is essential to an understanding of the work. The ambiguity of truth may result from Stravinsky's own status as an exile and his probable identification with the character of Oedipus.[28] In a religious reading of the opera, Oedipus is best regarded not as Christ himself, but rather as a Christian, as Stravinsky had recently become. Moreover, both protagonist and composer are exiles questioning their identity. In an article written in 1921 on his opera *Mavra*, Stravinsky reveals that he was greatly concerned about the meaning of being a Russian exile in Western Europe (he had left Russia for professional opportunities in Paris, but did not return because of the Russian Revolution). To reflect this state, he chose to subdue the romantic "raw individuality" of his early ballets and to take pre-existing formal models as the material for his compositions. This was the advent of his neoclassical style, where style itself is part of the message of the work. He described his preoccupation with style in his *Autobiography*. "The need for restriction," he says, "for deliberately submitting to a style, has its source in the very depths of our nature."[29] The nature that Stravinsky expresses, however, is an adopted one, a musical language foreign to his native palette. The arias in *Oedipus Rex* display an intentionally wide range of sources, from Handel to Verdi. However Italianate early Russian opera was, such sources were not the bread and butter of the pupils of Rimsky-Korsakov. The Italianate music expresses the subjectivity of an exile returning to Christianity and searching for the essence of his identity. In a Christian interpretation of Sophocles, this subjectivity is common to both Oedipus and Stravinsky. His Orthodoxy was intimately bound to his identity as a Russian. He said that "Perhaps the strongest factor in my decision to re-enter the Russian Church, rather than covert to the Roman, was linguistic. The Slavonic language of the Russian liturgy has always been the language of prayer for me."[30] The use in a composition of a "sacred language" (Church Slavonic in his Pater Noster or Latin in *Oedipus Rex*) had occurred to him, he said, since the time of his deracination.[31]

Defining Stravinsky's subjectivity with reference to his biography is not, I think, a method that Maritain would have prescribed for art critics. He intended subjectivity to convey "the substantial totality of the human person," not "the inexhaustible flux of superficial feelings in which the

---

[28] Stephen Walsh has also suggested an autobiographical reading of the work in *Stravinsky: A Creative Spring* (New York: Alfred A. Knopf, 1999), p. 443. Walsh's book appeared after the delivery of the first draft of this paper.

[29] Stravinsky, *An Autobiography* (New York: W. W. Norton, 1962), p. 207, anonymous translation of *Chroniques de ma vie*, 2 vols. (Paris: Denoel and Steele, 1936).

[30] *Expositions and Developments*, p. 65.

[31] *Dialogues and a Diary*, pp. 3–4.

sentimental reader recognizes his own cheap longings."[32] And yet Maritain himself took recourse in biography writ large at the end of *Creative Intuition* when he describes Dante's successes as a poet. He considers the general trends of the man and his times as influences on Dante's subjectivity and on his poetry, writing of Dante's luck to be so gifted and to be living at a time propitious for a summation of Christian thought like the *Divine Comedy*.[33] Critical methods in the last forty years have properly corrected the extreme disassociation of the artist from his or her work, a belief promoted by Maritain's friend T. S. Eliot and other advocates of the New Criticism that was popular during Maritain's lifetime. Though the biographical portraits I use to describe the subjectivities of Stravinsky and Messiaen are writ slightly smaller than was Maritain's practice, they are essential to the poetic knowledge experienced by each man.

The untidiness of Stravinsky's ambiguous harmonies and ambivalent meanings has led some Stravinsky scholars to try to impose order on Stravinsky's deliberately unsettled scores. Stephen Walsh, for instance, the author of the only monograph on *Oedipus Rex*, admits that the tonality in Stravinsky's neoclassical works is ambiguous. Nonetheless, he denies the ambiguity in the crucial passage at "Lux facta est":

> Why invent an ambiguity to express a certainty as divinely inspired as Oedipus' 'Lux facta est?' The answer must surely be that there is not so much an ambiguity as an enrichment, an opening out of possibilities.... The entry of light into that benighted soul called for some fresh musical initiative, and Stravinsky, typically, found one that is rich but lucid, direct but resonant.[34]

Walsh too easily brushes aside the ambiguous tonality. The confusion of B minor and D major is intentionally ambiguous; it purposefully does not sound like an "entry of light," for there is darkness in the truth of Oedipus' identity.

Stravinsky is highly self-conscious personally and stylistically, a condition Maritain claims is necessary for becoming aware of poetic knowledge. However, Oedipus cannot assert the truth without either denying it or destroying himself. This is the reason not only for the F-naturals that confuse the F#s, for the G-flats that confuse the F#s, and for the tonal ambiguity, but also for the sounding of so many dominant chords in the minor, an effect that Stravinsky said would be important for the work's critics.[35] For

---

[32] *Creative Intuition in Art and Poetry*, p. 84.

[33] *Creative Intuition in Art and Poetry*, pp. 274-81.

[34] Stephen Walsh, *Stravinsky: Oedipus Rex* (Cambridge: Cambridge University Press, 1993), p. 61–63.

[35] *Dialogues*, p. 28.

Stravinsky in the 1920s there was no certain home, faith, music, truth, or poetic knowledge.

Dieu parmi nous

The situation was in all respects reversed for Messiaen in the 1930s. Unlike Stravinsky, Messiaen never met Maritain, though by his own account he did read one book (probably *Art et scholastique*) by him in 1927.[36] He said it was "a book of high philosophy that seemed very difficult to me," but admitted having benefited from it.[37] Maritain's influence is suggested in Messiaen's views on artistic imitation, his skeptical attitude toward science, his apparent interest in Emmanuel Mounier's personalist movement, and his rhetorical use of terms such as "poetic intuition."[38]

Among Messiaen's early works, *La Nativité du Seigneur* (1935) most strongly suggests Maritain's influence in its Thomistic theme of truth. Like *Oedipus Rex*, *La Nativité* opens a window onto Messiaen's epistemology. Comprised of nine movements for solo organ lasting twice as long as any composition he had yet written, *La Nativité* quickly entered the organist's repertoire and remained one of his favorite works. Though it bears no dedication, Messiaen later said it was written in homage to his teacher Paul Dukas.[39]

---

[36] See Brigitte Massin, *Olivier Messiaen: Une Poétique du merveilleux* (Aix-en-Provence: Editions Alinéa, 1989), p. 178. Of Maritain's twelve books published by 1927, nine might qualify as "high philosophy" to the eighteen-year-old Messiaen. Only two of these were published in 1927, *Primauté du Spirituel* and the third printing of *Art et Scholastique*. Olivier Messiaen's father, Pierre Messiaen, did know Maritain, whose books quote English Romantic poetry in the father's translations.

[37] Massin, *Une Poetique du Merveilleux*, p. 178. Messiaen's full account of Maritain reads: "Je ne l'ai jamais rencontré. Mon père le connaissait. Moi je n'ai jamais fait que lire un de ses livres à dix-huit ans, c'était ma première année d'orgue. J'ai été malade plusieurs semaines, j'en ai profité pour lire Maritain, un livre de haute philosophie qui m'a semblé très difficile." Note that Messiaen claimed that he had read Thomas Aquinas as early as 1923 or 1924, making Maritain's influence on his love of Thomas indirect at best (see Massin, *Une Poetique du merveilleux*, p. 31).

[38] Messiaen says he likes the term "poetic intuition" in Messiaen and Claude Samuel, *Music and Color*, trans. E. Thomas Glasow (Portland, Oregon: Amadeus Press, 1994), p. 15. Note that Maritain had written a letter to Stravinsky, dated 28 July 1935, in which he explains his idea of "creative intuition" (see *Stravinsky in Pictures and Documents*, p. 222). Messiaen's interest in Mounier, a Maritain protegé, is most evident in his concern for liberty during his Jeune France years of the late 1930s.

[39] Brigitte Massin, *Olivier Messiaen: Une poetique de merveilleux* (Aix-en-Provence: Alinéa, 1989), p. 172.

At its premiere, Messiaen marked the significance of *La Nativité* by distributing a leaflet stating his personal artistic credo. This strange document shows Messiaen's philosophical self-consciousness toward his art, a circumspection that heightens the role of his subjectivity in his music. The manifesto reads with broken syntax:

> L'émotion, la sincérité de l'oeuvre musicale.
> Qui seront au service des dogmes de la théologie catholique.
> Qui s'exprimeront par des moyens mélodiques et harmoniques....
> Le sujet théologique? le meilleur puisqu'il contient tous les sujets.
> Et l'abondance des moyens techniques permet au coeur de s'épancher librement.

> [The emotion, the sincerity of the musical work.
> Which shall be at the service of the dogmas of Catholic theology.
> Which shall be expressed by melodic and harmonic means....
> The theological subject? The best, for it comprises all subjects.
> And the abundance of technical means allows the heart to pour out freely.][40]

The published score includes a lengthy preface that expands on the ideas in this manifesto and details his innovations in rhythm and harmony.

La Nativité's last and longest movement, "Dieu parmi nous" [God among us], explicitly links the idea of Christ with truth. The title is a pun on the word "Emanuel," which means "God with us," a phrase subtly distinct from "God among us," though the latter phrase (with the word "parmi") does refer to Christ in Luke 7:16 and John 1:14. Messiaen forged musical symbols depicting "the Incarnation" and "truth" by drawing from pieces by his teachers, the composer Paul Dukas and the organist-composer Marcel Dupré. Dupré's organ teacher, Charles-Marie Widor, had helped to foster this sort of musical symbolism in France by instigating his student Albert Schweitzer to write a book describing how the musical syntax in J. S. Bach's chorale preludes for organ imitates the hymn texts.[41] The best example, Schweitzer said, was in the chorale prelude *Durch Adams Fall*, BWV 637, where the fall of Adam is depicted with a sequence of descending sevenths. Schweitzer's book was widely read and

---

[40] Translation mine. The leaflet is preserved under the call number "Rés. Vmd. ms. 0094" at the Bibliothèque Nationale, Paris, and is reproduced in Nigel Simeone, *A Bibliographic Catalogue of Messiaen's Works* (Tutzing : H. Schneider, 1998), p. 46. An alternative English translation is printed in Madeleine Hsu, *Olivier Messiaen, the Musical Mediator: A Study of the Influence of Liszt, Debussy, and Bartók* (Madison and Teaneck, New Jersey: Fairleigh Dickinson University Press, 1996), Appendix D, p. 158.

[41] See Albert Schweitzer, *J. S. Bach*, trans. Ernest Newman, 2 vols. (New York: Dover Publications, 1966), vol 2., p. 3.

established a precedent for Messiaen's imitation of abstract ideas in the organ repertoire.

The influence of Schweitzer's interpretation of *Durch Adams Fall* is obvious in Messiaen's own description of "Dieu parmi nous," in which he writes that the descent in fourths of the theme of truth "is the glorious and ineffable fall of the second person of the Holy Trinity into a human na-ture—it is the Incarnation."[42] It descends, he says, "in imitation of Truth coming down from heaven to earth." Messiaen derived this musical sym-bol from Paul Dukas's opera *Ariane et Barbe-Bleue*, where it functions as a leitmotif for the heroine, Ariane, who in turn symbolizes truth. Ariane, the last of Bluebeard's wives, discovers the previous wives (who were thought dead) in the basement of Bluebeard's castle. Ariane urges them to leave the castle and to free themselves of their nefarious husband, but the wives are unwilling to go. In his 1936 essay on the opera, Messiaen relates this situation to a statement from the Gospel of John: "The Light [Ariane] shines in the darkness, and darkness has not understood it."[43] Messiaen calls the grand trombone entrance at the end of Act II the simplest version of the Truth theme, though the theme recurs in every act. He quotes the theme at the beginning of "Dieu parmi nous" (Examples 2a and 2b).

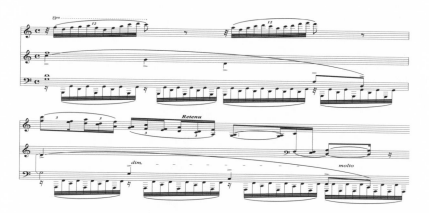

Example 2a. Dukas's "Truth theme" beginning in the middle staff, four measures after "Je vais tomber dans vos ténèbres!" at the end of Act II of *Ariane et Barbe-Bleue*.

[42] Messiaen, *Messiaen on Messiaen: The Composer Writes About His Works,* trans. Irene Feddern (Bloomington, Indiana: Frangipani Press, 1986), p. 13.

[43] Olivier Messiaen, "Ariane et Barbe-Bleue de Paul Dukas," *Revue musicale* 166 (1936), pp. 79–86. For more about Dukas' connection of truth and light, see Anya Suschitzsky, "*Ariane et Barbe-Bleue*: Dukas, the Light and the Well," *Cambridge Opera Journal* 9: 2 (1997), pp. 133–61.

Example 2b. Messiaen's quotation of Dukas's "Truth theme" in the pedal at the beginning of "Dieu parmi nous," the last movement of *La Nativité du Seigneur*.

This theme of descending fourths recurs at the end of "Dieu parmi nous" beneath the perpetuum mobile filigree of a toccata derived from Marcel Dupré's popular Christmas composition *Variations sur un noël*. Messiaen performed Dupré's work publicly in the Christmas season of 1935 and 1936, when he was composing his own Christmas work, *La Nativité du Seigneur*.[44] The similarity of these Christmas toccatas is unmistakeable. In Dupré's work, the left and right hands quickly alternate pairs of repeated notes while the pedal plays a familiar carol. Messiaen imitates this texture but replaces the carol with Dukas's Truth theme (Examples 3a and 3b).

Example 3a. Dupré's toccata texture set over a traditional noël, concluding his *Variations sur un noël*.

[44] *Le Guide du Concert* 22, no. 12–14 (20 and 27 December 1935, 3 January 1936).

Example 3b. Messiaen's toccata texture set over Dukas's "Truth theme," concluding his "Dieu parmi nous."

Both pieces conclude with the fireworks of a quickly repeating figure that is put into diminution, followed by a brief descending scale for a final cadence.

By setting his teachers' works in counterpoint, Messiaen purposefully ascribes truth to the Catholic notion of the Incarnation. Messiaen was preoccupied with the idea of truth. The most important aspect of his work, he said, was "the illumination of the theological truths of the Catholic faith,"[45] and one of his favorite aphorisms was that "God dazzles us by excess of truth; music carries us to God for lack of truth." This is a paraphrase of a passage from the *Summa Theologiae*: "Just as human reason fails to grasp the import of poetical utterance on account of its deficiency in truth, neither can it grasp divine things perfectly on account of their superabundance of truth; and therefore in both cases there is need of representation by sensible figures."[46] Messiaen's motto about truth recalls Maritain's view of poetic knowledge:

> At the culmination of our knowledge we know God as unknown, St. Thomas said, after the pseudo-Dionysius, with regard to mystical contemplation. We must say of the poet: at the source of his creative movement he knows things "as unknown" together with his own soul.[47]

Messiaen's belief that he could not "grasp divine things" did not discourage him from seeking truth, though Stravinsky's similar uncertainty is reflected in *Oedipus Rex*'s equivocation toward truth.

Like Stravinsky, Messiaen is stylistically self-conscious, borrowing from Dukas and Dupré, using the cyclical forms that César Franck had popularized in France, and subscribing to the tradition of writing toccatas for the organ. His manifestos, prefaces, and quotations from scripture in his publications all evince his awareness of his own work. Unlike Stravinsky, however, Messiaen's self-consciousness was not due to a feeling of loss or lack of identity, but to a surfeit of faith in the teachings of the Catholic Church. "I didn't have a sudden conversion, as did Blaise Pascal or Paul Claudel," he said. "For me, there was nothing of the kind. I've always been a believer, pure and simple."[48] He did not question or ironize the representations of truth and the Incarnation by Dukas and Dupré, but accepted them and built upon them.

---

[45] Olivier Messiaen, *Music and Color: Conversations with Claude Samuel*, trans. E. Thomas Glasow (Portland, Oregon: Amadeus Press, 1994), p. 20.

[46]Messiaen's paraphrase may be found throughout his many interviews. It is most famously quoted in the last scene of his opera *Saint François d'Assise*. The source of Messiaen's paraphrase has been uncovered by Camille Crunelle Hill, "Saint Thomas Aquinas and the Theme of Truth" in Siglind Bruhn, ed., *Messiaen's Language of Mystical Love* (New York: Garland, 1998): p. 145. Thomas' reference to "sensible figures" (I-II, q. 101, a. 2, ad 2) is, as the following quotation from Maritain indicates, taken from the Pseudo-Dionysius' *On Divine Names*.

[47] "Poetic Experience."

[48] *Music and Color*, p. 16.

Though he was self-conscious, a sincerity bordering on naïveté pervades Messiaen's writings. He called for a sincerity of expression in the leaflet and the preface for *La Nativité*, as well as in his manifesto for *La Jeune France*, a composers' collective he founded the following year. In Messiaen's music, truth is conveyed by deep conviction and powerful emotional expression.[49] Believing that he could not fully know the truth of a paradoxically transcendent yet immanent God, he composed in a highly personal idiom that shows certainty of knowledge through conviction of faith. For Messiaen, true knowledge came from faith and poetic knowledge derived from communion with God.

Messiaen's self-consciousness may also be traced to the period of his life when he wrote *La Nativité*. In the mid-1930s, he was beginning to build a reputation in Parisian musical circles. The year he wrote *La Nativité*, he crossed into a public life by co-founding the group *La Spirale* (which later became *La Jeune France*) and he defined himself against the prevailing neoclassical aesthetic, whose works he found anachronistic, insincere, and sometimes distastefully bawdy. To live in Paris in the politically polarized 1930s was to choose between fascist and communist ideology, urban and rural life, sacred and secular culture. Throughout the decade, Messiaen re-evaluated much of what he had been taught, and self-consciously fashioned himself as a successor both to the French organ tradition and to the tradition of exoticism prevalent in French music since Saint-Saëns and Debussy. He defined himself with the conviction of a highly gifted and independent young man in a divided society. The formation of his identity, of his subjectivity, was thus different in every way from Stravinsky's uncertainty of faith, home, music, and knowledge.

The different conceptions of knowing truth in Stravinsky and Messiaen are also evident in the texts that accompany their compositions. Stravinsky strategically set a Greek tragedy for its widespread familiarity, since he knew that he would not have been able to set the text in Latin if the story were not well known. Messiaen, however, prefaced "Dieu parmi nous" with a quotation from Ecclesiasticus (aka the Book of Sirach), a particularly Catholic text excluded from the Protestant and Hebrew Bibles. His ideal audience was thus more personal than Stravinsky's.

Messiaen called the story of Dukas's *Ariane et Barbe-bleu* "the tragedy of Truth misunderstood."[50] The misunderstanding results from

---

[49] For more on conviction in art, see Lionel Trilling, *Sincerity and Authenticity* (Cambridge, Mass.: Harvard University Press, 1972).

[50] Messiaen, "Ariane et Barbe-Bleue de Paul Dukas," *Revue musicale* 166 (1936), pp. 79–86.

Bluebeard's wives' lack of faith in finding a better world than the basement of Bluebeard's castle. Messiaen seems to have rectified Dukas's tragedy by associating Dukas's truth with the truth he found in Christ. The tragedy of Stravinsky's *Oedipus Rex* is that Oedipus will not accept the truth when he learns of Laius' murder at the crossroads. Messiaen conveys certainty, while Stravinsky expresses doubt. To repeat Maritain's distinction, Stravinsky grasped his subjectivity—and his music—as an object to be defined and redefined at will. The critic Boris de Schloezer disparaged him as a Pelagian for this reason.[51] Like Stravinsky, Messiaen drew upon his subjectivity as a source for his works. However, he did not manipulate it, but rather immersed himself within it. He surrounded himself with works that confirmed his identity as a French Catholic organist and so composed works that appear sincere, free of irony, and composed with conviction.

Maritain's writings claim that subjectivity is central to the expression of poetic knowledge in art, an idea confirmed in Stravinsky and Messiaen, where knowledge of their own identities is directly reflected in their ideas about truth and thus knowledge. Stravinsky's subjectivity was confused and his expression of truth ambiguous, whereas Messiaen's subjectivity was firmly planted and his notions of truth clear. Though Stravinsky's and Messiaen's notions of truth are different, subjectivity, as influenced by the world, determines their understanding of the nature of truth and so creates their poetic knowledge. The clear reflection of subjectivity in their work affirms Maritain's claim that subjectivity is a source of poetic knowledge, but Stravinsky's case contradicts and expands Maritain's claim by showing that subjectivity can also serve as the object of poetic knowledge.

---

[51] Boris de Schloezer's comment is related in Robert Craft, ed., *Stravinsky: Selected Correspondence*, 3 vols. (London: Faber and Faber, 1984), 2: 503.

The Recovery of the Symbolic

Steven J. Schloeder

My major interest and area of research is the question of the Catholic church building, in both its historical and its modern Vatican II contexts. Therefore, my intention in this essay will be to propose a return to understanding the symbolic aspects of the human person, especially in regard to how such an understanding might aid us to better design church building, create works of sacred art, and consider the liturgy in which the person participates. This recovery is necessary, I believe, to counteract the prevalent reductionistic views of the person—rooted in Enlightenment rationalism, and common in the academy—which the Church has let influence the discussion of what constitutes an appropriate approach to the questions of liturgy, sacred arts, and church architecture.

In an entirely other discipline, the great political philosopher Leo Strauss (1899-1973) proposed a rather simple remedy to the problem of modern rationalism in the social sciences. He wrote:

> The social scientist is a student of human societies, of societies of humans. If he wishes to be loyal to his task, he must never forget that he is dealing with human things, with human beings. He must reflect on the human as a human. And he must pay due attention to the fact that he himself is a human being and that social science is always a kind of self-knowledge.[1]

In this age since the Second Vatican Council, an era of increasingly banal and alienating Catholic church architecture, Strauss's exhortation can well be applied to the liturgical establishment in the West—the Episcopal conferences, diocesan liturgical commissions, professional liturgists and "liturgical designers," parish "art and environment" committee members, pastors, and church architects—all who in varying degrees of indiscretion, complicity, and culpability have contributed to the current architectural malaise.[2]

---

[1] Leo Strauss, "Social Science and Humanism" in *The Rebirth of Classical Political Rationalism* (Chicago: The University of Chicago Press, 1989), p. 6.

[2] One is tempted to recall Eric Gill's words about the bad repository art at the beginning of this century: "It is remarkable that things should get so bad without anybody being to

Across the twentieth century we have steadily moved away from the great tradition of church buildings that speak to the whole person, that respect the whole person, and that engage the whole person. In its stead we have church buildings that tend toward the spartan, the aniconic, and the functionalistic: more intended for a reductive view of the human person common to the social thought of the Enlightenment than to the rich and wonderfully complex understanding of classical Western anthropology. In short, to paraphrase Strauss, we have failed to remember that we are building *for* human beings, and that we should think about church design *as* human beings.

In order to recapture a robust, potent, and engaging tradition of sacred art and architecture, I will argue that it is first necessary to regain an understanding of the human being as symbol-knowing and symbol-using—a sort of *homo symbolicus*—which is integral to the fabric of the classical Catholic view of the human being, the material world, the liturgical experience, and the sacred arts tradition. Only in returning to our classical anthropological insights of the human person, a view that allows for and encourages the person to interact with the church building, with sacred art, and in the liturgy with one's whole being—body and soul, will and intellect, memory and imagination, emotions, appetites, passions, and senses—can we hope for true renewal.

The Loss of Architectural Symbolism

I will venture that the history of twentieth century church architecture will be seen in history as a peculiar time of loss of symbol structure, transcendent meaning, and appeal to beauty. How did this happen?

Since the end of the First Great War, practically all the major Western architects—the Futurists in Italy, the de Stijl in Holland, the Bauhaus in Germany, Le Corbusier in France, and Frank Lloyd Wright in America—were advocating functionalism and machine-inspired efficiency as the basis of architectural design. They saw ornament and the eclectic historical stylism of the 19th century as decadently bourgeois—hardly appropriate for the proletariat worker of the new society. Adolf Loos in Vienna was writing tracts comparing architectural ornament to tattoos on criminals and tribal natives. Marinetti in Italy saw the future of art, architecture, and civilization embodied in the automobile racing through the night toward a new dawn. Le

blame. For nobody is to blame. It is nobody's fault. No one need go to confession and accuse himself of sin." From Eric Gill, "Repository Art" in *Beauty Looks After Herself* (London: Sheed and Ward, 1933), p. 30.

Corbusier posited the future of architecture, indeed the truth of architecture, to be the efficiency of the steamship, the airplane, and the grain silo. The Church was not slow to be swept up in this movement. In the 1920s Auguste Perret explored the potential of reinforced concrete and modular building systems in the design of churches in France, while Rudolf Schwarz and Dominikus Böhm in Germany were obviously influenced by the Bauhaus concerns for efficiency, formal abstraction, and freedom from ornament. These architectural expressions were adopted by the pre-WW II Liturgical Movement in Germany through Rudolf Schwarz's close association with Romano Guardini. Their vision came to America by way of the writings of the H. A. Reinhold, and through the architectural projects of Barry Byrne, both of which were widely disseminated in religious and secular arts and architectural journals in the 30s and 40s.[3]

The 1950s saw the post war boom. The mass production techniques perfected in the wartime industrial complex were easily transformed to produce consumer items for the growing and affluent American population. Programmatic planning, developed by corporate America, came to bear on the architectural problem, and gave rise to campus planning for churches as it had developed for corporations, academic institutions, and government projects. The most important incursion of the corporate functional efficiency mentality into the world of sacred architecture came in 1960 with the publication of Peter Hammond's highly influential book *Liturgy and Architecture*, in which he argued for the same approach to designing churches as any other contemporary building. He wrote: "that good churches—no less than good schools or good hospitals—can be designed only through a radically functional approach."[4] Hammond's view was concisely summarized in his oft-quoted statement, "The task of the modern architect is not to design a building that *looks like a church*. It is to create a building that *works* as a place for liturgy. The first and essential requirement is radical functional analysis."[5] Hammond was clear that the traditional styles of architecture "have no message for the contemporary world."[6] For Hammond, rather, as long as the process of radical functional planning was done properly, the church building's "symbolic aspect can be left to take care of itself."[7] Thus, with a few strokes of the pen, the Liturgical Movement discarded as meaningless a 2000-year-old tradition of sacred architectural language.

[3] Michael DeSanctis, *Some Artistic Aspects of Catholic Liturgical Reform* (Ph.D. Diss., Ohio University, 1985), p. 20n.

[4] Peter Hammond, *Liturgy and Architecture* (London: Barrie and Rockliff, 1960), p. 7.

[5] Ibid., p. 9.

[6] Ibid., p. 3.

[7] Ibid., p. 7.

So it was that church buildings began to take on an increasingly schematic feeling. The efficiency of the machine replaced the wondrously organic
complexity of the human body—or the sacramental representation of the
Heavenly Jerusalem—as the basis for design. Driven by economic concerns,
multi-purposefulness and *multi-functionality* were the values of the day.
Classical architectural decoration was widely discarded along with the human figural elements in the arts. Amidst this tumult, much of the distinctly
human element of sacred architecture was lost.

The Pressing Need for Catholic Anthropology

Over twenty years ago, the Bishops Committee on the Liturgy (BCL)
issued a provisional document titled *Environment and Arts in Catholic Worship* (EACW), in which were set out guidelines for the contemporary ordering
and reordering of Catholic churches. Issued at perhaps the nadir of liturgical
architecture—at a time when the architectural academy was critically evalu-
ating the previous 60 years of increasing alienating architectural modernism
and was proposing various returns to a classical or at least "postmodern"
understanding of architectural tradition and multivalent symbolical meaning—EACW, despite its occasional rather obtuse references to symbol, beauty,
and mystery,[8] did little to further that academic movement among church
architects. Rather it enshrined a functionalist, stripped-down, liturgical aesthetic in intentionally nondescript,[9] aniconic,[10] and transient[11] barn-like
buildings.

In effect, the BCL (but more so the hordes of iconoclastic liturgists
who ransacked perfectly good and even beautiful traditional churches to
implement EACW) rushed headlong into 1930 by apotheosizing the
liturgical experiments of Romano Guardini and Rudolf Schwarz at Burg
Rothenfels. The castle at Rothenfels was the headquarters of the
"Quickborn" Catholic Youth Movement, which under Guardini's
directorship became a center for vibrant liturgical renewal, especially among
the laity. Liturgy was held at Burg Rothenfels in two places: the first was a
rather typical small chapel with an altar against the side wall (typical of
counter-Reformation churches), albeit rendered in a stripped down, Bauhaus

---

[8] Bishops' Committee on the Liturgy, *Environment and Art in Catholic Worship*,
(Washington D.C.: United States Catholic Conference, 1978), art. 12, 14, 34, and 67
[9] Ibid., art. 42 states: "The building or cover enclosing the liturgical space is a shelter or
'skin' for a liturgical action. It does not have to 'look like' anything else, past or present."
[10] Ibid., art. 98-99.
[11] Ibid., art. 100.

inspired, functionalist aesthetic. The larger liturgies were celebrated in a bigger multifunctional meeting room, called the "Knight's Hall." This was also a spartan, flat ceilinged, non-differentiated, assembly room. For Mass, sleek black cuboid stools were gathered around three sides of a portable table for celebrating *versus populum* in an atmosphere of convivial hospitality. The influence of the machine-inspired Bauhaus aesthetic then in vogue throughout Germany is obvious in three ways:

1. The flexible arrangement of the multifunctional room capable of being modifies to suit changing programmatic needs
2. The transient and provisional nature of the portable altar and the other liturgical furnishings, and
3. The clean, crisp, image-free quality of the space.

Now, it would be unfair to accuse Guardini of liturgical minimalism, or of promoting an egalitarian, demotic approach to liturgy. This was hardly his agenda, as his books, *Sacred Signs* and *Spirit of the Liturgy*, testify. Rather, he seemed interested in helping the idealistic Catholic youth, who had left behind the bourgeois decadence of the Weimar Republic, find meaning for their lives in the liturgy through engaging in a sort of chivalric quest: Guardini's project for the youth had far more to do with rebuilding a Christian civilization in the sprit of the German Romantic movement and the heroic ideals of the Round Table and the Grail legend—one thinks of Wagner's *Parsifal*—than with the reductivistic philosophy and socialism of the Bauhaus. These good intentions notwithstanding, the combination of Schwarz's sleek functionalism and Guardini's centralized liturgy has had widespread and enduring impact. At a *festschrift* for Guardini, no less a personage than Karl Rahner stated plainly, "It is a widely known fact that the Rothenfels experiment was the immediate model for the liturgical reforms of Vatican II."[12]

With this background in mind, it can be argued that that EACW's consideration of Catholic architecture owes at least as much to the *zeitgeist* of the Bauhaus (with its strong and deliberate socialistic anthropology and sociology undergirding it) as to a traditional Catholic perspective. EACW evinces that the principles of radical functional analysis have continued to inform the Church's approach to liturgical architecture even into the late 1970s.[13] And yet EACW—despite its unevenness, its time-bound agenda and artistic examples,

---

[12] Regina Kuehn, "Romano Guardini" in *Leaders of the Liturgical Movement*, ed. Robert Tuzik, (Chicago: Liturgy Training Publications, 1990), pp. 47-48.
[13] *Environment and Art in Catholic Worship*, art. 42.

and its vague and obtuse language—was not entirely devoid of merit. One of its almost completely overlooked clarion calls was to develop an appropriate anthropological basis for liturgy and church architecture:

> Like the covenant itself, the liturgical celebrations of the faith community (Church) involve the whole person. They are not purely religious or merely rational and intellectual exercises, but also human experiences calling on all human faculties: body, mind, senses, imagination, emotions, memory. Attention to these is one of the urgent needs of contemporary liturgical renewal.[14]

To my knowledge, in the past twenty years this "urgent need" has yet to be addressed in respect to the liturgical innovations and architectural arrangements.[15] Rather, the predominant model of the human person implicit in most recent Catholic architecture is that of the Enlightenment man: rationalistic, scientific, socially atomic, and rejecting of deep symbol structure. This tendency can be seen in the abstractive art of most contemporary crucifixes and stations of the Cross that bear no realistic idea of the human body (disregarding the difference between knowing "mental image" and knowing "concept"); and in the "universal liturgical spaces" (i.e., multifunctional assembly spaces) that disregard our capacity and desire for knowing things as discrete knowables (i.e., "church," "meeting room," "theater" become merged into one vague, functionally determined, "room" or "centrum"[16]). The tendency toward reductionism also gives us a certain univalency of emotional experiences in most recent church buildings, where we are given only well-lighted open assembly spaces for public gathering, with no more dark, intimate corners to find solace before a devotional shrine, or quiet, emotionally-laden chapels for times of grief, desolation, contrition, or contemplative silence.

The problems of Enlightenment consciousness, with its increased alienation of the individual in society, have certainly affected Catholic life and art, both from without and from within. Their deleterious effects on parish life have not gone unnoticed, even among the progressive members of the liturgical renewal. In a recent article, Rembert Weakland, OSB, Archbishop of Milwaukee, an acknowledged "progressive" in matters liturgical, questioned the work of the Reformists who have brought about the horizontalization and immanentization of the liturgy through the introduction of what he calls

---

[14] Ibid., art. 5.

[15] Indeed, two of the few texts to even look at the relationship between the liturgy and the human person are Dietrich von Hildebrand's 1943 classic *Liturgy and Personality* and Jacques and Raissa Maritain's *Liturgy and Contemplation*.

[16] To use Edward Sövik's phrase. See his *Architecture for Worship* (Minneapolis: Augsburg, 1973).

"the homespun creeds that have no regard for the tradition, eucharistic prayers that leave little room for God, the reading of questionable material in the place of Scripture and the like." He likewise questioned whether these tendencies have not contributed to the loss of belief in and respect for the Blessed Sacrament.[17] Similarly, a few years ago the theme of one of the national liturgical conferences called for a return to "mystery,"[18] and likewise, one now sees Jungian appeals to archetypal symbology in current liturgical journals.[19] More traditionally minded groups are calling for a restoration of classicism in church architecture,[20] and one also sees the obvious rise in popularity of Tridentine indult masses and other forms of traditional piety such as icons and Gregorian chant.

The Thomistic Model of Knowing

Across the centuries the Church has developed a working paradigm for understanding the human person: our composition, operation, purpose, and end. What I intend here is the view of person which St. Thomas and traditional Catholic anthropology uphold, and which Pope John Paul II's thought has further developed—that of a spiritual being of body and soul, with faculties of intellection and volition—a being in relationship. This paradigm has been foundational for the Church's moral theology, social teaching, spiritual counsel, and pastoral guidance. And yet, regardless of whether the discussion is among progressives or traditionalists, conspicuously absent from most recent discussions of Catholic liturgy, art and architecture is the matter of the human person. Few thinkers in matters liturgical seem to have grappled with the question of the human person *qua* person, the "urgent need" mentioned in EACW, in these discussions.

Such a broad topic needs containment (since its implications extend to *every* human activity imaginable), and so I wish to constrict this current discussion to the question of how man knows reality, and particularly how he participates in the experience of symbol. Thus, rather than dealing with the manifold problems of various fragmentary modern anthropologies (e.g.,

[17] Archbishop Rembert G. Weakland, "Liturgy and the Common Ground" in *America* (20 November 1999). Quoted from http://www.americapress.org/articles/weaklandliturgy.htm.

[18] Form/ Reform 1995, San Diego, California. Sponsored by Georgetown Center for Liturgy.

[19] E.g., John Buscemi who argues for chthonic holy water stoups imbedded in the floor, vaginal "birth canal" crucifixes, and other bizarre subversions of traditional iconography, in John Buscemi *Places for Devotion* (Chicago: Liturgy Training Publications). Cited in Irene Groot, "Places for Iconoclasm," *Adoremus Bulletin*, 3:3 (May 1997), p. 8.

[20] E.g., Professor Duncan Stroik at the School of Architecture, University of Notre Dame.

psycho-analytical, behaviorist, determinist, evolutionary, etc.), I will content myself to advance a classical Catholic understanding, one which is rooted in Aristotle, developed by St. Thomas, and implicitly continued in the contemporary teachings via the Universal Catechism. Time and space do not allow for a detailed explication, so it must suffice to concentrate on the power of the phantasm in the imagination as the locus of symbolic knowing which is pertinent to the question at hand. In brief, I wish to draw our attention to certain important considerations:

1) We first apprehend things through sense powers (sight, hearing, smell, etc.) that are seated in the sense organs (eyes, ears, nose, etc.).[21]

2) These external sensory data, or *sensibles*, are presented to the internal senses. The *common sense* apprehends the preliminary unity among the sensibles.

3) The next stage, presupposing the operations of the common sense and the cogitative sense, is the appearance of the phantasm in the *imaginarium*.[22] The phantasm, which is a sort of "mental picture," preserves and presents before the mind the material conditions of the thing perceived. The phantasm is deposited in the imaginarium for retention and recollection.

4) The imaginarium is a complex faculty for St. Thomas. It has the powers of:

   a) Storage: The imaginarium stores the phantasm with its record of sense data that are the material conditions of the thing perceived.

   b) Recall: The imaginarium has the power of phantasmal memory. The phantasms remembered in the imaginarium are conjoined to the concept in the intellect as integral to the symbol-understanding process.

   c) Synthesis: It is in the imaginarium, working in conjunction with the practical intellect, that stored images are manipulated and new ones created as part of our participation in the creative process.

   d) Emotion: The emotions are properly triggered through the imaginarium when a particularly meaningful phantasm

---

[21] Thomas Aquinas, *Summa Theologiae,* I , q. 78, a. 3; and I, q. 78, a. 4.

[22] I use the term *imaginarium* to express that this faculty is a sort of psychic locus, a "place" in the soul, wherein these operations occur, as distinct from the common usage *imagination* understood as the *ability* to conceive ideas or form images in the mind.

(either experienced or recalled) is conjoined with a clear and important concept. There seems to be a sort of potency, or a polar charge, between concept and phantasm, which activates emotional responsiveness when the two are conjoined in the imaginarium.

I will not go further into the operations of the intellect here. Suffice it to remind ourselves that:

6) When the agent intellect has stripped the material conditions from the phantasm, the resulting intelligible species actualizes the passive intellect, thus producing a concept. [23]

7) However, the end of knowing is not merely a concept, but *being* itself.[24] All the concepts are "mental words" by which we know being. It is these concepts that our mind apprehends, judges, understands, and retains in our consideration of *being*.[25]

8) Furthermore, we can also be reminded that vis-à-vis the material world there is no knowing of concepts without recourse to phantasm.[26] That is to say, there is no "imageless thought."

9) Thus it is necessary for human knowing to access *images*—either previously retained mental images or newly experienced physical images that we then convert to new mental images—for us to know.

This then is the anthropological basis of symbolic knowing: the image perceived recharges our imagination with a fresh or refreshed phantasm. Given that symbols per se speak to a whole constellation of ideas, the various concepts associated with the symbol—or in the case of liturgical art and architecture a whole *deep symbol structure*—are conjoined to produce a engagement of the person in the senses, the intellect, the memory, the imagination, and the emotions. With this epistemology in mind, I will simply posit that abstraction in sacred art frustrates this experience.

---

[23] The need for both agent (active) intellection and potential (passive) intellect is based on the aforementioned rule of powers corresponding to operation. Whereas the agent intellect (AI) causes understanding, the potential intellect (PI) formally understands; whereas AI is an active potency, *i.e.*, always ready to act, PI is a passive potency, *i.e.*, needs to be complemented before being fully ready to act. See Henry Koren, *An Introduction to the Philosophy of Animate Nature* (St. Louis: B. Herder, 1955), pp. 179-80.

[24] *Summa Theologiae* I, q. 84, a. 8: "our intellect's proper and proportionate object is the nature of a sensible thing."

[25] *An Introduction to the Philosophy of Animate Nature*, p. 182-83.

[26] *Summa Theologiae* I, q. 84, a. 7: "it is impossible for our intellect to understand anything actually, except by turning to the phantasms."

The Problem of Abstract Art

The abstract strains of modern art, which have so greatly influenced the production of sacred art in the twentieth century, fail to understand this operation, much to the loss of the art. Speaking only to the question of the necessary qualities of sacred art, and leaving aside the question of the value of abstract art in general, it seems that the very attempt to convey artistically a pure concept already abstracted from the material conditions of a previous phantasm can only short-circuit the fully human participation in the work of art.[27] From a stripped down phantasm, we might well be able to grasp the concept of the piece of work, say of a crucifix, but the lack of material conditions will possibly result in a dearth of recollected images to further engage our memory. Furthermore, since we know concepts by recourse to phantasms, the substitution of an already stripped down phantasm may only allow for a virtually "one-to-one correspondence" between the mental word and the mental image. The relatively close proportion between the mental word and the mental image may thus prevent the concept from activating the power of the imagination to engage the emotions in a fully human act of emotional response.[28]

So within the idea that a concept can be portrayed is the two-fold problem that (1) a concept, or "mental word," requires an associated phantasm, or "mental image," for it to be actually knowable; and (2) given the need for some sort of polar charge between concept and phantasm, the relative univalency in abstract art fails to charge the imagination to produce a meaningful emotional response. Even given the best of intentions on the part of the artist: say that the artist wants to provide us with a reductionistic image so as to allow our imagination to fill in the lacunae from its storehouse of image memories: the realities of faulty memory and wandering imagination tend to militate against this intention. In short, the human person is not made to be moved emotionally by abstract art, and the lack of material conditions related to history or events fails to engage our memory or imagination. Thus,

---

[27] Jacques Maritain, *Art and Scholasticism* (London: Sheed and Ward, 1930), pp. 144-48. See also my discussion on this in Steven Schloeder, *Architecture in Communion* (San Francisco: Ignatius Press, 1998), pp. 39-41.

[28] As was pointed out to me by a fine German philosopher, Anselm Ramelow, it seems that the modern artists may be fooling themselves in fancying that they are portraying concepts, when in fact they are portraying phantasms. Just as the concept must resort again to the phantasm, so the phantasm must resort via the external senses to the particular image to be better understood. Failing memory quickly reduces a phantasm of a particular to a generic, and our imagination thus needs to be "recharged" with sense data of particular material conditions.

from a Thomistic understanding of the human person, we can see how poor anthropology can frustrate the potential of sacred art to move the human heart toward greater love for God.

Anthropology and Liturgical Architecture

To conclude, I would ask why is it that, in general, we wish to keep returning to Chartres or Saint Peter's, each time seeing it anew as if for the first time, and not so with most modern buildings, let alone most modern churches? Having examined the problem of abstraction in sacred art, its inability to engage fully the human person, and its failure to move the human heart, we can begin to understand the analogous problem in recent church architecture that fails to move the soul. St. Thomas, following St. Augustine, teaches that the mind is meant for rest. It is a common human experience that once we sufficiently understand something, it ceases to attract pressingly our attention. Once we understand the essence of something, which is the goal of human knowing, the mind is content.

We have already seen how the valorization of abstraction can frustrate the fully human engagement in the arts. In architectural terms, much of modern architectural programming involves the reduction of things to only their functional aspects, these parts then to be considered one to another in respect of their functional relationships. Thus the modern building (properly designed according to functional planning principles) is somewhat "schematic," and it takes on the characteristics of concepts: it tends to be devoid of particular material conditions that should individuate it.[29] This explains why the typical schematically designed American parish church that we have been building lacks the vitality to capture our interest: the human, in quickly understanding it, quickly loses interest.[30] Conversely, this explains why buildings which are rich and complex, which are capable of supporting a wide of human emotions, with multivalent symbolism, and with a wealth of architectural details continue to intrigue us and engage us.

By failing to engage the senses with a wealth of images from which to draw phantasms in the imagination, the building fails to engage the heuristic process of the soul to understand that which it does not. As we have seen in

---

[29] Consider, for examples, the typical urban high rise, or the suburban shopping center and anonymous mass-produced tract houses.

[30] Conversely great art, be it Dante's *Divine Comedy* or Shakespeare's *Romeo and Juliet*, Michelangelo's *David* or Beethoven's *Ninth Symphony*, can be experienced again and again, each time anew.

the case of abstract art, because of the conceptual nature of the typical modern building, the soul does not apply from its storehouse of memory corresponding phantasms, concepts, and emotions to organically participate in the building.

If this Thomistic model of knowing is valid, and if the goal of church building is to create sacred spaces that engage the human community in a full range of human experiences toward one's loving participation in the things of God, then these would suggest a different approach to church building from that which we have been doing for the past seventy years. What might this entail? For instance, remembering that the external sense are ordered to perceiving *accidentals* (color, odor, texture, etc.), but the whole person is ordered to knowing *being*, this should suggest that we ought return to a more depictive way of sacred art. Rather than continuing the abstract tradition of reductionistic and fragmented splotches of colored glass, emblematic grape clusters and wheat stalks, and Stations which consist of geometric exercises—physical images which move virtually from the external senses to the intellect to inform us of concepts—our art should be rooted in reality of the human body both as subject and intended viewer. That is to say, by virtue of humanity we should be presented with physical images which engages not only the external senses with light and color, but can present to the imagination a potent phantasm so as to engage our intellect, memory, and emotions.

Church interiors should inflame our imagination with images of the holy, especially since our imaginations need to redirected and re-informed with sacred images to combat the consumeristic and often pornographic media with which we are daily assaulted. With careful iconological programming these images can all be properly ordered so as to support the liturgy and still allow for the subjectivity of the individual in the community.

In conclusion, if one of the major goals of the conciliar reforms is to help achieve truly "*active* participation," we should seek to engage the person on as many levels as possible in a truly human way. By returning to a fuller Catholic anthropology, one that engages the whole person, "body, mind, senses, imagination, emotions, memory," there is great hope for returning to a rich, robust, meaningful, and beautiful way of sacred architecture; which is still very much the unfinished business and "one of the urgent needs of contemporary liturgical renewal."

Maritain on the Song of Songs

John M. Dunaway

Several years ago I undertook to teach a Bible class at church on the *Song of Songs*. Like everybody else, I suppose, I had always been puzzled by this mysterious and controversial text and hoped the challenge of teaching it would help me understand it better. Its pure poetic beauty and its rich love allegory had always appealed to me, and I sensed a profound kinship between it and some of my favorite literary works: Dante's *Commedia*, for example, and certain other poems and novels where the metaphorical treatment of human and divine love recalls Paul's famous analogy in Ephesians between marriage and the relationship of Christ to his bride, the church. Ever since that project I have wanted to pursue the subject in a more scholarly vein, so I was delighted to rediscover Maritain's chapter on *Song of Songs* in *Approches sans entraves*.[1]

We are told that Saint Thomas Aquinas on his deathbed gave a teaching on the *Song of Songs,* no record of which, alas, has survived. And to those for whom the *Song of Songs* has become the most sublime love poem of all time, it would indeed seem a tragic loss. The man whose mystical union with Christ was so awe-inspiring that it caused him to refer to the *Summa Theologiae* as "so much straw" must have had a unique insight on Solomon's canticle. Yet it is perhaps appropriate that the celebrated "silence of Saint Thomas" should forever include this oral commentary; it might have been misunderstood, given the controversial history of exegesis to which the *Song* has been subjected over the centuries.

In any case, it is most certainly not happenstance that the twentieth century's greatest disciple of Saint Thomas wrote the very last chapter of his very last book on the very same subject. Maritain's meditation, which

---

[1] Jacques Maritain, *Approches sans entraves* (Paris: Fayard, 1973), "[En complément du livre 'De l'église du Christ, sa personne et son personnel'] Le Cantique des cantiques: une libre version pour l'usage privé," chap. 19, pp. 532-95. All translations of this chapter are the author's. For the English translation see *Untrammeled Approaches*, trans. Bernard Doering (University of Notre Dame Press: Notre Dame, Indiana, 1997).

figures as the concluding chapter of *Approches sans entraves*, was occasioned by his desire to compose a "free version for private use" of the biblical text, and this rendering is printed at the end. John Howard Griffin notes in *Jacques Maritain: Homage in Words and Pictures* that Olivier Lacombe read the then-unpublished text as part of Maritain's funeral mass in Kolbsheim in 1973.[2]

Maritain explains that he set out to produce a reading of the *Canticle* that would please him personally. "As far as all it brings to the spirit, I wanted its prophetically Christian meaning to appear explicitly and markedly enough to satisfy me in prayer. As far as what it brings to the ear, I wanted it to appear to me in the form of a French poem that would spring from a single, continuous thrust, in its incomparable beauty, thus satisfying my need for poetry better than generally do the literal translations."[3] He also notes that it really is not, properly speaking, a translation, since he did not know Hebrew or Syriac. Instead, he gathered all the existing French translations and compared them, coming up with the blend of them that best suited his aesthetic taste. He was particularly heavily influenced by the rendering of André Chouraqui, who notes in his preface that "the *Canticle,* which belongs to the wisdom writings whose definitive content was…determined at the time of the second Temple, has never ceased since then to be venerated by Jewish tradition and chanted at each Friday evening service at the synagogue as the sacred song *par excellence.*"[4]

Maritain insists his is not a "reflexive reading" of the *Song*, that is, a formal theological exegesis. He calls his interpretive remarks a *"lecture de premier jet,"* which might be translated a "first-blush reading." With a great enigmatic poem such as this, he avers, "it's not a matter of evoking ideas, but of obeying, in order to give it a voice, an entirely intuitive and supra-conceptual élan of the soul in which the resonances of language reverberate *ad infinitum*. It goes straight to its object, which is absolute love. It sings of love in its pure essence as its immediate signified."[5] Surprisingly Derridian terms for a Maritain text, although used in a decidedly un-Derridian way!

Maritain postulates three legitimate interpretations of the *Song* on three different levels of meaning, depending on who we understand the interlocutors of the text to be. It may be understood as a dialogue between:

---

[2] John Howard Griffin and Yves R. Simon, *Jacques Maritain: Homage in Words and Pictures* (Albany, New York: Magi Books, 1974), p. 64.

[3] "Le Cantique des cantiques, " pp 570-71.

[4] Ibid., p. 532.

[5] Ibid., p. 533.

1) Yahweh and the chosen people;

2) Christ and his Bride, the Church; or

3) "God and the soul wholly devoted to him in the secret of mystical contemplation" (534). This third interpretation, epitomized by that of St. John of the Cross, is one that works by analogy, however, whereas the first two operate on the basis of a *direct* reading.

What Maritain calls a reflexive reading according to the second interpretation would be concerned with "the spiritual experience lived out by the person of the Church, the Bride of Christ, in her innermost self, in her relationship with the Bridegroom, and at the successive phases of progress of her unfailingly holy love, with the vicissitudes, the purifying dark nights, the renewals of ever-deepening union with the Beloved."[6] Since, as he observes, the great commentaries of the patristic writers could not take into account the Church's historical itinerary through such vicissitudes and phases of progress, there has yet to be written a thorough and satisfactory reflexive reading according to the second interpretation. So Maritain evidently would have had no delusions about the definitiveness of St. Thomas's deathbed commentary.

One of the most significant details in which Maritain corrects the traditional readings concerns the sleeping of the Shulamite. Nearly all the commentators have agreed that her sleeping episodes signify "guilty torpors, due to the fact that she has forsaken the Bridegroom and must return to Him, and that these torpors testify of the infidelities and betrayals she has committed."[7] And indeed, such an interpretation would seem to fit the pattern of behavior of the chosen people decried by the prophets throughout the Old Testament, as well as the Church as Bride in her moments of greatest failure (evils of the Crusades, the Inquisition, her treatment of the Jews, etc.). Yet Maritain points out that the *Canticle* contains absolutely no reproaching of the Beloved (whether taken as Israel or the Bride) and that the word infidelity is never pronounced in it. "All beautiful you are, my darling; there is no flaw in you."[8]

For Maritain, the sleeping of the Shulamite Beloved is an allegorical picture of the spiritual faculty of vision that can take place only in the serenity of contemplation, as in the description of 5:2, where the Bride says, "I slept but my heart was awake." In 1:7, where she longs not to be like a veiled woman, Maritain gives us: "*Qu'il tombe enfin, le voile* [Let the veil finally fall," and adds "*Pour que je voie* [that I might see]!"[9] And

---

[6] Ibid., pp. 538-39.

[7] Ibid., p. 546.

[8] *Song of Songs*, 4:7. All biblical quotes, other than of Maritain's version, are from the New International Version.

in four separate passages having to do with sleep, his translation adds specific phrases to describe the sleep as contemplative rest—She "abandons herself to rest [*s'abandonnent au repos*] ... Her eyes rest in plenitude [*reposent en plénitude*] ... Let me dream in your arms ... Dream? But this is holy reality [*Laisse-moi rêver dans tes bras ... Rêve? Mais c'est la réalité sainte*]," and, finally, she asks how one could awaken love "now that in the Beloved, it exults forever beyond sleep [*maintenant qu'en l'amante / Il exulte à jamais au-delà du sommeil*]?"[10] Thus, Maritain rejects out of hand any interpretation that would suggest that the sleeping episodes signify any sort of *acedia* or truancy on the part of the Beloved, who instead is now seen by her Bridegroom as the one rendered perfect by her fixed gaze, the soul lost in the wonder of contemplation.

A key to understanding Maritain's approach to the *Song* is to remember that it has nothing to do with discursive knowledge. "It is thanks to the insightful emotion of the heart awakened in us by the poet; it is musically, if I may say so, not conceptually, that it reaches and enlightens us."[11] Maritain achieves his most remarkable insights thanks to what I consider one of his most exciting and fruitful epistemological building blocks. As we look at his "Many Ways of Knowing," we should be especially grateful for his development of the Thomistic notion of connatural knowledge. As he delineates it in *Art et scolastique* and in *Creative Intuition in Art and Poetry*, connatural knowledge is the secret of poetic creativity in all the arts. A non-conceptual mode of knowing, it is a "knowledge through affective union...or inclination, connaturality or congeniality."[12] The supreme rule for the artist is to love what one is making. "Thus art, like love, proceeds from a spontaneous instinct, and it must be cultivated like friendship."[13] In this regard, I like the quote from Alfred Sisley that Maritain cites in *Creative Intuition*: "Every picture shows a spot with which the artist himself has fallen in love."[14] And those who have tried their hand at drawing know the truth of that axiom.

Maritain explains the failure of traditional commentators to see certain facets of the text by "the fact that they exerted themselves in a totally reflex-

---

[9] "Le Cantique des cantiques, " p. 578.

[10] Ibid., pp. 580, 588, 592.

[11] Ibid., p. 541.

[12] Jacques Maritain, *Creative Intuition in Art and Poetry* (New York: Pantheon, 1953), pp. 115-17.

[13] Jacques Maritain, *Art and Scholasticism and The Frontiers of Poetry*, trans. Joseph W. Evans (Notre Dame, Indiana: University of Notre Dame Press, 1974), p. 41.

[14] *Creative Intuition in Art and Poetry*, p. 58.

ive and expressly allegorical reading of the inspired poem, without seeking...to enter into the character of the inspired poet."[15] Maritain, on the other hand, precisely by entering into the poet's character through connatural knowledge is able to understand that the poet of the *Song of Songs*, while he certainly was extensively and painfully aware of the many infidelities of the chosen people, was able to leave that knowledge buried in his subconscious during the composition of the inspired poem and to extol the Bride as being totally without spot or wrinkle. Equally striking is the prophetic quality of the poem, through which the Old Testament writer was able to speak, by the inspiration of the Holy Spirit, of the Bride—the Church—of which he had no natural foreknowledge whatsoever.

That the perfection of the Bride is a dominant theme in the *Song of Songs* is first a function of the literal level of meaning, where the poet is so madly in love with his betrothed. And, this applies at all levels: Yahweh loving his chosen people and Christ loving his bride, as well as God loving the soul who is totally devoted to him. With the notion of mad love (*l'amour fou*), I see Maritain again appropriating a language that is normally associated with a movement that is considered anything but Thomistic: namely, Surrealism. But as I have shown elsewhere,[16] André Breton's doctrine of the poetic consciousness is in some ways not terribly far from that of Maritain. Breton was fond of the phrase *l'amour fou* (along with *le merveilleux* and *le hasard objectif*[17]) to describe poetic inspiration. It is the contradiction of material determinism and logical discursive reasoning. This perfect, free spontaneity is what happens when beauty, in its supreme innocence, becomes "the perfect mirror in which all that has been and all that is called to be is admirably bathed in what is going to be this time."[18] For both Maritain and Breton, then, there is a magic moment of creative intuition in the poet in which something novel and unique is born through mad love.

In *Song of Songs*, God is so consumed with *l'amour fou* for his people that he forgets their transgressions. The Bride is so consumed with *l'amour fou* for Christ that she is able to pass beyond the trials and vicissitudes mentioned in the *Canticle* into a more perfect union with her Divine Beloved.

---

[15] "Le Cantique des cantiques, " p. 546.

[16] John Dunaway, "Maritain and Breton: Common Denominators in the Aesthetic Confrontation of Thomism and Surrealism." *French Literature Series*, vol. VI ("Authors and Philosophers"), (Columbia, South Carolina: University of South Carolina Press, 1979), pp.16-25.

[17] "The wonderful" and "objective chance."

[18] André Breton, *Les Vases communicants* (Paris: Nouvelle Revue Française, 1955), p.167 [Translation is the author's].

Here Maritain quotes Psalm 45:10, the companion piece to the *Song of Songs*, where the Bride is entreated to "Listen, O daughter, consider and give ear: Forget your people and your father's house" in order to cleave to her new Betrothed. Only for Maritain, the interpretation also applies to God, who is being entreated to forget the sins of his people. "Raise your eyes only on the Bride *restored to grace*. Why? Because in the poem everything belongs to love and is for love; because what it sings is absolute love, the love of Yahweh for the Bride he has chosen. And God himself, in his love stronger than death, and which asks only to pardon."[19]

The notion of the spotless Bride, then, is made possible in *Song of Songs* by the ruling power of *l'amour fou* in the creative consciousness of the divinely inspired poet. And it explains further the injunction of chapter 2, verse 7, where the Bridegroom warns the chorus not to awaken love. The sleep of the Beloved is a function of her love. She has fallen asleep in the satiety of *l'amour fou*. "'I adjure you, daughters of Jerusalem, by the deer, by the hinds of the fields, not to waken love until she wishes.' There is nothing but tenderness in this. And if instead of saying 'not to waken the Beloved' the Bridegroom says 'not to waken love,' it is because the Beloved in her sleeping as in her waking is entirely love herself."[20]

The Bride's first sleep in 2:7 is not even associated with night. She dozes off in the Bridegroom's arms, saying "I am faint with love."[21] This particular instance of sleep Maritain interprets as "the highest, most important, and most hidden activity in the life of the Church in her love-relation to Christ...the silent ardor of holy contemplation, eyes closed on all the rest."[22] Rather than a failure to remain soberly vigilant, as in the Gethsemane scene, where the disciples could not watch and pray for even one hour, it is a heightened mode of consciousness ruled by the second sight of the contemplative visionary. The intense desire of *l'amour fou* is its enabling precondition.

But perhaps the most noticeable aspect of Maritain's translation of the poem is its strengthening of the erotic language on the literal level. Five times he renders what in the English-language versions is described simply as "love" by "*caresses*."[23] Four times he adds references to love in terms of wine or intoxication.[24] In 1:2 the New International Version reads: "Your love is more

---

[19] "Le Cantique des cantiques, " p. 545.

[20] Ibid., p. 547.

[21] *Song of Songs* 2:5.

[22] "Le Cantique des cantiques, " pp. 558-59.

[23] *Song of Songs,* 1:2, 1:4, 4:10a, 4:10b, 7:13, although one of these also appears in the Louis Segond translation.

[24] Ibid., 1:2, 1:3, 2:4, 5:1.

delightful than wine," whereas Maritain's reading is: "*Caresses de ses mains meilleures / Que l'ivresse du vin fou* [His hands's caresses better / Than the intoxication of mad wine]." In 1:16, where the Bridegroom exults over his Bride: "How handsome you are, my lover! / Oh, how charming! / And our bed is verdant," Maritain adds two entire lines: "*D'un printemps éternel qui monte autour de nous; / Seul à seule! Deux dans un seul souffle d'amour* [With an eternal springtime that rises around us; / Alone, the two of us in a single breath of love]." There are several other passages whose poetic language in the Maritain rendering seems to me a clear improvement on the English-language versions, but it would be difficult to capture those improvements by again translating his translations into English![25]

My final comment on the spotless, perfect Bride of the *Songs of Songs* is that Maritain's interpretation really goes back to his fundamental premise in his 1970 book *De l'église du Christ*. The mystical *person* of the Church is the spotless Bride, and she is unsullied by the errors and excesses of the *personnel* of the Church. "The person of the Church is unfailingly holy, her personnel is not."[26] The very title of this chapter of *Approches sans entraves*, in fact, proclaims it to have been written as a complement to *De l'église du Christ*.

Maritain includes a gesture of ecumenical peace-making toward Eastern Christians when he says that he wishes to correct a previous statement in *De l'église du Christ* and include not only the Roman Catholic but also the Orthodox Church in his interpretation of the Bride of the *Canticle*. This is another evidence of the continuing evolution of Maritain's thinking on the church near the end of his life.

Another interpretive insight worth comment, perhaps, is the famous refrain: *Nigra sum, sed formosa*. Again, Maritain emphasizes the tenderness of the Bridegroom's attitude toward his Beloved and the lack of reproach. The Bride's blackness does not detract from her beauty. "Let us not imagine that she is black because of the faults of her members and her personnel. She suffers for those faults, she does penance for them, but they are totally foreign to her personality. If she is black, if she has darkened skin, it is because the sun of history has burned her."[27]

In 1:7, the Bride complains of her veiled face and wishes she could remove the veil in order to *see*. "She aspires to *see*, to pass, when the blessed hour of noon comes, beyond the knowledge of Faith in order to enter completely into the Vision of the divine essence."[28] The *Song of Songs* is, after all,

---

[25] Ibid., 4:15, 5:6, 5:16, 7:2, and 8:6.
[26] "Le Cantique des cantiques, " p. 549.
[27] Ibid., p. 567.
[28] Ibid., p. 570.

one of the most misunderstood books of the Bible at least partly because its evocation of the relationship between the Church and the Bridegroom pushes us, of necessity, beyond our present relationship with Christ to contemplate the direct, unmediated beatific vision in eternal glory. It is the love poem that goes beyond George Herbert, Graham Greene, Mauriac, or even the bold vision of Dante's *Paradiso*. And all literary texts that plumb the depths of meaning in the analogy of human and divine love are derived from it.

"For this reason a man will leave his father and mother and be united to his wife, and the two will become one flesh. This is a profound mystery—but I am talking about Christ and the church."[29] This great mystery of divine and human love is at the core of life's very meaning. Friendship, marriage, our relationship with our Creator—all these form the crucible out of which the character of God is developed within us. Knowing our friends, our spouses, or our Redeemer activates the connatural mode of knowledge that also enables us to imitate the Divine Artist as poets, painters, composers, or even perceptive interpreters. Jacques Maritain was often described as having a genius for friendship, and he was also a devoted husband who seemed only a shadow of himself in his grief over the death of Raïssa. I have said before that for me he is less a philosopher of art than an artist of philosophy. Of the many modes of knowing that he so masterfully distinguished in order to unite, I think the quintessential one is connatural knowledge.

There are also, of course, some changes or additions in Maritain's free version of *Song of Songs* that I have difficulty understanding, some that, in my desultory reading at least, don't seem to enrich or clarify. One mysterious example is in perhaps the most famous passage of the poem, the concluding panegyric to love in 8:5-7. "Many waters cannot quench love..." etc. What puzzles me is why he chose to omit the last line of verse 7: "If one were to give all the wealth of his house for love, it would be utterly scorned."

Near the end of the essay, Maritain confesses that most scholars will doubtless find his free translation a bit *farfelu*—a wonderfully untranslatable French word that roughly means "bizarre with just a hint of mischief." Yet he also confesses that he has always had a liking for the *farfelu*, and has always longed for an opportunity to do a project that would put the *farfelu* in the service of the rational and vice versa. I am certain that all true poets— and wannabe poets, too—will find such a confession congenial and salutary. And who cares about stuffed-shirt scholars!

Maritain also deletes the final verse in which the Bride asks the Bridegroom to flee far from her on the fragrant mountains. He sees this as an

[29] *St Paul's Epistle to the Ephesians*, 5:31-32

apocryphal interpolation from an overzealous priest or pharisee who was afraid that the picture of God in the *Canticle* is not sufficiently transcendent and otherworldly. While I'm not sure I agree with him here, I do find emotionally and theologically effective his choice of the passage with which to replace it. To conclude the *Song of Songs* with a paraphrase of Jesus's description of the Good Shepherd in John chapter 10 is an indication of the way Maritain apprehended, through connatural knowledge, the matchless love of Christ. And the last verse recapitulates the ecumenical spirit in which he wrote the last chapter of *Approches sans entraves*: "I have other sheep who are not of this flock. Those also I must lead, and they will hear my voice. And there will be only one flock and one shepherd."[30]

---

[30] "Le Cantique des cantiques, " p. 594.

Contributors:

George Anastaplo is Professor of Law, Loyola University of Chicago; Lecturer in the Liberal Arts, The University of Chicago; and Professor Emeritus of Political Science and of Philosophy, Dominican University. His most recent books are *The Thinker as Artist: from Homer to Plato and Aristotle*, *Abraham Lincoln: A Constitutional Biography* and *But Not Philosophy: Seven Introductions to Non-Western Thought*.

James Arraj is the co-director of Inner Explorations, an extensive website (www.innerexplorations.com) where Christian mysticism and metaphysics meet Jungian psychology, Eastern religions and a new sense of the earth. He is the author of a dozen books including *Mysticism, Metaphysics and Maritain, The Mystery of Matter* and *From St. John of the Cross to Us*.

Fr. Joseph M. de Torre, of the Opus Dei prelature, is the University Professor of Social and Political Philosophy at the University of Asia and the Pacific in Manila. He has published more than twenty books and hundreds of articles and essays.

Robert A. Delfino is Assistant Professor of Philosophy at St. John's University. He received his Ph.D. from State University of New York at Buffalo. His primary interests are in metaphysics and ethics, with special attention to Aquinas and Aristotle. He has recently published "Aristotle on the Value of the History of Philosophy for Philosophy." He maintains the official webpage of the American Maritain Association.

Raymond Dennehy is Professor of Philosophy at the University of San Francisco, where he teaches metaphysics, epistemology, bioethics and political philosophy. He is a former president of the American Maritain Association, editor of the anthology, *Christian Married Love* and author of *Reason and Dignity* and the forthcoming book, *Anti-Abortionist at Large*. He has also published many scholarly articles and is a frequently invited guest on television, radio, and university campuses to discuss contemporary ethical issues.

324

John M. Dunaway is professor of French and Interdisciplinary Studies at Mercer University in Macon, Georgia. His published writings have centered on French religious writers, especially Maritain, Julien Green, and Simone Weil. He has served on the Executive Board and as Vice-President of the American Maritain Association.

Robert Fallon is currently completing his doctoral dissertation in the musicology program at the University of California, Berkeley. An editor of *Repercussions: Critical and Alternative Viewpoints on Music and Scholarship*, he has written on twentieth-century musical cultures in France, England, Germany and the United States.

Desmond FitzGerald is Professor Emeritus of Philosophy, University of San Francisco. Born in Toronto, he studied at St. Michael's College, University of Toronto, where he attended the lectures of Jacques Maritain in 1942 and 1943. He received his M.A. in Philosophy from the Pontifical Institute of Mediaeval Studies, studying under Étienne Gilson and Anton C. Pegis. He completed a second M.A and his Ph.D. in Political Science at the University of California, Berkeley, writing on "The Political Thought of Jacques Maritain." He taught for 50 years at the University of San Francisco.

William J. (Joe) Fossati received his B.A. and M.A. degrees in history from the University of Arizona, and his Ph.D. in modern European history from the University of Kansas. His major field is the history of *La belle époque* in France, and has conducted extensive research on the philosophy of Henri Bergson. He has taught history at Rockhurst University since 1986.

W. Matthews Grant is a doctoral candidate in Philosophy at Fordham University and recently completed a fellowship at the Aquinas Center of Theology at Emory University.

Catherine Green is Assistant Professor of Philosophy at Rockhurst University in Kansas City. She has an M.S. in Nursing from the University of San Diego, as well as an M.A. and Ph.D. in Philosophy from The Catholic University of America. She has published articles and reviews on Yves R. Simon's theories of freedom and practical knowledge as well as on ethical issues in nursing and the health sciences.

James G. Hanink is a Professor of Philosophy at Loyola Marymount University, Los Angeles, and Associate Editor for the New Oxford Review. He is working on a study of the personalist movement, with a special focus on its implication for philosophy and theology. He is active in a pro-life ministry in Los Angeles.

Gregory J. Kerr is Associate Professor of Philosophy at DeSales University. He is a past editor of the *Maritain Notebook*, the newsletter of the American Maritain Association. Having received his M.A. from Boston College and his Ph.D. from Fordham University, he has published several articles on the aesthetics and epistemology of Jacques Maritain.

John F. X. Knasas is Professor of Philosophy in the Center for Thomistic Studies at the University of St. Thomas, Houston. He is the author of *The Preface to Thomistic Metaphysics: A Contribution to the Neo-Thomist Debate on the Start of Metaphysics* (Peter Lang, 1990) and of many articles on Thomistic metaphysical concerns.

John F. Morris is an Assistant Professor of Philosophy at Rockhurst University. His area of specialization is ethics and medical ethics, with a background in Aquinas and medieval philosophy. He has published several articles and is currently editing a volume titled, *Medicine, Healthcare, & Ethics: New Essays from the Christian Tradition*. He is currently a member of the Ethics and Human Values Committee at St. Joseph Health Center in Kansas City, and a member of the American Occupational Therapy Association's Commission on Standards and Ethics.

Ralph Nelson has taught philosophy and political science at the University of Windsor since 1961, and is now Professor Emeritus. His research and publications are in the areas of French moral, social, and political philosophy and in democratic theory. He is the author of numerous articles on Yves R. Simon and Jacques Maritain and is the co-editor of Yves R. Simon's *Foresight and Knowledge*.

Douglas A. Ollivant is an Assistant Professor of Political Science at the United States Military Academy and a Major in the United States Army. An Indiana University Political Science Ph.D., his research focuses on Catholic responses to contemporary liberalism. He has also done work on the American founding and in military ethics. He is a past Vice-President of the American Maritain Association.

Matthew Pugh is Assistant Professor of Philosophy at Providence College. He previously taught at Ohio Dominican College, Ohio State University, and the University of St. Thomas in Houston. His interests include Thomistic metaphysics, epistemology and ethics, and he is currently researching the connections between Aquinas' understanding of the transcendentals and his moral philosophy.

Steven J. Schloeder is a registered architect, writer, and Ph.D. candidate at the Graduate Theological Union in Berkeley. He is the founder of Liturgical Environs, an architectural company specializing in new and remodeled Catholic Church projects, and is the author of *Architecture in Communion: Implementing the Second Vatican Council through Liturgy and Architecture.*

Christopher H. Toner is a doctoral candidate in philosophy at the University of Notre Dame, and is currently writing a dissertation on virtue ethics. His research interests include contemporary ethics and political philosophy, medieval philosophy, and French neo-Thomism.

John G. Trapani, Jr. is Professor of Philosophy and Chair of the Humanities Division at Walsh University in North Canton, Ohio. He received a B.A. from Boston College and a Ph.D. from St. John's University in Jamaica, New York. He has written extensively on Maritain's aesthetics/epistemology, including his dissertation: "The Interrelation of Poetry, Beauty, and Contemplation in The Philosophy of Jacques Maritain." John served as President of the American Maritain Association, 2000-2001 and he is active as a professional musician and bandleader.

Henk E. S. Woldring is Professor of Political Philosophy at the Free University in Amsterdam. He is the author of many books, including *Karl Mannheid: The Development of his Thought.* In 1999 he was elected as a member of the First Chamber of the Netherlands Parliament.

Thomas F. Woods is professor of English at the University of Montevallo in Alabama, where he has taught since 1980. He is a graduate of John Carroll University, and studied English at John Carroll and Miami University before completing his Ph.D. in English at Ohio State.

Index